Evolution of Sickness and Healing

Evolution of Sickness and Healing

Horacio Fábrega, Jr.

University of California Press
Berkeley / Los Angeles / London

University of California Press
Berkeley and Los Angeles, California

University of California Press
London, England

Copyright © 1997 by
The Regents of the University of California

First Paperback Printing 1999

Library of Congress Cataloging-in-Publication Data

Fábrega, Jr., Horacio
    Evolution of sickness and healing / Horacio Fábrega, Jr.
        p.   cm.
    Includes bibliographical references and index.
    ISBN 0-520-21953-8 (pbk. : alk. paper)
    1. Social medicine.   2. Medical anthropology.   3. Sick—
Psychology.   4. Human evolution.   I. Title.
    RA418.F323   1997
    306.4′61—dc20   96-29318
                                                          CIP

Printed in the United States of America

1 2 3 4 5 6 7 8 9

This is for Andrea Melanie and Michele Marie, with deep appreciation and gratitude to Joan Rome

Contents

Preface

This book constitutes an attempt to provide a theoretical introduction to the comparative study of medicine as a social institution. I draw on work from many disciplines, including cultural and physical anthropology, sociology, social history of medicine, medical geography, economics, paleoanthropology, paleopathology, archaeology, historical epidemiology, and human evolutionary biology. I cover biological aspects of disease prevalence, characteristics of medical practice, lay and folk as well as practitioner orientations to illness, and the general cultural meanings of medicine in various types of societies.

A fundamental motivation behind the book is that there exists a need to conceptualize medicine in a theoretically integrated way. I am seeking the connections among the biological facts of disease and injury, the social and cultural facts of their expression in behavior that is meaningful, the social responses of healing, and the relationship of all this to characteristics of the society considered as a social structure. Furthermore, I seek a synthesis through an evolutionary formulation of medicine. Such a synthesis will provide unity and balance to the study of medicine, now split along the lines of different academic disciplines and traditions.

I attempt to accomplish this admittedly daunting task by conceptualizing the essence of medicine as centered on sickness and healing. And these basic concepts are handled in biological, social, and cultural terms. My goal is to view sickness and healing from an evolutionary frame of reference. I conceptualize sickness (the behavioral expressions of disease and injury) and healing (the culturally meaningful social responses aimed at undoing or preventing the effects of disease and injury) from the standpoint of biological/genetic and social/cultural evolution.

This evolutionary view of sickness and healing is what maintains the unity of my approach. In my formulation they constitute linked facets of a unique human adaptation developed during the biological evolution of the hominid line and expressed culturally in relation to the changing historical contingencies of social organization and complexity. Sickness and healing are ordinarily conceptualized as different phenomena that are linked, to be sure, in the event of medical care. However, I handle them as "two sides of the same coin." The dynamism of each enters into that of the other; they are constructed out of the same material; they are reciprocal; and they both originate in the same way. They are seen in relation to social and cultural evolution and are analyzed as expressions of an underlying biological adaptation unique to *Homo sapiens*. This "natural" integration of sickness and healing, natural because they were both sculpted together during evolution, provides a new vantage point from which to examine the institution of medicine.

In chapter 1, I describe some of the problems of studying medicine from a theoretical standpoint, review earlier efforts to conceptualize medicine in biological and cultural terms, including evolution, and set boundaries on what is to follow. In chapter 2, I discuss material related to the origins of sickness and healing during biological evolution. The idea that at the root of medicine one finds a complex but integrated adaptation for both sickness and healing is introduced and discussed using material from evolutionary psychology. The problems inherent in examining sickness and healing in an integrated way and as grounded in evolution are reviewed. In the next two chapters, I go on to review characteristics of sickness and healing during what I term the early and later stages of social evolution, beginning with early, village-level societies, proceeding through prestates, states, and civilizations, and finally including the modern European and postmodern eras. This material, which includes reviews of social organization of the societies, epidemiological and ecological factors, and aspects of sickness and healing in each of the selected social types, is discussed in chapters 3 and 4. Individuals living in family-level societies during the line of evolution to *Homo sapiens* are judged to have evolved a distinctive framework for medicine. This framework, consisting of orientations and behaviors related to sickness and healing, is judged to have been transformed as societies evolved and became more complex. The two chapters offer a summary account of how sickness and healing have been configured and played out in different types of societies. Some of these ideas on the evolution of sickness and healing are elaborated by discussing the role that active substances and drugs might have played in different historical periods (chapter 5). A more in-depth account of sickness and healing in different types of societies is illustrated by giving attention to somatopsychic disturbances (chapter 6). These are important medical disorders in biomedicine today, and there are good reasons for believing not only that they are universal but also that they constitute a good barometer with which to record the interplay of culture, society, and biology. This line of analysis is pursued in chapter 6. In chapter 7 I introduce the concept of a "medical meme" to refer to the basic unit of information pertaining to how sickness and healing are configured and played out. This concept serves as a bridge for linking the biological and cultural evolution of medicine and is used here and in later chapters as a way of giving substance and focus to the evolution of medicine. In this chapter I also consolidate earlier descriptive material by summarizing general parameters pertaining to sickness and healing in each of the different types of societies analyzed earlier. In chapter 8 concepts and principles are further elaborated in my attempt to conceptualize sickness and healing as well as the institution of medicine in an evolutionary frame of reference. The inner workings of the adaptation at the base of medicine are analyzed more fully. In particular, the role of medical genes in producing the machinery of the adaptation for medicine is discussed together with the relationship they are thought to have to medical memes, which produce the expressive, meaning-centered aspects of the adaptation. In addition, what I regard as the ontogeny of this adaptation is reviewed together with its implications. The adaptation is judged as providing the conditions that together with social environmental inputs pertaining to experiences with disease and injury during critical periods of development lead to the unfolding of sickness and healing orientations and behaviors. Finally, the tie between the material of the adaptation and the material that sociologists and economists have in mind when they discuss institutions and their social evolution is reviewed. All of this provides a way of integrating the study of the biological and cultural evolution of medicine. In chapter 9 I step back and examine aspects of the evolution of medicine from a broader point of view. I present a diagram for illustrating the various types of phenomena implicated in this evolution. The institution of medicine is conceptualized as incorporating differing materials and systems, beginning with genes and ending with social organizations, corporations, and material products. The institution of medicine is connected to other institutional sectors of any society, and these are included in a macrosociological schema of society. The changes in the differing components of medicine and in the society during evolution are summarized. In chapter 10 I discuss some of the implications of studying medicine from an evolutionary standpoint, giving attention to topics in social medicine, clinical medicine, and social theory. In chapter 11 I review my thinking and discuss ways in which an evolutionary perspective on medicine can be used to examine contemporary problems in biomedical practice. In the appendix I summarize my argument by providing an outline of the concepts and a description of the characteristics of the stages of the evolution of medicine.

A general view of my intellectual orientation is appropriate here. A common interpretation of evolution is betterment and progress. It is important to emphasize that with respect to medicine this interpretation is not promulgated in this book.

There unquestionably have resulted enormous gains in the treatment of many types of disease during the rise and development of biomedicine. And prior to this, one could reasonably claim that practitioners of many of the ancient "great traditions" of medicine, such as those of China, India, and the ancient Mediterranean societies, produced more enlightened, successful understandings of sickness and healing compared to other, smaller and less evolved traditions. Even the latter approaches cannot be said to be without their benefits as research studies centered on the value of native healing rituals and local, indigenous medicinal preparations continue to elucidate.

In conflict with a view of the unquestioned beneficial effects of social evolution on health and medicine is the body of work of physical anthropologists on the comparative nutrition and health of prehistoric and early historic populations. This line of investigation tends to support the relatively high nutritional status and physical health of foragers and hunter-gatherers. Moreover, and although this is contested, the consensus of opinion seems to point to possible relative declines in nutrition and health of populations in association with the major social and economic revolutions involving subsistence patterns and population density and size. Based on this line of thinking, then, it would be difficult to conclude that growth and "evolution" of a society's medical tradition and approach to disease, which one can equate roughly with the major social and economic revolutions of human groups across history and prehistory, always resulted in improvement or progress.

It needs to be emphasized, then, that the "success" of a tradition of medicine is difficult to establish and is much contested. Many of the gains in morbidity and mortality associated with the modern era, as an example, have been explained as resulting from improvements in sanitation, hygiene, and diet rather than from medical practice per se. And from a theoretical standpoint, an argument can be made to the effect that the value of a tradition of medical care should be measured in terms, not exclusively of epidemiological indices per se, but of those pertaining to how sickness problems as identified by that tradition are handled. With respect to the latter point, several factors linked to sickness and healing, not just success in eliminating or controlling the underlying disease or injury, should be taken into account, for example, success in relieving pain and suffering, success in facilitating the social losses occasioned by disease and injury, success in promoting sociopsychologic reconditioning, and success in providing for comfortable ways of dying in the event that healing is unsuccessful. Finally, it should not be forgotten that otherwise exemplary healing traditions can cause disease and injury (so-called iatrogenic medical problems) and these "losses" of an otherwise "scientific" medical tradition would have to be balanced with its gains in any strict accounting of its overall "success."

For these and related reasons, then, the conceptualization of an evolution of medicine proposed in this book should not be taken to imply progressive improvements in the handling of disease and injury. In fact I believe that there are many practices and orientations in contemporary medicine that are biologically "unnatural," constituting medical maladaptations. An advantage of formulating medicine from an evolutionary standpoint anchored in human biology is that it serves to more clearly profile the good and the bad of contemporary medicine. My frame of reference and proposal is also not in any strong way a functional one. I certainly do not believe that there is a purpose, function, or design and direction that explains why and how evolution has occurred in medicine. These caveats about medical evolution as progressive and having taken place for functional reasons are consistent with contemporary thinking on social evolution generally.

Rather, the conceptualization I propose aims to depict what aspects of sickness and healing differ in the various types of societies that are held to form, in a rough way, a continuum of size and complexity and to have constituted, in an abstract way, probable phases in the posited evolution of society, however controversial and contested this area of study might be. I aim to show, in other words, how the construction of sickness changes in relation to changing levels and degrees of social organization; and similarly, how approaches to healing change as a result of these types of social changes. In addition to describing sickness and healing in different types of societies, I attempt to explain how transformations in the configuration of sickness and healing might be presumed to have taken place. My aims, in short, are to offer a descriptive interpretation of the evolution of medicine, to provide a conceptual frame of reference for visualizing this evolution, and to propose a methodology for studying it.

It is important to emphasize that I identify my effort as an introduction. I see it as pointing the way toward a more theoretically integrated conceptualization of medicine. My approach is to use basic knowledge of disease, injury, and the social aspects of medical care to provide a better way of looking at how medicine as a social institution arose, unfolded, and transformed itself during the course of human evolution and history. I believe that this way of conceptualizing medicine provides a useful frame of reference from which to examine practical matters pertaining to medical practice and care and theoretical ones pertaining to the social sciences.

Acknowledgments

It is difficult to give credit to all persons who have provided help and support in this undertaking. I am especially indebted to Tom Detre for having enabled me, early in my career, to appreciate through his clinical brilliance the beauty and scientific integrity of academic psychiatry. He also provided me with support, continued intellectual interest, and goodwill during my academic work at the University of Pittsburgh. Since my medical school days, Howard P. Rome was a source of inspiration, encouragement, and renewal, and I am very pleased to acknowledge this here. Gene Brody is another person whose positive influence has been constant and sustained over the years and whose implicit encouragement I have valued greatly. In his unique "Latin" way Juan Mezzich has always been encouraging of my work, and this has been very sustaining. George C. Williams reviewed one of the chapters, and I found his remarks encouraging and illuminating. Tom Fararo and John Marx have read portions of certain chapters, and their warm endorsement of my thinking was instrumental in furthering my resolve in this project. Steve Gaulin's help in guiding me to relevant literature, his interest in my ideas, and his mental toughness in response to my queries have proven very helpful. My dealings with the Press were very positive: I am grateful to Stanley Holwitz for his continued encouragement and to Michelle Nordon for her patience and goodwill in shepherding the manuscript. Finally, I wish to acknowledge the patience, acceptance, and sheer hard work of my wife, Joan Rome Sporkin, whose dedication to shared pursuits of family goals provided me with the time and reclusion for my writing.

1

The Need for Theory in the Study of Sickness and Healing

Introduction

Members of all societies encounter disease and injury and develop social practices to cope with their effects. Social practices can also lead to disease and injury. The existence of medical problems and institutions to handle all of this can be regarded as a cultural universal (Brown 1991). Social scientists have described much variety in the way societies cope with disease and injury. There is a need for theoretical consolidation of this field. One of the principal tasks is to develop a frame of reference and a set of concepts in terms of which this variability could be organized and explained.

The basic material of medicine that requires explanation is that involving sickness and healing as these are configured and played out in different types of societies. As social and cultural phenomena, sickness and healing need to be studied from a holistic standpoint: The dialectic is between the physical environment, disease/injury as biological phenomena, and sickness and healing that are constructed as a function of the preceding and of social organization itself. This, in essence, is the enterprise of this book, with the added intention of interpreting changing aspects of medicine in terms of biological and social evolution. The purpose of this chapter is to discuss some fundamental issues, both methodological and conceptual, that pose problems for one attempting to develop a comparative approach to sickness and healing.

Visualizing the Material Content of the Medical

A clear hindrance to the development of a unified, comprehensive, and theoretical approach to the institution of medicine has been the sheer difficulty of incorporating in one frame of reference the different kinds of disease problems that exist and the variety in the way they can be expressed in one society, regardless of its level of complexity or modernity. This would include the range of injuries, neuromuscular dislocations, anatomical fractures and contusions, and like phenomena that can befall people as a result of physical happenings. It would also include the range of infectious problems, systemic and local, that populations are vulnerable to, infections that vary as a function of a society's geography, characteristics of the physical habitat, dietary intake, level of social stress, and level of social organization and complexity. Besides infectious problems, there exist a plethora of disease processes involving metabolism, disorders of physiological function (e.g., gastrointestinal, respiratory, cardiovascular, genitourinary), and diseases of unknown etiology (e.g., cancer, multiple sclerosis, varieties of arthritis). Finally, one would have to include so-called emotional and functional medical problems that constitute a very large percentage of what physicians actually observe and are forced to treat in some way. This would include a large amalgam of somatically, psychologically, and behaviorally expressed ailments that in biomedicine today are not clearly classified from a causal standpoint. The amalgam would include a large segment of somatic conditions traceable to stress as well as most of the more clearly profiled psychiatric disorders, all of which prominently include somatic problems and very often still make their initial medical appearance in primary care settings because they manifest somatically and are so interpreted (e.g., depression, anxiety, dementia, psychoses of different types).

That these medical problems are dealt with by a large number of different types of biomedical specialists (clinical practitioners and public health oriented) and are thought of as different precisely because of the way they are defined, classified, and dealt with by the respective medical disciplines creates further difficulty for one intending to formulate a satisfying (i.e., comprehensive yet parsimonious) theoretical approach to medicine. At the very least, this heterogeneity of problems, although obviously neatly packaged biomedically, refers to highly diverse human phenomena of suffering that disable and incapacitate in different ways, that persist for different degrees of time when manifest, and that can be ameliorated from a symptomatic standpoint (short of acute surgical or pharmacologic intervention) to differing degrees and for different amounts of time. All of these problems, in short, create the formidable profile of morbidity and mortality that constitutes a society's medical burden and that one intending a theoretical amount of the medical must attend to.

A way of coping with the problem of the complex and variegated nature of the material content of the medical is to divide the theoretical labor and handle the material in different modes. From the standpoint of researchers in epidemiology and clinical medicine, the task is to identify the profile of medical problems that these scientists as well as physical anthropologists, archaeologists, and paleopathologists equate with societies classified as to level of social organization and complexity as well as ecology or physical habitat.

Societies, of course, are not neatly isolated "things" one can study as though their approaches to the medical were unique. Nor is the structure of any society exactly like that of another, given the range of factors that can affect them. Rather, and despite apparent similarities and insularities, societies differ in any number of ways and are always in contact with each other. Medical phenomena in any one society and at one point in time reflect spread of diseases and cultural borrowings from other societies (McNeill 1976, 1992). A comparative, unified view of how societies construct and play out sickness and healing requires that one adopt an abstract frame of reference and a set of typologies that facilitate analysis.

One can assume that a particular "social type," namely, a society characterized by a distinctive set of structural properties, has associated with it a more or less distinctive profile of medical problems that constitutes the material content of the medical. In any theoretical account of medicine, this material would have to be in some way referenced since it constitutes the base out of which a people think about, approach, and cope with the medical. On the other hand, from the standpoint of a comparative social and cultural approach to the medical, the task is to rely on root concepts in terms of which one is afforded a way of fruitfully organizing and conceptualizing this material content of the medical of any particular society in social and cultural terms. In short, abstraction, reduction, and theoretical economy and precision are necessary here as well.

Illness, an individual's perception of a medical problem, sickness, the social construction of a condition of illness, disease, or pathology, what exists from a physical/organic standpoint, and healing, the range of medicines, procedures, and rituals by means of which a people try to prevent, undo, or minimize morbidity, are basic concepts that have been used in the past in medical anthropology and will be adopted here (Fabrega 1974; Frankenberg, 1980, 1986; Good 1977; Kleinman 1980). In later chapters, these basic concepts are supplemented by others that will serve to cast medicine in a more suitable theoretical frame of reference as the occasion demands.

The Problem of Data

Good ethnographies of sickness and healing are basic requirements for theoretical discussions of medicine that are truly comparative. The field of medical anthropology contains many in-depth studies of sickness and healing. Several studies can be cited as classic examples (Glick 1963; Harwood 1970; Lewis 1975; Nash 1967; Ngubane 1977; Turner 1963). Recently, there has taken place a surge of interest in the medical traditions of Asia. Characteristically, this interest has expressed itself in textual analyses of beliefs about sickness and healing practices, looked at as complex and elaborate systems of symbols (Dols 1984a; Farquhar 1987; Sivin 1987; Unschuld 1985, 1986a, 1986b; Zimmermann 1987). Emphasis on the richness of medical topics and their potential value for the study of rituals, spiritual concerns, and political happenings, staple themes in cultural anthropology, seems to have had the effect of directing efforts toward systematic in-depth studies (Young 1976).

Most ethnographies concentrate on only certain aspects of comparative medicine, for example, aspects of beliefs or meanings of illness, and not on concrete aspects of healing. Sometimes, the reverse is observed. Descriptive accounts predominate, making it difficult for one to evaluate how frequently a practice or an explanatory model is implemented. Ethnographers also differ in terms of orientation; some may prefer ritual aspects of healing, others semantic themes pertaining to illness, and still others the kinds of diseases that are encountered and their effects on the population.

With respect to literate traditions of medicine, such as those of India, China, and Islam, anthropologists' efforts overlap with and parallel those of historians. The anthropologists' interests obviously center on observed behaviors and contemporary practices, whereas those of historians center on what can be inferred from documents. The study of the social history of Western medicine has attracted a great deal of interest in the last fifteen years, far exceeding that of China, India, or Islam (e.g., Porter 1985; Wear 1992). Nevertheless, social histories of medicine deal with beliefs and practices and frequently rely on concepts and perspectives developed in anthropology. A basic limitation of these studies is the lack of material on the actual dynamics of behaviors associated with sickness and healing in earlier historical epochs. It is usually the case that important documents that reveal aspects of sickness and healing are translated and interpreted. Whereas this is indispensable for formulating some parameters, they simply do not address others. It is very likely that the actual processes of healing, including the kinds of organizations that may have existed among healers and the nature of relations between healers and their sick patients, are not recorded and may never be fully understood.

Since much of the data collected on sickness and healing are contemporary in nature, be these of small-scale societies or pertaining to the "great traditions," the problem posed by the competing, often dominant biomedical tradition is vexing. It is difficult to separate native cultural perspectives on medicine from biomedical impositions. The following questions illustrate this point. How much of a certain tradition's approach to healing is a result of the competition with or emulation of the biomedical? Were one to attempt to determine the kinds of sickness problems that a tradition handles "well," how is one to establish this if patients have resorted to other forms of healing? Since industrial capitalism is becoming the dominant political economic system in the world, how do its tenets erode, undermine, and tarnish aspects of healing and medical practice that a more pristine tradition would have displayed?

These and related questions point to the kinds of data that are needed. A general theory about sickness and healing must overcome limitations in the quality and amount of data pertaining to medicine. Its goal is to explain how the medical is configured in different types of societies and how it changes in response to social, ecologic, and historical considerations. The study of sickness and healing has been strongly influenced by contemporary biomedicine and its cultural presuppositions. Consequently, theory about medicine must incorporate biomedical insights but also strive to handle biomedicine as but one (highly influential, to be sure) cultural approach to medicine. The approach to medicine in "pristine" societies not affected by biomedicine should ideally be given special consideration, although, as already noted, such types of societies are at best abstractions and approximations.

Delimiting the Medical

In an analytic sense, one can delimit the medical as that which encompasses the problems of disease and injury in a society. However, this formulation immediately makes evident one's ethnocentric bias. Diseases as conceptualized in biomedicine and played out in contemporary societies are reasonably well demarcated. For the most part they are easily separated from the political, the legal, and the religious, as an example. One who studies such phenomena comparatively, however, learns quickly that in many societies problems of sickness and healing are not separated from other concerns but blend imperceptibly with phenomena that in European, biomedicine-dominated societies are institutionally separated.

Some problems in delimiting the medical in different societies can be illustrated. Many "diseases" of European societies may not be recognized or handled as sickness in other societies (Fabrega 1974; Payer 1989). The personality disorders of psychiatry constitute good examples of this, although similar generalizations can be made about other "diseases." Conversely, most "folk" illnesses are not easily equated with Western medical diseases (Johnson and Sargent 1990). However, that they can implicate traditional medical categories has been well documented (Guarnaccia 1990; Jenkins 1988; Topley 1970). Another example is provided by misfortunes involving domesticated animals or crop failures. In many societies these are conceptualized and handled in ways that are very similar to misfortunes of human sickness. Obviously people are able to tell the difference between sickness and other misfortunes; however, the point is that ways of understanding these diverse problems and attempts to undo their consequences share a basic ontology and epistemology in the culture. Something that an outsider might think of as "not medical" might be the object of terminologies, explanations, and procedures that are also reserved for problems of sickness. Conversely, in modern Anglo-European-influenced societies, problems of obesity, unwanted facial or scalp features, undesired gender characteristics, or what is judged as an unattractive bodily organ may be the object of medical treatment. In this case, it would appear that sickness of morale and satisfaction with self-image or social confidence underlie and motivate medical treatment. In other words, something that would hardly be recognized as medical or sickness in many societies has taken on these labels in Anglo-European-influenced societies.

Finally, one can consider other items of social behavior that flirt with the medical. In many small-scale, elementary societies, conventions pertaining to hunting, foraging, and harvesting are invested with sacred directives and rules that operate as safeguards against sickness (and a host of other misfortunes, to be sure). What one could term "the medical" thus appears to be spread out, intruding into the social, political, and economic. As a contrast, one can consider the profound effects on thoughts and behavior that have taken place in modern society as a result of the way public health officials promoted the germ theory of disease. A host of attitudes and behaviors toward the body, hygiene, and private functions were altered dramatically and medicalized as a consequence of learning about the germ theory of disease. Given the profound influence that ideas of health and disease have on social experience and identity generally (Giddens 1991), it is difficult indeed to draw the line between health/disease concerns and those pertaining to identity, appearance, and behavior generally. It is obviously the case that in these instances, also, the medical is spread out and intrudes into highly social and private spheres of human behavior. In both instances, then, one can say that the boundaries of the medical are problematized.

The problem of delimiting the medical in society has to be viewed as part of the more general problem of reification of structures and entities as separate sorts of "things." An important tradition in the social sciences draws attention to the recursive nature of social life (Bourdieu 1977; Giddens 1984). Human action and practice is reflexively under review and influenced constantly by knowledge that it essentially reproduces. Problems of sickness and healing are, of course, no different, yet for one intending a theoretical approach to medicine both conceptual categories and culturally organized behaviors need to be dealt with abstractly and formulated systematically.

The problem of delimiting the medical poses obvious difficulties for one intending to articulate a comprehensive yet unified theory. How can one be provided with a frame of reference and a set of concepts for integrating, analyzing, and comparing the way people in different societies instantiate sickness and healing if the material is so fluid and variable that it seems to militate against valid categorization? There is, in fact, no way of avoiding these quandaries, although different strategies can be surmised.

One way is to adopt a frame of reference such as biomedicine in terms of which one defines the medical and, with it as a measuring rod, proceed to analyze and compare how societies handle sickness and healing (the concrete social phenomena that instantiate disease and its effects). This epidemiological, public health approach has been undertaken and is not without its merits. However, since one starts out with a preconceived definition of the medical, one can only encompass phenomena covered by it and of necessity might have to exclude problems of sickness and healing that do not conform to biomedical definitions.

The approach suggested here is to start with abstract definitions of what sickness and healing consist of viewed in biological, social and cultural terms and allow them to identify and locate the medical across societies and cultures. Provided one is sufficiently specific, such a procedure can serve to delimit important areas of the domain of the medical that facilitate analysis. In this instance one may fail to include certain problems of disease (viewed biomedically) that are not conceptualized as problems of sickness and healing in a society. However, if the diseases produce bodily symptoms, physical signs, or behavioral breakdowns, it is very likely that they will be conceptualized as sickness and dealt with accordingly in the society and culture.

Measuring the Impact of Sickness in a Society

Many factors affect the level of sickness in a society. What one could term bioecologic factors have received most attention. Research has indicated that complex genetic structures of populations, the ecology of its physical habitat, its way of procuring and processing food and water, and the level of social organization of a society, including in particular the density of its population and its social institutions pertaining to the availability of fresh air and the disposal of wastes, are all important. All of these and related factors will influence the level and kinds of disease that are prevalent, and the latter bear a direct relation to the level of experienced illness in the population and hence the impact of this in the form of sickness and healing on the members of the society.

Were one to limit oneself to measuring the level of malaria or dysentery in a society, measures derived from epidemiology would suffice to assess impact of sickness. However, were one to be interested in what sickness is made of as a social and cultural phenomenon, then what members of a population perceive as sickness and how they explain it, which entails orientations toward and understandings of the body and its functions as well as the problems of disease (which reflect purely bioecologic factors), all are relevant.

What is important to emphasize is the role played by social and cultural factors in constructing and reconstructing sickness and healing. This involves not only influencing and shaping threshold levels of what is to count as sickness, a basically cognitive/psychophysiologic matter, but also negotiating and re-creating knowledge structures through social practices wherein experience and reality are reflexively monitored. These factors can be conceptualized to operate more or less independently from the purely bioecologic ones pertaining to the epidemiology of disease and injury and to changes in physiology. In other words, even if sickness and healing are conceptualized as rooted in biological factors and as having evolutionary implications, one must still study them from a comparative standpoint as socially and culturally constructed. There is much controversy here about how one is best to regard the biological and the cultural that will be dealt with in later chapters (Barkow, Cosmides, and Tooby 1992; Bourdieu 1977; Giddens 1984, 1990, 1991).

In the way of a generalization, if the social aspects of sickness and healing are emphasized, this means that the way in which they are thought of and played out in social conflicts or interpersonal relations can be studied comparatively with the strictly biomedical end of things kept separate. Moreover, a social and cultural framework allows one to consider under what conditions of social organization actors might be motivated (consciously or unconsciously) to express personal or social conflicts in sickness phenomena that are then played out during processes of healing. In this instance, then, the degree to which sickness is played out socially and interpersonally, a practice factor, influences the level of perceived sickness and end points of treatment, a more cognitive one; and the actual pathology underlying all of this needs to be recognized but can be left out of the analysis. Other parameters of sickness and healing that reflect cultural meanings could be studied, for example, attitudes about the body or remunerative aspects of healing. Finally, specific parameters of sickness and healing can be compared in different societies.

In summary, sickness and healing have a form and content that are a function of society and culture. Societies and cultures are, of course, not unitary things, nor can eventuations of sickness and healing be regarded as homogenous and representative "entities" even if they were. These complexities need to be kept in mind whenever medical phenomena are dealt with in terms of social types. Nevertheless, the interplay of cultural categories, social practices, and the reflexive, recursive nature of eventuations of sickness and healing need to be dealt with theoretically: Their diverse aspects in relation to types of societies need to be formulated and explained. A way of looking at sickness and healing comparatively so as to explain the diversity will be presented in later chapters.

On the Ontology of Sickness and Healing

An evolutionary perspective on behavior and adaptation, and, indeed, on the way physiological systems function, urges one to adopt a holistic, systems theory point of view. In this light, an individual is judged to respond to environmental stress by means of changes in connected systems that describe him or her hierarchically. Sickness and healing as evolutionarily conditioned are thus constituted in a unity one could describe (given our linguistic bias) as psychosomatic and somatopsychic. What this means is that there is a natural tendency for problems of adaptation to be manifested in terms of physiology, emotional experience, and behavior. Biomedical science and the intellectual tradition that spawned it have created an emphasis pertaining to sickness and healing that has been characterized as ontological (Temkin 1963). The hallmark of sickness and the key target of healing is disease, a thing or object thought of as having a separate existence: an identity in anatomy, physiology, chemistry, and the like; a cause separated from itself; and an extension in time or "natural history." The ontological perspective or emphasis is said to constitute a watershed in the modern theory of disease and foundational to its understanding and epistemology (Rather 1959).

A key logical corollary of the ontological emphasis is that the entities and processes that make up disease have a physical essence and of course come to occupy and take place in the physical body. Given this interpretation, disease is thought of as somehow different from things mental, behavioral, or psychological. Dualism thus seems to be entailed by the Western epistemology and ontology of disease.

Dualism as a symbolic property of Western culture is structurally embedded in the contemporary practice of medicine. The education of physicians at the graduate and undergraduate levels and the emphases of the different specialties within medicine reflect a dualistic, mind/body dichotomy. Since physicians are socialized with this bias, their clients are reinforced for it, a cultural bias that is widely prevalent in the society to begin with. Dualism is thus a conditioning factor in the way sickness and healing are played out in Western society. Problems that have come to be conceptualized as "somatization" illustrate this point. This term refers to somatic problems that cannot be explained adequately in anatomic or physiological terms. The biological sciences stipulate a basis for disease that "somatization" problems fail to conform to or elude. One thus finds individuals sick with somatic problems that are compelling to patients and families but fail to meet criteria for disease. Such problems are now constituted as mental disorders, and their treatment is partly impeded because they carry a social stigma of mental illness that plagues patients with these disorders.

The basic holistic perspective on persons has implications for a theoretical approach to medicine. One is that to develop a theory, a unified schema and a comprehensive frame of reference is needed. A systems theoretic approach has been adopted. The second is that in constructing a social theory of the medical one is required to appreciate the dialectical interplay among the parameters of sickness and healing, on the one hand, and altogether different features of the society, such as its organization/complexity and culture, on the other. In other words, holism implies interconnection, so that if a culture chooses to single out, say, purely the physical, then given psychosomatic mediation and the powerful shaping effects of social symbols, the material of sickness and healing will come to prominently display this facet. However, other components of the holistic material of sickness and healing, say, the emotional and mental components, remain present but masked, labeled differently, and expressed in a form that is dictated psychophysiologically by and consistent with the emphases conditioned by the semantics of the culture. One who attempts to construct a theoretical account of the medical is thus forced to analyze how the holistic basis of sickness and healing is shaped, modified, and labeled semantically in relation to "external" factors pertaining to society and culture.

In summary, from a theoretical standpoint, cultural conventions pertaining to ontology and epistemology give material content to sickness and healing. This material needs to be analyzed as meaningful and adaptive. However, to compare and formulate theoretically the cultural material of sickness and healing, it must also be studied in relation to scientific, etic understandings that are comprehensive and hierarchically organized.

Comparing Medical Knowledge Structures

To be able to compare how sickness and healing are configured and played out in different societies, a way of categorizing and measuring these is needed. With a procedure for quantifying the medical in one society conditions are created not only for comparison across societies but also for predicting trends in the way the medical is likely to unfold across time and in relation to factors that impinge on the medical and are likely to alter its course.

One intending to use a classification of medical problems runs into problems of bias and cultural relativism. What frame of reference is to be adopted, and how can one validate it for comparison since of necessity it reflects the culture and political economic status of the analyst? Epistemological problems such as these when applied to medicine can essentially paralyze efforts aimed at scientific analyses (Spiro 1986), which of necessity require categories and classifications. With respect to sickness, a common scheme of classification pertaining to causes has included such categories as natural, supernatural; also, magical, religious, empirical, and scientific (Fabrega 1974; Johnson and Sargent 1990). These are obviously rather general and abstract categories. More detailed ones might include such things as physical environmental (e.g., heat, cold, level of moisture), social interpersonal (e.g., jealousy/envy, acts of hostility), actions perpetrated by spiritual/otherworldly agents (e.g., punishment by ancestors, godlike beings, malevolent spirits), psychological/mental states (e.g., hostility, worry, sadness), social/political happenings (e.g., work difficulties, setbacks associated with subsistence), and finally ethnophysiological, which might include reference to distinct bodily structures (e.g., organs, conduits), substances (e.g., the humors, vital energies), or processes (e.g., fermentation, pressure differentials, movements and flows of materials of different types). A complementary set of semantic categories for describing the way healing is understood to occur and actually implemented can be surmised. These would include such things as the ways medicines are believed to work, the processes that need to be neutralized or energized in order to counteract the causes of sickness, or the actual procedures used by healers. Healing, in other words, entails carrying out physical, social, or verbal actions that are believed to set in motion distinct processes and/or mechanisms and these could be categorized semantically and as information.

A system of semantic categories provides a static classification of a society's knowledge structures pertaining to sickness and healing. These structures are of course continually reframed, restructured, and reinterpreted (Bourdieu 1977; Giddens 1984, 1990) and for one interested in capturing the essential "thickness" of the medical, such structures need to be handled conservatively. Systems of knowledge nevertheless provide one way of depicting the way the sickness and healing are configured and played out across time. Not only the richness of categories embodied in the knowledge system could be formulated but also which categories tend to carry the burden of explanation across time. A hypothetical occurrence of sickness could be conceptualized as embodying a quantum of uncertainty that members of a society attempt to reduce or eliminate by means of their knowledge structures pertaining to sickness and healing. The information required to accomplish this is embodied in its knowledge structures (Fabrega 1976a, 1976b, 1976c). The preceding illustrates one way of coping with the problem of comparing sickness and healing in different societies.

A system of classification for describing and comparing the way societies configure and play out sickness and healing could not easily deal with the effects that sicknesses produce; or, alternatively, with the efficacy of healing actions. Abstract schemes such as the ones suggested are just that—devices for describing or quantifying what constitutes the cultural and social reality of sickness and healing of a people. They cannot provide information about physiological effects. For the latter, an entirely different schema would be required. Standard epidemiologic measures of mortality and morbidity immediately come to mind. The latter schema, of course, would be used to answer questions altogether different from those asked of a symbolic schema. Cultural and symbolic schemas pertain to how knowledge structures about sickness and healing are configured and used, whereas epidemiologic ones pertain to the effects of these structures on the lives of persons who use them. The one provides cultural information about social processes of sickness and healing, whereas the other provides biologic information about the effects of disease and injury. It is the former schema that is developed here. In a complete theory of the medical, these two types of schemas and many others pertaining to the way knowledge structures work in a society would be required.

Medical Pluralism

What has been termed a theoretical perspective on medicine as a social institution involves the use of an explanatory frame of reference for comparing sickness and healing. Of necessity, then, it involves comparisons of *whole societies,* and this runs into the problem of the diversity of ways of thinking and acting with respect to the medical realm that exists in societies that differ in terms of social and cultural complexity. Is it possible to describe how sickness and healing are configured and played out in a (particular type of) society when that society seems to show a pluralism with respect to medicine?

Consider that a member of a small-scale society can explain illness in terms of several different causes by means of which he or she could make sense of the illness and seek to heal it. Insofar as each orientation is different in terms of content and required practices, is even this type of simple society "pluralistic" with respect to the medical? While any of a number of "pluralistic" interpretations are possible, together, presumably, they form a coherent part of the one cultural reality of medicine of the society. In other words, all members of the society share in this cultural reality and see alternative causal explanations as part of their one coherent picture of medicine.

An idea of medical pluralism makes more sense when an individual has access to more than one cultural approach to sickness and healing. Each approach need not constitute an organized system, leaving aside for the moment the problem of how one is to conceptualize what exactly is an "organized system" pertaining to sickness and healing (Press 1980). Suffice it to say that when individuals are able to distinguish between more or less separate ways of explaining and handling the medical, ways that differ in terms of basic propositions, explanatory mechanisms, procedures, and personnel, one can begin to speak more comfortably of medical pluralism.

Related problems can be given focus by considering how one will define "medical pluralism." To start with, one can entertain the following question: What would constitute the obverse of medical pluralism? "Medical singularity"? For example, could one ever describe a society that demonstrated a pristine, uncontaminated singular medical tradition or approach to sickness and healing? Even an isolated, family-level society could be said to have borrowed at least part of its knowledge of sickness and healing from nearby groups, rendering its approach somewhat eclectic. With time, it might evolve its own distinctive approach to sickness and healing but along the way is likely to assimilate elements from nearby groups.

Societies larger and more complex are likely to contain ethnic groups, lineages, or clans that have had different experiences with sickness and healing and hence are probably in possession of different bodies of knowledge and practices. Even an ethnically homogenous society is likely to be made up of groups that differ in terms of economic factors and given a modicum of complexity is likely to have access to different types of healers with approaches that differ. It is arguable whether one could meaningfully speak of a society with but one integrated, continuous tradition pertaining to sickness and healing. What one is likely to find instead are societies with several distinct approaches to the medical, each tradition constituting an amalgam of ideas, explanatory frameworks, and healing practices. The information of a tradition is likely to contain elements shared with other traditions found in the society, the latter linked to indigenous approaches, pagan themes, magical/religious tenets, and the like. In short, it is probably the case that medical pluralism is a constant feature of any complex society. Even the so-called great traditions (e.g., Ayurvedic, Galenic, Chinese) may themselves have been mutually enriched from borrowings at different points of their history. That they were found in societies characterized by having any number of lay, indigenous, magical/religious as well as empirical approaches to sickness and healing in addition to the "Great Traditions" has been well described (Dols 1984a; Leslie 1976; Unschuld 1985, 1986a, 1986b).

Given that medical pluralism is a social property of most if not all (certainly complex) societies, how is this to be dealt with in a theory of medicine? At the very least, it forces one to avoid speaking as though there existed one or even a dominant tradition of medicine. The control and dominance of biomedicine today, a dominance made possible partly as a result of a de facto state enforcement consisting of regulation, subsidy of research and education, and the co-opting of biomedical experts as policy makers/advisers, is unprecedented in the social history and cultural evolution of medicine. Competing traditions in the medical marketplace constitute the reality pertaining to a society's approach to sickness and healing. A theory about sickness and healing and medicine, more generally, must allow for the existence of medical pluralism and the resort to different traditions must be taken into consideration.

In comparisons of the medical across societies or within societies across time, the extent of pluralism, its architecture across social groupings, the degree to which traditions shift in importance in relation to other social factors, and the relative impact that different traditions have on the workings of other social institutions would ideally need to be taken into consideration. It is likely that parameters that make up sickness, such as definition of sick role, semantic meanings of sickness, or expectation of relief, will vary in relation to what tradition is selected. If more than one tradition is used, then the effect of conjoint use on these or related parameters should also, ideally, be considered. Simply describing how the different groupings of a society cope with pluralistic alternatives or whether there exists a pattern in the way different traditions are used in the event of different types of sicknesses would prove illuminating in the comparison of sickness and healing across societies.

It should be clear that comparing the way persons orient to and make use of differing traditions of medicine in societies that differ with respect to degree of medical pluralism would constitute an enormously difficult undertaking. One way of coping with these and related problems is to focus on sickness and healing purely as abstract concepts and describe their properties in a generic way. Basic parameters in terms of which these concepts are configured and the semantics that serve to orient, give meaning to, and structure sickness behaviors and practices of healing would be emphasized. Of necessity, this requires formulating sickness and healing in terms of ideal actors of a particular type of society.

Social and Psychological Implications of Sickness and Healing

Many of the issues discussed thus far can be looked at in terms of the social psychology of sickness and healing. Two related factors are worth considering. First, conceptualizations of sickness (and healing as well) do not operate or function in a vacuum; rather, they are integral to a people's sense of social reality, which itself has religious, political, economic, and ideological as well as strictly psychological overtones and dimensions. Second, to the extent that one's approach is concerned with cultural configurations, it requires taking into account how medical symbolization, medical action, and medical organization stand in relation to these other realms of experience, more specifically, how the view of the medical is affected by and affects the wider view of social reality.

As social, structural, and cultural characteristics of societies change, so do also myriad other characteristics. And all of them are dialectically incorporated in basic outlooks and orientations to the world and ideas about the meaning of an individual's life (conceptions of personhood). This is so because sickness underscores and heightens man's sense of uncertainty and thus brings into play how persons are seen to relate to the ultimate conditions of existence (Fabrega 1977). Of necessity, then, symbolizations pertaining to religion and cosmology are implicated in a basic way in the medical (Bellah 1964).

Religious symbols implicate the operation of governing agencies and the meanings they impart to social life. They also presuppose, shape, and are shaped by basic conceptions pertaining to human identity that can be expected to affect responses to sickness. This would include such things as conceptions of self, of objects of the behavioral environment, and of social activities that provide meaning to everyday life. As an example, how unified or differentiated selves are felt to be determines how they orient religiously to this world; and both affect what can possibly be made of a condition of sickness and the opportunities presented by healing. Similarly, how persons are politically constituted, which is to say what they judge is possible in a civic, worldly sense, is not only intrinsic to religious action and experience but also critically shapes what persons and their healers think about a condition of sickness and possibilities for a return to health. Finally, the structures that comprise everyday life and experience, from the social divisions within the population through the way subsistence is patterned and carried out and on to the way reciprocation is contextualized, all affect the experience of sickness since they all determine what can be expected in the way of healing and how it can be accessed.

In summary, what has been referred to as a theoretical account of medicine as a social institution cannot but constitute a restricted enterprise insofar as its object is material that is also influenced by many other dimensions of a people's way of life. The theory's domain is social and psychological behaviors surrounding sickness and healing. The context of the medical underscores uncertainty and the essential powerlessness of human striving. The uncertainty of disease is colored by the society's way of conceptualizing such basic things as persons, the purposes of existence, the causes of human suffering, and the possibilities for betterment offered by worldly human actions. All that incorporates the sacred and the worldly is brought into play by sickness and healing. The topics relate to questions that are empirically contestable and theoretically highly controversial. As indicated earlier, a theory of sickness and healing should ideally incorporate material that only with difficulty can be separated from myriad other phenomena that condition human symbolization and action.

An elaborate historical account of the subject of illness considered in relation to social and cultural factors has been provided (Herzlich and Pierret 1987). Its emphasis is limited to Western societies and primarily those of the modern era, that is, orientations found in European societies during the eighteenth and especially the nineteenth centuries. However, this account contains material about views of illness in earlier European epochs, and it also includes empirical material that is contemporary. It draws attention to the central importance of epidemic diseases as setting the tone for how members of a society think of illness and orient to it.

One of its claims is that prior to the advent of tuberculosis during the nineteenth century (the "Ancien Régime of Diseases"), sickness and healing viewed in terms of the self had played a comparatively unimportant role in intellectual circles and in the society at large: "It is our hypothesis that in the nineteenth century, and particularly with the advent of tuberculosis, the figure of the sick person crystallized existential and socially, assuming its modern form. This figure emerged as an individual with his or her concrete experience yet also, and by the same token, as a social phenomenon. Henceforth the sick person was to be defined by his or her place in society" (Herzlich and Pierret 1987: 29).

It is not appropriate here to discuss more fully the many related and rich accounts of illness developed by Claudine Herzlich and Janine Pierret. It is relevant, however, to draw attention to how their orientation differs from the one followed here. They are primarily concerned with tracing the modern perspective of illness and the self. Moreover, they concentrate on intellectual and what one could term ideological aspects of illness. The widely prevalent (indeed, the dominant) symbols and social imagery about illness that are found in European societies are their principal concern. In this presentation, attention is given not to actual, descriptive properties of how illness and healing are played out (in Western or non-Western societies) but to a general, abstract account of such phenomena viewed from a comparative, evolutionary point of view.

Sickness and Healing and the Problem of Social Change and Evolution

A neglected topic in social studies of medicine is that of comparing sickness and healing and medicine, more generally, in different types of societies considered from a structural, macrosociological point of view. Despite anthropology's and sociology's interest in social organization and the call for systematic comparisons, the appropriateness of whole medical institutions or traditions as objects for comparison does not seem to have been given much attention. A prevailing emphasis in the social sciences on meaning-centered analyses and on theories of practice, with persons and interpersonal networks seen as creating and re-creating knowledge, has naturally deflected attention away from the study of institutions as whole structures. That sickness and healing as social and cultural phenomena might show different characteristics as a result of differences in the size and complexity as well as culture of a society has not been systematically addressed. An emphasis on comparison and difference raises the question of how medical traditions might be expected to change and why.

Various terms have been used to designate the medical domain of a society. Some examples are health systems, sectors of health systems, medical systems, medical institutions, medical care systems or structures, adaptive health systems. The terms are not always used consistently, nor do they have similar meanings (Press 1980). One problem is the ambiguity of the concept "system" (e.g., how ordered and interconnected must a set of units be to qualify as a "system"?). Another factor contributing to ambiguity has been whether a medical or health "system" is handled as one of potentially several social units of a society (e.g., a structure, institution, or corporation) or whether it is used to designate the total approach to medicine of the society as a whole and the separate medical units within this overarching system then being handled as sectors or subsystems (Janzen 1978a). All of the terms that have been used can be viewed as attempts to codify the variety and complexity of the social meanings about and resources pertaining to sickness and healing; or the health prevention/preservation rationales and procedures that exist in societies in a more or less ordered form.

A comparative approach to health systems was initially set forth vigorously by Fred L. Dunn (1976). He pointed out that health systems could be local (e.g., a particular lay, folk variety), regional (e.g., the Chinese, Ayurvedic), and cosmopolitan (e.g., worldwide, namely, the modern, Western, biomedical) and that regardless of type they all addressed basic factors related to health. He listed a number of factors, including health education, public health/sanitation, prevention, curing, and rehabilitation. Dunn emphasized that "each medical system evolved to meet a people's conception of their health needs" (1976: 142–143) and that it did so to varying degrees depending on which of the several areas of health promotion and medical care one chose to emphasize. Importantly, Dunn drew attention to the fact that a health or medical system (he used both terms interchangeably) could meet disease/mortality/morbidity needs of a population (termed by him biological needs) and also needs pertaining to outlook in areas related to health and well-being, including such things as life satisfaction, social support, and joy (termed psychosocial needs). Systems of medicine also differed in terms of their integration and stability given the structure of the population and the features of the environment (he referred to this as a system's adaptedness) and in terms of their capacity to respond constructively to exogenous insults (he referred to this as their adaptability).

In his formulation, Dunn raised a number of intriguing questions about the way in which health systems function. Some examples are the following: "Is a medical system more likely to be adaptable-capable of responding to new insults—if it is closely associated with other medical systems? Or is it likely to become rigid and unresponsive in such circumstances, to protect its integrity? . . . How, in general, are degrees of cultural homogeneity and heterogeneity related to the biological adaptive value of a medical system, to the capacity of a system to respond to new conditions, and to its ability to maintain psychosocial equilibrium?" (1976: 144). In this pathbreaking presentation, Dunn concentrated on characteristics of the Chinese, Ayurvedic, and Arabic-Persian medical systems. Although raising the question of variety, complexity, and differences in health systems, Dunn did not address the matter of how such systems change across time and dealt primarily with the contemporary scene, although his description and comparison drew on historical sources and examples.

An implicit and sometimes explicit (as in the case of Dunn) assumption that exists in the minds of workers in this field is that these so-called social systems of medical care are each governed by cultural symbols and meanings, that they are more or less systematized and coherent, and that they provide individuals of a society with constructive ways of dealing with a medical problem or illness. This is why such social modalities of medical care are sometimes spoken of as "adaptive systems" and thought to promote "cultural healing" insofar as they provide for a way of cognitively, emotionally, and even psychosomatically shaping and controlling sickness and healing episodes (Kleinman 1978; Kleinman, Eisenberg, and Good 1978). At the same time, it is widely appreciated that the different sectors of a health system or different social systems of medical care of a society are not all consistent in a cultural/symbolic sense and, furthermore, can give rise to conflicts that impede the resolution of sickness episodes, perhaps even leading to the causation of sickness (hence the term "cultural iatrogenesis").

An important, neglected topic in this field of inquiry is that of conceptualizing and measuring change in "social systems of medical care." In other words, given that systems of medical care differ across societies and cultures, the question can be raised of differences across prehistory and recorded historical periods and also the question of how and why such social systems of medical care change. This particular area of the comparative study of medicine, also thought of as the historical sociology of medicine, has not received much attention from researchers.

One person who has dealt with this aspect of comparative medicine is John M. Janzen (1978a), who in his discussion of health systems as adaptive systems used examples of change in Zaire during the modern era. Besides underscoring the importance of this problem of change in health systems, Janzen provided useful guidelines for conceptualizing the social medical units of a society that could initiate and or be affected by this "systemic" change in approach to sickness and healing (termed corporate category and corporate group and roughly denoting the increasing degree of social definition and empowerment of a medical unit, such as that of practitioners of a certain type). He also discussed in a general way larger factors and processes that could also prompt change in health systems (e.g., political economic, historical). Janzen's efforts are perhaps the most focused attempts yet to concentrate on the topic of change in health systems. In doing so he of necessity drew attention to the need to concentrate on societywide events and processes. Arthur M. Kleinman has dealt in particular with the topic of complexity in medical systems and alluded to factors that could bring about change in them, largely by implication. His efforts have, like Janzen's, also involved the modern era. In his discussion Kleinman indicated that epidemiological factors must also be considered important in addition to historical and political economic ones.

The formulation of Zdzislaw Bizon (1976) carries forward the perspective of health or medical systems in terms of function and adaptation and offers a way of conceptualizing social change and evolution. Although concentrating primarily on the workings of the medical profession during the modern era in European societies, his framework is applicable to all medical systems regardless of historical era or type of society.

Bizon indicates that the function of a medical system is to meet the goals for which it was set up and these consist of (and he is vague on this point) diminishing the morbidity and mortality associated with sickness and disease. Here, his formulation parallels that of Dunn. The goals are defined by the "environment," which in effect is constituted by the larger, suprasystem of which the medical system is part. The society and culture can be conceptualized as an important suprasystem, defining the functions of the medical system by providing the goals of improved health, decreased pain, restoration of function, and the like. These are targeted and managed by medical interventions and actions, which are defined as the basic units of the medical system.

The goals and functions of a medical system are framed in systemic and broad terms. In effect, they are properties of the society or of its dominant powers. Similarly, the medical system is framed in a corporate manner as consisting of groups with effective medical power. The medical profession is Bizon's classic example. However, these abstractly formulated goals and corporate units can be visualized in more concrete terms. Goals of the medical system are internalized in actors of the society who seek well-being through healing from the medical system that is actualized in its various healers. Sick persons in effect hold individual healers (implicitly or explicitly) accountable to the general goals and functions of the medical system as actualized in the actions of the healer.

Bizon introduces two important concepts in the study of medical systems. Function has already been considered and refers to a relationship between the medical system and the suprasystem or environment. The connectedness or fit captures this abstractly. The setting of goals is the key issue. Adaptiveness refers to the dynamic quality or ability of the medical system to maintain itself across time, not unlike the ideas of Dunn. In other words, as a result of change, evolution, or historical contingencies of any type, the suprasystem is constantly framing new functions and goals (or reframing old ones) in relation to changing needs and values of the population. A measure of adaptiveness of a medical system is how well it manages to keep itself functional in the light of inherent difficulties and/or inadequacies of its resources and capabilities. A basic assumption of Bizon is that only modern medical systems have been able to begin to meet their goals whereas earlier ones have been less successful, having to conceal and negotiate this matter. The medical system maintains adaptiveness through what Bizon classifies as adaptive mechanisms. These are classified in two categories that are not clearly separable. One consists of defense mechanisms, devices designed to protect the medical system from its dysfunctionality. Example of this are attempts to limit controls, obfuscate goals, and promote new goals which in effect conceal its dysfunctionality. The other consists of social and political actions designed to promote itself. These enable the medical system to counterbalance and/or compensate for its dys-functionality. Political action designed to obtain a monopoly is one way in which a corporate unit of the medical system can counterbalance its failures of resources and capability. Promoting defense mechanisms (e.g., "desirable" goals) as new definitions of a medical reality would constitute another exam-ple. "As a result of these activities, the profession [or any unit of a medical system] managed to counterbalance its ineffectiveness in influencing the natu-ral, biological reality by exerting an effective influence on social reality; to re-place the objective dysfunctionality of the medical system with the myth of its functionality in the social consciousness; to substitute for bio-technically in-effective action socio-technically effective activities" (Bizon 1976: 334).

One group of social scientists who also bring into focus the problem of so-cial change in health systems is that which emphasizes a "critical approach" to medical anthropology (Singer 1989a; Singer, Baer, and Lazarus 1990). A dominant interest of these researchers is in some of the limitations and indeed sometimes the perniciousness of biomedicine and its exclusive emphasis on disease/organic factors and treatment to the detriment of an appreciation of how social factors consistent and supportive of biomedicine lead to the pro-duction of these diseases. A corresponding theoretical focus is on how politi-cal economic and class-related aspects of a society lead to systems of medical care that foster and perpetuate class systems and systems of oppression in a society.

In using critical theory when discussing society and medicine, these re-searchers draw emphasis, if only by implication, to the importance of this the-ory in providing a way of examining what factors bring about a restructuring of social relations of medicine within a society. In sum, critical theory provides a potential way of examining in some detail how health systems and aspects of sickness and healing change and "evolve." The analysis by Andrew T. Scull (1993) of how approaches to mental illness changed and of the corresponding growth of psychiatry during the eighteenth and nineteenth centuries consti-tutes a landmark of this approach to the topic of change in health systems using critical theory as its basic approach. The rationale of critical medical the-orists has also brought about an interesting and probing critique of medical ecological theory, a theory that takes account of the notion of health systems as adaptive systems (Singer 1989b). This critique has led to important reformula-tions of medical ecology aimed at meeting these criticisms (Armelagos et al. 1992).

Critical medical theorists are obviously aware of the idea that health sys-tems are "dynamic," that there exist interests and factors that render such systems "functional," and that, by implication, health systems are capable of "dysfunctioning" and changing. However, although possessed of a theory of social change and cultural evolution, these researchers have thus far concentrated primarily on modern and contemporary societies and on changes linked to biomedicine. Nonetheless, in underscoring the overriding importance of political and economic factors in bringing about change in health systems, critical medical theorists emphasize the need to pay attention to societywide factors, and in this respect their emphases parallel those of Janzen, Kleinman, and medical ecologists like George J. Armelagos and Dunn.

The preceding constitutes a brief summary of previous efforts aimed at explaining the question of complexity and change in the way sickness and healing are configured and played out in different societies. All of these efforts, insofar as they deal at all with questions of social change, are primarily concerned largely with contemporary or at least modern developments. The work of Renée C. Fox (1988a, 1988b) and Alexander Alland (1970) is to be contrasted to these efforts insofar as both of the latter are concerned not only with change in so-called health systems but also with the question of whether such systems can be said to evolve over long intervals of time. Fox and Alland both have brought into focus the idea of social and cultural evolution of medicine. Their efforts are nearly mutually exclusive in the sense that the interests and emphasis of each exclude but complement those of the other. Fox is exclusively interested in a sociological approach to the question of evolution and change in medical orientation and approaches consistent with stages of social complexity and does not address medical epidemiological/ecological issues. However, her analysis of how medical uncertainty has evolved is not only richly evocative but compelling and potentially useful to one interested in capturing medical phenomena "in the field," that is to say, as a way of conceptualizing how sickness and healing change and evolve.

Alland's (1970) work pertaining to medical anthropology is unique in that it focused directly on evolutionary questions. Alland drew on a tradition in medical anthropology (Polgar 1962, 1963) and on his interests in human evolution (Alland 1967), evolutionary theory, and cultural ecology. His contribution was that he emphasized the importance not only of different types of disease pictures linked to the environment but also of a population's behavioral systems (his apparent gloss for society, culture, and social structure) in affecting its (i.e., the population's) adaptation to the environment. He was thus clearly concerned with the relations between biological and cultural evolution as these processes were affected by the need to surmount problems of disease posed by the physical and biological environment of man. Alland correctly emphasized that to deal with the question of how populations cope with and surmount problems of disease, activities of individuals that are not limited to their conception of the medical needed to be taken into consideration. Political economic, ritualistic, and strictly subsistence issues together with medical beliefs and practices needed to be brought into the cultural ecological equation if the goal was that of understanding how populations were adapted to the environment.

A very thoughtful and challenging theoretical exposition of the evolution and history of medicine has been provided by Timothy Johns (1990). His presentation differs from those of such researchers as Janzen, Kleinman, and Bizon and the critical medical anthropologists considered earlier in that biological evolutionary factors play a determinant role and empirical data pertaining to animal and human biochemistry are influential. The chemistry of plant and animal foods, the role of enzymes in intermediary metabolism, and the consequences of all of this for the meeting of energy requirements as well as for impairments in health status through toxic effects are his primary concerns. Johns sees the interplay of these factors as setting the stage for what he terms the chemical ecological context of subsistence, adaptation, and eventually medicine.

In his discussion of the origins and evolution of medicine Johns does not give concerted attention to social and cultural factors as do other social scientists who have been discussed so far. His formulation could be said to complement and elaborate that of Dunn and Alland in handling traditional medical practices as manifestations of an adaptive system for maintaining health. The actual behavioral characteristics of sickness and healing, including their meaning-centered features, are not a prominent concern. Rather, Johns gives primary attention to the relationship between social practices affecting nutrition (equatable as healing) and biochemical and physiological processes of organisms that affect health and well-being (Garcia, Hankins, and Rusiniak 1974; Rozin 1976, 1980).

I am giving considerable attention to the content of Johns's formulation here because it is complementary to the one I will be developing in subsequent chapters. During the evolution of the hominid line, food procurement strategies included reliance on a variety of plants that contained secondary chemicals, termed allelochemicals, that affected in a positive way the growth, health, and behavior of organisms through *detoxication* of plant allelochemicals. During cultural evolution, changes in human food procurement practices that decreased the amounts of these useful allelochemicals of plants are seen as related to the more elaborate use of herbal products for specific medicinal purposes. In effect, the latter are more concerned with the *detoxification* of the effects of plant and animal substances. Shifts to animal flesh and products, bacterial contamination of food, and the role of bacteria in the flora of the small intestine all mediate the chemical ecology of adaptation and health that points to the importance of herbal medicine.

Johns (1990) links, and seems to equate, the origins of medicine, which he defines as a cultural institution, to biological mechanisms of animals and higher primates involving ingestion of food substances and the special use of plants for medicinal purposes (see chapter 2). However, he seems to at times equivocate in the way he relates biological and cultural factors in the evolution of medicine, sometimes judging that a continuity exists between these two types of processes and at other times suggesting a correspondence. The following quotes summarize the issue.

> I argue that such use of plants is the biological prototype for human medicine. Similarly, the ingestion of clay to adsorb plant toxins has a biological basis. However, unless these behaviors have a cultural component, they are, strictly speaking, not medicine. When humans began to rely on learned knowledge and to communicate it from generation to generation, their use of plants evolved from a biologic, genetically determined behavior to a cultural practice. (Johns 1990: 258)

> The overlap of culture and human biology makes it difficult to say which of our medicinal behaviors have a specific genetic basis. A more important aspect of our biology in relation to the evolution of medicine is our ability to learn. (Ibid., 274)

> As plants and plant secondary chemicals preceded animal foods as determinants of human evolution, so it is reasonable to assume that herbal medicine—with its direct analogues in animal behavior—was the original form of medicine. However, which of the surgical or pharmacological roads of medicine is of greatest antiquity is really a meaningless issue. Early rudimentary practices would have provided only a predisposition for the elaborate medical practices that arose late in history. (Ibid., 260)

Regardless of how he judges relations between biology and culture in the evolution of medicine, it is clear that Johns sees herbal medicine as the original human medicine and relates this to biological factors manifest in the hominid line of evolution.

The major part of Johns's treatise concentrates on chemical and nutritional factors related to food procurement and preparation practices as these might have affected early hominids. However, in a final chapter he discusses in summary fashion the actual evolution of medicine considered now as a cultural institution. For each of the major stages of cultural evolution, for example, the transition from hunter-gatherers to agriculture and from preindustrial societies to modern ones, Johns discusses how changes in living style, nutrition, food availability, exposure to bacteria and parasites, and cultural practices of eating, including the forming of conditioned and learned food aversions, affected health status and the need for herbal medicines. Implicit in his formulation, then, is how social structural factors connect with biological ones in affecting health status and the practice of medicine. Like William S. Laughlin (1963), he judges that the knowledge of anatomy that is needed for surgical medicine developed in association with hunting and butchering of animals but [relying on suggestions of Landy (1977)] indicates that such knowledge could have been useful only as a last resort because of pain and surgical shock and infection.

It is useful to emphasize briefly here themes that I will be developing in later chapters which complement Johns's exposition. He leaves the actual behavioral material or content that make up sickness and healing largely out of focus. In other words, Johns is not concerned with the variety of practices, roles, institutions, and social psychological behaviors and the like that in their totality configure sickness and healing in any particular society, nor is he concerned with the transformations that have taken place during cultural evolution in the parameters of sickness and healing. I give primary attention to these sorts of themes. Similarly, although Johns is clearly motivated to link biological and cultural factors in the evolution of medicine, his emphasis on chemical ecology and his healthy empiricism appear to dissuade him from offering an actual methodology for conceptualizing the evolution of sickness and healing and for medicine more generally. It is precisely the incorporation of these quintessential social science themes with biological evolutionary ones as they pertain to the theoretical study of medicine that concern me and that I will be developing in later chapters.

There is little doubt that the fields of paleoanthropology, paleopathology, historical epidemiology, behavioral archaeology, and cultural materialism as well as chemical ecology have a bearing on any attempt at a comparative and evolutionary approach to sickness and healing (Cockburn 1971; Cohen 1989; Cohen and Armelagos 1984; Fabrega 1974; Harris and Ross 1987; Johns 1990). Researchers in this field have presented compelling generalizations about morbidity and mortality pictures in prehistoric and early recorded populations. They concentrate on the material base of the medical, and although they exclude from their consideration issues about culturally grounded "health systems" and behavioral issues handled here as sickness and healing, they nonetheless provide indispensable material that one interested in general, abstract theories of medicine has to make use of.

Scope of Presentation

It is important to emphasize that I do not attempt a comprehensive, descriptive account of how medicine has evolved and changed across pre- and recorded history. Ideally, such a full account would describe and summarize what is known about disease epidemiology and social medical practices in ancient populations in each of the major geographic regions of the world. Beginning with analyses of paleopathological remains of very early human societies in different regions, such an account would describe the presumed mortality and morbidity patterns of the population and go on to trace the effects of increasing social complexity and contact with adjacent societies on epidemiological and clinical disease profiles. An interpretation of the interplay between strictly epidemiological factors, on the one hand, as compared to social and cultural effects of disease on behavior and adaptation as well as on social organization, on the other, would need to be discussed (based on inferences from representative, extant studies of hunter-gatherer and traditional, preindustrial societies) to complete the picture.

At the point when historical periods of certain societies were reached in such a narrative account, recorded information or actual observational data on the morbidity and mortality of disease might be available for some societies. Ideally, and balancing this type of epidemiological material, one would have available information pertaining to social medical practices in the respective societies. Thus epidemiological facts would be integrated with social and cultural facts. Such a "full" account of the evolution of medicine would summarize, describe, and analyze how the then-prevailing epidemiological pictures were expressed and dealt with (e.g., beliefs about disease and practices of shamanism and healing) in each of the major geographic settings of the world that were heavily populated.

A final chapter of this "full" story about the evolution of medicine would go on to describe the growth and development of biomedicine in early modern to modern European societies and end by analyzing its rise to prominence in the nation-states and its eventual spread over the world where it has either displaced or merely competed with the various indigenous medical systems. The political economic as well as scientific causes and implications of all of this would need to be discussed and, it is hoped, untangled.

The full account just presented constitutes a comprehensive, descriptive picture of the world history and evolution of medicine. For reasons already suggested, such an account is not possible. Paleopathology and historical epidemiology are fields that have grown considerably, but as yet the lack of empirical information and difficulties of interpretation of information that is available render generalizations difficult and tentative. A number of theoretical studies of the "great" medical traditions of antiquity are available, and this field of study is expanding to include aspects of medical practice, at least for European societies. However, little is known (and much may never be known) about how individuals actually coped with disease and injury and went about obtaining medical care in their respective communities in prehistoric and early historic groups. Information obtained in medical anthropology studies of contemporary "traditional" societies is available to complement this lack, but such information is naturally affected by modern conditions of living and by competition and modifications of ancient traditions brought about by diffusion and modernization.

In addition to the unavailability of pertinent data about epidemiology and social medical practices of prehistoric and early historic groups (deficiencies that with time will probably be lessened), there is the obvious difficulty of being clear about the process of social evolution itself. Major social transformations have occurred in different geographic locations of the world and during different periods of time. However, a clear understanding of how some of these social transformations actually took place in any one region is not available and is also much contested. This is the case, for example, for that involving the transition from foraging/hunter-gathering to early agricultural societies and for that involving the shift from agricultural to urban societies, with the exception of many European ones.

This, then, constitutes an outline of what an empirically satisfying ideal picture of the evolution of medicine might look like and a review of some of the difficulties of studying it in a satisfying way. Something quite different is attempted in this book. A compromise is adopted. I handle the medical in terms of behaviors referred to as sickness and healing, for it is this interrelated set of meaningful human activities that, in my estimation, needs ultimately to be explained in any theoretical social and cultural account of medicine. Sickness and healing are viewed both as biologically evolved and as culturally evolved phenomena and a theoretical interpretation that regards them as expressions of a human adaptation is presented.

Instead of actually reviewing what is known descriptively about the medicine of different societies and epochs, a daunting and extraordinarily complex if not impossible undertaking (at this stage of historical and anthropological understanding), I rely very heavily on an evolutionary typology of societies and summarize abstractly how the medical is configured in each of the posited social types based on reviews of pertinent literature. It is important to stress that I aim to provide a conceptualization of and a methodology for the study of medicine from an evolutionary standpoint, not a "full," descriptively accurate account. Of necessity, I have had to be selective in what I discuss and analyze and, at times, abstemious as to details of how medical happenings were or are actually played out in each of the societies that my typology encompasses.

The chapters that follow complement and expand on the earlier approaches to the study of health systems that were reviewed above. In a most fundamental sense, any attempt to analyze the medical, socially and culturally, in relation to a particular "social type" is grounded on probable medical ecologic factors affecting morbidity and mortality. Principal attention is centered on sickness and healing as social phenomena, and an attempt is made to describe the ways in which these are conceptualized, behaviorally expressed, and played out in different types of social types. Second, emphasis is given to the fact that societies and cultures (handled here, descriptively, as whole entities possessed of complexity that problematize sickness and healing) change and evolve and that, as a function of this, sickness and healing as social phenomena also change, and in a more or less systematic way. In effect, the approach assumes the existence of change and evolution of health or medical systems reflected in the way sickness and healing are configured and played out. And such systems are handled as units that analytically are separate from whole societies. However, primary attention is not on health systems or on the adaptive characteristics of these systems (viewed ecologically, epidemiologically) but rather on parameters of sickness and healing as these change in relation to social and cultural evolution. The analysis assumes that there exists an important relation between social and cultural evolution, on the one hand, and change or evolution in health systems, on the other. More specifically, that factors pertaining to sickness/healing can operate as potential causes of social and cultural evolution; and, conversely, that factors pertaining to societies (historical, political economic) as well as to the environment (climatic, soil depletion, epidemics) that promote social and cultural change or evolution can bring about change in health systems.

In table 1 is found a partial classification of types of societies that are given attention in later chapters. Some of the ethnographies and related medical studies that are used to draw generalizations pertaining to sickness and healing are listed in the table. The material constitutes some of the data on the basis of which comparisons of sickness and healing are carried out in later chapters. Material on the medical orientations of societies during the modern period and in the contemporary postmodern era are also discussed in later chapters, but the relevant material or "ethnographies" for these are presented in the text.

Some groups straddle categories. I handle the Aztecs (Ortiz de Montellano 1990) as a state and not as a regional polity (my civilization/empire) because their medical tradition seems to have been less influential regionally. This is contestable. Hunter and gatherer groups are typically classified as family-level societies, a convention I follow, but some show features that I regard as those of phase two of the evolution of medicine. For example, Aboriginal Australians (Elkin 1977), and the Batek (Endicott 1979) and Chewong (Howell 1989) of Peninsular Malaysia are all hunter-gatherers. In all three, most adult males are shamans (in the Batek, even females are shamans), which I link with phase one. Yet all three, unlike other hunter-gatherers, appear to also show a specialist healer role (which I equate with phase two). Among the Batek, strong feelings within the group can lead to sickness, and part of healing involves personal apologies and exculpations that seem to go with phase two, as is the case with the Gnau (Lewis 1975). All three groups show how knowledge of ecology, practices of health maintenance, and notions of personhood and well-being come together and function like formulas that are shared and that program behavior in ways that bear on concerns of sickness and healing. The material evokes a lucid picture of how "simple" yet also "advanced" and penetrating the earliest approach to sickness and healing can be and could have been structured during prehistory.

Table 1.   Sickness and Healing Literature Sources

Family-level Societies	Village-level Societies	Empires and Civilizations
Aboriginal Australian: Elkin 1977	Ainu: Ohnuki-Tierney 1981	China: Gwei-Djen and Needham 1980; Porkert and Ullmann 1988; Ruey-Shuang 1989; Unschuld 1979, 1985, 1986a, 1986b; Yanchi 1988a, 1988b
Andamanese: Cripriani, Cox, and Cole 1966; Radcliffe-Browne 1922	Dinka: Lienhardt 1961	
	Gimi: Glick 1963	
Batek Negrito: Endicott 1979	Gnau: Lewis 1975	England: Cook 1986; MacDonald 1981
Chewong: Howell 1989	Huli: Frankel 1986	
Efe Pygmy: Bailey 199	Nuer: Evans-Pritchard 1940, 1956	Europe: King 1963; Russell 1979
General: Dunn 196		
	Nupe: Nadel 1954	Greece: Cohn-Haft 1956; Phillips 1973
Hadza: Woodburn 1959, 1970	Safwa: Harwood 1970	
Khoisan: Barnard 1992		Greece and Rome: Kudlien 1970
	Yanomamo: Chagnon 1977, 1992	
!Kung: Katz 1982; Lee and DeVore 1979; Marshall 1969		India: Dube 1978; Filliozat 1964; Kakar 1982; Kutumbiah 1969; Zimmermann 1987
Machiquenga: Johnson pers. comm. 1993		Islam: Dols 1984a, 1984b
Mbuti: Turnbull 1961, 1966		Italy: Cipolla 1976; Park 1985
Siriono: Holmberg 1969		Middle Ages and Early Renaissance: Siraisi 1990
Walbiri: Meggitt 1955, 1965		Rome: Scarborough 1969

2

Origins of Sickness and Healing

Vulnerability to disease, be it through infection, altered metabolism, neoplasia, or degeneration, can limit an organism's reproduction, ability to care for relatives, and general social functioning. Hence disease and injury, which can interfere and nullify these basic activities, play an important role in evolutionary theory (Darwin 1869; Williams 1966; Wilson 1975). However, in evolutionary accounts of disease and injury, what usually constitutes the main focus is not social behaviors stemming from medical happenings and their role in the evolutionary process but, rather, purely genetic and physiological factors that affect natural selection.

The evolutionary origins of sickness and healing are the focus of this chapter. Social behaviors of organisms that manifest disease and injury and those of conspecifics that aim to improve the condition are analyzed from an evolutionary standpoint. It is argued that social behavioral manifestations of disease and acts of medical caring constitute *special* elaborations of a basic sociality and are rooted in biological evolution.

On the Value of a Biological Adaptation for Medicine

Acts of caring involve helping relatives and conspecifics in times of need and distress. They include such things as helping a conspecific to carry a heavy object, helping someone struggle along a difficult uphill course, or furnishing a healthy comember with insulative covering in the event coldness and discomfort are perceived. The acts can be accounted for by existing concepts of evolutionary biology since the underlying mechanisms would appear to also account for social behaviors such as stroking, grooming, and bonding more generally.

What one can term medical behaviors, namely, acts of helping and caring directed at a conspecific who shows disease or injury, might appear similar to those reviewed and to require no special adaptation. The same evolved mechanisms pertaining to sociality and cooperation could account for these "medical" behaviors, rendering the actual presence of disease or injury irrelevant. In short, the evolutionary jump from helping and "social" actions, generally conceived, to seeking and giving care for disease and injury, the latter constituting the essence of medicine, might appear to be trivial, hardly requiring any specialized biological machinery. This viewpoint would accord well with the prevailing intuition in the social and biological sciences that medicine is a purely social and cultural institution.

When examined carefully, however, medically relevant behaviors will be found to consist of far more than mere social helping. Medicine is a social institution constructed around sickness and healing, and the latter, it is argued here, constitute *interpretive behaviors*: relatively complex expressions of suffering, need, and help seeking together with corresponding acts of compassion and help giving. Sickness and healing unquestionably are based on fundamental regulatory processes and responses common to primates, but their biological basis does not stop there. They are viewed as complex elaborations of these lower-order psychobiological mechanisms, that is, as naturally evolved adaptive responses based on specialized neural mechanisms. All of this is most fully realized in *Homo sapiens,* judged to have an evolutionary history and posited to constitute an adaptation different from but related to "social helping" and cooperation in nonhuman primates.

The biologically based, symbolic behaviors that are at the root of the medical consist of physiological changes in the body's functioning, changes in the flow of social events, interpretations of the meanings of all of these changes with respect to ongoing social and emotional behavior, and constructive actions aimed at coping with resulting problems. One root of the medical is to be found in primate responses, also manifest in one- to two-year-old children, having to do with the development of empathy, sympathy, and pro-social behaviors more generally (Batson 1987; Fox 1989; Kopp 1989; Zahn-Waxler and Radke-Yarrow 1990). Medicine as a social institution is also rooted in sensory perceptive processes and physiological mechanisms found in primates that mediate the procurement of food and that are concerned with the regulation of internal states through the incorporation of nutritional requirements and the elimination of unwanted toxins of plants and parasites (Eaton and Konner 1985; Garcia, Hankins, and Rusiniak 1974; Johns 1990; Rozin 1976; Williams and Nesse 1991). As will be discussed in this chapter and more fully elaborated in later ones, these "innate," "wired in" responses constitute the base material out of which a special sickness healing adaptation is constructed by natural selection and reinforced by cultural learning.

Ensembles of sickness and healing entail self-awareness, self-other distinctions, social and ecological knowledge, and social attributions. Many of these desiderata have been described for the higher primates, although the exact nature of behavior traits and mechanisms is controversial and contested (Cheney and Seyfarth 1990; de Waal 1982, 1989; Gallup 1970, 1985, 1991; Goodall 1986). In other words, sensory motor and especially higher nervous system levels of function are implicated in sickness and healing and these have a phylogeny in the animal kingdom, especially in nonhuman primates. The contention here is that such neural machinery and its products are vitally implicated and necessary for and integral to what is held to constitute a biological adaptation for sickness and healing.

The uniqueness of a biological adaptation for sickness and healing, hereafter termed SH, rests on the fact that it constitutes an amalgam of the biology of self-regulation, caring/altruism/compassion, and the organismic and behavioral effects of disease and injury. A natural and adaptive behavioral feature of sickness (the behavioral expression of disease and injury) is seeking relief and healing, including "self-healing" (Clayton and Wolfe 1993; Huffman and Wrangham 1994). The behavioral analogue and complement of this is "other healing," that is, providing acts of SH to others who are sick. These seemingly separate parts of the medical, showing/expressing sickness and seeking/giving healing, are handled as integrated features of a trait or biological adaptation underlying medicine.

Positing an "adaptation" for or at the base of medicine is not only controversial but also runs counter to the criticisms leveled at the adaptationist program in general (Gould and Lewontin 1979). Its ultimate scientific validity would need to be established by controlled observations and experiments involving nonhuman primates and by studies in human developmental biology and psychology that emphasize disease/injury factors as well as psychosocially contextual ones. What is required is a program of interdisciplinary study focused on how biology and culture mutually influence the way individuals come to shape orientations, dispositions, and responses to the effects of disease and injury. Visualizing disease and injury being molded by the biology of caring and altruism during human evolution so as to produce a unitary adaptation integrates thinking about sickness and healing and provides a theoretically satisfying way of conceptualizing medicine as a social and cultural institution of society that is rooted in biology. It is presented here not only because it offers a plausible "adaptationist narrative" but also because it unifies thinking in the biological and social sciences and will prove to have value for explaining medicine as an institution from a general evolutionary standpoint.

It is posited that SH rests on a machinery more specialized than that for social helping: the complex behavioral material of sickness constitutes its rationale and object. What an SH adaptation may be held to have possibly solved or ameliorated in the environment of evolutionary adaptedness is developed. The SH adaptation is posited to be anchored in animal and especially primate adaptations and to substantially elaborate on basic trends that mark advances between the protocultural and cultural evolutionary line.

The Behavioral and Evolutionary Rationale of the SH Adaptation

An adaptation for sickness and helping is an outgrowth of a tendency to respond to manifestations of disease and injury in ways that promote healing. An organism's appetitive, physiological, and immunological systems are designed to react adaptively, which is to say, constructively as well as protectively, when they are disturbed or injured by biological or physical stimuli (Williams and Nesse 1991). The topic of self-medication, one organism's defensive use of substances produced by another species, is receiving attention from parasitologists, botanists, and chemical ecologists (Clayton and Wolfe 1993). The complementary roles of biology and social learning, or "culture," in the shaping of appetite and food procurement strategies, on the one hand, and the regulation and maintenance of internal states, on the other, have been modeled and supported by Johns (1990). These seemingly "natural" activities of primates are judged here to constitute possible biological analogues of behaviors that in a more elaborated form are expressed as sickness and healing.

In the descriptions of the behavioral activities of any number of organisms, one finds references to the "helping" or "caring" activities directed at ill conspecifics (Trivers 1971; Wilkinson 1984, 1988). In the face of weaknesses displayed by an organism, a conspecific is sometimes said to render help and support, provide nurturing, and become less aggressive and more cooperative. Benjamin L. Hart (1988, 1990) has recently reviewed behavioral adaptations in animals to pathogens and parasites. While his analysis draws attention to adaptations of sick animals in the context of natural selection, in a special section, "Helping Sick or Injured Animals," he reviews material indicating that conspecifics respond to sickness by adjusting travel pace, saving and sharing food, and actively helping (see Goodall 1986; Huffman and Siefu 1989). Caregiving behavior (termed epimeletic) has also been described for cetaceans (Caldwell and Caldwell 1966). It includes the assistance by one or more organisms to a sick or traumatized conspecific. The offering of food by a healthy adult organism to an ill comember may constitute an example of succorant behavior, one of the types of epimeletic behavior (adult to adult versus nurturance, adult to infant) summarized by Melba C. Caldwell and David K. Caldwell (1966). Such behaviors are an example of a class of behaviors that have been widely described in a variety of other species (African wild dog, social carnivores, and some higher primates as well as several cetacean species [Johnson 1982]). The evolutionary adaptedness of SH in the hominid line could thus be viewed as having a phylogenetic pedigree. In constituting a link in the chain of reciprocity, it could yield special advantages to the giver besides reciprocated acts of "goodwill" (Trivers 1971).

There are several ways in which a behavioral trait like (or cognitive capacity for) SH can make sense in an evolutionary frame of reference. Drawing on evolved, "innate" behavior propensities to heal one's own state of sickness, propensities that are by definition adaptive, acts of SH promote healthier and more harmonious states of convalescence in the self and the other, the receiver. It consists of providing food, water, and other forms of care (taken up later) based on inherited behavioral tendencies to heal that underlie, promote, and lead to the accumulation of cultural medical knowledge of the group. In offering care and support to a group member in the event of sickness, the healing aspect of SH can improve physiological well-being.

In the evolution of the hominid line, the need to maintain balance between increased longevity and demographic parameters (birth spacing, infant dependency, gestation, and sexual maturity) required a reduction in the crude mortality rate. As a result, mechanisms of adaptation favoring the reduction of deaths caused by predation, accident, war, and disease would have become prominent and been selected for at the level of individuals. For example, in a group facing hostility from neighbors, the preservation of a critical mass of conspecifics for optimal functioning might select for acts of SH since these could promote personal survival even if such acts were not reciprocated in the future. The SH adaptation is viewed as constructing disease and injury as meaningful social phenomena and when interpreted it is held to elicit helping and medical caring. The adaptation involves communications between self and conspecifics geared to the understanding and melioration of disease or injury via the social construction of sickness and healing. The effects of the adaptation can be considered to have, on balance, depressed environmentally induced mortality and hence to have played a positive role in the avoidance of extinction (Lovejoy 1981).

Constructing disease and injury eventuations as socially meaningful phenomena (in a manner to be reviewed later) could have proven beneficial in a direct physiological and psychological sense; that is, the construction of sickness/healing could redress and meet specific deficiencies and needs. Indirectly, by means of the process of psychosomatic mediation, SH responses from conspecifics would induce hormonal and related general physiologic changes that would improve function and sense of well-being in the sick person.

Disease and injury undermine the necessary cooperation and deliberateness needed to pursue survival tasks (undertake and carry out basic subsistence and survival activities). In this context, an adaptation for the meaningful construction of sickness and healing might in principle potentially further distract from the productive effort of foraging in the environment of evolutionary adaptedness. However, given a measure of freedom from want and/or an elementary division of labor that would allow planning how best to provide healing responses, SH could prove advantageous in a purely social sense. This is so because behaviors like SH that afford care, protection, and dispensation to the sick organism validate its status (what one could term the analogue of a role pertaining to sickness; see later discussion) and this can weaken, if not nullify, group frictions that would otherwise arise during crises of sickness. In brief, if offered during a time when the hardship of sickness was demoralizing and divisive in the group, SH would also have been stabilizing and improved morale.

In constituting acts that communicate sickness and elicit interpretations that direct healing efforts, then, SH responses can also be viewed as providing basic conditions for the creation of a social adaptation to a state of sickness in group mates. Parsons (1951, 1975) and a cadre of sociologists following his insights have given emphasis to a role of sickness prevalent in modern, Anglo-European societies. The literature in medical anthropology supports the cross-cultural applicability of such a concept, although a number of additional concepts have been proposed to better articulate behaviors associated with disease and injury (see chapter 1). Here, I extend the use of this concept "sick role" and apply it broadly. I would posit that human, prehuman, and early human groups manifest a "preparedness" for special social changes in response to disease and injury that one can equate (loosely, to be sure) with a sick role (to be elaborated later in this chapter and in succeeding ones). In other words, group mates and conspecifics appear to respond to and make allowances for those manifesting and communicating sickness; and conversely sick members show a "natural" disposition to expect/anticipate/elicit nurturing and caring responses from others. These dispositions are judged as "wired in" biologically and reflect the posited SH adaptation. As will be elaborated presently, these innate pre-, early, and fully evolved human responses are elaborations of nonhuman primates' responses to the distress of others and reflect emotional contagion and empathy.

With respect to the fully evolved SH adaptation, the changes in behavior in the setting of disease and injury involve acts of caring and treatment, they communicate concern and support, and they elicit behaviors promoting the conservation of energy, acquiescence, and passive acceptance and in general, more or less, validate and thereby authenticate the condition of sickness. In other words, while sickness persists and is made the target of SH behaviors of a conspecific, the organism showing sickness temporarily suspends usual activities and is allowed dispensation for this.

However, it is not claimed here that the SH adaptation merely involves intentional, premeditated behavior, in other words, that organisms willfully enact sickness to simply solicit healing. As elaborated later in the chapter, the adaptation is viewed as biologically conditioning the meaningful display of sickness and as reflexively eliciting healing (in the self and conspecifics): Something "hard" and "wired in" in the human organism produces SH responses "naturally." (This theme is elaborated in another section of this chapter.)

If exclusively "willful" communication is what constituted SH, it would imply that diseased/injured organisms act entirely differently when among group members compared to when alone. As reviewed later, this has been suggested to be the case for chimpanzees (de Waal 1982, 1986; Goodall 1986). Since a feature of communication is the presence of interactants (i.e., more than one agent), on purely intuitive grounds, one anticipates that greater expressivity about disease/injury would take place in the presence of conspecifics. In this light, the phylogenetic roots of the SH adaptation could be clarified by conducting experiments in field situations or in more controlled environments to determine how diseased/injured primates behave when alone compared to when in the presence of conspecifics.

Indeed, since a biological adaptation implies proximal as well as distal ultimate causes (the latter being the focus of this chapter), a range of questions pertaining to the developmental unfolding of SH and the possibility of "critical" periods and necessary "environmental triggers" for its realization require explication and underline the need for research involving sickness/healing conducted from an evolutionary standpoint (this point is elaborated in a later chapter). The whole question of the ontogeny of the SH response (in humans and nonhuman primates) could be clarified by conducting studies among organisms in different stages of the life cycle in the setting of disease and injury. There is some literature in clinical and social medicine pertaining to illness behaviors, sick role behaviors, and developmental factors that may have influenced all of this. I am suggesting a reformulation of standard interpretations of this topic by positing the operation of an inherited, biological adaptation to show, interpret, and respond to disease and injury. This topic is discussed in later chapters.

In general, the topic of actively soliciting healing from others (i.e., SH) raises the question of "cheating" and the SH adaptation, which, in turn, requires one to cautiously specify what about disease/injury is "communicated" in the setting of illness, "interpreted" meaningfully as sickness, and then gives rise to healing responses "naturally." Furthermore, it should be kept in mind that not only sickness but also healing can be fabricated. In other words, besides reaping advantages from others by exploiting a so-called sick role, individuals will be tempted to spuriously fabricate healing to deceive others and reap social advantage of this same SH adaptation that conditions both sickness and healing. This touches on the question of a possible evolutionary basis for deception in medical caring and practice. Other issues pertaining to the question of sick role deception and healing deception, implicating questions about the authenticity of sickness and healing behaviors, respectively, are taken up in a later section.

Sickness and Healing in Chimpanzees

Nonhuman primates, particularly chimpanzees, are generally held to constitute living "relatives" of *Homo sapiens*. Their behavior can be assumed to provide an approximate picture of the behavior of a common ancestor of man. It is thus instructive to review some of the observations that have been recorded about chimpanzees in the general area that pertains to sickness and healing. In this particular section I have relied heavily on the observations of Jane Goodall (1986). For related observations about the social behaviors of chimpanzees in communities, behaviors that suggest psychological and interpersonal sensitivities that would render an adaptation for sickness and healing comprehensible, the classic studies of Wolfgang Kohler (1925) and Robert M. Yerkes (1943) and the more recent analyses of Frans B. M. de Waal (1982, 1989, 1996) were also consulted (see also Temerlin 1972). The treatise of Dorothy L. Cheney and Robert M. Seyfarth (1990) contains a very useful analysis of related themes (with principal emphasis on vervet monkeys) and of the need for caution in making inferences about mental states in nonhuman primates. The chapter by Michael H. Huffman and Richard W. Wrangham (1994) provides a résumé of chimpanzee use of medicinal plants. The controversies and difficult interpretive issues in this field of study cannot be dealt with in detail in this presentation.

It should be mentioned at the outset that the responses of nonhuman primates and especially chimpanzees and monkeys that I am relating to sickness and healing are viewed as special elaborations of sophisticated abilities and specializations that underlie the generation of and response to emotional displays. Nonhuman primates and very young children respond to strong emotional displays in others with personal distress, and this reaction is termed emotional contagion. A more elaborated expression of this disposition is the ability to show empathy toward the distress of others and, following this developmentally, to respond with concern and nurturance. This general ability to communicate and interpret social signals and assess motivations in self and others constitutes a neural apparatus developed during evolution. In humans, it has been hypothesized to generate a psychological model of others that mediates social cognitions and behaviors. Researchers in this area of comparative developmental neurobiology do not concentrate on sickness and healing per se. Instead, their main focus and goal is to clarify the neural mechanisms and descriptive parameters relating to how humans and nonhuman primates acquire the capacity of basic emotions such as fear, aggression, and guilt as well as pro-social behaviors (Brothers 1989, 1990; Eisenberg 1977; Eisenberg and Fabes 1990; Kling and Steklis 1976). I am positing that this neurobiological machinery is foundational to and an integral part of a special adaptation that involves organisms' reactions to the effects of disease and injury. Sickness and healing and the whole institution of medicine are ordinarily conceptualized as involving learned, cultural information (see chapter 1). While culture and social structure are extremely influential in how individuals and groups configure and play out sickness and healing (to be explicitly dealt with in later chapters), I am nonetheless conceptualizing these basic medical facts as expressions of a special biological adaptation built out of and around, as it were, even more basic neural mechanisms and behaviors involved in social cognition and body awareness. With this as background, let me move on to discuss material bearing on sickness and healing in chimpanzees.

Sickness in chimpanzees clearly has a social impact on the group and signals interference in social functioning, and this is manifest in changes in behavior. "Individuals suffering from [in this instance, respiratory] symptoms . . . often lay in day nests for several hours at a time, rose late in the morning, traveled only short distances, and retired early at night. Flo [a particular female chimpanzee] on two separate occasions was too ill to climb trees and lay on the ground, scarcely moving, for several days and nights in succession, twice in heavy rain" (Goodall 1986: 92–93). "A number of factors influence the distance traveled in a day. . . . [H]ealth-sick individuals do not travel far" (ibid., 209). "Ill health can affect the time spent feeding, for very sick individuals eat little or nothing; the same is true of new mothers" (ibid., 241). "Chimpanzees typically travel, feed, and sleep in parties of five or less (excluding infants and juveniles)" (ibid., 154). "Some males may become more solitary during old age [when they show debility and constraints resulting from diseases; see subsequent quotes]" (ibid., 167).

A generalization in social studies of medicine is that conditions of sickness are undesirable and give rise to a need for corrective action (Fabrega 1974). This, I would contend, can safely be regarded as a human cultural universal (Brown 1991). Observations of chimpanzees support this generalization for the condition of sickness is associated with emotional changes that underscore its burdensomeness, its undesirability, and, even, its disruptive effects on group harmony/organization. "When chimpanzees are sick, they sometimes seem to be especially irritable and often direct mild forms of threat, such as the arm raise or head tip, at individuals who approach them too closely or annoy them in other ways. Pain can elicit an immediate aggressive response. . . . It tends to increase irritability: a mature male who had a broken toe repeatedly threatened noisy youngsters who played nearby" (ibid., 335). Further observations that underscore the social meaning of the effects of disease and injury are reviewed in what follows.

Curiosity about sickness, some fascination with its manifestations, a com-
passionate appreciation of its burdens, and attempts to reverse its morbid effects are hallmarks of the SH adaptation as I conceptualize it. At the very least,
a preadaptation for this ensemble appears to characterize chimpanzees' responses to disease and injury. Some of Goodall's (1986) observations and
comments that bear on this theme follow. "Chimpanzees have a deep-rooted
need for contact with a friendly conspecific in times of physical or emotional
stress" (p. 358). "Submissive behavior directed up the dominance hierarchy
can be readily understood when considered in relation to the deep-seated need
for reassurance contact experienced by an emotionally or physically distressed
chimpanzee" (p. 361). "Chimpanzees often lick their wounds if these are on
hands or feet or other easily accessible parts. Or they may repeatedly touch the
lesion with their fingers, which they then lick. Often they dab the wound with
a handful of leaves, which are then usually sniffed and dropped, but may be
licked and reused. Infants and juveniles have been seen to lick their mother's
wounds, but an adult usually grooms carefully around the wound of a companion—though he may stare at it intently" (p. 98). "In order to feel compassion,
an individual must have some understanding of the wants or needs of the suf-
ferer. That chimpanzees have the cognitive ability to empathize, at least to
some extent, has been shown" (pp. 385–386). Goodall's remarks when listing
ecological benefits of social relationships are appropriate here: "B can clean
A's skin and remove parasites. . . . B can care for A when A is sick, keeping
flies from wounds and grooming, thereby removing fly eggs or maggots from
festering sores" (p. 201). In another context, Goodall states the following:
"Kohler [1925] also described the concern shown by the female Rana when
her small companion, Konsul, became fatally ill. As he lay on the ground,
Rana approached and invited him to accompany her, but he hardly moved" (p.
382). Goodall goes on to quote directly from Kohler [1925: 242]: "She grew at-
tentive, first lifted his head, and then, putting her arms around the little fellow,
carefully lifted his weak body and seemed by her bearing and her look so
deeply concerned that there could be, at that moment, no doubt whatsoever as
to the state of her feelings" (p. 382). In the following material Goodall draws
further inferences from her review of the literature. "If Temerlin or his wife
was ill and vomited, Lucy [the name of the chimpanzee living with the Temer-
lins] would run to the bathroom and stand by them, trying to comfort them by
kissing them and putting her arms around them. Once when this failed to alleviate the symptoms, Lucy slammed down the lid of the toilet, hitting it while
screaming loudly" (pp. 382–383). If Jane Temerlin was sick in bed, Lucy
would "show tender protectiveness, bring her food, share her own food or sit on
the edge of the bed trying to comfort her" (Temerlin 1972: 164–165, cited in
Goodall 1986: 382–383).

The apparent selective basis of sickness and healinglike behaviors must be
noted.

At Gombe, concern for sick, injured, or distressed individuals is observed primarily among members of the same family. Mothers care tenderly for their sick infant. When Olly's month-old infant lost the use of his arms and legs because of polio, she supported him carefully and each time he screamed she cradled him at once, solicitously arranging his limbs so they would not be crushed. The moment he died (or, at least, lost consciousness and no longer cried out), she began to treat the body in an extremely careless way, flinging it onto her back, holding it by one leg, and allowing it to fall to the ground (Goodall 1986: 383).

Maternal grooming, however, continues to calm and provide reassurance even when the recipient is fully grown. When twenty-three year old Figan screamed loudly after hurting his wrist in a dominance conflict, his mother, Flo, was about half a kilometer away. Old as she was (it was not long before her death), she ran to him. Figan, still screaming, approached her and she began at once to groom him. Gradually his screaming died away until he was quiet (ibid., 402).

After being fatally attacked by the Kasakela males, Madam Bee [a particular chimpanzee] lay, scarcely able to move, until she died five days later. During this time her adolescent daughter, Honey Bee, remained nearby, grooming her mother and keeping away the flies. And when old Mr. McGregor was crippled by polio and unable to walk, he too had a faithful attendant in the younger Humphrey (possibly his nephew). As I have described, Humphrey, in defense of his friend, not only dared to attack the higher-ranking and powerful Goliath, but stayed near Gregor for several hours each day throughout the last two weeks of the old male's life (ibid., 385).

The complex, context-dependent bases of behaviors associated with disease and injury in chimpanzees living under natural conditions are underscored by the following remarks. "Care of the sick, as mentioned, is rarely observed among unrelated chimpanzees at Gombe. Mr. McGregor was shunned by those individuals he approached for social grooming. . . . When Fiji had a gash in her head, which became infected, those individuals to whom she presented the wound for grooming seemed fearful and moved away. In a captive chimpanzee group, however, the situation is different—perhaps because members of the group so often are raised together and are as familiar as close kin in the wild. Kohler's (1925) chimpanzees zealously squeezed pus from wounds and removed splinters and . . . [Goodall here cites several literature sources] . . . have described similar behavior. As Kohler (1925) noted, such manipulations are undoubtedly prompted in some measure by a fascination with the lesions themselves. The results, however, are beneficial and it is easy to see how such behavior would have led to altruistic health care in humans" (ibid., 385).

Christophe Boesch provides information that suggests that sickness/healing behaviors of chimpanzees are not only specialized, they are also not limited only to relatives and kin.

Tai chimpanzees, however, totally independent of kin relationship, were regularly seen to tend wounded animals for extended periods of time. Once this care was observed for more than 2 months. . . . Individual reactions tend to indicate that they are aware of the needs of the wounded, e.g., they lick the blood away and remove all dirt particles with fingers and lips, as well as preventing flies from coming near the wounds. In addition, empathy for the pain resulting from such wounds was clearly demonstrated by the reaction of other group members: After having received fresh wounds from an attack of a leopard, the injured individual is constantly looked after by group members, all trying to help by grooming and tending the wounds. Dominant adult males prevented other group members from disturbing the wounded chimp by chasing playing infants or noisy group members away from his vicinity. In addition, as wounds handicapped the movements of the injured animal, group members remained with him as long as he needed before he was able to begin to walk again; some just waited whereas others would return to him until he started to move (three times the group waited for four hours at the same spot). Whenever he stopped they waited for him. Such a difference with Gombe chimpanzees may be explained by the high predation pressure Tai chimpanzees suffer from leopards. (Boesch 1992: 149)

The SH adaptation presupposes that the self and group mates constructively orient to disease and injury so as to promote healing. As reviewed previously, at least some of the responses of chimpanzees to disease and injury appear consistent and suggest a possible preadaptation. I have posited that the SH adaptation includes and provides for responses elicited from the death of a group mate devolving from the effects of disease and injury. Consequently, how chimpanzees deal with death has a relation to the topic of the phylogeny of sickness and healing. In addition to those reviewed earlier, the following observations are relevant in this respect. "Sick individuals are sometimes sniffed repeatedly at many parts of their body. Dead chimpanzees have also been smelled carefully, as were places where a dead body had lain. Drops of blood spattered onto the vegetation during a fight may be intently smelled (and licked). Leaves a chimpanzee has used to wipe dirt or blood from himself may be picked up and sniffed by other individuals" (ibid., 139). However, most of Goodall's information pertaining to the death of group mates from disease and injury comes not from direct observation of sickly and emaciated subjects during their terminal period but, rather, from inferences about events not directly observed. For example, having observed a sick chimpanzee who then is lost to observation frequently leads Goodall to infer that particular individual died, but exactly how this happened and the responses it occasioned among group mates are not described and may have not been evident. Goodall presents very little material pertaining to the actual death of a chimpanzee from a condition of pure sickness. In other words, we are not able to obtain a good picture of how chimpanzees accommodate to terminality in a group mate who had shown progressive sickness.

That the effects of disease and injury among chimpanzees do not always lead to behaviors I have grouped together as SH responses needs to also be appreciated. "Chimpanzees are quite fastidious, and if their bodies become soiled with dirt (feces, urine, mud and so forth) they often use leaves to wipe themselves. They also use leaf napkins to dab at bleeding wounds and (occasionally) to rub themselves during or just after heavy rains. . . . The Gombe chimpanzees, in fact, seem to have an almost instinctive horror of being soiled with excrement and only very rarely have been seen to touch feces (their own or another's) with their bare hands. If a chimpanzee accidentally becomes smeared with the feces of another, the offending substance is wiped off carefully with leaves" (ibid., 545).

Living under natural, "wild" conditions can be arduous and competition and selfish self-interest often operate even under conditions of (perhaps, in these nonhuman primates, especially *because of*) disease and injury. This is clearly documented by the following material. "In 1966 Jomeo appeared one day with a badly wounded foot. He was unable to put it to the ground for almost a month, and to this day all the toes are curled under. We do not know what happened, but it marked an abrupt end of his attempts to intimidate adult females" (ibid., 436). "One factor that is of overwhelming significance for the rank of a female at Gombe, outweighing all other variables *except extreme sickness or extreme old age,* is the nature of her family—and which family members are with her when she encounters another female" (ibid., 439; emphasis added).

The case that Goodall describes of the chimpanzee named Figan is instructive, for it illustrates the potential role of context and individual differences in behaviors related to sickness and healing. "Figan, from early adolescence on, had seized every available opportunity to get the better of his superiors—when they became sick, were injured, or showed any sign of weakening—even if it only gave him a temporary advantage" (ibid., 426). "In those days Faben [the older, presumed brother of Figan] was obviously the more dominant of the brothers, but very few aggressive incidents were observed; the two enjoyed a relaxed relationship and often played. Then in 1966, Faben was stricken with polio and lost the use of the one arm. Figan, taking instant advantage of the situation, began to challenge his brother. . . . It was after this [an incident when Figan aggressively intimidated Faben] that Faben was first observed being submissive to his young brother, greeting him with pant-grunts" (ibid., 178). That individualistic, competitive exploitation of disease and injury is found in chimpanzee communities is also illustrated by the following. "Passion [a particular chimpanzee] on her own was able to seize Gilka's infant in 1975—but Gilka was small and weak, having sustained partial paralysis of one arm and hand during the polio epidemic, and was suffering also from a fungus infection of nose and brow. When Gilka was again attacked the following year, her fungus infection was greatly improved and she put up a much harder fight" (ibid., 287–289).

These latter observations, in contrast to those reviewed earlier, suggest that disease and injury (perhaps simply the strength-depleting consequences of these, for the individuals in question appear not to have actually been in distress) can sometimes elicit aversion or create opportunities for rivals to exert pressure and seek advantage. Compassion, support, and caring (hallmarks of the posited SH adaptation) do not seem to underlie the activities of these particular chimpanzees in these particular contexts. Thus it may be the case that the anergic/amotivational and purely physical or more "mechanical" effects of disease and injury do not play as important a role in eliciting putative SH responses as compared to those that communicate actual distress, suffering, and need and that bring into play the effects of social cognitive states (e.g., compassion, empathy). Alternatively, it could of course be the case that group happenings, the sheer context of disease and injury, are what are pertinent in the possible triggering of putative SH responses. Finally, it must be conceded that features, or at least refinements, of the SH adaptation are not always manifest in chimpanzees.

It would appear that so-called SH responses are not the only qualitatively different behaviors that can be produced by sickness and injury. A chimpanzee can also be made fearful of, at least, some of the deleterious consequences of disease, injury, and death, especially when these are sudden and unexpected. "A change in the appearance or movements of an individual due to injury or ill health may affect the way he is treated by his fellows. Gross change in appearance or gait, as shown by polio victims, or complete cessation of movement, as when an individual dies, is likely to provoke fear or aggression or both" (ibid., 122–123). "When the other chimpanzees saw these cripples for the first time, they reacted with extreme fear; as their fear decreased, their behavior became increasingly aggressive, and many of them displayed toward and even hit the victims. . . . When adult male Rix fell from a tree and broke his neck, group members showed intense excitement and anxiety, displayed around the dead body, and threw stones at it; they also directed many aggressive acts at each other" (ibid., 330). These observations are important because they highlight the complexity of responses occasioned by the effects of disease and injury and reinforce the point made earlier about the potential importance of cognitive states in the mediation of sickness and healing.

The following more general observations proffered by Goodall (1986) are pertinent for they bring to mind complexities and ambiguities of chimpanzee behaviors that are relevant to the origins and uses of an adaptation for sickness and healing. "Chimpanzees have good memories for spatial and environmental locations and for conspecifics. They also show evidence of a cognitive ability for planning for a future that exists in their 'minds'" (p. 31). This generalization would suggest the possibility of a sustained interest in and concern for a diseased or injured group mate, with intentions of offering continuing healing. "Chimpanzees, without doubt, gradually learn the calming effect that their own grooming behaviour is likely to have on others. Grooming can then be used with *intent* as a manipulative tool. Over and above this, chimpanzees at times show some understanding of the significance of grooming interactions between others" (p. 406; original emphasis). Since grooming is either a feature of or a preadaptation for SH responses, its constructive, manipulative use has obvious implications for how sickness and healing are played out. Related to the giving/caring function of grooming is the "asking" function of begging, a feature of social behavior that is not well understood. "Begging behavior has not yet been analyzed in detail. However, a preliminary survey of the data reveals clear-cut differences between the adult males in the extent to which they are *prepared to beg* from their companions. . . . Similar differences, as we shall see, are found in the females" (p. 304; original emphasis). With respect to the social integrative effects of sickness and healing, the following is pertinent. "Chimpanzees can readily remember who helped them (as well as who sided against them) from one occasion to the next, even when the occasions are separated by long time intervals" (p. 330). Finally, that cultural traditions could underlie the possible existence of group differences in sickness and healing behaviors even among chimpanzee communities is suggested by the following. "Some of the . . . dissimilarities in the diet of the Gobe and Mahale chimpanzees may result from intraspecific variation in plant chemistry, which can affect food selection even in a single population. . . . Most of the differences however, are probably due to tradition. . . . [Y]oungsters, with their more flexible behavior and their predilection for exploration, are the most likely age class to introduce a new feeding tradition" (p. 265). "It is precisely this sort of behavior—curiosity and the practicing of learned patterns in new contexts—that can, because of the chimpanzee's ability to profit from chance experience, lead to innovations. And because chimpanzees are captivated by unusual behavior in their companions, new patterns can be passed from one to another through the channels of observation, imitation, and practice. This is the dawn of *cultural* evolution; it means that performance of a gifted individual can spread through a group and quite rapidly become part of its tradition" (p. 591; original emphasis). These latter generalizations about the behavior of chimpanzees, then, have relevance for an understanding of the possible origins of a group's tradition pertaining to sickness and healing and underscore the biocultural basis of sickness and healing.

The observations and interpretations of de Waal (1982, 1986, 1989) are pertinent with respect to the question of possible deception in the context of disease and injury. "Other instances of falsification among the Arnhem chimpanzees illustrate the use of these criteria [about modalities and examples of deception]. The first example occurred after Yeroen had hurt his hand during a fight with Nikkie. The wound was not deep, but Yeroen was limping. He did so for about a week. In the course of time we discovered, however, that he only limped if he could be seen by his rival. For example, Yeroen walked past Nikkie from a point in front of him to a point behind him. He hobbled piti- fully until he passed Nikkie, and changed to normal walking once he was behind him. Obviously, this limp must be classified as deceptive behavior. However, this sequence may have resulted from a prior sequence of stimulus- response contingencies, such that Yeroen might have learned from incidents in the past that his rival was less hard on him during periods when Yeroen was (of necessity) limping. It is impossible to know whether Yeroen's behavior in- volved more than knowledge of these beneficial effects, i.e., whether he be- lieved that the other chimpanzee believed that he was hurt" (de Waal 1986: 237–238). This particular chapter by de Waal (1986) contains any number of observations pertaining to the topic of deception in chimpanzees and of prob- lems of interpretation raised by attempts to attribute mental states, all of which are implicated in any claim about exploitation of sickness. The discussion by Cheney and Seyfarth (1990: esp. chaps. 7, 9, 10) is pertinent in this regard.

Finally, it is worth considering behaviors of chimpanzees that suggest a relationship to actual curing and healing. Johns (1990) reviews material pre- sented by Richard W. Wrangham and Toshisada Nishida (1983) and Wrang- ham and Goodall (1987) pertaining to the apparent use of plant substances for medicine by chimpanzees. These latter researchers have provided circum- stantial evidence that *Aspilia* is important to chimpanzees for its antiparasitic properties. Johns's interpretation of this work is pertinent.

> Associations made between plants and their perceivable effects on various body functions are clearly important for understanding how chimpanzees learned to use *Aspilia* or other plants for their medicinal properties. A stimulatory effect of *Aspilia* leaves on the nervous system has been suggested and could be easily un- derstood in terms of the kind of conditioned learning that characterizes animal interactions with plant chemicals. . . . This kind of learned behavior could then be maintained in a cultural fashion. Euphorics could be among the plants used in this way. If, on the other hand, parasite control is the primary function of this be- havior, it is harder to explain how the animals know to do this. Positive effects on well-being would come from reducing parasite loads, although the feedback is less rapid than that associated with direct effects on the nervous system, blood pressure, blood sugar, et cetera. Conscious awareness of parasite loads combined with awareness of the consequences of ingesting a particular plant are not likely to be learned through conditioning-type experiences. It is difficult (although not impossible) to imagine chimpanzees making these kinds of associations. . . . It is likely, then, that the general ingestion of specific leaves for a nondietary purpose is an evolved behavior that is expressed in situations where parasite control is called for; the specific focus on *Aspilia* would be a culturally transmitted re- sponse to a biological need (Johns 1990: 256–257).

In summary, observations of natural behaviors of chimpanzees in the con- text of disease, injury, and death suggest at least five generalizations. First, some of the basic behaviors I have included as part of the SH adaptation are present in chimpanzees and, thus, may constitute so-called preadaptations or may have already been selected for in the common ancestors of chimpanzees (and possibly other nonhuman primates) and, hence, in the line of evolution leading to *Homo sapiens* (e.g., emotional contagion, empathy, interest in and accommodation to sickness, compassion, "pro-social" caring for conspecifics, and possibly medicinal use of plants). Second, some of the behaviors of chimpanzees in the setting of disease and injury (e.g., aversion and fear to some of their sequelae, differences in caring responses depending on who is diseased/injured, and capitalizing on weaknesses of others) appear different from and, in some respects, inconsistent with those grouped as SH responses; hence, the behaviors might possibly constitute phylogenetically rooted routines that later evolution modified. In very young children, as an example, suffering in others seems to first elicit personal distress and this is followed by empathic concern and, even later, more differentiated caring/helping. A not unrelated developmental progression is that of concern for caretakers and family members, with concern for nonrelatives coming later (Zahn-Waxler and Radke-Yarrow 1992; Zahn-Waxler et al. 1992). (Alternatively, it could be the case that only experiential factors—thus interpretable as cultural and reflecting cultural evolution—are able to block out "wired in" responses that are inconsistent with sickness/healing.) Third, on balance, however, behaviors classified as SH responses are natural and innate and were most probably progressively sculpted during later phases of human evolution. Fourth, social ecologic context (e.g., predators, availability of food) and individual differences (e.g., involving intelligence, compassion, temperament) influence when and how SH responses are to be played out. And fifth, SH responses are constituted of material that can easily lead to the elaboration of group differences (i.e., cultural traditions) in the social domain of medicine (i.e., involving sickness and healing); it is possible that chimpanzees display a natural tendency to deceive others about the effects of disease and injury when this is possible.

Behaviors of nonhuman primates that are interpreted here as constituting early forms of or preadaptations for an SH adaptation are generally interpreted by primatologists and ethologists as examples of mutuality, altruism, and efforts at group integration. The link between these behaviors and such topics as attachment, bonding, parental care, affiliation, succorance, and nurturance, on the one hand, and human behaviors connoting sympathy and empathy, on the other, have been discussed by Frans de Waal in his recent book *Good Natured* (1996). He presents a number of additional examples of what I would view as SH-related behaviors of nonhuman primates; for example, those directed at handicapped, injured, and diseased group mates and responses to death.

At no point in his analysis does de Waal raise the question that these prosocial behaviors could be part of a special psychological adaptation for sickness/healing. Instead, de Waal's analysis of these and related behavior provide a foundation for his discussion of the roots and origins of human morality in biological evolution. The prevailing point of view in the human sciences about this general topic concerns the importance of human sociality, which takes into account such things as attachment/bonding, sympathy/empathy, and, more generally, social intelligence. Positing that the behaviors in question are part of a special adaptation to cope with disease and injury involves making a distinction and elaborating upon the general topic of sociality as it is conceptualized in general biology.

The SH Adaptation and Human Evolution

The capacity for SH may be hypothesized to have evolved in the line leading to *Homo sapiens* that followed a protocultural stage (Hallowell 1965). As suggested by the review of the previous section, early members of this line of evolution showed behaviors that can be viewed as early manifestations of SH as well as preconditions for its more evolved forms. Behavioral observations of nonhuman primates, especially chimpanzees, have drawn attention to capacities that are implicated in what has been termed sickness/healing, which constitutes SH (Goodall 1986; Hart 1988, 1990; Huffman and Siefu 1989). The ranking patterns and status behaviors of chimpanzees have been claimed to involve a "near-human mixture of traits" (Shafton 1976). Behavioral restraints, perceptual mechanisms linked to status determinations, the capacity for self-awareness and self-other differentiation, and modalities of social communication all attest to capacities that took place early in the evolutionary line of the hominids (de Waal 1986, 1989; Gallup 1970, 1985, 1991; Goodall 1986; Povinelli and Godfrey 1993; Premack and Woodruff 1978). As discussed earlier, a chimpanzee-like grade of evolution in the strictly human progression constitutes the evolutionary baseline that provided the conditions from which the special SH adaptation was progressively sculpted by natural selection.

Selection for SH is hypothesized to have played a central role in the selection of a suite of behaviors that descriptively can be thought of as transitional between the protocultural and cultural, that is, as marking advances beyond the chimpanzee grade. The specifics of these behaviors are discussed later in greater detail, but general features need emphasis now. As an example, the essence of an adaptation such as SH presupposes some cognitive understanding of what sickness is and portends, what distress and suffering mean, and what constitutes care and provisioning of sickness. While much of sickness and caring for self can be thought of as an adaptive response to disease and injury, the other-healing dimension of SH is a conspecific's expression toward others of this adaptation and implies a recognition and appreciation of sickness. Elements of the advanced design features of a system of communication are hypothesized to have been implicated in the SH adaptation as well as something resembling the beginnings of a normative orientation and associated notions of self and other (Hallowell 1965). In brief, the more evolved form of the SH adaptation needs to be seen as an integral part of the evolution of a social language and other "higher cortical" functions (the human psyche) that are tied to the eventual full development of culture (e.g., the construction of social scenarios, elaborations of sick and healer roles, the conceptualization of death).

The possible evolutionary pressures that may have accounted for the selection for SH need attention. Social competition with phylogenetically related species (e.g., earlier hominids, nonhuman primates) and with conspecifics (whether sporadic, sustained, or "runaway") and activities related to foraging, scavenging, and predation generally were important in the behavioral ecology of early hominids. The social scenarios that are implicated in these activities entail processes of immediate reciprocity, sharing, and social exchange in addition to the capacity for extended cooperation, all of which imply more advanced systems of communication and a capacity for choosing alternative courses of action (scenario building) (Alexander 1979). All of these sets of activities are complementary to and reinforcing of the purely social and communicational aspects of SH and are posited to have been dialectically involved in the selection of its more evolved form.

In a more specific sense, a putative adaptation like SH would need problems that were common, recurring, and likely to be solved in ways that enhanced inclusive fitness so as to be selected for. In the human line of evolution, social competition, warfare, foraging generally, and any hunting practices that existed can be expected to have increased the prevalence of conditions of disease and injury that constituted the evolutionary environment that selected SH (see next sections). Many of these conditions of sickness can be expected to have good outcomes, provided sick organisms were protected, physically stabilized, groomed, cleaned, and provisioned with water, food, and comfortable settings for rehabilitation. Competition and hunting depend on the establishment and maintenance of male coalitions, and the occurrence of injuries (as well as infectious diseases and illnesses more generally; see below) would have rendered such coalitions unstable, if not opportunistically propitious for cheating and for usurpations of authority relations and for alliances more generally. A progressively refined biological trait like SH (complemented, to be sure, with purely cultural learnings) would have proven beneficial to providers and recipients since it is a factor that besides potentially contributing to physical/psychical well-being also promoted reciprocity and cooperation more generally. It is conceptualized as predisposing to and helping promote social reciprocity, which has been singled out as characteristic of early human groups.

Conjuring Up the Archaeology and Prehistory of Sickness and Healing

A brief review of the phases of human evolution is needed to contextualize later discussions of sickness and healing. A sampling of the relevant literature reveals the complexity of the posited evolutionary trajectories leading to modern humans. Remains of craniums and other skeletal parts of specimens held to conform to separate genuses and species as well as a variety of lithic materials and stone implements prepared according to established forms and even industries are found. Most important, it appears to be the case that the chronology of these two sets of material remains cannot be correlated with each other, nor can either be graded in a consistent linear fashion leading to the present.

I will be guided by the synthesis provided by Clive Gamble (1993), who posits three main phases of hominid evolution. The first phase, termed "early hominids," is held to follow the split from the pongids and to have extended from around five million to one million years before the present. A separate genus, the australopithecines, and early representatives of the hominidae, particularly *Homo habilis* and *Homo erectus,* are held to constitute the early hominids. The second phase, termed "the Ancients," extended from approximately one million to 50,000 years before the present. Representative forms of this phase include *Homo erectus,* "archaic" *Homo sapiens,* early and classic Neanderthals, and some anatomically modern humans. Gamble divides the period of the ancients into three parts, but I have condensed these into one. The final phase consists of "the Moderns," or anatomically modern humans, and spans the period from 40,000 years ago to the early beginnings of agriculture, approximately 10,000 years before the present.

Gamble's categorization can be used in conjunction with that of Merlin Donald (1991), which deals more centrally with forms of cognition, memory, and the representation of experience and knowledge in the context of human evolution. For purposes of exposition, I hold that Gamble's early hominids show a progression beyond the strict episodic culture that Donald attributes to the great apes. He emphasizes the latter's alleged inability to willfully "bring to mind" and constructively use stored representations of past occurrences, but I am conceding this ability to the early hominids. I equate Gamble's Ancients with having a more or less fully developed mimetic culture as described by Donald as well as some capacity to conceptualize and communicate by means of a protolanguage as propounded by Derek Bickerton (1981, 1990, 1995). I equate Donald's next stage, "mythic culture," with Gamble's Moderns.

Early Hominids

Cognitive and behavioral traits that have been described for the chimpanzees can be assumed to have also characterized early hominids. An opportunistic, free-living, group mode of existence is assumed. The earliest prepared lithic specimens are ascribed to around 2.5 million years ago. The term "Oldowan" has been used to refer to this rather primitive enterprise; how one should best characterize it is controversial (Ingold 1993). A very low level of effort seems to have been expended in the preparation of their stone products, which are assumed to have been manufactured to meet immediate needs.

Scavenging of carcasses from carnivore kills is held to constitute an important source of food. Natural means of food storage were used as carcasses lasted but a few days. Contaminated food sources can be assumed to have caused a variety of gastrointestinal infections. It is possible that varieties of australopithecines and early hominids had means of using fire for meat preparation (certainly found in later phases of evolution), and this may have ameliorated food poisoning. Although no direct evidence is available pertaining to the use of plant foods, they are believed to have supplemented the diet. The remains of early hominids are best described as scatters and patches in the landscape rather than true sites that would suggest permanent occupation.

A harsh, precarious existence is suggested by the presence of early hominid remains with teeth marks, most likely the result of the actions of carnivores. While early hominids may have hunted prey as a means of subsistence, still a somewhat controversial point, they clearly were also hunted by predators and were part of a diverse animal community. Most paleoanthropologists and archaeologists emphasize that early hominids were capable of coordinated subsistence activities and displayed elementary, "shallow" forms of planning. This implies a more advanced form of social communication than that of chimpanzees. This was probably accomplished by means of gesture, facial displays, and elementary vocal signals that could have functioned as lexical units for naming and reference, although a truly mimetic culture as conceptualized by Donald (1991) appears to correspond more closely to the group Gamble (1993) terms Ancients. The consensus is that the early hominid groups did not have a true language or speech as we understand it, although this is a highly contested topic (Gibson and Ingold 1993; Karlin and Julien 1994; Pinker and Bloom 1990; Schlanger 1994; Wilkins and Wakefield 1995).

Many of the characteristics of sickness and healing as described for chimpanzees can be assumed to have characterized early hominids. A refinement of social communication, a more fully developed sense of self, and a clearly established capacity to attribute mental states to group mates probably emerged during this phase of evolution, and all of this can be expected to have heightened an appreciation of the suffering and pain of sickness so vividly described for chimpanzees. Knowledge about the medicinal properties of plants must have become more focused and precise. Whereas a rudimentary sense of intentional self-healing may have characterized the common pongid/hominid ancestor, this trend toward a better definition of sickness and a corresponding need to undo its manifestations (undoubtedly conceptualized in very global terms) by ingestion of "medicines" and associated specific actions focused on the self "must have" been enhanced among early hominids.

An interesting question is the extent to which active *healing of others* took place in early hominid groups. Chimpanzees show concern for the suffering of others, most particularly kin, and rudimentary actions aimed at cleaning wounds have been recorded, although the associated mental states are difficult to interpret. The cognitive and protocultural developments of early hominids must have included more directed actions at physical lesions and wounds of group mates as well as some active responsiveness to general, systemic forms of suffering, however generally they may have been expressed. As with the Ancients, to be discussed later, trauma, infections, and the consequences of predator attacks constituted the most common forms of disease and pathology. The tenuousness of subsistence, the harshness of life, and the absence of elaborate symbol systems obviously militated against the likelihood of any public, protracted scenario of sickness/healing, and few individuals probably lived to advanced age. Important markers of sickness and healing in earlier human groups and their overall significance are taken up later in this chapter.

The high prevalence of carnivore predators, vulnerability to environmental hardships and extremes, competition among fellow hominid groups, and the overall tenuousness of existence and survival overshadowed strict concerns about sickness and healing. Nonetheless, more than a strict concern with on-going events and the here and now, the hallmark of the episodic culture of the great apes (Donald 1991), can be assumed to have constituted the way of life or "protoculture" of early hominids. When one applies this form of representation, memory, and experience to that of the known, overt behavioral consequences of disease and pathology and conjoins all of this with an emerging and better-developed sense of self compared to other, and associated social attribution and the like, one can conclude that a somewhat more active, focused, and elaborated form of sickness/healing adaptation (rudimentary, to be sure, but discernible nonetheless) prevailed in early hominids well beyond that posited for the common ancestor with the pongids and assumed to be reflected in the chimpanzees.

Hominid Expansion out of Africa and the Emergence of the Ancients

This development is held to have taken place approximately one million years before the present. Changes in social behavior and social organization are held to have played a critical role in this expansion/colonization. Generalist *Homo* groups perfected the process of calculated migration based on the sharing of information provided by selected foragers who would leave the main group and explore nearby habitats. Elaboration and refinement of skills of social and emotional communication as seen in nonhuman primates and further developed among early hominids is held to have made calculated migration followed by colonization possible with the Ancients. These changes in social complexity and communication are held to be associated with important biological changes that produced longer periods of infancy; in turn, this made it possible for greater behavioral plasticity and social learning, expansion of the neocortex, increases in manual dexterity, and refinements in stone working to take place.

This period included a number of glacial/interglacial cycles and involved movement into higher latitudes. Thus cold winter weather posed a major hardship. This entailed not only obvious requirements for overcoming physical hazards but also special means for coping with diminished and variable food sources due to curtailment of plant growth, hibernation of animals, and migration south of the major herd species. The key issue is how the Ancients could have migrated/colonized and then persisted while living under such extreme conditions; many explanations have been proposed (Dibble and Mellars 1992; Geist 1978; Mellars and Stringer 1989; Trinkaus, 1989).

Gamble (1993) emphasizes that population stasis, exhaustion of surrounding food sources, and social conflicts result when large groups are situated around water holes for several months of the year. This was presumably an important setting for emerging scenarios of sickness and healing. By contrast, if groups were to break apart for long periods of time during the limiting winter to look for dispersed food sources, problems of recognition and competition would result. According to Gamble (1993:123),

> The solution would be for individuals to combine the roles of information and subsistence foragers. But this could only be achieved if the social networks were somehow intensified to cope with greatly increased separation, which could lead to a failure to recognize group members, as a penalty of extended fission. . . . [W]e can see that social relationships such as alliances, partnerships, and kinship are a form of storage. They are an insurance policy against the bad times and greatly extend an individual's range and chances of survival through participation in the construction and reproduction, in a social as well as a biological sense, of a human group.

Nevertheless, sickness and healing would have constituted burdensome interferences for those undertaking foraging excursions, and diseased or injured group mates would have either desisted or constituted vulnerable victims to predators and the elements.

In summary, changes in social organization are held to have constituted the factors that allowed this phase of hominid migration and colonization. This entailed a strengthening of social bonds, the development of strong family ties, the emergence or extension of kinship systems, and the solidification of social alliances and partnerships—in short, overall changes in group organization. In a general sense, since sickness and healing constitutes a socially elaborated biological adaptation, all of these changes in social organization undoubtedly were associated with more focused, extended, and socially complex medical scenarios.

When carnivores migrated in pursuit of herd species, the Ancients operated as mobile foragers of animals that had died through natural means (e.g., old age, disease, accidents, predation). Scavenging natural stores would have constituted a predictable source of food provided individuals and subgroups engaged in exploring the environs looking for food for the larger group. Limited knowledge of the surrounding ecology, including knowledge of medicinal substances, would have sufficed. Technology appears to have been relatively unimportant and to have been developed and used episodically as food sources were encountered. The depth of social planning remained relatively shallow but clearly exceeded that of early hominids so that a rudimentary form of planning for ways of combating the effects of disease and pathology can be surmised.

The Ancients can be held to have had more fully established mimetic forms of representation and expression and to have developed some sense of group identity, group memory, and even group knowledge (Donald 1991). All of this clearly deepened and enriched the capacity for a more elaborate sense of self and attribution of mental states to others. The attainment of a fully mimetic form of cognition and culture along with a protolanguage undoubtedly gave group mates a sense of group vulnerability with respect to the inevitability and consequences of disease and pathology. It is debatable whether the Ancients displayed forms of burial, which would signify a clear-cut symbolic awareness of death and its existential implications (Chase and Dibble 1987). If this were the case, then one could assert that they relied on clearly established rituals and beliefs pertaining to forms of sickness and healing as was certainly the case for the Moderns. Nevertheless, the existence of more articulated forms of self, other, and group as well as the clearly more dense and elaborated social bonds that enabled an emerging sense of group identity and corresponding recognition of group mates would have rendered scenarios of sickness and healing richer, more focused, and more detailed. The combination of these factors can be assumed to have contributed to the evolution of sickness and healing.

Generalizing from material pertaining to chimpanzees and material conjectured to have pertained to early hominids, one can assume that the Ancients showed some rudimentary appreciation of what constituted sickness, of what it entailed in the short and the long run, and of its potential duration, reversibility, and possible eventuation in death and that they developed a more or less equally focused and concerted set of actions aimed at undoing or neutralizing manifestations of disease and pathology both toward the self and others. Evidence of healed fractures in the remains of some Neanderthals attest to the capacity of group individuals to cope with pain and adjust their movements and actions so as to allow for healing. Such forms of paleopathology in skeletal remains can also be assumed to reflect social toleration toward those who showed disease and pathology as well as the willingness of group members to support and minister to the needs of mates who were injured and diseased.

The Moderns

Contemporary discussions of the emergence of modern *Homo sapiens* necessarily commingle with the tenets of the two competing theories to explain the various transitions and particularly the status of the Neanderthals. The first of these theories posits one major line of evolution leading to *Homo sapiens* following the migration out of Africa approximately one million years ago (the theory is often termed "Out of Africa II"). This theory regards the Neanderthals as having been essentially replaced by the Moderns (Mellars and Stringer 1989; Stringer and Gamble 1993; Trinkaus and Shipman 1992). The second theory accounts for modern humans in terms of various separate lines of evolution in different geographic settings (termed "multiregional evolution") culminating in the various races of mankind. This theory posits some gene flow across regions and lines, or regional evolution, and also emphasizes biological convergence in response to common cultural and environmental forces. Multiregional theorists hold that Neanderthals constitute the population of "archaic" humans that culminated in modern *Homo sapiens* found in Europe today. The details of the implications of these two theories will not be pursued further. Instead, emphasis will be given to generally agreed upon common characteristics of modern *Homo sapiens,* principally behavioral ones.

Modern humans are held to have emerged approximately 40,000 years ago, although there is controversy about this dating. In most respects, the Moderns are viewed as conforming in an anatomical, behavioral, and genetic sense to contemporary human populations. Language and associated forms of cognition are held to constitute defining features of the Moderns. As already indicated, there is much speculation and controversy about what exactly constitutes the quintessential features of the "modern" mind, how they developed during evolution and the role of language in all of this. There exists a prominent trend within linguistics and evolutionary psychology to view human mentation as involving the gradual acquisition of a complex, hierarchical special "mental" organ in the operation of which a language module played a complementary if not controlling role. (For a fuller discussion of this topic, see Bickerton, 1981, 1990, 1995; Davidson and Noble 1989; Dennett 1995; Donald 1991; Gibson and Ingold 1993; Jackendoff 1994; Lieberman 1991; Pinker 1994; Pinker and Bloom 1990; Plotkin 1994; Trinkaus 1989; Wilkins and Wakefield 1995.) Archaeological material used to establish the emergence of the Moderns in different geographic settings consists of new, more refined forms of manufacture of stone implements; the use of bone, antler, and ivory material; the existence of burials and organized hearths; evidence of spatial organization in dwelling locations; and prominent forms of artistic expression as revealed in carved figurines, ornaments, jewelry, the use of pigment, and paintings on walls and ceilings of caves (Chase and Dibble 1987; Pfeiffer 1982; Trinkaus 1989).

Sickness and healing in the Moderns is held to have been manifested and played out in scenarios analogous to those of contemporary hunter-gatherer, family-level societies. Since the way of coping with disease and pathology among the Moderns can be inferred using ethnographic material, it will receive special emphasis here as the earliest stage of sickness and healing. This will be covered in the subsequent chapter.

Comment

The view that sickness and healing was a biological adaptation that had its roots in the common ancestor of pongids and hominids, took on a more discernible form among early hominids, became focused and amplified among the Ancients, and then continued to evolve raises the obvious question of when and how expressions of the adaptation came to constitute a cultural institution. To raise this question is to bring to mind a more basic one concerning the origins of culture and human society itself. This constitutes a complex and controversial topic that is fundamental to biology and the social sciences and that has not directly been examined from the standpoint of disease and pathology.

I am proposing here that disease and pathology have played a critical role in human genetic evolution and would suggest that it is possible that its effects, a biological adaptation for sickness and healing, when contextualized behaviorally and symbolically, may have provided conditions for the establishment of culture itself. To elaborate on this, I would say that a sickness and healing adaptation could have operated as a root structure that generated such basic human experiences as those involving vulnerability, suffering, need, hope, faith, solicitude and caring, mortality, privation and loss, bereavement, and perpetuity. These and related experiences are elementary and powerful and at the core of what culture defines, conceptualizes, works with, and "assimilates" for humans. The experiences motivate rituals and mythic narratives. They can also prompt political agreements, rules, and contracts that are foundational to the maintenance of social structural continuity across generations (Knight 1991). In short, a sickness and healing adaptation when expressed in symbolic behavior can arguably be regarded as having played a central role in the emergence of culture. The interplay between biology and culture in relation to genetic and cultural evolution as it pertains to the medical is touched on later in this chapter and taken up in some detail in later ones.

On the Ecology of the SH Adaptation

Biological Material Favoring an
SH Adaptation

What sorts of biological changes were likely to be found among early hominids which co-occurred with, in fact caused, the elements of sickness that were instrumental in selecting SH? The following are relevant: (1) traumatic injuries to the body, including fractures, dislocations, and abrasions associated with widespread tissue damage; (2) destruction of body parts such as that occasioned by warfare and predation; (3) noxious plant and animal substances for which the body's natural defense systems were unprepared; (4) heavy loads of parasites and virulent microorganisms capable of invading the body, overwhelming its defenses, and producing infection with fever and associated behavioral responses. These factors, constituting the social ecology of disease and injury in the early hominids, are likely to have been prevalent and to have also figured prominently in the causation of states of sickness.

Small bands (and temporary aggregations of them) are held to have constituted the form of social grouping that in an evolutionary sense led to early human forms (Barnard 1992; Lee and DeVore 1968; Price and Brown 1985). Paleoarchaeological and contemporary anthropological studies suggest that ancestral groups developed pictures of disease that were quite different from those of modern, civilized populations (Black 1975; Cohen 1989; Eaton, Shostak, and Konner 1988; Johns 1990). Zoonotic infections, for example, were probably important, as were infections or toxic conditions stemming from plants as well as forms of parasitation causing chronic infections. Moreover, these kinds of diseases varied greatly in relation to the kinds of physical environments inhabited by early prehuman groups (Cohen 1989). A group's diet can obviously render individuals vulnerable to disease; although this also varied in relation to physical habitat (as well as season of the year), food appears to have been plentiful and nutritious. The mobility of early prehuman groups probably exposed its members to repeated infections caused by microvariants of parasites. Much less common in the disease picture were chronic conditions, such as cancer, hypertension, and atherosclerosis, the so-called diseases of civilization, that are typically seen today. In addition, viruses associated with epidemic diseases that play significant roles in large, sedentary populations were not likely to have been a part of the ecology of disease in early prehuman groups (Cohen 1989). Finally, all indications are that diseases and infirmities in the elderly and in adults who were handicapped probably occasioned less concern since individuals with these conditions proved especially burdensome to other group members and were not contributing actively to subsistence. Diseases affecting those that were highly functional to the ongoing and future well-being of the group were likely to have been of central concern.

In summary, insofar as early human groups probably resembled hunter-gatherer groups of today, the ecology of disease of these groups needs to be examined for clues about the states of disease and injury that selected for SH. This area of study has produced information that is comprehensive and complex and indicates that plant toxins, infections, and traumatic injuries played a significant role whereas diet-related and so-called degenerative conditions played a comparatively much smaller one. The existence of detoxication allelochemicals from plants and physiological and learned, conditioned avoidances to selected food substances did much to protect against the effects of plant toxins (Johns 1990). Some of the infections produced systemic diseases that were probably severe and rapidly fatal, others produced ones that were more chronic and localized. This type of ecology, then, underwrote the sickness conditions that could have selected a putative SH adaptation.

Aspects of Disease and Injury Comprising SH

The SH adaptation comes into play during sickness and healing. Manifestations of disease and injury that can elicit healing constitute one set of components of the adaption. The following sorts of things are relevant: (1) changes in physical appearance indicating marked distress with or without frank pain; or simply weakness, lethargy, loss of interest, and disability; (2) states of somnolence and actual sleeping during normal periods of wakefulness; (3) other physical manifestations of changes in the level of consciousness and arousal; (4) changes in facial appearance and expressiveness and in locomotion resembling malaise; (5) physical increases in temperature or changes in behavior associated with fever (e.g., anorexia, diminished motivation, shivering, sweating); (6) physical changes in the color of exposed parts of the body (coating of hair, skin, sclera, mucus membranes; (7) structural changes in the appearance of the body (malposition of extremities, swellings, lacerations); (8) bleeding from bodily orifices or from lesions on the body; (9) tenderness to palpation; (10) changes in the diameter of the pupils and pupillary inequalities; (11) changes in gait; (12) changes in physiological functioning, involving respiration, excretion, urination, and heart rate and rhythm (this would involve such things as hematuria, diarrhea, vomiting, coughing, rhinorrhea, dyspnea, and rapid pulse rates). The preceding encompass changes in physical appearance, functioning of the body, and social expressiveness that can be regarded as the physical components of sickness.

From the standpoint of SH, that sickness behaviors have a public basis is important. The public or social basis of sickness may signal its cause, and it is for this reason that visible lesions, inflammations, and wounds together with behaviorally and physically well-marked disordered physiologies can be considered centrally important in eliciting an SH response from conspecifics and thus, ultimately, in serving as the evolutionary basis for medical institutions. As an example, the occurrence of fever and anorexia would appear difficult to fabricate and can be considered to signal sickness "physically." The same could be said for diarrhea and vomiting. In other words, in directly signaling its cause, the lesions and the visible "signs" of disease impart a measure of authenticity to the condition of sickness. The same applies to other sickness manifestations. For these reasons, the phenomena listed earlier comprising the behavioral morphology of sickness would seem to constitute anchoring percepts of any computational theory of SH (see below).

In hominids that displayed evolved cognitive capacities and social structures, sickness behavior can include, in addition to issues reviewed earlier, motivated willful symbolic references to the state of the organism. The organism, in other words, can communicate that it is in a state of sickness so as to elicit behaviors geared to promote help from conspecifics or group mates. This naturally entails the possibility of cheating, for the organism may project a state of sickness only to accrue undeserved advantages. The problems posed by the "protohypochondriac" constitute a basic constraint on the cognitive capacity for SH. The provider would need communication skills that would enable it to see physical manifestations of sickness and accurately "read" authentic distress, suffering, and impairment. The physical components of sickness reviewed earlier can be thought of as bringing into play the language that communicates authentic states of sickness. In effect, conspecifics have been selected to effectively encode and show/communicate it as well as read/interpret and decode its messages and respond to them in socially adaptive ways.

One question that arises is the medium through which sickness is communicated to conspecifics. A purely visual channel implies that the perceived physical components of sickness are basic. Olfactory and somesthetic channels are also relevant. Similarly, one can envision a proto- or early linguistic channel in which verbal or gestural elements are used to symbolize and point to the state of sickness, its implications and possible causes. Linguistic competence, however elementary, would have aided in the communication of information pertaining to the ingestion of substances producing vomiting and diarrhea, thus complementing innate dietary preferences, "natural" phobias of new foodstuffs, and learned conditioned avoidances of deleterious plants that protected against sickness (Garcia et al. 1974; Johns 1990). Clearly, there exist universals in the expression and recognition of affect through facial musculature, and to the extent that such emotions, in conjunction with pain and other physiological responses involving disgust, nausea, vomiting, and diarrhea, are part of the behavior of sickness there is a basis for believing that sickness is communicated in this way (Craig, Prkachin, and Grunau 1992; Ekman and Friesen 1975; Ekman, Friesen, and Ellsworth 1972; Johns 1990; Prkachin 1992). One can judge all of these as playing a role and thus envision the channel through which sickness is communicated as multimodal. However, as elaborated later, the essence of the SH adaptation is its cognitive character. It enables the provider to appreciate sickness by interpreting changes in physical appearance, physical behavior, emotional behavior, and related signals of distress and disability.

Aspects of Healing Comprising SH

Organisms have inherited adaptations that are geared to minimize, control, and undo states of sickness. A host of intraorganismic changes come to mind; for example, physiological, biochemical, hormonal, immunological, inflammatory, and reparative changes and mechanisms (Williams and Nesse 1991). However, special emphasis is placed here on acts of self-caring and use of substances having medicinal properties that could have a broad representation in animals (Clayton and Wolfe 1993; Johns 1990). With respect to prehominid groups, self-caring or self-medication would include such things as protecting injured body parts; promoting loss of excess heat and fluids; maintaining warm body temperature; inducing vomiting or gastrointestinal evacuation; and seeking medicinal substances to relieve symptoms, such as using acquired knowledge stored in memory systems or searching the environment for natural products that relieve symptoms of illness and that promote changes in wellbeing and communications to conspecifics that medical help is needed. It is this set of adaptations that when elicited and directed at the self or at conspecifics constitutes the biological roots of SH.

It is emphasized that to the potential provider of SH, sickness behavior (the target, what elicits SH from a conspecific) has both physical and symbolic meaning. This is different from the claim that the sick organism must willfully communicate about its state of sickness to elicit SH. It has already been pointed out that the possibility of cheating about sickness renders a capacity for SH problematic. Not only must the caregiving organism perceive and respond to sickness, but in addition it would have to detect cheating. The pitfalls associated with this (the risks and benefits of being right or wrong) in the setting of states that are potentially life threatening create obvious problems. In settings involving trauma or acute severe illness, the social communication of a need for SH may not be possible. Furthermore, the advantages of an adaptation for SH would obviously involve giving care to the very young who may not as yet have acquired the necessary verbal/linguistic/cognitive skills. In short, for a number of reasons that would also include theoretical economy and precision, the eventuations of sickness that elicit SH are assumed to constitute biologically based physical and behavioral changes in the sick organism that are intrinsically symbolic or communicational to the provider of SH but that do not require willful, self-referential communications. The latter, however, are likely accompaniments of sickness and would need to be taken into account in the computation of possible acts of SH. Further problems relating to cheating in relation to SH are taken up later.

The elicitation of the SH adaptation would lead to rendering care that is helpful and ensuring that the organism's recuperative powers are maximized. As an example, in the event of injuries and trauma, immobilization and the cleansing of open wounds would constitute actions linked to SH. The provisioning of splints and supports for locomotion would be part of this effort. So also would be the resort (by the organism itself or by conspecifics) to plants having medicinal properties. These could be directly helpful (by providing needed detoxification chemicals or antiparasitic remedies); and the use of plant euphorics could improve morale and well-being, however temporarily, during the time prior to the activation of immunological mechanisms and physiological responses that would inevitably follow. In the event of illnesses with fever, the sick organism may be provided with insulation and protection from loss of heat through radiation, convection, or conduction. Thus covering could be provided as well as placement in locations that are insulated and not windy. Selection of microclimates to maximize the effectiveness of the fever response would be the goal. The treatment of fever in human groups has undergone changes. Although antipyretics were frequently used in the past, this practice has been reevaluated. Data on how higher primates react to febrile responses of conspecifics as well as other physical manifestations of sickness, already highly suggestive, would prove useful in helping to clarify properties of an SH adaptation. Data from contemporary hunter-gatherers might also help, although in them cultural developments might very well mask or override the more basic, "wired in" responses. In other words, although there should ideally exist a complementariness between the processes of biological (i.e., genetical) and cultural evolution, there is no reason to suppose that medical care actions stemming from cultural evolution always complement those sculpted by natural selection. Issues such as these that involve the interplay between the processes of evolution and possible coevolution are taken up later in this book.

In the event of weakness and lassitude, provisioning of food and water ensures conserving energy and preventing excessive negative energy balances. As discussed in chapter 1, the search for plants and botanical specimens with medicinal properties in the event of sickness might constitute a behavioral trait that was selected for during evolution (Huffman and Siefu 1989; Johns 1990). Any rudimentary knowledge that the group might have acquired about the positive medicinal effects of plants and herbs (for relieving pain, controlling gastrointestinal symptoms, cleansing wounds, etc.) would have been used by the sick organism and by conspecifics to attempt to heal sickness depending on manifestations and circumstances. Strategies of resource provisioning would be matched by strategies for predator avoidance. To promote physiological homeostasis, the sick person's psyche should also be "provisioned." This would involve the communication of support and caring and the avoidance of communications that are stressful since the latter (given psychosomatic mediation) would be deleterious. All of the above and other aspects of SH are costly to the provider of SH since the actions involved not only contribute negatively to fitness but also in the case of infections expose the provider to their spread.

Although costly in a general evolutionary sense, many of the component activities of the SH suite of behaviors that has been posited here are analogous to activities already observed in animals and some primates (see Goodall 1986; Hart 1988, 1990; Johns 1990; and discussions in chapter 1 and above). Such costs were partly borne by earlier adaptations that produced behaviors resembling SH and that may have provided conditions for its selection. In short, what has been here termed the SH adaptation is seen as consistent with an evolutionary trend that may have begun in animals and that became specialized in the hominid line. Many behaviors involved in "caregiving" that were associated with earlier adaptations were elaborated.

On the Machinery of the SH Adaptation

SH has been conceptualized here as an adaptation to sickness in the self and in a conspecific. It is rooted in the caregiver's own behavior dispositions regarding sickness in itself, which are to self-heal and self-medicate. Both the disposition to heal oneself and the disposition to heal another are judged to constitute a product of natural selection and to be complemented by cultural evolution. In a metaphorical sense, the communicative messages of sickness can be thought to elicit defenses on their behalf. In this regard, SH can be viewed as an adjunct "social defense" to the defensive systems that natural selection has provided organisms in order to promote the propagation of those genes that operate them. In short, SH is like a host defense in that it protects against the costs of disease, injury, and related biological conditions. However, it is also a "defense" added to those of the organism by the actions of altruistic conspecifics.

A basic feature of the behaviors subserving SH is that of knowing who is a legitimate recipient and when. On the one hand, this involves recognizing states of sickness in the self and in conspecifics. On the other hand, the provider of SH to a conspecific should have an awareness of mortality. When elicited, SH is directed at living (not dead) conspecifics, and organisms offering it should ideally be capable of distinguishing sickness from imminent death to render SH economical in an inclusive fitness, evolutionary sense.

This discussion raises the question of the necessary cognitive distinctions that a provider of SH must make to interpret a condition of sickness and respond accordingly. The following issues are relevant: (1) a capacity for self/other differentiation; (2) an ability to detect sickness in self and react through sickness-relieving behaviors; (3) the capacity to differentiate self from other and to impute mental states to self and other; (4) a capacity to recognize that a subset of distinctive physical changes in a conspecific constitutes evidence of sickness and that there exist different varieties of sickness; (5) an awareness that the needs of sickness and the response of SH entail not taking advantage of or exploiting the other in its state of incapacity and dependence; (6) awareness of when sickness terminates in death rendering further SH in a strict sense unnecessary but bringing into play social adjustments and accommodations consistent with mourning and grieving (see below); (7) a memory system capable of having stored previous instances of sickness and medical caring; (8) a cognitive system that facilitates observational learning from previous exposures to conditions of sickness and medical caring; (9) an awareness that sicknesses entail distinctive courses or prognoses if left unattended; (10) attempts at protecting the sick conspecific from environmental hazards, including weather changes, predators, and deprivation of needed foodstuffs and fluids provided these factors do not unduly endanger the organism.

Much of the machinery of SH takes into account the topic of an organism's theory of mind. In humans, it entails such things as a concept of self, social attribution (assuming the perspective of others), capacity for genuine caring and compassion, empathy, the development of values, and the cognitive underpinnings of ethical behavior. Such issues are being actively researched in human infants and comparatively in nonhuman primates. Clearly, the machinery underlying all of this has implications for understanding not only the evolution of medicine but also human evolution and behavior more generally. Thus far, however, despite the relevance of these themes for sickness and healing as formulated here, researchers in this field have concentrated mainly on psychological questions and issues pertaining to evolutionary ethics (see Povinelli and Godfrey 1993 for a recent review).

As mentioned earlier, a key factor in the computation of the significance attached to a state of sickness and in the activation of the behavioral suite subserving SH involves the likelihood of the "sick" person surviving the state of sickness. There are suggestions that female chimpanzees and dolphins find it hard to separate from deceased offspring (Connor and Smolker 1990; Goodall 1986). This suggests difficulty in defining death or difficulty in shutting off epimeletic or caregiving behavior. On the other hand, organisms avoid intimate contact with critically ill associates and in many instances of possible significant cost to the group entailed by a state of sickness may abandon the sick organism or let it fend for itself (Cheney and Seyfarth 1990; Fabrega 1974; Goodall 1986; see also chapter 3). All of this implies that associates may be able to surmise the imminence of death. Such an eventuality signals an imprudent and costly expenditure of SH. Thus the SH adaptation entails evaluating, in however an impressionistic way, when investments of healing are likely to prove advantageous to the sick person (Shafton 1976). Conversely, when the condition of the sick conspecific signals imminent death or hazards to the group or organism delivering SH, an investment in medical caring would appear to be contravened unless it were to be linked with related social and cultural imperatives (see below).

A programmed suite of behaviors such as that posited for SH would have been selected for if (1) it proved specially beneficial to sick members, and in the long run, to the caregiver; and (2) its value was not vitiated by cheating (see below). Because medical deception is always a possibility, the phenomenon of pain poses some problems. Pain is obviously a fundamental biological property of evolved species that is replete with significant information regarding the need states of an organism and its capacity for adaptive behavior. It constitutes a hallmark of sickness and can elicit caring and nurturing. And most important, there appear to exist common, perhaps universal, ways in which pain of different modalities is registered in changes in facial musculature. This points to common ways of communicating and decoding pain (Prkachin 1992). Moreover, the relief of pain must have been a stimulus for the search for pharmacologically active substances in the physical environment. However, pain behavior can be feigned, and for this reason it poses a problem to a potential caregiver who guards against exploitation of the sick role. An ability to evaluate pain behavior and the communicative messages that are implicit in that behavior would seem to constitute a key component of the SH adaptation. In summary, pain behaviors—perhaps distinctive types of pain behavior—must be viewed as essential components of sickness and are integral features that point to a sociobiology of sickness and healing.

Cheating and the SH Adaptation

Sickness Cheating

Deception, manipulation, and cheating can be viewed as features of social behavior and as biological imperatives. With respect to SH, they can be ascribed to the sick organism or to the would-be caregiver, that is, to the recipients and to the providers of SH, respectively.

It has been argued already that the possibility of cheating with respect to sickness probably was a factor in the way the SH adaptation was initially sculpted. The perceptions and cognitions necessary to make SH "work" as an adaptation, and so avoid the cheating that might undermine it, would have required an anchoring more on the material substance of sickness than on its "mere" overt display or phenomenology, which can be more easily feigned. Moreover, one can assume that SH was initially selected for during a period in the evolutionary progression when the capacity to willfully elaborate symptoms of disease for self-advantage (sickness "fabrications") may not as yet have been fully realized in the protohuman repertoire of behavior and or sharply repudiated by group mates and conspecifics. In later developments of self/other discriminations and attributions, sickness fabrications were undoubtedly problematic. This is implicit in my emphasis on perceptions and cognitions that require careful, subtle, and "objective" probings of sickness episodes, probings that would have excluded being easily manipulated and exploited into providing self- and group-defeating caring. Careful assessments of sickness are also implicated as safeguards against providing wasteful expenditures of caregivers on conspecifics likely to die (discussed later).

That an evolutionary adaptation that underlies social behavior can serve as a basis for instances of cheating, deception, and the reaping of selfish rewards goes without saying. However, one may judge sick role exploitation (as indicated earlier, in a loose sense since this concept was defined for special modern societies; see Parsons 1975) as a later development in human evolution, an aspect of sickness and healing strongly influenced and complemented by cultural and social evolution. The formulation of sickness in social moral terms and the playing out of sickness in the social arena of the group, typically seen in sedentary societies that are socially complex, are both implicated, as is the commercialization and monetarization of medicine and life more generally. This theme is dealt with in subsequent chapters.

The potential for self-advancement implicit in the unconscious or consciously fictive manufacture of sickness, which bears a relation to the idea of "secondary gain" that is associated with the sick role, should not be allowed to detract from the potential importance of an evolutionary adaptation such as SH that is argued for in this chapter. The implications of unconscious manufacture of sickness and the unconscious but "real" psychosomatic bases of some sicknesses in the evolutionary progression of SH constitute a later chapter in the story of sickness and healing. This topic will be addressed in subsequent chapters that deal with sickness and healing in different social formations.

One final point needs emphasis. It is true that disease and injury in the environment of evolutionary adaptedness are held to have, in the long run, "naturally" selected for behaviors geared to a lessening of mortality and morbidity. However, the adaptation implies economy and efficiency, which necessarily also implies that trade-offs were involved in the "calculation" of the "costs" and "benefits" of sickness and healing. And to recall an earlier theme, all of this took place *in a distinct type of ecology and social environment*. Consequently, the adaptation was necessarily sculpted with an awareness of the possible outcome of death. This means that social biological constraints of group living in Pleistocene conditions set "natural" boundaries to the expression of SH. An individual's cheating of sickness constitutes a group burden under the conditions posited. Diseased and injured organisms as well as conspecifics, in the process of expressing sickness and healing, had in consideration possible wasteful, costly, and burdensome behaviors along different points in the continuum which signaled the inevitability of death. This, in turn, means that on crossing a "critical" point of sickness and healing, preparing for this inevitability was integral to the adaptation. All of these considerations undoubtedly influenced interpretations about the authenticity of sickness and the value of healing. Authentic SH, in other words, meant expressing and reading biologically compelling signals in the environment of evolutionary adaptedness.

Fraudulent Healing

The converse of the above is that healing also had a biological rationale in the special environment of human evolution. The adaptation, to recall, constitutes a holistic response to disease and injury: sickness and healing are integrated and reflexive in the individual. Just like individuals had in mind the calculation of authentic sickness, so also did conspecifics have in mind the calculation of "authentic" healing; more specifically, healing that could potentially help and that was not wasteful. This can be viewed as the "natural," authentic boundary to healing.

It is intuitively self-evident that deception, manipulation, and cheating can easily come into play with respect to the provider of SH. Two varieties of such self-interested acts need to be singled out. One can posit that (1) conspecifics in general were (and are) motivated by self-interest and engaged in fabricated, fictive acts of SH to incur advantages from others and also that (2) special individuals in a group who appropriated or were assigned tasks or "roles" as SH providers ("protoshamans") exploited its potential for resources, power, or special privileges. In this chapter emphasis is mainly given to aspects of SH that implicate the first type of potential deceiver. One can judge the second type of deceiver, the unauthentic healer, as part of later developments in the evolutionary progression of the SH adaptation in man. However, the argument pursued here necessarily contains an implication that the origins and evolution of healing exploitation have roots in evolutionary biology. The full pursuit of this aspect of the problem can be construed as part of cultural evolution and is discussed in subsequent chapters (see also later discussion for related issues).

As has been suggested earlier, an instanciation of SH entails spotting "authentic" sickness and providing "truly" and "economically" efficacious acts of SH. All entail the mediation of symbolic, cortically based behaviors. In being geared to the physiology of sickness, SH is held to have constituted an understanding of sickness that was, by definition, adaptive.

A thorough understanding of adaptive behavior triggered by disease and injury of a conspecific requires further investigation naturalistically and experimentally. Thus far, the essential purpose of directed chimpanzee searches for medicinal plants appears to be "self-medication," whereas SH as conceptualized here is also "other directed." The seeking for medicinal plants and their ingestion at times of sickness would seem to require a measure of self-awareness, as postulated by Gordon G. Gallup (1970, 1985, 1991). Moreover, material reviewed in an earlier section suggests compassion with respect to the effects of disease and injury and other changes that is analogous to and can be viewed as a preadaptation for or early manifestation of sickness and healing (Goodall 1986). In other words, the material reviewed suggests the operation of a trait already incorporated in the earlier phases of protoculture characteristic of ancestors of early man. To the extent that it is purposeful, sickness and healing also implies the possibility of relief, which takes into consideration temporal/spatial binding. Given the integrated, reflexive character of the SH adaptation and response, the directing of healing efforts to sick conspecifics, which clearly implicates subtler aspects of self/other distinctions and attributions, would constitute a refinement of these behaviors.

The progression of self-caring to other-caring essentially underscores a biological continuity between sickness and healing. This continuity explains the relationship that exists between the SH adaptation and what has been described as Darwinian medicine (Williams and Nesse 1991). One may take the latter to mean the behavioral and bodily changes that accompany disease and that constitute adaptive responses of the organism. These "natural" manifestations of disease, when examined in the light of biological evolution, can be shown to have a rationale that promotes self-healing. SH constitutes an extension and projection outward to a conspecific or group mate of this innate self-healing response. Darwinian medicine informs of responses geared to control or undo disease in the self; SH incorporates these Darwinian responses and extends them outward to conspecifics.

SH as conceptualized here constitutes an adaptation that is common to the evolving genome, being widely shared in the population. Insofar as SH is conceptualized to be based on the recognition of "authentic" sickness, one can hold that a complementary authenticity on the part of the provider is required. An analogy between self-medication "cheating" and provider "cheating" of SH might prove illuminating here. Self-medication (as described for higher primates) would appear to constitute an "authentic" adaptive act. Yet such an act could in theory be conceived of as either (1) fabricated or (2) misinformed. In the former instance, the act could be construed as designed to exploit conspecifics; in the second instance, as impulsive or wasteful, given the inevitable margins for error in the physiologically based changes that might trigger SH (or any evolutionary adaptation for that matter). At any rate, these construals would seem to point to boundary conditions for the cheating or antisocial. One may contend that analogous acts on the part of providers also point to boundaries between the social and antisocial or cheating with respect to healing. In other words, an act of other-directed medical altruism can also be construed as fabricated or misinformed, with similar interpretations and construals. In both cases, cheating is possible, but SH is defined so as to limit these selfish exploitations.

SH is based on perceptions and cognitions linked to the physiological and psychological material of sickness and entails a measure of intentionality to act in an adaptive way, which implies redressing aspects of sickness. It of necessity brings into play levels or degrees of intentionality (Dennett 1987). One may add that elaborated exploitations of healing (as for sickness as well) are more properly to be included in the chapters of medical caring that are part of cultural evolution. When SH becomes the basis of a special social role and economic incentives attach to its performance, all of which are later developments of cultural and social evolution, powerful influences favoring exploitation are created. These can override the more natural, biologically rooted or "innate" aspects of the SH adaptation. On more general philosophical grounds, sickness and healing need to be understood as having played a role in marking the boundaries for cheating and exploitation in the human line. The pursuit of this topic is well beyond what is possible and suitable for this presentation.

Summary

The important points pertaining to cheating/deception are that SH (1) builds on acts of sociality that are biologic and symbolic; (2) builds on, adds to, and applies to conspecifics' and group mates' evolved innate knowledge based on self-perceptions of illness and innate tendencies to care for (and medicate) the self; (3) entails elaborated capacities for self/other distinctions and attributions of intention; (4) involves responding adaptively to perceptions of sickness behaviors of conspecifics; (5) offers safeguards against spotting fabricated sickness scripts; (6) in a logically complementary way, entails safeguards against its own fictive enactments ("unauthentic sickness"); and (7) like sickness (given possibilities provided by culturally more elaborated scenarios), is subject to fabrication and deception; and (8) the biological boundaries of sickness and healing are set by wasteful, costly behaviors directed at terminally ill organisms. Indeed, the question of whether cheating of sickness or healing/caring applies to contemporary hunter-gatherer societies is at all clear will be discussed in chapter 3 (see also Fabrega 1979a).

Social and Emotional Considerations

The factors considered so far underscore the point that the provider of SH is likely to have achieved a substantial cognitive capacity and to have been extensively socialized, that is to say, is likely to be a member of a population that is group living and possessed of a home site or home base with the communicational and early cultural features described above. In short, although the ability to recognize authentic sickness behavior, the essence of SH, is anchored in psychology, SH is actualized in a quintessentially social context of interpersonal bonding.

What are some of the social ecological conditions that prevailed in the environment of evolutionary adaptiveness that served as necessary conditions for the selection of SH? Many of these have already been alluded to but can be briefly summarized (Cheney and Seyfarth 1990; Goodall 1986; Shafton 1976). The following factors seem relevant: (1) a social group characterized by a considerable measure of cohesion and solidarity; (2) the involvement of significant group members well known to each other, which implies a measure of group stability; (3) the prevalence of high and sustained levels of social cooperation and reciprocity within groups and competition against outsiders (e.g., as favoring a critical mass of conspecifics); (4) the existence of a more or less safe and stable place of residence or home base where sick comembers could be attended; (5) the ability to acquire and use social and ecological knowledge; (6) the availability of food, fluids, and other materials deemed necessary for convalescence and recovery, which implies an abundant habitat, or the capacity to store and transport bare necessities; (7) the ability to accumulate and share knowledge about sickness and its care, however rudimentary; (8) instrumentalities that protect against inclement weather and other environmental hazards, including predators.

The nature of the cognitive processes and social contexts entailed by SH and intuitions about it and the settings eliciting it raise the question of the possible emotions surrounding the provisioning of SH. Emotions can be viewed in this context as mediators if not as elicitors of actions provoked by situations that are evolutionarily significant to the organism (Hamburg 1968; Nesse 1990). In this account, emotions are mental states that were selected by important environmental contingencies. They are important design features of adaptations. It is quite likely that emotions would have been implicated in the evolution of SH. If this is the case, what emotions are likely to have been associated with the perception of states of sickness that served as the natural elicitors of healing? At the most basic level, there is the state of suffering, pain, and distress that is integral to SH. This constitutes an emotion and the capacity to respond to it, a trait of empathy and compassion that is intrinsic to altruism and SH. Clearly, emotions signaling danger would be implicated, which suggest fear and anxiety. A sense of worry and concern, if not sadness, about the threat posed by sickness might be implicated as well. One can suggest that something resembling "positive" emotions, such as optimism, trust, confidence, faith, reassurance, caring, and hope, are presupposed by, implicated in, and evolutionarily elaborated through an adaptation such as SH. Finally, one must include feelings of loss and grief necessarily aroused in the context of terminality. The essence of SH is that it is a social action and hence many of the so-called social emotions should be expected to have played some role in help-ing to program and mediate the suite of behaviors here described as SH.

Early Forms of SH in the Human Line of Evolution

There are several reasons for believing that an adaptation such as SH would have originally been most prominently displayed in females, targeted at se-lected infants and children, and focused on kin (i.e., genetic relatives). First, social processes favoring kin selection among early hominids were part of the evolutionary environment that provided conditions that selected SH. With respect to caregiving in the setting of sickness, a well-established behavior pattern was already present the purpose of which was the protection and car-ing of the newborn, infant, and child during its period of dependence. SH di-rected at the young may be viewed as a specialization and elaboration of pa-rental investment.

Second, an altruistic act such as caring, protecting, and generally supporting life mechanisms and processes in a young and biologically dependent organism at nontrivial costs to the parent is obviously effective from the standpoint of inclusive fitness. In effect, these are the organisms that share the organism's genes to the largest extent. (Care for parents and siblings, of course, may also increase an organism's inclusive fitness, which is another reason to expect that SH may have been initially centered in the family.)

Third, one may consider that in order for a trait such as SH to be selected for, it ideally should also be advantageous in the short run. The behaviors labeled SH would need to have been elicited sufficiently frequently and for the benefit of an organism likely to be benefited by and to survive its effects. Infection in newborns, infants, and the very young is common. The period of passive im-munity provided by placental transfer and later by antibodies in nutrients pro-vided by milk is naturally limited. Many infections during the gradual decay of passive immunity can be expected to have been of low grade since the waning phases of the immunity would have afforded some protection. All of the pre-ceding would render actions subsumed as SH likely to have been beneficial to receivers, the very young, and hence to have been naturally selected.

Fourth, as indicated earlier, the SH adaptation has ultimate, distal causes as well as more proximal ones involving common experiences during develop-ment and, thus, must be held to have required critical triggering and some learning early in the life span. In caring for the young and responding to their needs and suffering, parental figures would be helping to shape the SH adap-tation. As researchers in evolutionary psychology contend, there is no in-consistency between ideas pertaining to instinct and learning, between that which is "hard wired" and that which requires shaping through experience (Barkow, Cosmides, and Tooby 1992). That SH has an ontogeny as well as a phylogeny points to infancy and early life experiences as crucial periods during which behaviors implicated in sickness and healing would have been shaped and streamlined.

Finally, and more speculatively, one must consider that the very young constitute a potential focus for the joint efforts of *both* parents. An adaptation such as SH would have been selected more strongly in both sexes if they were both already predisposed to care for the young. In other words, each mate would have been rewarded by the display and activation of SH, a quintessential instance of maternal and paternal investment. To the extent that male and female hominids were bonded, and males engaged in parental care, this would have enhanced selection for the special SH adaptation.

Food sharing and reciprocity more generally between the sexes were traits that provided the social context for a putative SH adaptation. Any male parental investment that may have existed in the human line would have entailed favoring and provisioning care to pregnant females or mates. In fact, any genetically related organism would benefit from such an investment. The "sickness" of the pregnancy carries a high probability of remitting provided an accommodation is made to the pregnant woman's need for rest and relief from overtaxing subsistence activities. The needs of such a "sick person" are also not elaborate and difficult to meet since much of evolutionary history has gone into ensuring the success of pregnancy. All of these and other factors can be expected to have in some instances rendered pregnant females possible targets for SH on the part of mates (and other relatives in the nuclear group). The whole question of male parental investment and behaviors directed at pregnant mates and relatives is not well profiled in the primate literature. The suggestion here is that pregnancy resembles sickness and that offering SH might be fruitfully examined in relation to behaviors toward pregnant females and parental investment behaviors more generally. The latter can be viewed as social behaviors that might have preceded, contributed integrally to, and helped elaborate the SH adaptation. When these behaviors expand in focus and meaning to encompass reciprocation for altruistic acts, generally, as well as for acts of care administered during earlier or preexisting states of sickness, one glimpses the emerging social architecture of SH.

In summary, an adaptation develops because through natural selection it favors the replication of the genes that control it. The organism "housing" those genes can benefit from this process. Although initially linked to a discrete problem, the genetic ensemble producing the adaptation can expand its focus or target so as to encompass related problems. It has been hypothesized that the very young may have served as the initial, basic recipients of SH and that the latter may have subsequently been a factor in contributing to any paternal investment that was manifest. Pregnant women, it can be hypothesized, would have constituted another possible target of SH for many of the reasons listed above. From an initial focus on the young and possibly pregnant females, the behaviors subsumed as SH could have expanded in focus to include other

members of the group in the logic of reciprocal altruism. In addition to prov-
ing physiologically and psychologically beneficial, this would promote social
reciprocity. For all of these reasons, it would seem that SH might have constituted a form of behavior that would have been complementary to or in-
strumentally efficacious in the emerging behavioral repertoire of the hominid
lineage that has been described in an earlier section.

Later Stages in the Evolution of Medicine

This topic will be discussed in greater detail in subsequent chapters. Here it
is appropriate to present a general account of later developments in the evolution of medicine so as to highlight important issues that will be given attention
later in this book.

A basic consideration to keep in mind is that the SH adaptation is rooted in
biology and genetic evolution and provides the material for subsequent elaboration during social and cultural evolution. In other words, while the adaptation
is genetically based and, hence, "hard wired," it also requires and facilitates
learning about sickness and healing. In short, SH constitutes the foundational
material for the elaboration of medicine as a social institution (which, as alluded to earlier in the chapter, can have maladaptive consequences—a theme
dealt with explicitly in later chapters). In visualizing the evolution of medicine
one must keep in mind that both biological/psychological and social/cultural
factors have played a role and that the SH adaptation is the bridge that integrates these complementary processes.

Initially, the healing component of SH can be visualized as a "natural response" of conspecifics located in the proximity of the sick. All witnesses to
an event of trauma or illness would have responded with efforts directed to
help, ameliorate, and support the sick organism. One development would involve the coordination of efforts on the part of conspecifics, with some individuals taking a more active role in rendering care. More than likely, immediate family members would assume greater responsibility and those more
distantly related or genetically unrelated would adopt a more passive, supportive, and retiring role. Given an evolved means of social communication, a
pooling of information would no doubt take place, perhaps with one or a few
individuals taking a leadership, coordinating position toward the sick person.

Two developments that can be expected to have followed involve elaborations in the knowledge domain pertaining to sickness and healing and elaborations in the mode of provisioning medical care to the sick. Initially knowledge of sickness, curing methods, and curing expertise may have been applied
and administered by immediate or extended family members, perhaps adult

females, although any senior respected family members would be involved. Next, the provisioning of care may have moved outside the immediate family. Either because of prestige and power stemming from non-sickness-related activities, because of socially perceived medical expertise, because of personal interest, or because of acquired knowledge and acumen, one or a few of the members of the group came to be identified as more expert than their comembers. The skills of these early "protohealers" or "protoshamans" would combine with the accumulated sickness/curing experiences in the group to establish a body of knowledge and lore pertaining to medicine. Localized lesions or ailments or symptoms would come to be distinguished from more extensive problems that involved the whole person. The implications of part sicknesses as compared to whole "self" sicknesses may have been differentiated, as an example. Concepts about sickness analogous to our concepts of minor/serious, acute/chronic, traumatic/nontraumatic, safe/dangerous, and so on, would occupy the emerging semantic space of medical knowledge.

Along with these early concepts (in reality, conceptual refinements) there would probably develop differences in the type of curing practices. Initially offered informally and in an egalitarian social setting, medical curing and care would come to be offered in a more selective fashion. In other words, caregiving would encompass relationships that were slightly more specialized: a shift from informal, egalitarian giving to more personalized and specialized giving. It is not unlikely that the shift in the mode of provisioning SH would parallel the type of sickness that was made the object of care. The more serious/dangerous/encompassing, and so on, the sickness, the more specialized the setting of care with group- or self-selected persons (the group experts or "healers") administering it. All of these early human forms of medical care and practice are seen as elementary elaborations of the structure of early group relations and of the process of social reciprocity more generally. They do not yet involve the establishment of a true healer role, much less the establishment of curing rituals or ceremonies that involve organization, elaborate preparations, and the like (Fabrega 1974).

The preceding developments are viewed as the earliest elaborations of SH and emerging from the logic of kin selection, reciprocal altruism, and general social reciprocity in a setting of caring, helping, the development of a sense of group identity, and the like. In other words, these early cultural aspects of SH are judged as natural extensions or elaborations of the basic psychological adaptation that is at the base of medicine as a social institution. Further developments that place the evolution of medical care and practice well within the process of social or cultural evolution (or the coevolution of genes and culture) would include such things as the establishment of a true healer's role, extension of clientele beyond the immediate group, more personalized relations between the sick and the healer, the rendering of special compensation or remuneration for the delivery of healing, competition between healers, and the specialization of practice on types of medical problems. Associated with the development of specialization and remuneration for medical care and practice are a whole range of economic factors that come to alter the character of SH as a psychological adaptation and early form of healing, as is evident in preindustrial as well as modern contemporary societies. These developments, part of the whole story of the evolution of medicine, will be covered in subsequent chapters.

So far, aspects of "other healing" have been emphasized in the evolutionary progression of the SH adaptation. Since this adaptation has been conceptualized as interconnected, that is, as encompassing both sickness and healing in a coordinated way, it is understandable that extensions of SH related entirely to other healing would have their counterpart in orientations and behaviors of the sick person. In other words, the evolving behavioral material of SH is constituted in learned information that is, to a large extent, shared by all members of the group. What the relevant audience of potential healers can provide the sick person, then, is part of what he or she can expect from them, and it is precisely such expectations or cultural models of SH that shape the behaviors of sickness. The evolving information pertaining to SH is internalized in all members during enculturation and, as codes regulating behavior, comes to shape in a complementary way its evolving material. In short, with further extensions of the biocultural evolution of medicine one can expect to observe systematic changes in the structure of sickness itself, changes that complement the cognitive implications of developments pertaining purely to healing. New developments in the control of pain, for example, will be reflected in new ways of expressing and communicating it. Similarly, to the extent that the causes of illness change and come to be ascribed to possible malevolent actions of group members (for example, as a result of cultural changes secondary to sedentarism and social complexity), to that extent how the sick person behaves in relation to such group members also changes. That specific persons can cause a sickness means that they will have to be addressed and in some way incorporated as part of the healing enterprise. Finally, should certain types of manifestations of sickness (e.g., the purely somatic, as compared to the "mental") come to be accorded important and significant meanings, then during episodes of protracted sickness and healing such manifestations will come to be more prominently displayed since they may be judged in the group as more authentic. In sum, SH constitutes a biocultural and psychobiologic unity that can be expected to more or less systematically change during social and cultural evolution encompassing all behaviors of sickness and healing.

Earlier it was mentioned that positive emotions may have been integral to the healing component of the SH adaptation. An emotion of hope and one of faith associated with or elicited by SH raises the question of possible propitiatory actions on the part of conspecifics rendering SH. In this regard, an adaptation for SH is linked to or may serve as a precondition for seeking outside specialist help (e.g., ancestors' spirits), invoking ritual activities, and using emerging concepts about the otherworldly domain. In other words, SH can be viewed as a pivotal adaptation that required or promoted other adaptations associated with the movement from protoculture to culture. Medical care and practice as observed in elementary groups are very much intertwined with group ritualistic activities, propitiation, and the invocations of supernatural interventions as well as with strictly instrumental activities directed at the condition of sickness. These are all quintessentially cognitive, symbolic, and/or cultural activities that implicate religion, the supernatural, the longing for protection in the face of danger, the concern over mortality and the changes taking place after death, and the like.

In this context, that the strict evolution of the SH suite of behaviors had a link to the awareness of death and the beginnings of an appreciation of mortality more generally raises a number of questions. If sickness terminates in death, is the healing component of SH thereby nullified? Are the healing behaviors of SH extinguished as a result? I have indicated that SH entails resignation about and preparations for an accommodation to the inevitability of death from disease and injury. How accurately must death be recognized? At what point is death a certainty? Could not a variety or elaboration of SH be provided to conspecifics already deceased: The care of the deceased can be viewed from two standpoints. On the one hand, it can constitute an integral part of the healing component of SH itself. In other words, in association with emerging ideas about the spiritual domain and notions of an afterlife, "medical" activities on behalf of deceased who earlier were recipients of SH can be viewed as mere extensions of the basic SH adaptation. Providing for a departed relative or group member may have simply been construed as further healing. On the other hand, SH can be viewed as itself instrumental in the evolution of concepts pertaining to the spiritual domain and afterlife and religion more generally. On this account, SH is seen as a key link in a series of cultural developments that cover not only strict medical altruistic acts but also acts of propitiation and worship that are more properly considered integral to the evolution of religion. In either case, sickness and its biological consequences need to be considered as related not only to evolutionary questions pertaining to medicine but also to key questions about the evolution of society and culture.

Summary

The essence of sickness is that it is associated with distress and suffering and poses a threat to life. Given human rationality and the natural tendency to use it in coping with misfortune, one anticipates that individuals will regularly resort to the care of persons who are sick. Indeed, such medical practices constitute a human universal. Medicine could be viewed as an example par excellence of culture and its evolution the result of cultural evolution, with heritability imposed by learning. In this chapter a contrary position has been adopted with respect to the origins and universality of medical care and practice. It has been linked to a biology of sickness, altruism, and healing in the form of an adaptation arising from the standard Darwinian process of natural selection based on genetic variation and selection later to be elaborated during social and cultural evolution. The possible roots of an SH adaptation in animal and primate behavioral routines was discussed. The ecology of disease and sickness behaviors that may have constituted part of the selective environment of SH in the hominid line were reviewed. The role that an SH adaptation might have played in the evolution of related cultural behaviors in hominids and early man was given some attention as well.

The topic of human evolution and, in particular, the nature of human adaptation during the Lower and especially Middle Paleolithic periods, has been the object of considerable attention from biologists, linguists, evolutionary psychologists, cultural ecologists, paleoanthropologists, and archaeologists. The frame of reference adopted to study the topic has broadened to incorporate traditional concerns of zoologists, community ecologists, and zooarchaeologists. All of these scientists are coming to broaden evolutionary biology with the tenets of niche and optimality theories as appreciation is reached concerning the similarity between the nature of hominid and archaic human adaptive strategies and analogous behaviors of nonhominid social carnivores with which hominids competed. A surprising gap in all of these studies is a singular absence of any emphasis on sickness and healing. The selective implications of disease and injury constitute the main point of contact between human evolutionary studies and medical phenomena. The perspective adopted in this chapter has relevance to the studies of paleoanthropologists, archaeologists, and general biologists. Sickness and healing, properly formulated as an SH adaptation, constitute a point of conjunction between the biological and cultural and can be viewed as just as foundational or basic as other more traditional themes pertaining to human adaptive behavior (e.g., attachment, bonding, empathy, sexuality, cognition). The general implications of viewing sickness and healing and, indeed, the institution of medicine as a whole from a coevolutionary standpoint is taken up in later chapters.

3

Early Stages of the Evolution of Sickness and Healing

As reviewed in the previous chapter, sickness and healing involve a sick person and medical caregivers or healers and entail certain common features. These would include such things as a social context of suffering, worry, and disappointment and, potentially, of fear and danger; a desire and need for help and relief; a complementary desire to help and relieve; a setting of mutual trust and a moral economy pertaining to need and help giving; and a framework of meaning pertaining to the nature and causes of sickness and the rationale of healing. Sickness elicits acts of healing that are geared to simply supporting, helping, cleansing, and provisioning. These basic, "natural" and "altruistic" acts of healing are complemented by special acts that are directed at undoing the sickness. Thus an additional component of the sickness/healing ensemble is a set of expectations that special acts of healing, carried out in terms of the prevailing framework of causation pertaining to sickness, might bring about either a set of hoped-for improvements in health and well-being or a suitable termination of suffering with the promise of socially appropriate transitions to future states however these might be conceptualized.

Natural selection in the human line of evolution has shaped a distinctive genotype and phenotype as this pertains to vulnerability to disease and to effects of disease (Black 1975). There is wide appreciation of the fact that this evolution took place under distinctive types of social organization and with exposure to distinctive types of physical and biotic environmental hazards (Williams 1966; Wilson 1975). All of this had the effect of conditioning what kinds of features of the environment proved deleterious to health and well-being and, in particular, how states of compromised health were realized and manifested in behavior. Stated briefly, when the physical apparatus and its mechanisms break down in the face of disease and injury, more or less universal patterns of pathophysiology and behavioral alterations take place.

Given the fact of biological differences pertaining to such things as genetic polymorphisms, physical appearance, and physiologic responsivity, it would be unusual indeed if the various populational groupings of humans did not also differ with respect to vulnerability to disease and in the way in which diseases manifested as signs and symptoms. The fields of epidemiology, medical psychology, and clinical medicine chronicle differences in disease prevalence and disease manifestations across societies and social groups (Cohen 1989; Fabrega 1974). However, except for some well-known genetic diseases (e.g., sickle cell disease), whether and, if so, how disease pictures (i.e., vulnerability and manifestations) could be said to differ in relation to specific genetic characteristics of social groups are difficult to establish precisely. A range of factors, including such things as environment, social class, cultural orientation, gender, and characteristics of the society (its degree of modernity) as well as strictly genetic properties of race/ethnicity, affect the kinds of diseases of a population and how these diseases manifest in illness pictures of morbidity.

While the role that the genetics of a population plays in its disease pictures is extremely important, it is also complex and problematic. For purposes of this chapter, an assumption is made that the anatomical, biochemical, immunological, and physiological processes set in motion by disease and injury are universal in man, and that this was so to a large extent during evolution. In other words, one assumes that if a "Japanese neonate body" is allowed to develop in America, or a highland New Guinea one in South Africa, the manifestations of disease (including altered biochemistry, physiology, signs of disease, and behavioral symptoms) in the corresponding child, adolescent, or adult body will be more or less similar to those disease manifestations of adults of the respective "adoptive" societies provided physical environmental factors were similar. The literature informs that there do in fact exist ethnic differences in psychophysiology and autonomic responsivities and other allegedly genetical characteristics relevant to disease manifestations (Fabrega 1981b)—and also, that untangling what is biological (nature) from what is cultural (nurture) is not only difficult but theoretically problematic if not nonsensical. However, from the standpoint of how the genetics of disease affects manifestations of sickness and healing, I will assume for heuristic purposes that such genetical differences can be ignored in favor of sociological, ecological, and cultural factors.

An assumption that genetics do not affect manifestations of disease allows me to concentrate analytically on matters external to genetics (i.e., ecology, culture, and social organization) that can possibly influence the kinds of medical pictures found in different types of societies, how these manifest, and how institutions of medical healing might be structured and operate in them. More specifically, it allows me to examine and compare sickness and healing in different types of societies from the standpoint of ecology, culture and social organization rather than from strictly genetic and populational points of view. It is the way sickness and healing are configured as cultural and social phenomena in different types of societies that is of interest rather than the sheer genetic constraints underlying them.

Sickness and Healing in Societies of Family-level Foragers

Social, Ecologic, and Cultural Characteristics

Societies with foraging economies have the simplest form of subsistence production (Fried 1967; Johnson and Earle 1991; Lee and DeVore 1968; Service 1975). They depend on gathering wild plants and (to a lesser extent) on hunting wild animals. In the typical case, they show a low population density (usually less than one per square mile) and little sense of territoriality (Bailey 1991; Barnard 1992; Price and Brown 1985; Upham 1990). Although they are subject to seasonal and periodic hardships (with decreased availability of water, plants, and game), for the most part their members are said to display limited needs that can be satisfied by working but a few days a week. The family is the basic subsistence and social unit. The technology used to gather and hunt is small-scale, multipurpose, portable, and personal, generally being available to all families. When resources are plentiful and uniformly distributed, one or a very few families are said to live together and to manage to procure their own bare needs. The division of labor is elementary, being based on age and gender; and labor required for procurement activities rarely extends beyond the family. In times of scarcity, several family units come together in camps so as to better coordinate their subsistence activities, but these camps usually dissolve when resources become more plentiful. Family units are generally opportunistic, coming together or dissolving depending on availability of resources. They maximize flexibility and minimize structural constraints such as those imposed by territoriality, leadership, and elaborated divisions of labor. On the whole, informal and flexible social relations exist between families. Elaborate ceremonial activities are generally not found in the typical family-level forager groupings except at times of formation of camps when subsistence activities need to be coordinated.

Characteristics of Disease and Sickness Pictures

Infections.   A nomadic society of family-level foragers and hunters can be infected only by certain types of parasites (Black 1975; Cohen 1989; Eaton,

Shostak, and Konner 1988; Fiennes 1978; Lovejoy 1981; McNeill 1976). Infectious organisms must rely on plants or animals as a way of maintaining themselves and sporadically intrude on humans, producing the so-called zoonoses; or, they can live within humans, affording themselves a long time to bring about transmission from person to person, in which case they account for slow-acting, chronic diseases.

The kinds of zoonotic diseases that might have affected early humans (and do affect contemporary hunter-gatherers) are protean in their physiological effects, long term and short term. These diseases include the following: rabies, tularemia, toxoplasmosis, brucellosis, salmonellosis, trichinosis, tapeworm infestations, typhus, yellow fever, malaria, and encephalitis. As outlined by Mark N. Cohen (1989), the zoonotic and soil-borne diseases have the following characteristics: (1) they do not claim many victims; (2) they can have a severe impact on the body; (3) their rarity precludes individual immunity or resistance; (4) their independence from humans means that there has taken place no selection for less virulent forms compatible with human life; (5) they are more likely to strike adults and productive members (as compared to children) who venture into the wild, away from the camp, with severe economic and demographic consequences for the group; and (6) they have limited geographic distribution. There are a number of theoretical and informative summaries of the ecological balances that have existed between early human (and, later, fully human) communities and parasites and microorganisms of environments located in different regions of the world (Boyden 1970, 1987; Dunn 1968; Eaton, Shostak, and Konner 1988; Fiennes 1978; McNeill 1976; Wadsworth 1984).

Early family-level foragers and hunters were less vulnerable to infections that were based on a fecal-oral mode of transmission since they moved frequently and accumulated less human wastes at any one site. However, their nomadic mode precluded elaborate housing structures, rendering them more vulnerable to extremes of precipitation and temperature.

Dietary Factors and Health Implications.   As discussed in chapters 1 and 2, early hominid groups undoubtedly inherited an array of food procurement practices and dietary preferences that reflected evolved "health maintaining" routines. These were complemented by other innate biological traits involving physiological responses and disposition to form learned conditioned avoidances of plant toxins and contaminated food substances, whether of plant or animals. These processes, mechanisms, and reactions that account for the healthy maintenance of an organism's chemical ecology have been viewed as constituting a biological predisposition toward or antecedent of medicine (Johns 1990). Here, it is only necessary to add that special food preparation technologies (e.g., leaching, washing, pounding, cooking) constituted extra protections against noxious effects of ingested plant and animal material.

The foraging subsistence mode is said to constitute a comparatively efficient way of producing food (Cohen 1989; Eaton, Shostak, and Konner 1988; Lee and Devore 1968). Provided population density remains low and large game animals are not scarce or exhausted, hunters and gatherers are able to obtain a high caloric yield of foodstuffs per hour of expenditure of effort at procurement. The quality of diet associated with foragers is said to be healthful, characterized as offering varied, balanced intakes of nutrients, vitamins, and minerals (Wadsworth 1984). Signs of malnutrition are generally mild and not very common, but the adequacy of caloric intake can be uncertain. Although controversial, it is generally believed that societies showing this mode of subsistence have reliable and ample sources of foodstuffs but depending on local supplies are subject to periods of famine and deprivation.

The foods eaten by family-level subsistence foragers are ordinarily coarse and tough. This produces a heavy wear on teeth, protects against caries, and can prove problematic to individuals with few or no teeth, namely, the very young and the very old. There probably existed a high reliance on human breast feeding to supply the nutritional needs of infants and toddlers, with weaning onto foods prechewed by parents. While this provided healthy diets for the child, it contributed to a heavy caloric and mineral drain on the mother with possible deleterious health consequences or at least vulnerabilities. Despite these factors, contemporary hunter-gatherers are relatively successful in rearing their children to adulthood, although life expectancy is low compared to modern standards.

In general, the relatively low caloric yield of the high-volume diets of foragers limits the accumulation of body fat, which means that leanness as compared to obesity was common. Thus their generally varied, healthful diet plus its high fiber content means that diseases such as atherosclerosis, diabetes, and cancer are comparatively rare. The relative lack of energy body reserves in the form of fat, the low energy yields of diets, and a reliance on prolonged breast feeding means that fertility among family-level subsistence foragers is comparatively low.

Other Types of Medical Problems.   A figure of around 200 deaths per 1,000 infants is cited as the average rate of survival among family-level subsistence foragers (Cohen 1989). This means that approximately 50 to 65 percent of all babies are reared to adulthood. These figures naturally vary in relation to the physical environment. Although the figures do not compare favorably with those of contemporary industrial societies (infant mortality averages around 10 deaths per 1,000 infants), they match and in some instances are better than levels achieved in the historical past, especially in urban settings of civilizations. The pattern of mortality in hunter-gatherers varies in relation to the physical habitat. It is appropriate to here quote Cohen: "[There is] a changing distribution of causes of death with latitude. In the tropics, indigenous infections are a significant source of mortality, but by most accounts starvation is rarely a cause of death, and accidents are relatively unimportant. Malaria and other diseases of greater antiquity account for a significant fraction of deaths in some societies. Hunting accidents appear surprisingly unimportant as causes of death. Such accidents as falls, burns, and (more rarely) snakebites are mentioned more frequently. In high latitudes, in contrast, famine and accidental death are significant sources of mortality" (Cohen 1989: 102).

Studies of contemporary family-level foragers indicate that so-called degenerative diseases (heart disease, cancers, hypertension, diabetes, and bowel disorders such as peptic ulcer and diverticulitis) are comparatively rare, as are also epidemic virus diseases (influenza, parainfluenza, mumps, measles, polio, whooping cough, rubella, tuberculosis, and smallpox); the former largely a result of diet and the latter of the small size, isolation, and migratory lifestyle of the group. Studies of contemporary hunter-gatherer societies (which rely on some agriculture to be sure) strongly suggest that skin diseases, either due to insect bites or to infected injuries with resulting abscess and ulcer formation and chronicity, were an important consideration.

Given the size, social organization, and cultural ecology of small-scale forager groups, one can surmise that any number of medical events and circumstances special to such groups will influence the character of healing in them. The high level of parasitic infestations and exposure to toxins that is found in these groups (particularly among those living in low latitude) suggests that short-lasting episodes of acute illness are common. The group would have acquired experience in coping with and treating such illnesses, in the process acquiring tolerance for their manifestations. It is likely that skin lesions were common, as were secondary infections with ulceration and chronicity. Upper and lower respiratory tract infections as well as gastrointestinal infections were likely to be common. The latter were probably a result of improper cooking and contamination, although it is likely that fecal oral contamination within the group did not play a significant role.

Implications for Sickness and Healing

There exist few studies that concentrate in depth on characteristics of sickness and healing in family-level, subsistence foragers and hunters (Fabrega 1979b; Holmberg 1969; Katz 1982; Lee 1993; Marshall 1969; Woodburn 1959). The classic generalizations of Ackerknecht that I have reviewed elsewhere contain a range of material that is useful in deriving a picture of sickness and healing in family-level societies (Fabrega 1974), as does also the work of Laughlin (1961, 1963). The following generalizations about sickness and healing are based on the material that is available and on an extrapolation from characteristics of the group that bear on sickness and healing.

The literature indicates that sickness considered in a general sense (including minor ailments as well as more serious illnesses) is a common occurrence. Most of these occurrences are not the object of elaborate causal explanations and attempts at treatment. An accounting of the mode of injury or a simple description of the concrete circumstances that evolved into an infection or lesion with its attendant ill health is sufficient. In short, nothing in the studies that are available contradicts the idea that members of the group frequently resort to naturalistic explanations and remedies for many episodes of sickness. This is especially the case with respect to such things as localized skin lesions, infections, ailments, and pains the causes of which are visible and fixed in concrete experiences. An uncomplicated, naturalistic approach to sickness also applies to nonserious, recurring, short-lived systemic sicknesses involving the respiratory and gastrointestinal systems and about which the groups are familiar.

The literature indicates also that spiritual agents external to the immediate group (e.g., major "guarding" or "evil" spirits, spirits of ancestors) or identified persons/enemies outside the group may figure in the explanations of more persistent, worrisome sickness pictures that have proven unavailing to the commonly trusted everyday remedies. In general, the number of causes of sickness is small and propositions pertaining to causation and pathology are unelaborated, having a rationale that is concrete, direct, and localized and that stems from everyday experiences. For example, localized pains "are" the sicknesses and can be moved via massage, removed by sucking out the evil, or ameliorated by scarification applied to the specific location. Sicknesses produced by systemic diseases, or any serious sickness for that matter, need to be neutralized or released by the spiritual agent causing it, hence invocation or prayer.

Knowledge of sickness and healing is common to all adults. Most conventions pertaining to subsistence and social behavior operate as prescriptions to avoid illness. Previous experiences with sickness, as well as interest, and intelligence of a particular (more often, many) group member(s) correlate with greater knowledge and trustworthiness pertaining to diagnosis and treatment. Most adult males function as healers, and among the Batek (Endicott 1979), the women do, too. However, a special social role of healer is generally not found (Howell 1989; Lee 1993) although there are notable exceptions (Elkin 1977).

In the event of early manifestations of sickness adults initiate treatment themselves, be this a modification of activity and diet as well as self-medication or the seeking of help from significant others, most usually members of the nuclear family or otherwise members of immediate households. Many types of procedures (e.g., scarification, massage, application of plant substances, ingestion of medicines) are resorted to by the sick person or through efforts of significant others. When sickness persists and worsens it takes on an ominous significance. It is these sicknesses that occasion apprehension and anxiety, which lead to more penetrating inquiries regarding causation, and which elicit striking cooperative efforts at healing (Lee 1993).

Allan R. Holmberg (1969) indicated that the Siriono took to bed and the family did not provide treatment. Yet his illustrations and anecdotes showed clearly that family members provided acts of caring, support, and treatment that qualified as forms of healing as conceptualized here. It was when persons were moribund that the Siriono avoided healing altogether. Lorna Marshall (1969) indicated that the !Kung have what she terms "special curing" for serious sicknesses. The general curing dances of the !Kung have many functions (e.g., celebration, prevention of sickness, spiritual regeneration). However, her observations suggest that when general curing dances were aimed at specific instances of sicknesses, these were usually of a serious nature. In summary, most sickness elicits healing aimed at direct symptom relief, usually undertaken by the person sick but with the help of immediate family members. It is mainly in the event of rather serious sickness, when persons are debilitated and impaired, that elaborate healing takes place. Yet most cultural rationales appear to have at least some indirect link to health (Howell 1989).

No studies have given the impression that group members begrudge the condition of sickness in an adult, previously healthy group member and withhold treatment. However, features of small-scale forager groups set clear constraints on the meaning, value, and expectations of healing. This is covered later. As already implied, there are data to suggest that little in the way of a special role of healing is found. More properly, it would appear that each group has many individuals (or "roles of healer" or "shamans") that are called upon to heal, being able to provide expertise and conduct dialogues with the preternatural world to effectuate cures. In some groups it seems that sickness episodes can occasion group ceremonies of cure that involve all of these "shamans" as well as most adults of the group.

Dyadic relations between a healer and a sick "patient" do not constitute the typical mode of healing in family-level societies. Although a dyadic or circumscribed approach to healing (i.e., involving few participants) may characterize episodes of sickness that are mild or stages of illness that are evolving, it would appear that highly evolved, more persistent and worrisome episodes that pose a potential hardship to the structure and functioning of a family and especially a group occasion concern and more formal efforts at control. In some groups, this takes the form of large-scale ceremonies that involve many adults from several families (Lee 1993). Sickness and healing are generally public, as compared to private. The fact of publicness involves sharing of efforts (in the way of knowledge, experience, supernatural exploration, etc.) as well as responsibility for its outcome. This orientation is a result of circumstances pertaining to maintenance of the group's integrity and functioning. All group members are tied together to furthering subsistence and presumably are partners in the effort to overcome misfortunes like sickness. Serious episodes of sickness appear to engage the group as a whole, occasioning inquiries regarding causation and concerted efforts to provide special healing. When persons are moribund, healing diminishes, persons may be abandoned, and efforts are started to prepare for disposition of the corpse (Dunn 1968; Holmberg 1969).

The ethos of a group that is active and "on the go," with a persistent requirement of food procurement, means that members do not indulge themselves extensively during episodes of mild or fleeting illness or for minor ailments (Bailey 1991; Lee 1993). A "sick role," if one might use this concept to signify any group's sanctioning of withdrawal from subsistence and social activities in association with sickness manifestations and behaviors, is unlikely to be resorted to for trivial and mild symptoms; instead, it is likely to be justified or well earned and deserving, possibly with clearly marked behavioral boundaries. This suggests that what in biomedicine are termed organic problems are likely to command attention of (public, visible) healing as compared to so-called functional ones, with phenomena such as somatization, conversion, and secondary gain less prominent or absent.

There is little likelihood that in family-level societies truly specialist or "renowned" healers can be consulted. These are the healers that in theory would occupy clearly demarcated roles and would be likely to entertain different interpretations and models of sickness and approaches to healing and to be little acquainted with the sick person. By contrast, actual healing relations and transactions are informal insofar as they engage parties that know one another and are involved in everyday procurement activities. Although focused on preternatural phenomena, healing in small-scale forager groups is rooted in and geared to concrete and practical results (what could be termed "cures"). Death as the eventuation of sickness or traumatic injuries is an expected possibility. It is interpreted as failure of efforts to overcome overpowering spirits as much, if not more than, as a negative result of healing. There exist limited expectations of what healing can accomplish. The practical link of sickness and healing to the group's integrity points to limited toleration for ambiguity and disabling illness/problems.

The playing out of "relationship difficulties" through the medium of a semantics of illness or idioms of distress is, thus, not highly elaborated. On the other hand, one is likely to find that frictions and problems of relationships and intragroup tensions may contribute an etiological "psychosomatic" vulnerability to disease, which then provides an opportunity for resolution through group healing arrangements. There is ample documentation in biomedicine of the importance of purely psychological (e.g., mental, spiritual) factors in influencing the outbreak of disease, however this might be defined (Engel 1977). There is no reason not to believe that such "downward causation" influenced sickness in early human groups and was also influential in healing. The point here is that this facet of the moral and political economy of sickness and healing was not highly elaborated (or "exploited") in early human groups and is most likely a feature of later stages in the evolution of sickness and healing. A delicate balance undoubtedly existed between stress-producing vulnerabilities to "real" organic disease and a practical orientation to and expectation of healing which disavowed ambiguity and sick role perpetuation.

Episodes of protracted illness in adult members who are not centrally involved in procurement activities or related pursuits of crucial value to social success (older subjects, the handicapped, the debilitated) are not tolerated (Dunn 1968). Together with the practical approach to sickness that is likely to prevail, this indicates that such individuals when sick are passively dealt with, ignored, or abandoned (Lee 1993).

Imperatives of Sickness and Healing Conditioned by Evolution

Family-level foragers constitute the simplest form of human social group. They are held to approximate the conditions of life during the Pleistocene era when *Homo sapiens* evolved their distinctive characteristics. The environment of evolutionary adaptedness of early humans consisted of so-called hunter-gatherer groups showing an ecology, pattern of subsistence, and social organization similar to that of contemporary family-level societies, although there is controversy about this (Lee and DeVore 1968). On the basis of what is known about sickness and healing in these societies, one can construct a general picture of social practices related to sickness and healing that may be regarded as the earliest social and cultural form of what is here construed as a basic human biological adaptation (which was termed SH). The following set of generalizations, which are not mutually exclusive but rather overlapping in their content, may be held to describe the evolutionary foundations and imperatives of sickness and healing in human societies. In a basic sense, they constitute what natural selection has sculpted into *Homo sapiens,* and it is these features that later developments of cultural evolution modify, transform, and elaborate.

1. *Sickness/healing was family and small-group oriented and had a public character.* This generalization is logically entailed by the size and behavioral ecology of protohumans and early human groupings. Sickness gives rise in the self to distinctive behavioral reactions such as nursing wounds, withdrawing from social activities, limiting energy outputs, and seeking relief of symptoms of disease. Self-healing and self-medicating are part of this behavioral reaction and are associated with or followed by similar efforts on the part of family and immediate group members. The gathering of group members and the expression of sympathy, concern, and ideas about causation and healing were natural accompaniments of sickness. Group members were visitors who came to help

and heal. The fact of face-to-face interactions among all group members means that behavioral reactions of sickness involved the sharing of practical information about sickness, health, and medicines. Informality and practical considerations of relief and return of function probably dominated these initial efforts. An explanation of the cause of the sickness was an intrinsic part of discussions, but in many instances these were not elaborated beyond the mere description of circumstances of how lesions had occurred or symptoms developed (see below).

In the event sickness was more protracted, and especially when it was more debilitating and serious in its implications, explanations became more elaborated and involved a review of recent happenings to the self or immediate group that might have prompted actions by agencies capable of causing injury. In these instances, the special help of persons outside the family but of the camp (possibly of a nearby camp) might be sought. Family-level foragers have access to nearby groups with which they have a loose relationship; it is likely that persons experienced with sickness and healing who resided in such groups would be called in for consultative help in cases of serious and extended sickness, especially if it affected a key group member.

In its most elaborated aspects, healing might entail a group effort that would include ceremonies and supernatural inquiries and dialogues. Family-level societies appear to include many "shamans" possessing knowledge and expertise, and these could be consulted and may have cooperated. In the event of serious/protracted conditions of sickness occurring in important members of the group, then, healing might have engaged the efforts of those in the camp and perhaps others not too distant who were regarded as allies.

In summary, rather than being formalized, closed, and private, healing was an open affair in which many could participate; it was not restricted to a select few. A healing role, by which is meant a more or less differentiated social identity marked by a specialist orientation to curing on the part of an identified person, was not a structural feature of healing in the environment of evolutionary adaptedness of early human groups. The lack of a distinct healing role, the public character of healing, and the participation in what was a group effort implies that payment for service was not a feature of healing. Healing was rather part of the moral economy of the group and of social exchange, a component of kin-directed altruism and also altruism of unrelated individuals who expected to be reciprocated in the future for their help.

2. *Knowledge of sickness/healing was not systematized.* Participants in the scenarios of sickness and healing were comembers of face-to-face societies or groups that all shared a common set of basic concepts. The concepts can be described as "natural" in that they were also used in everyday life to explain social relations, existential questions, and vulnerability to other misfortunes besides those of disease and injury. What are termed "natural" concepts are to be contrasted with theoretical and abstract concepts pertaining to the body,

sickness, and healing which are features of knowledge structures that are sys-tematized, elaborated, more complex, and separated into special domains such as "the medical," and all are features of larger-scale societies.

The mental representations or internalized schemas about sickness and healing consisted of concepts that were ordered in terms of relationships that were taxonomic, functional, and probably redundant. By this I mean that causes were differentiated and had definable modes of operation but appear to have been relevant to several if not most sicknesses. What one can term *sickness types,* that is, socially recognized and labeled distinctive pictures of sickness based on cause and manifestations and mode of healing, were not a prominent part of the medical experiences of people of family-level societies. Sicknesses could be graded as to severity and related to environmental hap-penings or violations of taboos; and healing rationales obviously made logical and empirical sense to comembers. In this sense, then, the knowledge of sick-ness and healing was for the most part self-contained, more or less shared among comembers, and patterned. However, such knowledge was limited in scope and not systematic, with basic propositions pertaining to sickness and healing that were probably unelaborated, redundant, and inconsistent if exam-ined on external, scientific grounds. All of this follows the fact that groups were small, changeable in composition, and hence limited as to the shared experiences of sickness and healing that they could acquire; and the individual memory capabilities of individuals set boundaries on what could be recalled and used in the event of sickness and healing. Stated differently, knowledge was not highly elaborated, abstract, and conceptual in the sense of taking group members into realms outside the bounds of everyday happenings and interpre-tations. The behavioral environment of the group formed boundaries for the knowledge pertaining to sickness and healing.

Equally important, the knowledge pertaining to sickness and healing was not separated from that of other concerns of the group. It did not pertain exclu-sively to sickness and healing but was part of the knowledge used to explain other unwanted, dangerous, and potentially threatening phenomena of the world.

These characteristics of the knowledge of sickness and healing imply that the body was not an elaborated structure that figured importantly in the way episodes of sickness were explained. The ethnoanatomy, ethnophysiology, ethno-pathophysiology, ethnopsychology, and ethnopharmacology pertaining to sick-ness and healing were limited in scope. Exigencies of survival and subsistence procurement dominated group concerns and together with the relatively lim-ited experiential contents (group representations) pertaining to sickness and healing imply that groups were not able to construct elaborated structures of knowledge about the body and about medicines. Such knowledge as existed was memorable, concrete, practical, and geared to the exigencies of sickness and healing as played out in the group and to the group's ecology.

3. *Sickness/healing had a practical and unelaborated character.* Features

and happenings in the physical habitat and negative actions of spirits, ancestors, or enemies probably figured importantly as causes of sickness. The social and emotional atmosphere of healing for serious/protracted sickness was shrouded in ambiguity, concern, and potential danger, but its underlying logical calculus probably stipulated a more or less explicit binary form: the sick (or injured) person would recover (and be restored eventually to a "normal" state) or would not, with permanent disability or death constituting a real and overtly considered alternative. Similarly, medicines collected from the habitat and positive actions of powerful (supernatural) agents were sought to counteract causes.

It is unlikely that malevolent actions or moral failures of comembers in the immediate group figured as significant causes of sickness or that healing exegeses entailed the direct probing of intragroup tensions. Certainly, there is a tendency for forager groups to fractionate and reincorporate, and outcomes of illness-based exegeses might point to attributions of causality among comembers as a significant factor. However, the high interdependence of forager groups and their kin orientation would render these happenings the exception. In the event that out-group hostility, warfare, and unpremeditated attacks were common eventuations, then, it is likely that individualized malevolence by enemy comembers would be invoked as causes of sickness.

Although immediate group members may not have been explicitly considered as sources of sickness and health misfortunes, it is not unlikely that personal, unconscious conflicts on the part of a member resulting from intragroup pressures might, by a form of "psychosomatic" mediation (through stress), contribute vulnerabilities to sickness. In other words, strains within a group may have figured as potential underlying causes of sickness by rendering an individual vulnerable, although it is unlikely that such strains would have figured as explicit causes in the explanatory models of group members.

4. *Sickness/healing was constructed as an acute, as compared to a chronic, eventuation.* A concern with relieving the symptoms of sickness validated healing, meaning that it was crisis oriented and focused on phenomena that were interfering in subsistence pursuits. Episodes of sickness no doubt varied in their perceived severity and importance, some viewed as minor and a nuisance and others as major and threatening. Any and all such episodes could be occasions for forms of healing. However, regardless of their qualification, it is likely that their content was signaled by manifestations that were visible and compelling.

The close interdependence among members of these groups and their preoccupation with subsistence themes, especially with food procurement/production, means that minor sicknesses, although objects of self- and family healing, were not likely to be the object of elaborated attention, much less of curing rituals. It is worthwhile underlining one of the main implications of this generalization. I have in mind here the negotiation (via the process of sickness and healing) of the morality and social status of the sick person in the group, as is seen in (sedentary) societies that show a more elaborated social organization. In the latter societies, such constructions of sickness and healing occur in the context of protracted nondisabling symptoms or in the context of slow, even progressive chronic sicknesses that (at least in their early phases) are not incapacitating or visible and compelling. Sickness and healing dramas constructed for these purposes were unlikely occurrences among early human, family-level foragers, except possibly in the event of serious, threatening sicknesses of key group members.

In summary, sickness and healing in family-level foragers was primarily geared to occurrences of disease and injury that were somatically disabling and that intruded visibly into the productivity of a group member. Chronic or even acute problems that were not disabling did not occasion much concern. Except for serious disabling problems affecting key productive members of the group, healing did not involve elaborated exegeses encompassing the management of social identity and moral status.

5. *Sickness/healing was short term.* The goals of healing were dictated by its social biology and involved improvement and relief, with full restoration of function desired and its possibility anticipated in the event healing was deemed successful. Just like the instanciation of sickness was predicated on relatively sharp, clear, and unambiguous boundaries, so was the termination of healing predicated on such clear, unambiguous boundaries. The preceding two points imply that neither health management, in the sense of offering comprehensive schemas for the maintenance of an ordered life of social spiritual and physical well-being, nor elaborated curing rituals encompassing social exegeses, as discussed earlier, were likely to constitute a directive of healing predicated by its evolutionary biology.

The short-term, acute sickness orientation does not mean that there did not exist health practices or forms of "quasi-healing" that can be thought of as preventative. Such curing ceremonies have been described for !Kung Bushmen (Katz 1982; Lee 1993; Marshall 1969). The maintenance of health was a dominant concern equal in significance and meaning to the protection against environmental catastrophes of all types. The prevention of all such misfortunes was undoubtedly a central concern to the group and entered into the rationale of subsistence practices and practices of social exchange as well as in-group activities of recreation and healing (Endicott 1979). It is clear that such rationales had spiritual or moral components and were framed in meaningful rituals. Whatever made up the culture of forager groups, it had a social rationale that included ecologic, religious, and economic as well as strictly "medical" considerations. Such "social practices and rituals of health maintenance" undoubtedly had emotional implications and cathartic consequences that added to the well-being of group members. However, the more mundane instances of sickness and healing were linked to distinct practical exigencies of relief and immediate cure. Discrete organic medical problems that caused disability are

the units I am giving attention to here. The basic point is that in this type of social and ecological environment, sickness and healing had a provisional, rather
than stabilizing, character: Its goal was to eliminate or prevent illness and
not to condone or equilibrate it. All of this implies that healing did not prolong
the dependence of sickness, nor could it be said to have caused conditions of
sickness and dependence. In this sense, one can think of sickness and healing
among early small-scale family foragers as "antihypochondriacal." Taken in
concert with earlier generalizations, this one also implies that if psychosomatic
mediation figured importantly as an underlying cause of disease processes, it
produced sickness pictures that were highly visible and dramatic and, consequently, might have been amenable to quick resolution.

6. *Sickness/healing was framed in light of the possibility of death.* The conditions of life of early human groups were punctuated by acute illnesses and
traumatic injuries that could cause visible pain and suffering and that frequently
claimed the lives of group members. Physical competition with other early
human groups and with nonhuman primates and the rigors of avoiding predation and hazards devolving from inclement weather and limited, changing
food sources created onerous and burdensome living conditions that rendered
disease and injury common and disabling realities. Consequently, death was
an ever-present and immediate eventuation. This meant that participants shared
in the awareness of the very limited resources of healing that were available,
knowing and anticipating that death could ensue.

In light of the small size of the group and the shared, public nature of hardships including sickness, this means that healing, arranging for death, and
planning for death's aftermath (protection of the corpse, "final diagnoses,"
proper burial, reequilibration of group membership) were not sharply bounded
social enterprises. They were probably part of what was "naturally" conceptualized as intrinsic to sickness and healing. In other words, they were encompassed within the "protomedical" institution of human groups. Just like healing
had a "practical" and focused goal of restoring or undoing sickness, it must
have also had a practical approach to death that involved planning for its eventuation and promoting the adjustment of survivors. The ethos of these groups
included frank, publicly reinforced evidence that disease and injury were dangerous, could produce agony and suffering, could lead to physiologically/ana-
tomically disfiguring changes in appearance and demeanor, and very often
could not be contained. Resignation to an often unavoidable and grim-visaged
demise constituted an integral component of the cultural script of sickness and
healing. In summary, preparing for death, watching over its occurrence, ensuring an optimal transition to the afterlife, easing the anguish and burdens that all
of this produced, and providing for the continuity of surviving family members were part of the social construction of sickness and healing in early human
societies.

7. *Sickness/healing was personal status oriented.* It was already mentioned

that the scope of healing was influenced by the symbolic as well as the bio-logical character of sickness. The nature of "medical" knowledge and the exi-gencies of healing meant that a group's typology of sicknesses (considered as taxonomic types) was not the significant object of concern but rather real suffering, endangered sick persons as well as the group itself. Acute and inca-pacitating sicknesses were the object of extended and elaborate attention. It is very likely that the scope of healing was determined by who developed sick-ness as well as by properties of the sickness.

Infant and childhood mortality due to infectious diseases was probably quite high despite the advantages to the newborn of extended breast feeding. Infan-ticide was often practiced. It is probably the case that sickness and healing ex-egeses in the very young were not very elaborate. Similarly, it is very likely that sicknesses in the very old and in the already incapacitated were not the object of elaborate, extending healing. By contrast, sicknesses in a productive adult occasioned great concern.

8. *Sickness/healing was not socially divisive.* The public character of sick-ness in a member well known to the group and the sharing of information and efforts aimed at restoring health implies that sickness and healing did not frac-tionate or splinter the cohesiveness of a group; instead it was more likely to or-ganize and unify it (at least during the phase when its outcome was uncertain). Causes of sickness were ascribed to agencies outside of the group as compared to actions of individuals within it. This would include such things as spirits, deceased ancestors, and enemies located in hostile, nearby groups in competi-tion with the group in question.

The lack of social divisiveness of sickness and healing is a corollary to points above regarding the practical, short-term, and public nature of healing. It can also be surmised that sicknesses and the healing that resulted were not likely to be socially stigmatizing. The kinds of symptoms and signs of disease or injury that a person developed might have frightened and alarmed comem-bers, especially if they had not previously been exposed to them. The "awe-some" or alarming character of such manifestations may have occasioned spe-cial explanations (harm from malevolent agents, possession by spirits, etc.), but given the social connectedness that existed and the integrated character of the group, it is not likely that such sicknesses would have proven socially dis-crediting and stigmatizing.

9. *Responsibility for the outcome of sickness/healing was limited and shared.* The public nature of sickness and healing logically entailed that re-sponsibility for their outcome was not focused on one or a few ("failed" or "esteemed") healers. Rather, it was seen as a natural and not unexpected out-come of the limited concrete resources of the group, including its limited abil-ity to elicit supernatural support. As already discussed, minor and less serious sicknesses probably occasioned little concern whereas serious and threaten-ing ones occasioned major concern. In the latter instances, the scope of healing

increased, involving a greater number of healers and thereby probably spreading and balancing the responsibility for its outcome. The preceding implies that the kinds of manifestations of sickness that a person showed must not have constituted impediments to undertake healing. Individuals who ordinarily would constitute objects of healing concern (e.g., adults, males) would not have been denied this because of the serious or disfiguring nature of sickness. An exception here might have been cases of highly traumatic injuries (or overwhelmingly acute, fulminating infections) that patently implied certain death. In these instances, healing as such was probably judged unnecessary, and the inevitability of death merely expected as a matter of course.

In summary, sickness and healing constituted a form of cost-efficient, group risk management; planning for its eventuation and accounting for its possible outcomes engaged a large number of group members, thereby limiting personal responsibility.

10. *Sickness/healing did not contribute to long-term dependence.* It is possible that early human groups enjoyed periods of much leisure and the luxury of inactivity and repose as has been described for some contemporary hunter-gatherers and as is also reported for some nonhuman primates (Goodall 1986). However, one can assume that for the most part living conditions were harsh and demanding. The generalization pertaining to potential psychological consequences of disease and injury was alluded to above, but it is worth delineating further because it contrasts sharply with what is known about sickness and healing in more complex societies. The basic point is that sickness and healing had a narrow, practical dimension with expectations that were bounded sharply by behavioral conditions of sickness and wellness: It was expected to eventuate in the restoration of well-being, or to fail to forestall the inevitability of death. Its provisional character was a safeguard against the perpetuation of sickness states that could be depleting of resources and undermining of the morale needed to undertake group efforts aimed at maintaining a bare livelihood. A consensus prevailed that sicknesses were socially, economically costly affairs that strained resources of the family and associated kin and group mates. Neither the individual who experienced sickness nor the group members who constituted the healing audience fashioned undo dependency and problems of social and psychological morale as tolerable correlates of disease and injury. In other words, except for rituals and dances or ceremonies having explicit, life-affirming (e.g., preventive) functions (as described, for example, for the !Kung), the medical was framed in terms of a heavily somatic idiom that presupposed motivation to overcome infirmity and not pose immoderate burdens.

Social strains and physical hardships imposed constraints and challenges on members of a group resulting in social and psychological stress. Constructions of sickness and healing incorporated actions designed to limit, if not resolve, such stresses. However, the biological components of sickness in the form of debility, pain, visible lesions, pallor, physiological malfunctions, and the like, constituted the markers that served to inform the group about the course and prognosis. The permissible levels of social and psychological dependence associated with sickness and healing were calibrated in terms of such biologically rooted manifestations. The script of sickness and healing did not include resources for or indulgence of symptoms that could not be related clearly and unambiguously to disease and injury.

11. *Sickness/healing did not lead to active social regulation.* Family-level forager groups of early humans probably had what one may term a passive, fatalistic orientation to sickness. Locked into one basic (although culturally shaped) reality of subsistence and persistence that was arduous and trying, they naturally viewed impediments to success as calamities that were imposed on them. Misfortunes of any nature altered the economy of food procurement and production in a negative way that needed to be corrected, and this naturally applied to sickness. Hence the practical, activist, and focused nature of healing, at least in its early phases before death was imminent and expected. Healing, in short, was concentrated on restoration of well-being or on accommodation to and resolution of deficiencies in the event of death. The causes of sickness more than likely were projected outward, modeled in terms of persecution and victimization. This means that healing most likely did not entail an activist orientation toward the regulation of group relationships.

Sicknesses might have also been attributed to personal wrongdoing or punishment for failures, in which case healing required remorse and conciliation. But such practices of atonement, even if also transformed into moral directives to ensure stability and continuity of life, applied to all misfortunes equally. Ideas pertaining to the causes of sickness and conduct of healing most likely did not play a unique and dominating role in the economy of survival and success. In short, it is unlikely that cognitions and directives linked exclusively to sickness and healing figured in a special way in the direct regulation of everyday life. On the other hand, the possibility of sickness undoubtedly served as a source of anxiety that group members dealt with through ritual activities and social practices involving the natural and supernatural world. In this indirect, general way, the possibility of illness (along with other misfortunes) functioned to regulate behavior.

Sickness and Healing in Village-level Societies

Aspects of Social Organization

What are termed village-level societies are larger and more complex than family-level foragers (Fried 1967; Johnson and Earle 1991; Service 1975). For one, they are confined to well-defined territories, they show a greater density of population, and the units that comprise them are more integrated. They are generally regarded as an evolutionary extension of family-level foragers. This type of society encompasses a variety of subtypes that vary with respect to size, density, social organization, and mode of economic subsistence. Such terms as local groups, villages, clans, corporate groups, and big man collectivities are generally used to describe variations of the type under discussion. A reason for handling these societies as a unit is that they form a convenient category from the standpoint of sickness and healing. In contrast to the relative autonomy of the family unit or of that of a connected group of related families, village-level societies show a measure of integration among neighboring groups, be these hamlets, actual villages, or larger collectivities. There may exist a living community that houses officials and chiefs and operates as a ceremonial center. The families manage risks attendant on subsistence by resorting to agriculture in a more intense and diversified way than family-level foragers. Hunting for wild game generally plays a comparatively smaller role in the food economy, as does also the gathering of wild foods. They may rely on pastoralism and, depending on the habitat, on fishing and group hunting but typically do so by cooperating with nearby groups for purposes of large takes that then are stored to be used during periods of scarcity. These enterprises require a measure of cooperation and leadership since they entail a pooling of labor efforts and technology. A measure of political centralization goes along with the sedentarism of village-level societies.

Village-level societies show a preoccupation with competition and warfare with nearby groups over scarce resources. These factors together with the need to coordinate subsistence activities and manage economic risks mean that they show the beginnings of social differentiation in the form of true leaders or "specialists" who are distinguished by their prowess in battle and hunting and their political skills. The latter are displayed in the mediation of conflicts and the foraging of the cooperation needed to fight enemies and ensure the protection and storage of surplus foods that allow spreading the risks of subsistence.

Aspects of Disease

The literature suggests that village-level societies are characterized by a heavier burden of disease (Boyden 1987; Chagnon 1977, 1992; Cohen 1989; Fiennes 1978; Lewis 1975; McNeill 1976). Sedentarism may reduce the variety of infections that a population is vulnerable to and allow members a better immunologic adjustment to infective organisms that are now more or less endemic. However, newer technologies of pastoralists and horticulturalists directly propel man into contact with complex life cycles involving worms and multicelled parasites as well as bacteria, protozoa, and viruses, all of which can prove toxic. Malaria, schistosomiasis, hookworm disease, and related diseases, admittedly problems for larger, more complex societies relying on more advanced forms of farming, are examples of the new disease pictures attendant with social evolutionary development. In addition, because of their integration and contact through trade or warfare with adjacent groups, people of village-level societies are vulnerable to exposure to a greater number and variety of infectious diseases that are transmitted from without. An increase in the density of population encourages the spread of disease, and since these societies do not generally show facilities that reflect a concern with hygiene and sanitation, fecal-oral modes of transmission of infection are very common. Gastrointestinal infections that can be acute and fulminating or ones that produce only mild, short-lasting disability probably increase in prevalence. That individuals live in close proximity also increases the prevalence of airborne infections. All of these considerations mean that village-level societies are prone to epidemics in the event the population is exposed to new organisms from without (being too small to provide for a ready supply of uninfected persons who can render epidemics emergent in the society). However, the groups in question were not large enough to sustain infective agents that could periodically infect vulnerable individuals not previously exposed to infection.

In short, these societies characteristically produce an alteration of the landscape and these changes can result in new disease pictures such as malaria, yellow fever, and schistosomiasis. Alteration in food-producing techniques can increase food contamination by adding new steps in the scheme of food preparation. The domestication of animals that is usually found in the larger, more complex village-level societies exposes the population to new diseases as well. Finally, sedentarism is generally associated with a reduction in the variety and quality of food, bringing about an increase in risk for vitamin and mineral deficiencies as well as a greater susceptibility to disease in general.

Material reviewed by Cohen (1989) suggests that with the advent of farming and village-level societies, the health of populations decreased as compared to that of family-level societies. It is unclear whether the level of trauma, violence, and degenerative changes as revealed in bone remains increased or decreased as a result of the advent of farming. However, evidence observable in bone, fecal remains, and intestinal parasites (as noted in mummies) suggests that infections (e.g., treponemal, tubercular, bacterial, and parasitic) became more prevalent with the advent of farming. The quality of the diet decreased and together with increased levels of parasitization contributed to anemias (and presumed states of debility) as revealed by porotic hyperostosis. The stature, size, and robustness of adult members seem to have decreased as well. Food may have become more reliable and episodes of mild hunger less frequent, yet other bone changes suggest that periods of severe episodic stresses did not decline as a result of the shift to farming.

Aspects of Sickness and Healing

The special social, ecologic, and cultural features of village-level societies may be expected to introduce some modifications and elaborations of the character of sickness and healing compared to that discussed for family-level societies (Chagnon 1977, 1992; Glick 1963; Lewis 1975). The sedentary character of the societies is likely to be associated with a greater knowledge of, sense of territoriality about, and conceptual delimitation of regions of the immediate habitat. Concretely differentiated habitats are likely to be culturally elaborated and related to in ritualized ways. This, in turn, is likely to mean that local spirits and guardians as well as conventions or taboos pertaining to the travel across and use of the environment are likely to figure more importantly in explanatory models pertaining to sickness and healing (see also Howell 1989).

Given the relatively larger role that ceremonialism with respect to religious and ancestral agencies plays in these societies where the earliest traces of corporateness and lineages are to be found, it is also likely that these essentially protective and benevolent agents may play a more central role in explanatory models of sickness. The more precarious and vulnerable nature of local group societies with respect to enemies and competitors certainly suggests that putative acts of malevolence attributed to those enemies will continue to play important roles in cognitions about sickness.

When sick in ways that exceed the healing capacities of the self, family members, or members of the immediate camp or hamlet, members of village-level societies are likely to have access to healers possessing greater expertise and knowledge who reside in nearby groups. Such healers, while possibly not related through kinship, may nonetheless be viewed as part of the larger corporate group. This means that what are termed village-level societies may be said to show the beginnings of specialization of knowledge and rudiments of a healer role. By no means is this knowledge abstract and systematized, nor can healing be said to constitute an occupation. The sought-after healer is not likely to be distinguished merely by his medical prowess. Ability and competence in planning and conducting local group affairs, and the prestige and power that this brings, are more than likely the basis for an assumed expertise in healing along with advanced age. This follows from the similarity in the organization of village-level groups and that of family-level ones, from the fact that many shamans exist in both types of societies, and from the fact that at the village level of group social organization, power and efficacy in the management of conflict and misfortune come to be differentially associated with selected persons who function as quasi leaders. This power and expertise is likely to encompass sickness and healing.

The more settled nature of village-level societies means that it should be easier to care for members who are sick. Sedentarism entails that groups persist settled and have access to agricultural and other foods. The absence of a need to migrate and continually, actively search for food across large territories means that families and groups can "tolerate" impaired, disabled persons. Thus protracted sickness and healing scenarios become a possibility at this level of organization. Furthermore, given a more or less permanent habitat, more persons are likely to know and to have accumulated knowledge about sickness and healing and to be available for consultation and actual caregiving. Healing is thus likely to encompass more individuals, whether these be involved in one-to-one caring; in a gathering of comembers to express concern, sympathy, or consultation; or in more extended rituals and ceremonies of healing. In addition, in these groups there may begin to take place in a more or less systematic way the bringing together of selected individuals for purposes of making decisions about how to go about obtaining consultation and planning the actual course of healing. Even in smaller, family-level foraging groups, serious episodes of sickness and associated healing efforts were public and "managed" by comembers. In village-level societies, however, because of a greater variety of options, one might find that special-purpose healing managing groups may begin to assume informal responsibility for the healing of serious and protracted cases of sickness. These are likely to coordinate efforts, to seek outside consultation, and to plan and mediate the process of healing during illness or following it in the event that death ensues and final divinations or diagnoses are judged necessary.

Many of the characteristics of sickness and healing found in small-scale foragers will be found in village-level societies, for example, the practical focus of healing and its short-term character, the emphasis on acute illness, the possibility and importance of death in framing healing transactions, and the unsystematized, basic, and natural concepts pertaining to sickness. However, many factors are likely to be different. Some of these will be a function of the ecology and epidemiology of disease. These groups probably experience a lower level of general health and well-being; a larger volume of sicknesses; more pictures of chronic sickness; more sicknesses that spread from person to person, rendering the idea of an environmental personal or social focus more pertinent; and gastrointestinal ailments that result from fecal-oral routes of contamination. The fact of more apparent contagion reinforces the idea that comembers in the group can cause illness to occur in others, and this perception undoubtedly influences ways of explaining and healing sickness.

Since in village-level societies one is likely to observe an intensification of intragroup rivalries and conflicts, details of these are likely to intrude into the network of explanations for sickness and in the deliberations aimed at undoing those sicknesses that are protracted. This is another way of saying that at this level of social organization one may begin to see sickness and healing functioning as social and political dramas in the moral and behavioral economy of the society.

The greater competition and rivalry among group members are likely to be reflected in mutual suspicions. One of the ways in which the latter dynamic of group life is played out is in attributions of the causes of sickness (and other misfortunes as well, of course), in negotiations surrounding healing, and in the consequences of sickness, particularly when these lead to permanent disability and especially when they terminate in death. Such a group and interpersonal perspective on factors influencing sickness and healing reflects the effects of sedentarism and social complexity. It also complements an idea roughly analogous to our contagion which is mirrored in the epidemiology of disease and illness of these types of societies.

It will be recalled that among family-level foragers, sickness and healing activities are shared enterprises focused entirely on sick persons per se and on the outcome of treatment. These are by nature cooperative, group-validated enterprises that are not radically altered with respect to conduct and responsibility in the event of death. However, the introduction of an intrasocial, interpersonal, and political dimension to the accounting of episodes of sickness and healing, such as is emergent in and even likely to be accentuated in village-level societies, can be said to constitute a significant transformation in the construction of sickness and healing.

In short, it is not unlikely that some of the highly morally charged nature of sickness and healing stems from the unique set of social characteristics that begin to achieve relevance in village-level societies. Sickness begins to reflect moral/ethical concerns of the group and the status of social relations within it. These associated social factors are played out in terms of religious convictions.

An individual's status in the society is reflected in the sicknesses he or she or family members are prone to and may develop and the healing exegeses that follow. Frictions in the community are played out in the way sicknesses are explained and in their outcome. The highly socialized character of sickness and healing in village-level societies means that in them one may begin to perhaps see the beginnings of sickness stigmatization: Certain pictures of sickness may serve to qualify the moral worth of the person sick and his or her immediate family and group.

All of the preceding implies that in village-level societies one sees an expansion, complexification, and problematization of the sick role. The social and moral character of sickness means that individuals can now manipulate consciously or unconsciously a state of sickness on behalf of their own or their family's prospects. That perceived social grievances or moral transgressions figure importantly in the way status and relations are negotiated means that all sicknesses are potentially able to take on such dimensions. This suggests that sicknesses may increase in duration pending the resolution of social and moral breaches. The restoration of purely biologic function may now become but one of the end points of sickness and healing. To this is now added the restoration of psychosocial distress, social function, and status of the sick person and significant others whose crises may have figured importantly in causation and vulnerability.

In short, what Dunn (1976) has termed the "psychosocial needs" of individuals and populations begin to play a more visible and perhaps important role in the functioning of health and medical systems in village-level societies. A social function attached to sickness, healing, and an expanded sick role means that the scope of healing is also changed. Whereas the scope of healing in family-level societies was probably correlated with the status of the person sick, in village-level societies one may begin to see the sicknesses of relatively minor social actors in the economy of a family group playing larger roles in healing exegeses. This is the case because they increase the opportunity for the playing out of social and moral conflicts and can sometimes serve as indirect, concealed, but nonetheless symbolically involved actors of village political life.

What one can begin to term, on the basis of externally imposed standards of accounting, to be sure, medical scapegoating and "hypochondriacal" behavior may owe their roots to the structure of sickness and healing in village-level societies. It should be clear that although acute sicknesses and death may continue to importantly determine the focus of healing and frame its conduct in village-level societies, the preceding discussion implies that other factors can potentially play important roles. Chronic diseases are certainly made more possible since nutritional deficiencies predispose to this; since larger, settled living arrangements associated with sedentarism facilitate reinfection; and since the exigencies of life make it easier to provide greater attention and caring to those who are sick. It is also possible that adults live longer in these types of societies, although the level of child mortality probably did not appreciably change as compared to family-level societies. All of this implies that while the young and adult members of societies may have been especially selected (in the sense of having overcome childhood stresses and infections) they nonetheless may have had greater opportunities to have experienced chronic, low grade infections and other diseases common to older age groups.

Finally, since other than purely biologic factors, namely, truly social and cultural agendas, come to influence sickness and healing in village-level societies, opportunities are created for the psychosocial production of sickness and its social perpetuation and for modes of resolution of healing other than total normalization or death.

Since immediate family member "healers" are no longer exclusive participants of healing, their lot being supplemented by others in the hamlet, village, or larger collectivity, this has implications for how the outcome of healing is calibrated. With healers limited to one of many of similar rank involved in a healing enterprise, all share in the ordeal of neutralizing the evil of sickness, and all are equal participants with their cohorts in the implications of the outcome of sickness. Outside healers who are consulted or brought in to the healing enterprise and who may assume a major role in its conduct will be more active and deliberative. By definition, they are now more responsible agents who are brought in because of their greater expertise in healing and social/political mediation. They are expected to negotiate the conflicts that now figure more importantly in causation.

These differences in the way structural factors shape the morphology of sickness/healing scenarios imply two things that will figure more importantly in larger, more complex societies. First, the healer role becomes differentiated and thus social power is added to knowledge of healing "power" in the exegeses of healing. In other words, individuals selected in part because of their psychological, social, and political as well as strictly medical talents are operative in sickness/healing scenarios. Second, the new structural factors also mean that individual persons or protohealers are in a position to now profit from positive and favorable outcomes of healing. Opportunities for self-aggrandizement and exploitation now become potential elements of healing. In short, the identified cultural evolutionary conditions make possible the beginnings of a significant interpersonal, "psychotherapy" component in healing as well as conditions for the origin of the deceptive healer. While the former is generally regarded a "benefit" associated with social complexity, the latter may well constitute a social maladaptation as Roy A. Rappaport (1979) has construed this aspect of cultural evolution. Furthermore, in the event efforts of healing are unsuccessful, "specialist" consultants or healers may come to be held accountable for the perceived grievances that are held to underlie sickness and for those that result from what divination activities reveal are social and/or moral failures of persons entrusted with healing. Adopting a social evolutionary frame of reference, one can say that the seeds of much of the complexity of sickness and healing are sown at this level of social organization. It clearly reveals that the behavioral ensemble for sickness and healing that was sculpted by natural selection, namely, the unfolding of the SH adaptation as discussed in the previous chapter and earlier in this one, is broadened and complexified. New cultural, ecologic conditions begin to virtually transform the parameters of sickness and healing as these evolved in family-level prehuman and early human groups.

4

Later Stages of the Evolution of Sickness and Healing

Sickness and Healing in Chiefdom, Prestate, and State Societies

Aspects of Social Organization

These societies are larger, denser, politically integrated, and centralized (Fried 1967; Johnson and Earle 1991; Service 1975). Members of the population are differentiated with respect to status, prestige, and economic resources. The settled nature of social life and the fact of size, density, and social differentiation mean communities have fairly elaborate and clearly defined rules and norms pertaining to marriage, kinship, and social relations more generally. Competition, rivalries, and social strife are all not only more prevalent but also subject to greater regulation and control. In relation to this and as a sheer consequence of the higher level of social organization that characterizes chiefdoms and prestate societies, one finds elaborate and well-articulated cultural representations pertaining to religion, cosmology, and moral directives. These representations achieve a measure of standardization in the society. What one can term specialists, whose concern is the formulation and protection of such sacred knowledge, are found. This means that knowledge is not equally shared across the population and that some of it is the exclusive province of important personages. Revelation, social power, and the mandate to intervene, regulate, and enforce moral/religious tenets and social conventions are found in these societies embodied in distinct individuals and in distinct social roles and political positions.

Aspects of Disease and Medical Ecology

Research in the fields of historical epidemiology and archaeology strongly suggests that the trends described above for village-level societies with respect to changes in disease patterns and nutrition are more pronounced and clearly manifest in chiefdoms, prestate, and state societies (Cohen 1989; Eaton, Shostak, and Konner 1988; Fiennes 1978; Harris and Ross 1987; McNeill 1976; Mascie-Taylor 1993). In fact, it is probably in these larger, more complex societies that also show greater density of population that the picture of health and the properties of the disease pictures described earlier are found to operate in a more prominent way: a less nutritious and balanced diet, increased prevalence of bacterial, viral, and parasitic infections, lower general health and well-being, higher volume of sickness and disease, more chronic pictures of sickness, lower thresholds for the definition of sickness, prominent spread of disease, ideas of contagion or of sicknesses that are directed at the group as a whole (epidemics), and prominent gastrointestinal infections. Life expectancy at birth is comparatively low due to the very high infant and childhood mortality. On the other hand, those who survive this period appear to live longer lives (on the average) compared to people of smaller-scale societies. Diseases of older adult ages thus become prominent in chiefdoms, prestates, and states and, of course, in empires and civilizations (see below).

Aspects of Sickness and Healing

General Considerations.   The size and especially the social complexity of chiefdom, prestate, and state societies have their medical complement in the fact that knowledge of sickness and healing has a broader sweep and is more systematized (Fabrega 1979b; Fabrega and Silver 1973; Harwood 1970; Serov 1988; Ward 1977; Warren 1974; Winkelman 1984). Important also are the changes in the physical environment and ecology brought about as a result of increased density of population (Alland 1970), an increased burden of disease secondary to agriculture and sedentarism, and a systematization of knowledge and belief pertaining to cosmology, religion, and the sacred as well as medicine. This underscores an important dialectic in the study of sickness and healing: How does a group's demography and ecology of disease and corresponding burden of sickness influence the growth of knowledge systems devoted to explaining and handling sickness? This problem is one that could be clarified by the use of the standard cross-cultural sample, although thus far only general aspects of medical beliefs and cultural practices have been studied (Murdock 1980).

Emergence of Specialist Healers.   The social and political differentiation, the greater division of labor, and the delineation of experts and their empowerment that is found in chiefdoms, prestates, and states means that an opportunity is created for individuals to become true medical practitioners and "specialists." What one could term a craft or occupation pertaining to healing, even if only part time, begins to become a reality in these societies. In an admittedly modernizing society (the Techiman-Bono of southern Ghana in the southeastern Ivory Coast) but one still showing many traces of the traditional roles of healing, Dennis M. Warren (1974) applied ethnoscientific methods of elicitation and was able to obtain a large number of terms describing herbalists, general practitioners, and priests and other healing types.

Special individuals are selected for the healer's role. The factors promoting recruitment to healing have not been studied systematically in anthropology. The general problem of recruitment has important implications for the comparative and especially evolutionary study of medicine. As will be elaborated in later chapters, this problem involves the interplay between biological genetic factors (embodied in the machinery for the SH adaptation) and social cultural inputs (experiences with disease and injury) during critical periods of development. In general, factors of recruitment are thought to include parental/family influences, special experiences with sickness, and supernatural experiences. To these factors, one can now add that some individuals who are selected may be endowed genetically with a special complement of SH or have had unusual experiences with disease and injury during childhood or early adulthood. In other words, genetic loadings of SH can promote through epigenetic rules special experiences with sickness and healing, channeling persons into the society's healing roles.

The presence of specialist healers means that systematic and sustained thought can now be applied to sickness and healing. As an example, empiricism and a heavily somatic idiom pertaining to sickness and healing was a common and recurring feature of the information uncovered by Warren (1974) among the Techiman-Bono of Ghana. In these types of societies, special individuals are provided with the opportunity to examine and analyze many episodes of sickness and to compare them with respect to their properties. The beginnings of a codification of sickness types is made possible by the creation of more or less special medical personnel. Out of this, given the prevailing modes of explanation, emerges a body of medical knowledge that is more elaborated, specific, conceptually organized, and systematized. Returning to the material uncovered among the Techiman-Bono, as an example, Warren (1974) was able to obtain 1,266 lexemes that defined these people's system for defining and classifying unhealthy states. Generalizations drawn from many similar anthropological studies suggest, in short, that in these types of societies one finds a dialectical interplay between social complexity, the epidemiology of disease, the prevalence and importance of sickness pictures, and the development of general and specialist cultural knowledge that one can describe as quintessentially medical, with associated cosmological, religious, moral, and sociological features as well, to be sure.

The origin of specialist healers means that specific *individuals* begin to acquire leverage over sickness and the course of healing. Their special role, social status, prestige, and charisma, independent of family and immediate group, constitute an independent, external psychological influence on healing. An individual psychotherapy component becomes prominent in healing, although this is limited by the biology of disease, by the interpersonal rootedness of sickness, and by the conscious and unconscious (psychosomatic, somatopsychic, and sociosomatic) motivations toward sickness that sociocentric societies can generate.

In less complex (and evolutionarily "earlier") social formations, sick persons and their surrogates commanded equal if not dominant power in the enterprise of sickness and healing: In other words, they could select, choose, comply with, reject, cooperate with, or co-opt any outside "healer" or "specialist" that might have been involved. At most, the family and sick person commanded and at worst shared the burdens and responsibilities of healing. With the emergence of true specialists and distinctive social roles of healing, this changes and the latter begin to acquire a modicum of independent influence in the course and outcome of sickness and the conduct of healing. Sick persons continue to dominate healing, however, and it is not until the modern era that healers become dominant (Jewson 1974).

Emergence of the Domain of the Medical.   Whereas in group-level societies, knowledge pertaining to sickness and healing is not systematized and focused on a domain that is identified as separate and special (i.e., the "medical"), in these societies such specialization of knowledge begins to appear. The absence of literacy means that highly elaborated stores of "encyclopedic" knowledge are not possible and that memorial capacities of individuals still operate as natural constraints on the degree of abstractness, complexity, and organization of knowledge structures. Nevertheless, at this level of social organization, one finds the early beginnings of an "institution" or "system" of medicine, acknowledging the complexity of these terms (Lewis 1975, 1993; Press 1980).

An emerging definition of the medical as a separate domain in chiefdom, prestate, and state societies is reflected in a number of ways. The following are examples of this: the presence of specialist knowledge of sickness and healing, the emergence of social roles pertaining to healing, the existence of more or less well defined modes of training/apprenticeship of healers, the production of varieties of types of healers (e.g., priests, practitioners, herbalists, bonesetters, midwives, and diviners) whose principal job is healing the sick and dealing with biological crises more generally, the beginnings of standards with respect to medical practice, and a means of evaluating the performance of healers. Persons occupying such healing roles cannot be said to operate "full time" or as limited to strictly medical matters; diviners, as an example, are consulted for many problems, not just medical ones, and practitioners may possess power not only to cure but also to cause illness as well as other calamities. Nevertheless, some specialization of effort on the matter of sickness and healing separates and distinguishes certain individuals who are socially rewarded and compensated for their efforts in the way of prestige and material.

Systematic medical knowledge of sickness and healing continues to embrace aspects of cosmology, religion, and morality. However, some of this knowledge is now more directly linked to naturalistic, empirical, and phenomenologic aspects of sickness. For example, a greater exposure to disease outbreaks and to what in reality can be termed true epidemics means that a more important place is given to sicknesses as natural phenomena; sicknesses that may "just happen," although it is very likely that cosmological, religious factors continue to exert some influence in general interpretations. Moreover, the concrete, empirically determined aspects of sickness and healing become more relevant, elaborated, and standardized. As an example, what one can term the content or "material" of sickness, the more specific signs and symptoms of organismic malfunctioning (disease in the biomedical sense), now figure somewhat more directly and elaborately in models of explanation of what is perceived of and socially labeled as an episode of a type of sickness.

In these groups one can begin to more profitably distinguish between (1) illness, the private aspects of a medical problem; (2) sickness, the more abstract, socially typified, and semantically elaborated if not standardized aspects of illness that reflect political economic factors as well as widely shared, culturally represented medical knowledge of the society; and (3) disease*, the more formal and theoretical account of a sickness problem that is stipulated by specialist practitioners of the society as a result of consultation/diagnosis/treatment and that of course becomes part of the common knowledge of the group. (The term "disease" is marked by an asterisk to distinguish it from its biomedical analogue, disease, which constitutes our Western theoretical account of sickness; see Fabrega 1976a, 1976b, 1976c; and Eisenberg 1977, for further discussion.)

In a way that complements the preceding, social practices of healing involve rationales that include such things as distinctive social rituals, concrete procedures, and actual medicines and their modes of use/application. Body parts and locations become the loci for the application of medicinal substances that themselves become more standardized and widely used (e.g., poultices, emetics, inhalants) (e.g., Warren 1974; Ortiz de Montellano 1990). Procedures of a more explicitly preventive or strengthening nature are elaborated. Thus not only is a more elaborate conceptual technology of sickness found but also a more elaborate technology of healing that is tangible, formulaic, systematic, and explicitly linked to distinctive aspects of sickness, illness, and disease*. The body as a concrete object is given more salience in healing, reflected in the fact that surgeries, scarifications, and ingestions and applications of medicines become more prominent and elaborated. Even after death, the body is regarded as important in accounting for and containing clues of sickness and disease* as reflected in the performance of autopsies in some groups (see Harwood 1970 for an example).

One can posit that at this level of social organization, a condition of sickness begins to be seen as containing clues of its nature and identity. All of this means that in chiefdoms and prestate and state societies one is likely to find the beginnings of culturally more elaborated medical knowledge pertaining to anatomy, physiology, pathophysiology, pharmacology, and prevention as well as sickness and specific curative practices including medicines. Although this knowledge is still not complex and none of it may be truly "empirical," but rather analytical and strongly marked from a ritualistic standpoint and is most ideally articulated and standardized by specialists of the society, some of the elements of it are to be found shared across adults of the population (e.g., involving herbs, common remedies, etc., as among the Aztecs; see Ortiz de Montellano 1990).

In short, what one could term "consumers of medicine" have a more articulated basis on which to conceptualize sickness and plan healing. This, in turn, means that from a purely symbolic point of view, episodes of sickness can be played out in socially more elaborated ways. There are more ways in which persons can visualize the prospect of sickness, more ways in which they can express crises and "psychosocial" stressors (Dunn 1976), including even political needs in a bodily/sickness or somatized mode, and more ways in which intercurrent factors of a social nature can enter into the equation of healing and course of sickness.

The Sociocentric Dimension of Sickness.   From the standpoint of systems theory, an individual's health can be visualized as biologically based and a product of linked, open, hierarchical systems. In all types of societies, but especially those characterized as at the family level of social organization, an individual's health is very much dependent on the stability of the family and group (of related families). A holistic unity underlies and is manifest in a person's responses to bioecologic stressors and states of sickness. This adapted, healthy state is interpreted culturally as a sense of connection of the self with the family, group, and setting. Serious disruptions of this interaction of mind, body, and social experience constitute sickness, manifested as a psychosomatic and somatopsychic unity. This is interpreted in the group as a perturbation of the person's centeredness in his or her world. Because of the group's stability and interdependence among its members, conflicts appear to be not as common or striking an influence in sickness vulnerability and causation compared to more complex societies. In village-level societies, the integrated, holistic mode of functioning and responses of sickness remain important, although as discussed earlier, one finds the beginnings of intragroup social stressor influences on sickness and healing. In chiefdoms, prestates, and states, one finds an elaboration of what one can now term a sociocentric influence in medicine. As in village-level societies, illness is viewed as an outcome of the moral and ritual state of the person (or his or her family or group). However, in the societies considered here, such moral factors are complemented by an emphasis on empirical factors (i.e., physically concrete manifestations) and sociological factors (i.e., intragroup social relations). Indeed, it is perhaps the integration of the concrete, objective, and physical aspects of disease and injury with the cultural and sociological elaboration of sickness that distinguishes the institution of medicine in chiefdom, prestate, and state societies and will grow in salience in societies that are more complex (see later discussion).

The relative complexity of a society, its more settled and stable nature, the prominence of disease, and the probably higher prevalence of psychosocial conflicts means that there is likely to exist more sickness and opportunities for their visibility and attention through healing exegeses. With this comes greater opportunity to explain sickness in terms of divisions and conflicts in the society. Causes of illness are likely to prominently embrace social rivalries and jealousies. Types of sorcery and witchcraft are elaborated, and they are likely to have their realization in intragroup social dynamics. Specialists involved in the divining and diagnosis of such causes are likely to exist along with more "empirically" oriented specialists in internal diseases*, pregnancy and parturition, herbal modes of healing, and bone setting.

Finally, given the greater social problematization of sickness and healing and the fact that it comes to be viewed as having a more complex material (i.e., bodily, symptomatic) and explicitly social/moral dimension, a dimension that by definition potentially embraces and marks the immediate group, means that what was earlier termed sickness and healing "family and group management" groups are given a more important role to play. Indeed, such informal groups consisting of immediate family, kin, and ritually related comembers come to play a central role in the economy of sickness (for an example of how these groups function, in very different types of societies to be sure, see Janzen 1978b). They help to define the nature of a sickness condition, clarify and establish the terminology of sickness that is suitable, and help work out a strategy with respect to how to go about establishing its formal identity as a sickness "type" or even a disease* and eventual cure.

Associated with healers and true practitioners of medicine are found modes of behavior and conduct that are more conventionalized in the domains of sickness and healing. Sick persons or their surrogates have more elaborate strategies of how to cope with sickness, whom to consult, and when, where, and how to do this. Although ordinarily thought of as a characteristic of more complex societies, what has been termed a "hierarchy of resort" to medical care probably begins to constitute a feasible construct in chiefdoms, states, and prestates (Rommanucci-Schwartz 1969). Rules and conventions of how one should go about seeking care, how the resort is carried out, are known in the community so that social expectations and practices pertaining to medical help seeking and medical caregiving begin to be more or less standardized.

Complementing this are more standard ways in which practitioners behave with respect to sick persons. These practitioners have an awareness of the hierarchy of care seeking resorted to by families and behave accordingly. In other words, they are aware that competition exists for the services they provide and that different types of healers are usually consulted in the event of (protracted, serious) conditions of sickness. Because they are now more accountable personally for the outcome of sickness, they adopt more circumspect and formulaic ways of framing diagnostic insights and healing advice.

The sociological elaboration of illness, the fact that sickness and healing are often played out as social and political dramas in the community, means that social arbitration, social regulation, and social intervention become dominant parts of sickness and healing. Moreover, that social relations and associated conflicts/feelings within the group can become an integral component of sickness and healing means that in these societies one begins to see social exclusivity and the exchange of private information or confidentiality integrated into what one can tentatively and loosely term "the practice of medicine."

Characteristics Associated with the Sick Role.   It has been pointed out that in chiefdoms, prestates, and states sickness and healing are rendered more abstract medical and sociological objects of the society. They come to acquire fairly standardized and conventionalized social meanings and to play equally important symbolic roles. This is a natural function of the size and complexity of the society. However, a measure of standardization of sickness and healing is complemented and facilitated by the fact that, compared to less evolved societies, in these one observes a general abatement in the onerous, harsh, and demanding conditions of life. This has the effect of removing some of the crisis, life/death, and menacing implications of sickness and healing. Social differentiation and the availability of kin and lineage group mates who can help and offer support render sickness and healing less of an immediate threat to subsistence in many groups of people in these societies. A consequence of all of this is that a scenario of sickness and healing is less prominently shrouded with an ethos of urgency, circumscription, and overt danger.

Provided one keeps in mind that cultural and social circumstances still frame the medical in moral/spiritual as well as secular/empirical terms, that is, in an idiom very different from that of modern societies, one can rely on what was in an earlier chapter referred to as the "sick role" as a useful concept with which to analyze medical happenings in chiefdom, prestate, and state societies (Parsons 1975). Indeed, it can be said that the sick role becomes more visible and easily manipulated socially. There are several reasons why this is the case. First, the systematization of medical knowledge means that medical vocabularies and sickness and disease* types become objects of common knowledge. Second, the pictures and trajectories of sickness become more clearly profiled given that sicknesses are more common and many of them are chronic and less than lethal or even of serious proportions. Third, given the larger size, greater social divisions, and greater opportunities for social pursuits, individuals interact more and more with frank strangers or true strangers. All of this means that since economic, interpersonal, and psychosocial conflicts are more prevalent in these types of societies, sicknesses will come to be expressed in a more elaborated and social idiom of distress. The result of these and related factors is that the social causes and consequences of sickness become more evident, defining elements that can enter into the causation and/or computation of the "secondary gain" of sickness. Vulnerability to others of the behavioral environment becomes more heightened and, also, the motivation to be sick becomes a more easily visualized, sought after, and realized goal. This expanded ecology and social economy of sickness, illness, and disease* promotes coping by accentuating the need for healing. Thus what many may term (loosely) the social functions of sickness become more prominent and elaborated and this can lead to an enhancement of the appeal of sickness.

These factors relate to what one might conceptualize as the push toward sickness and the adoption of the sick role. At the same time, one must keep in mind that the "social pull" generated by practitioners and the psychological favors they can bestow begins to exert influence on the generation of sickness (see earlier discussion on specialist healers). What are often termed (sometimes too loosely) problems of somatization or "psychosomatic" and "sociosomatic" sicknesses, some associated with more or less consciously perceived political economic hardships, if not frank malingering, become potentially important factors in the social economy of medicine largely because of the independent influences exerted by sociological factors. All of the above addresses the person's conscious intentions and motives and the potential charisma of healers.

The preceding point can be stated differently: the social rationale of sickness is more defined and its rewards increased. The psychosocial needs and conflicts of persons become more important influences in the occupancy of the elaborated role of sickness. In addition, and perhaps inseparably related to this process, "unconscious" factors begin to play a more important role in the social economy of medicine. In other words, because conditions of sickness become prominent symbolic objects in the social and political arena of a community, they function psychologically so as to facilitate the shaping of physical and psychological stress toward the unconscious production of sickness and eventually disease*.

All of the preceding means that the social ecology of these types of societies create different inputs for the way the SH adaptation comes to be constructed in sickness and healing. As an example, whereas death and termination were entailed by sickness and healing scenarios and a short-term crisis ethos colored medical exegeses, all of these features of the way the SH adaptation evolved during Pleistocene conditions (see earlier chapter), now under very different social and cultural conditions death and termination begin to recede in salience and dominance. Individuals, be they sick or drawn to heal others, begin to be provided with an altogether different calculus or set of rules in terms of which sickness and healing can be configured and played out. One can say that the meanings, rationales, and functions of medicine all begin to change as (what I have termed) a sociological emphasis with amplification and complexification of the sick role begins to operate in the society.

In summary, social conflicts, rivalries, and jealousies are very prominent features in societies at this level of differentiation. States of physical vulnerability are enhanced, as is also the opportunity of contracting infection. Individuals can be said to live in a more precarious, compromised state of physical and psychological health. The psychological and physical stress that is a product of these sociological, cultural, and ecological conditions can be held to predispose toward, if not promote, the outbreak of disease. Moreover, the preceding mix of factors also facilitates the construction of conscious and unconscious motives for sickness and healing since this promises attention to and the possible resolution of social and psychological strains through the intervention of charismatic healers.

The Emergence of Medical Pluralism.   Finally, it would appear that in chiefdom, prestate, and state societies there exists the beginnings of what one could term medical pluralism. A form of "pluralism" could be said to exist even in small forager groups who have available to them different approaches to the understanding and formulation of sickness and healing. However, this pluralism is clearly but the reflection of the diverse elements that constitute their approach to the "medical," which does not constitute a systematized or separated area of human concern. Pluralistic interpretations of sickness and healing form connected texts in the one larger extended text that addresses sickness and other human misfortunes. In chiefdoms, prestates, and states, on the other hand, one sees the beginnings of truly separate approaches to the medical: Not only does it constitute a more or less distinct, autonomous area of human concern but there exists practitioners whose formulations of sickness and approaches to healing differ one from the other.

One can posit that during cultural evolution in these types of societies there existed a dominating ideology pertaining to the sacred. Since problems of disease were very prominent and visible and true epidemics devastating possibilities, such problems became integral aspects of how sanctity and groupwide rituals were conceived and played out. One can speculate that these societies were characterized by the beginnings of a religiously dominant ideology pertaining to sickness and disease that must have had associated with it ceremonial centers that operated as the central foci of early "medical policy planning." Priests and, at hierarchically lower levels, practitioners of the orthodox ideology functioned in the protection against and healing of sickness. However, as discussed above, the complexity associated with this expanded economy of sickness and healing means that healers of different varieties existed. The regional basis of chiefdom, prestate, and state societies necessarily means that there existed opportunities for different conceptual approaches to sickness and healing. There no doubt existed types of practitioners for different types of illnesses who could resort to different schemas of diagnosis and healing for the same illness. Diviners contrasted with herbalists who contrasted with potential experts in sorcery and witchcraft. Specialists may have concentrated in diagnosis as opposed to pure healing, on adult females as opposed to adult males. The training requirements of different practitioners differed, further emphasizing the more or less distinctive approaches to understanding sickness.

In summary, in this social type a medical "organization" or "system" is discernible. It entailed a structuration that rendered true medical pluralism a natural property of the overarching approach to sickness and healing. In civilizations and empires, of course, with their literate, academic, scientific, and more or less official medical tradition played out against the lay, folk, popular, and indigenous (given the reality of ethnic diversification) varieties, medical pluralism reaches its full complexity. Nevertheless, the seeds of this pluralism are found in chiefdoms, prestates, and states.

Sickness and Healing in Empires and Civilizations

Aspects of Social Organization

As with previous social types, it is intellectually awkward and also difficult to summarize the characteristics of civilizations and empires in a succinct way (Crone 1989; Fried 1967; Johnson and Earle 1991; Jones 1987; Service 1975; Tainter 1988). The requirements of parsimony dictate that one bring together societies with highly different ecologic, cultural, and political characteristics. For example, in the category discussed here, one is forced to bring together classical, medieval, and early modern societies of Europe as well as societies within the sphere of influence of the civilizations of ancient China, ancient India, and medieval Islam. Any social history text or any of the many treatises dealing with the historical epidemiology, theories of disease*, and medical practices of these highly distinctive societies will reveal sharp differences across the spectrum of medicine. A truly comprehensive history of the evolution of medicine would have to integrate these developments that are separated in space, time, and regions of cultural influence. As already indicated, I judge such a comprehensive enterprise as premature given the state of knowledge in the very diverse fields that are relevant to its exposition. Moreover, I am concerned to summarize, integrate, and abstract knowledge in order to fully embrace the problem area and provide a general conceptualization and methodology for studying medicine from an evolutionary standpoint.

Life as it is lived in most societies today conforms in many ways to that of the civilizations and empires, and an enumeration of their distinctive features compared to smaller and less complex societies would require extended treatment. In general, societies of the type considered in this section are very large and populous, territorially fixed, and marked by well-defined and politically important boundaries. They are highly centralized politically and show well-established, bureaucratized structures of government, law, religion, and commerce. Power is concentrated and the maintenance of social order becomes a dominant concern of established rulers who are usually revered in special ways. Official and civil servant operatives are increasingly influential in public affairs and policy formation.

Although earlier and less complex varieties of these societies were predominantly agricultural, large urban centers were present. In civilizations and empires, one finds the beginnings of industrialization, considerable growth of mercantilism and commerce, well-defined social groupings if not frank social classes, occupational specialization, and systematization of commercial routines and knowledge, both secular and cosmological/religious. The high density of the population means that problems of sickness are more visible and prominent in the lives of residents of empires and civilizations. Ethnic, linguistic, religious, and economic diversity divide the populations of these societies.

The presence of literacy in many of these societies makes possible the systematization and standardization of social practices, economic activities, and litigation of the inevitable conflicts and infractions of social order that are found. The effects of literacy on social organization, the organization and production of knowledge, the growth of science and technology, and cognitive functioning, all of which relate in an important way to life in empires and civilizations, is a subject of immense complexity that cannot be discussed in detail here.

Aspects of Disease

The trends described above for prestates, chiefdoms, and states are, if not clearly and unambiguously accentuated, certainly larger in scope in the societies described as civilizations and empires (Cohen 1989; Fiennes 1978;

McKeown 1988; McNeill 1976; Riley 1989). First, high infant and child mortality, more chronic diseases that produce debilitation and lassitude, and general symptoms of malaise with gastrointestinal problems are prominent. Second, there is the matter of food. Although problems of agriculture and food storage are managed in a very elaborate way and state representatives are able to protect granaries, the risk of resource failure and starvation may not have been reduced, contrary to what is generally believed. Thus it is unclear whether the diets of the populations of civilizations and empires were more reliable. Vulnerability of domestic crop species to climatic variation and other natural hazards and the ease with which stored resources could be politically expropriated were threats that worked against a stable source of food. In addition, the nutrition of individuals living in highly sedentarized communities of states and empires may have declined further, among other things, because an increasing amount of productive energy was used in the maintenance of intragroup order and the celebration of the community.

Third, with respect to sickness itself, the introduction of new diseases from one region of the world to another rendered these populations highly vulnerable to epidemics and, more generally, very high rates of debilitating morbidity and mortality (Crosby 1972; McNeill 1976). Periodic plagues could devastate the population. Except for epidemics and in the short run, populations of civilizations and empires may have coped better with acute, potentially virulent infections because their size allowed epidemic diseases in time to become spread out and endemic. It is arguable whether this promoted the genetic selection of resistance (see McNeill 1976: chaps. 1 and 2 and Cohen 1989 for a review of this topic). However, with endemicity, many infections become prevalent during childhood when they tend to be less severe. The settled nature of these populations and the fact that only a fraction of the population is vulnerable mean that, in the event of infection, family and community resources are not as disrupted and individuals can be better cared for. One way of interpreting these generalizations is to say that (excluding plagues and major epidemics) civilizations and empires may have experienced less devastation in the way of mortality from infection but may have actually experienced a greater amount of controllable sickness from infection because of endemicity and the ease of transmissions of infection via air, direct contact, and fecal-oral pathways. That many persons may have lived longer in these types of societies (provided they overcame the health hazards or childhood infections) and not all were vulnerable to an infection (because of acquired immunity and better means of supportive care) means that those infected were probably cared for better.

Fourth, in these populations the prevalence of chronic, so-called diseases of civilization (e.g., diabetes, coronary heart disease, hypertension, cancer) may be higher. These diseases are classically said to be found as features of industrialized, Western societies, where they are said to define an "epidemiologic transition" that complements the demographic transition (see Omran 1971). However, there is a dearth of information pertaining to these types of diseases in earlier Western and non-Western civilizations and empires. Knowledge drawn from contemporary medical anthropological studies underscores the richness of medical vocabularies and idioms of distress, the differing social appearances of sickness, and the symbolic and behavioral complexity of sickness pictures. Many so-called diseases of civilization are expressed as "folk illnesses" and "culture-bound" sickness pictures. There is no compelling reason to believe that such diseases were absent from earlier (Western and non-Western) states and civilization if the age structure of the populations included a significant number of adult and aging individuals. The complexity of disease* nomenclatures and the highly elaborated degree of medical knowledge, including the central role played by symptoms of all varieties in the medical compendia of these societies, provide additional support for the possibility that "diseases of civilizations" were prevalent in earlier epochs and played somewhat important roles in the social economy of sickness and healing.

Civilizations and empires very likely included individuals who suffered from diseases generally equated with poor bowel function, such as appendicitis, diverticulitis, hemorrhoids, and hiatal hernia. Many of these diseases can become chronic. Finally, adult life expectancy probably increased among some groupings, at least, in civilizations and empires, which from the point of view of this chapter basically means that there was greater opportunity for members of the population to experience all types of sickness. In general, overlooking the devastations produced by epidemics, the bioecology of nutrition and disease in states and empires creates conditions for the population to experience more medical problems that are characterized by less acuteness/virulence, more chronicity, endemicity, but moderate levels of morbidity. As indicated above, one can anticipate that social scenarios very different from those sculpted by natural selection during the move from protoculture to culture are made possible by the conditions prevailing in civilizations and empires.

Fifth, in these societies one finds distinct differences in mortality and morbidity across ethnic, religious, and socioeconomic segments of the society. This creates different sickness pictures that correlate with pluralistic ways of conceptualizing them and carrying out healing. It no longer is possible to isolate a modal type of sickness/healing scenario given the complexity and pluralism of the society.

Sixth, the trend already manifest in prestates and states pertaining to the higher prevalence of psychosocial needs and conflicts that could culminate in sickness pictures of diverse types (problems of somatization and psychosomatic, somatopsychic and sociosomatic sickness pictures) was undoubtedly more pronounced in civilizations and empires. The implications of this point are taken up later in this chapter.

Finally, it is probably the case that in civilizations and empires what today constitute bona fide psychiatric disorders begin to have a discernible social effect in the community (Fabrega 1991a, 1991b). This is not necessarily a result of any increase in incidence, although that in these societies stress is said to be more common might positively affect incidence levels (but not only of psychiatric disorders, of course). Rather, an increase in the amount of psychiatric disorders is a result of their chronicity and the social conditions that are found, including in particular the greater visibility/acceptance of sickness generally and growth of humanitarian, ethical medical ideologies in many civilizations and empires in particular. In other words, many persons who are likely to have been neglected or abandoned under more stringent living conditions live longer, and the fact that they are generally cared for better allows a greater accumulation in the numbers of the psychiatrically disordered (an increase in prevalence as compared to incidence). In addition, as a result of the concentration of the population in often very large preindustrial and frankly industrial urban complexes, psychiatric disorders become more visible in the community. The possibility that with heavy urbanization there may take place a breakup in the cohesiveness of the extended family also worked to the disadvantage of the psychiatrically ill, affecting both incidence and prevalence. Their visibility and dependence were increased. In general, for these and any number of additional reasons (which would have to include conditions shaping a somatic emphasis on distress and suffering as well as sheer sickness exploitation), the social problems posed by what today we term psychiatric disorders became a more prominent part of the picture of sickness and healing in civilizations and empires.

Given the size and differentiation of the population and its segmentation along a number of different lines, one can anticipate that the social visibility, prominence, and effects due to the bioecology of disease differed markedly across the segments of the population, depending on such things as ethnicity, religion, climate, geography (i.e., rural vs. urban centers), and socioeconomic resources. However, it is likely that the generalizations noted here were to some extent manifest across the society. In a strict sense, wealthy classes could enjoy a level of health comparable to that found in the better-off classes of modern societies, but the large mass of the population appears to have suffered very high burdens of disease.

Aspects of Sickness and Healing

General Considerations.   Civilizations and empires are important because in them one finds an official, scholarly, academic, and more or less elitist tradition of medicine of great scope, complexity, and systematization, all of which is made possible by writing. The traditions were based on a large corpus of writings and commentaries that had accumulated over time. The traditions of India, China, the Mediterranean (i.e., Galenic), and medieval Islam are classic

examples. These medical texts contained much information that was often inconsistent, redundant, and not necessarily organized systematically. Repeated
syntheses of this information yielded material that will be regarded here as
more or less canonical and coherent. Textual knowledge structures of great
complexity and scope pertaining to elaborated aspects of sickness and healing
clearly distinguishes these traditions from those of simpler social formations
(see Dunn 1976; Janzen 1978b; Leslie 1976; Press 1980). An example is appropriate here.

In his masterful synthesis of the culinary, ecologic and climatic underpinnings of Ayurvedic medicine in ancient India, Francis Zimmermann (1987)
captures nicely a holistic orientation to sickness and healing and emphasizes
the interconnection between a range of factors involved in the "clinical practice" of medicine in civilizations and empires. Moreover, Zimmermann associates all of this to other great traditions of medicine. The following material
illustrates this.

> We should at this point remember the context within which the doctor of antiq-
> uity practiced his art, in India as in Greece. Anatomy and physiology were quasi-
> inexistent, and the medical practitioner had no truly biological knowledge on
> which to base his actions. What pathology depended on, instead, was what the
> hippocratics called *prognosis,* the science of the course taken by illness and of
> the signs that herald accident, crises, and solutions. . . . He was consequently less
> concerned to recognize the nature of a disease than to foresee its development,
> taking into consideration the most general conditions of life: climate, seasons,
> customs, postures. Ecology was an integral part of this practical context. His
> knowledge of the patient's environment, including the flora and fauna, enabled
> the doctor to anticipate the course of the disease and to take action on it. (Zim-
> mermann 1987: 20)

Later, Zimmermann extends his argument: "In India as in Greece, as early as
the pre-Socratic period, ideas about justice and political harmony were associated with the idea of health. . . . Medicine is a form of politics" (p. 31). A more
physiological, functional analysis of ancient Indian medicine that does not
minimize the comprehensiveness or the quintessentially clinical emphasis of
this tradition is presented by P. Kutumbiah (1969). This particular work presents in a very succinct way the enormous physiologic knowledge that one
finds in "great" traditions of medicine and complements Zimmermann's more
literary, exegetical emphasis. The study by Sudhir Kakar (1982), which concentrates on healing and the emotionally sensitive approaches of Ayurvedic
practitioners, a study rich in its evocation of the psychological sophistication of
this tradition, makes accessible themes relatively deemphasized in the works
of Zimmermann and Kutumbiah that focus more on ecological/climatic and
medical/physiological themes, respectively.

The material on Ayurvedic wisdom can easily be matched with material pertaining to ancient China. The writings of Nathan Sivin (1987), who is more concerned to present the underlying "ethnophysiological" thinking of ancient, traditional Chinese medicine than is Zimmermann (1987) with respect to that of ancient India (but see Kutumbiah 1969), are relevant here. The following is pertinent:

> In connection with . . . *ch'i* . . . some of the aspects of normal body function had been defined by the third century B.C. . . . Recapitulating these aspects along with others that became important later gives us a general outline of what for the past thousand years has constituted health in classical medicine [of China]. . . . Energies are continuously extracted from food and breadth and the residues are expelled. . . . Vital energies penetrate throughout the body in an equitable, unimpeded circulation. This metabolic circulation maintains not only life but order and invulnerability to invasion. . . . Vital substances are sealed within the body and heteropathy sealed out, without interrupting normal ingestion and excretion. . . . The mind is centered and free of inappropriate, immoderate emotions. . . . A dynamic balance maintains itself among somatic functions, among emotional functions, and between the two aspects. . . . This endless process of renewal is spontaneous and ordered, cyclical in character, its daily and seasonal rhythms in accord with those of the environment. . . . The orderly character of this process depends on an orderly life. The understanding of order came to include not only physical and mental hygiene, but moral discipline, spiritual purity, and a life lived in harmony with the physical environment, governed in turn by the cosmic order. (Sivin 1987: 96–98)

A study that complements nicely the presentation of Sivin by providing a description and interpretation based on contemporary science of some of the basic therapeutic procedures of ancient Chinese medicine is that of Lu Gwei-Djen and Joseph Needham (1980).

In civilizations and empires, then, medicine emerges as a major organization or system of society associated with a corpus of knowledge pertaining to the nature of sickness, disease*, treatment, and ethical imperatives of medical practice. This means more sickness terms, more disease* terms, a greater number and complexity of basic assumptions and beliefs pertaining to sickness and healing, and an increase in the number of specialized medicines including herbal preparations and technical procedures for healing. A rough picture of the complexity and elaborateness of medical knowledge for chiefdoms, pre-states, and states by Warren (1974) was profiled in an earlier section. Suffice it to say that in the societies under review here the scope of medical knowledge about disease* and healing is greatly increased through the literate preservation of the writings of esteemed practitioners and theorists.

A result is that the body of the person and its many parts and openings become defined as important landmarks of sickness and healing. An increase in the number and complexity of abstract and theoretical concepts evolves which address the health of the person in a comprehensive frame of reference.

Specialist healers become more socially empowered, independent, entre-preneurial, focused, and skilled about sickness, the empirical features of which begin to dominate the center of the medical stage. With this comes a maturation of their resourcefulness as diagnosticians and healers and psychotherapeutic abilities. The preservation, systematization, expansion, and complexification of medical knowledge made possible by literacy means that the intellectual consequences of this "revolution" profoundly augment and transform under-standings of sickness and lead to the development of elaborate texts, scenar-ios, and protocols of healing. Since literacy makes possible such things as lists, formulas, recipes, prescriptions, and even experiments, the effects of this in the production and organization of medical knowledge can be anticipated (Goody 1977, 1986, 1987).

In some civilizations and empires, the state begins to take a hand in the con-duct of medical practice, in some instances hiring practitioners for elitist groups and providing free or nominal care for the poorer segments of society, espe-cially during periods of famine and epidemics. There also is a concern with so-cial policy toward the health of the public, a concern that spans prevention and treatment of widespread epidemics that periodically devastate the population (Amundsen 1977; Cipolla 1976; Dols 1984a, 1984b; Miller 1985; Needham 1970; Russell 1979).

Variability and Complexity in the Configuration of Sickness and Healing. A literate, theoretical, and "great" tradition of medicine operates as a standard in the society. However, its pure form or expression may be accessible to only a small (economically relatively well-off) segment of the population. There exist other "traditions" of medicine that may or may not have their origins in the ethnic, linguistic, and religious diversity of the population (Bynum and Porter 1987; Unschuld 1985, 1986a, 1986b). The diversity includes various indigenous peoples, aliens, or nonnatives and slaves. They are found congre-gated together in the large urban, "preindustrial" and industrial, commercial cities of these societies or in outlying areas of colonial domination or in rural hamlets and villages.

Many of these latter social groups have access to medical traditions of their own (carryovers from earlier phases of social differentiation) that can com-pete with or complement the more official and scholarly one, although many of the "little" traditions are also elaborate and could be rendered in some form of writing. There exist also many lay, folk practitioners who rely on popular and more explicitly magical/religious ideas that constitute remnants of less complex societies that have been incorporated through political domination. A complex picture of medical pluralism is thus a striking feature of civilizations and empires (Cooter 1988; Press 1980).

The increase in the number of practitioners of different orientations in-creases the options that a sick person and his or her family have in the event of sickness. The availability of diverse specialties of healers means that the members of the population are aware of alternative perspectives on sickness and that disease* vocabularies are available in terms of which families and individuals can make sense of sickness and proceed to plan and undertake healing. Family managing groups play a far more strategic role in the planning of healing in the case of serious or protracted instances of sickness.

These societies create at least a two-tiered system of medical practice. The differentiation of the population in terms of occupation, education (which is made formally possible for a small segment of the population, mainly men), and economic resources is reflected in resorts to different types of practitioners who are distinguished by their social rank, cost, and associated credentials and paraphernalia of diagnosis and treatment. Inequality in states of health, prevalence of sickness, and recourse to healing specialists is a distinctive picture of civilizations and empires.

Finally, in civilizations and empires there exists a great deal of rivalry among medical practitioners and specialists. Economic incentives in the practice of healing surface as important, if not dominant, factors in this competition. Despite the absence of regulation, control, and centralization of medicine, it could almost be said that sickness and healing become veritable industries in civilizations and empires. In some instances, groups of practitioners constituting what could be termed "protoprofessions" emerge which vie with one another. The issue of a healer's morality, trustworthiness, theoretical orientation, learning, and authenticity becomes an important concern in the society. Sick persons and their surrogates are forced to choose practitioners in an open market, relying on their own cultural orientations and knowledge based on hearsay, repute, scholarly credentials, economic cost, or epistemologic orientation.

Much literature about issues pertaining to early professionalization of medicine and competition is available for European civilizations and empires (Bullough 1966; Cook 1986, 1994; Freidson 1970; Gelfand 1980; Park 1985; Siraisi 1990). The conduct of medical practice in other, "non-Western," civilizations and empires, particularly with respect to the matter of professionalization and state regulation, control, or support of practice (and competition) is not as well understood and controversial (Farquhar 1994; Sivin 1987). As an example, Michael W. Dols (1984a) makes a point of emphasizing that physicians were not regulated in medieval Islam. In ancient China, there existed a tradition of scholarly medicine and many government officials were trained in medicine, but whether they were employed to treat the poor, regulated by the state, or formed actual corporate groups like guilds that managed competition and standardized practice is not clearly established (see Needham 1970; Sivin 1987, 1992a, 1992b).

Medical ethics is a paramount concern of practitioners of the "great" traditions, which suggests that issues of competition, authenticity, commercialization, frank quackery, and the like were not only prevalent but also of considerable concern in many civilizations and empires, not just the European (Fabrega 1975, 1990c). This emphasis on morality and invidious comparison of the reputable to "quacks" and "unorthodox" practitioners clearly suggests a sense of humanitarian concern and ethical responsibility but also, it needs to be recognized, a concern with economic rewards and competition. Thus practitioners of civilizations and empires begin to form more or less distinctive groups differentiated as to mode of training, scholarship, and repute; that they shared a social identity of some sort is also clear. However, the market for healing was generally an open one and its regulation and control were limited until the modern era in European societies (see Needham 1970 for the issue of certification of practitioners in China; for related issues in Islam and Byzantium, see Dols 1984a and Miller 1985, respectively). Even in Western European countries and in England (Cook 1986; Garcia-Ballester, McVaugh, and Rubio-Vela 1989; Jackson 1988; Miller 1985; Nutton 1983), the effectiveness of regulation and control of practice seems not to have been significant. This means that the influence of healers as well as sick persons and their surrogates on the course of sickness and conduct of healing was significant, if not determinate. Sickness and healing, in other words, were relatively open ended and under informal local control (not formal or official). This feature of the configuration of sickness and healing is different from that found in the modern period, as will be described later.

Finally, the evidence pointing to a preoccupation with morality, ethics, exploitation, and authenticity of healers and of medicine more generally suggests certain features about the phenomena of sickness and healing. In a general way, it underscores not only the increasing commercialization of medicine but also the expansion and attraction inherent in sickness and healing as a social, political, economic, and psychological enterprise. In other words, ethical codes can be regarded as early forms of regulation and advertisement of medical practice under conditions that underscore high commercialism and exploitation; all of this implies expansion of the medical market and congested social traffic in the pursuit of health and well-being. Consequently, not only does there arise an awareness that healers can and do exploit, but one must assume that there exists an awareness that sickness itself constitutes a vulnerable condition that individuals may be led to exploit and that curbing undue exploitation of sickness constitutes an obligation of ethical healers.

Aspects of the Sick Role.   The trends promoting an exploitation of the social role of sickness, facilitated by elaborated medical models, languages, and routines, described for chiefdoms, prestates, and states are more pronounced in empires and civilizations. Along with an increase in the amount and variety of healers, there was an increase in the sheer amount of sickness. Similarly, given the nature of the social conditions prevailing as well as the epistemology pertaining to sickness and disease*, there was probably a continuation, if not intensification, of sociological emphases, implications, and functions with respect to medicine that were discussed earlier with respect of chiefdoms, prestates, and states. I would like to elaborate on this point.

One could plausibly maintain that the existence of an official, academic, scholarly, and scientific tradition of medicine associated with elitist backing might operate to set constraints on the degree to which individuals can exploit the sick role for their own conscious and unconscious needs. In other words, scholarly, respected, official, and more or less standardized knowledge structures pertaining to sickness/healing and the existence of individual practitioners who are knowledgeable in all this and hence socially empowered (in some instances, more or less administratively recognized, if not certified) to validate the nature of sickness as disease* might be expected to set constraints on sickness behaviors, providing, as it were, grounds for establishing authentic versus unauthentic states of sickness. This, however, does not appear to have occurred and may have been precluded by the kind of ontology and epistemology associated with medical theory and general cultural orientation (Fabrega 1990b).

The model of disease* and sickness that was found in earlier civilizations and empires prior to the advent of the modern European era was what social historians of medicine term "functional." Symptoms of sickness were all-important in defining the nature of a medical problem (Temkin 1963). The content of sickness behaviors and symptoms together with careful examination of the body constituted the material out of which practitioners constructed their formulations of disease* by means of their elaborate epistemologies. The ultimate bases for determining the identity and boundaries of sickness and healing were the experiences of individuals who in reporting bodily and behavioral malfunctions defined themselves as sick and suffering.

In civilizations and empires, and to some extent in prestates, chiefdoms, and states as well (see earlier discussion), the "healer," or more properly the *expert,* continues to acquire and gain therapeutic leverage as a persona in the economy of sickness and healing. Stated differently, the persuasiveness of the expert healer, *independent of the support of family and group,* begins to exert influence on the course of sickness. The roots of the potential beneficial effects of the "doctor-patient relationship" are thus found well defined in these larger-scale societies. However, there are limits to what an expert can accomplish. These are set by pressures exerted by the sick person, the family, and the immediate group—all of which acquire the time and means of exploiting the role of sickness for purposes of resolving social and political problems.

All of this reflects a fully elaborated sociologic and interpersonal dimension of sickness and healing in empires and civilizations. More specifically, authentication of sickness and constraints on occupancy of the sick role are limited by the following factors: (1) the biologic imperative of suffering is so strongly ingrained in individual healers (perhaps selected because of their greater genetic loading of the posited SH trait that underlies medicine) that he or she is simply unable to withhold support and offers care, thereby endorsing and supporting an individual's messages, idioms, and scenarios of sickness; (2) a commercialized ethos and the imperatives of economic incentives of the practitioner's role are commanding, tempting the practitioner to selfishly cheat and exploit (consciously or unconsciously) the sick person and his or her family for his own economic ends (and, as elaborated earlier, it needs to be recalled that it is precisely in these social types that ethical codes are more or less officially promulgated by groups of healers probably in response to just such exploitation [Fabrega 1990c]); (3) the nature of the ontology and epistemology of sickness operates to preclude the practitioner from being able to evolve independent, objective, technologically based evidence of disease* that could serve as a litmus test of authentic sickness and suffering (e.g., no radiographic examinations were possible); and (4) the state did not (in reality, was not yet able to, given the constraints of [3]) intervene in the way the system of medicine operated (e.g., by gaining power through the sponsorship of procedures for the acquisition of knowledge, supporting education and research that then allowed it to impose standards for "authentic" sickness and healing, the regulation of practice, etc.).

In summary, the cultural ontology and epistemology undergirding sickness and healing had the effect of contributing to the production and prolongation of sickness and healing. One cannot deny that healing in civilizations and empires "worked" or was effective, a topic of considerable scientific and philosophic complexity that cannot be dealt with fully here. The claim is merely that the epistemology of sickness and healing of the "great" traditions did not appear to have evolved a technology for the authentication of sickness independent of its enactment and acceptance by the healer. Obviously, such a technology was not fully available even in biomedicine, although much of medical care today does bring into play the question of "secondary gain" of sickness and need for "objective" disability determination, which implicates the topic of authentication (see later sections and chapters) (Fabrega 1990b).

Knowledge and Technology about the Course of Sickness: The Beginnings of Clinical Medicine.   Traditionally, clinical medicine is thought to be a result of developments that took place during the nineteenth century in European societies (Ackerknecht 1942a, 1942b, 1945a, 1945b, 1946a, 1946b; Golub 1994; Hudson 1983; Lesch 1984; Riese 1960; Shryock 1969). There can be little doubt that with respect to our contemporary, biomedical perspective on sickness and healing, this is correct. However, one can suggest that a version of what one can term the "science" of clinical medicine was found in societies described in this section.

This intellectual approach to "clinical medicine" is captured nicely with respect to Chinese medicine by Sivin.

The Chinese conception of visceral systems of functions was from first to last an attempt to understand the workings of physical organs. Nothing in historians' or anthropologists' current understanding of the origins of medicine supports the old prejudice that early curers thought of the body in an empirical way unaffected by preconceptions. Archaic Chinese preconceptions are obvious enough. In the pre-Confucian classics the heart and liver appear more often as loci of emotions than as innards, to give only one example. This granted, we do find in such writings a more concrete approach to the viscera than in the high medical tradition or even in the philosophy of 100 B.C., simply because by 500 B.C. overarching philosophic schemes did not yet exist. . . . From organs to visceral systems, was one of the more striking leaps of abstraction in Chinese intellectual history. The outcome was well adapted to predominantly functional thought about vital processes. Traditional physicians gave remarkably little attention, early or late, to structure, location, and lesion. This emphasis on function is perhaps the most fundamental difference between classical medicine in China and Europe. (Sivin 1987: 168–169)

Whereas holistic, functional emphases characterized Chinese medicine, it should not be assumed that this entailed a relative disregard for more standard features of a clinical orientation. Gwei-Djen and Needham (1980) provide a detailed interpretation of the Chinese medical procedures of acupuncture and moxibustion relying on contemporary scientific thinking in anatomy and physiology. Judith Farquhar (1994) also underscores the strong clinical/symptomatic emphases of contemporary Chinese practitioners of traditional medicine. The compendium on Tibetan medicine prepared by Rinpoche (1973), although admittedly much less elaborate for this special system of medicine compared to India and China, points nonetheless to similar emphases on function, and in a section entitled "Tokens of Approaching Death" (pp. 47–49) one finds material of central clinical concern to all healers which involves an acquaintance with terminality. Other material pertaining to the medicine of China is supportive of this general emphasis on function and clinical phenomenology as well as broader themes pertaining to cosmologic orientation (Chiu 1990; DeWoskin 1983; Porkert 1974, 1983; Ruey-Shuang 1989; Unschuld 1979, 1985, 1986a, 1986b; Ware 1966; Yanchi 1988a, 1988b). This general perspective about sickness and healing is consistent as well with writings pertaining to the ancient, classical Mediterranean traditions and to the medieval European and Islamic traditions (see, e.g., Dols 1984a, 1984b; Jacquart and Thomasset 1988; Lloyd 1978, 1979; Ullmann 1978; Von Staden 1989). It should be recalled that a holistic, comprehensive approach to sickness and healing and to features that can properly be characterized as clinical description is also found in the medicine of the societies of Mesoamerica, which I handle as states (Lopez Austin 1980; Ortiz de Montellano 1990).

One can arguably claim that in civilizations and empires there takes place a systematization of medical practice. It needs to be acknowledged at the outset that there exist marked differences in the emphases and concerns of Galenic physicians, the various types of Chinese practitioners, and Indian practitioners of Ayurvedic medicine. Each operated in terms of theories that stipulated different material substances, agencies, and pathophysiological mechanisms as well as therapeutic doctrines. It is not the content of how sickness and healing were conceptualized but the more abstract process that took place in medical dialogues that I am concerned with here.

The course of sickness becomes an object of analysis as a function of the greater visibility and emphasis of the medical and the specialization of healers into crafts and quasi professions. In this sense, they are better able to delineate and also influence the boundaries and end points and dictate the flow of sickness and healing. The sheer practice of medicine, including the concrete features of the *course of sickness and illness* as a result of healing interventions, becomes concretized and empirically more visible and better defined and articulated. Together with the factors reviewed earlier pertaining to specialist identity and the acquisition of scholarly knowledge, what one can term an *epistemology and technology of medical practice* signals a potential increment in the power that specialist healers can exert on the perceptions, dispositions, and motivations of persons who are sick. In other words, from an academic and scientific standpoint, the cause, course, and response to healing all become important properties of a sickness condition and disease* and its typology. Healers begin to see sickness and pictures of disease* longitudinally in relation to holistic aspects of the person, including responses of symptoms to previous interventions and to intercurrent social and interpersonal influences. All of these factors imply a continuity of experience with the trajectory of sickness and a familiarity with its vicissitudes in the person. All of these factors also reflect an increase in the healer's potential influence on sickness and on the sick person and surrogates; and vice versa, on the power and compellingness of the pursuit of healing on the part of consumers of an evolving medical industry.

When one adds to this picture the fact that there were few, if any, "magic bullets" in a healer's armamentarium, or safe, definitive procedures that might have shortened and focused healing, one begins to appreciate the necessary integration that existed in this "early" science of clinical medicine between social, psychological, and somatic emphases pertaining to sickness and healing. The science of clinical medicine thus evolved in a holistic context for this is what the epistemology and ontology of sickness, disease*, and healing stipulated. Extended dialogues between healers and sick persons that incorporated psychosomatic and somatopsychic features of experience and reasoning were integral to clinical medicine; prevention and treatment were united; and active intervener as well as general adviser were aspects of "doctoring." This characteristic of healing and clinical medicine is implicitly recorded in the great medical texts that invariably reflect a holistic orientation toward disease* in the ancient traditions. In subsequent phases of medical evolution, medical epistemologies and ontologies yield to the objectivity of disease mechanisms and to the primacy of the technical as a means of calibrating clinical medicine, and this is reflected in the character of healing dialogues.

An enhancement of the healer's influence, knowledge, and sensitivity to the properties and especially the course of sickness, what one can term the beginnings of a science of clinical medicine (or, alternatively, an early stage of clinical medicine), had its disadvantages. As emphasized earlier, this power and influence could work to create, reinforce, and perpetuate sickness. This result of the healer's power was made possible by the social validation of their model of disease* and of their role in society (i.e., their power to sanction and shape sickness). As a result, their visibility and accessibility in society created opportunities and role scripts for persons experiencing psychosocial conflicts. At the same time the economic temptations of their role as elite healers allowed them to exploit occupants of the sick role. This state of affairs, with healing promoted and enhanced at the cost of producing or perpetuating sickness, may be viewed as a social maladaptation as Rappaport (1979) has described this concept.

A Commercialization of the Healing Enterprise.   The changes in the character of sickness and healing imply that the practice of medicine became more commercialized. The evolution of actual crafts and professions of healing, with their associated social markers and access to detailed, specialized, and learned knowledge, enabled the healer to command economic compensation in an increasingly monetarized and standardized form. This incentive of healing clearly must be held to have competed with the basic biologically rooted adaptation toward healing (what in an earlier chapter was termed SH) that is posited to have constituted the basis of sickness, healing, and medical practice more generally. On balance, it can be said that in civilizations and empires the social contingencies of practice and the nature of medical knowledge operate so as to allow sick persons to continue to constitute and dictate the material of sickness and the end points of healing; and that although healers may potentially have gained greater efficacy over chronic forms of sickness and somatization problems, they also were able to reinforce and perpetuate them. As a result of psychological dispositions and behavioral routines imposed by social and cultural evolution, sickness and healing clearly expanded beyond the boundaries carved by genetically canalized or "pure" biological evolutionary processes. Stated more succinctly, the distinctive social environmental inputs that affect the way the SH adaptation unfolds in individuals of this type of society make possible altogether different scenarios of sickness and healing than those found in the environment of evolutionary adaptedness. Sickness and healing are not just dangerous, life and death, crisis-oriented affairs of great existential import but, in many instances, social scripts that when played out exert enormous influence, significance, and power on the life and social adaptation of residents of a community. The biological adaptation for sickness and healing thus has the opportunity to grow and expand to accommodate and medicalize the stress, suffering, and distress associated with social and political hardships of many different origins.

The Higher Prevalence of Psychiatric Disorders.   Specialization of healing in civilizations and empires extends to those who suffer from mental illness (Dols 1987; Dube 1978; Foucault 1965; Haldipur 1984; Milns 1986; Ng 1990). Continuing the trend described earlier for chiefdoms, prestates, and states, so-called psychiatric disorders and mental illness more broadly conceived accumulate as a result of the sheer size and concentration of the population and the fact that persons are better cared for and can live longer. The unique, purely social/psychological manifestations of some psychiatric disorders may actually have earned them a separate, stigmatized identity and definition within the domain of sickness, illness, and disease*. However, this was certainly not the exclusive or even the dominant social response to such types of disorders.

Although data are lacking for many earlier civilizations and empires, it would appear that psychiatric disorders producing a sickness picture of madness and insanity (e.g., mood disorders, chronic psychoses, organic mental disorders) were given an identity as special sicknesses or diseases*. As currently interpreted in biomedicine, these pictures of sickness result from a small set of psychiatric disorders that are severe, chronic, and usually progressive. Psychiatric stigma pertaining to this subset of disorders was and is a palpable reality in many civilizations and empires (see Fabrega 1990a, 1991a, 1991b). However, what today are termed psychiatric disorders encompass much more than varieties of madness and insanity. They include very diverse emotional, behavioral, and somatic symptoms that are persistent and that wax and wane in relation to social and political hardships. All of these latter varieties of our contemporary nonpsychotic mental disorders were incorporated in the pool of general sicknesses, illnesses, and diseases* of empires and civilizations.

In summary, it is when psychiatric disorders result in senseless, bizarre, and violent behavior or social marginality and dependence that they tend to become marked in special ways (stigmatized). However, for psychiatric disorders of lesser severity and more varied manifestations (e.g., those now termed depression, anxiety, somatization) this was not the case.

In general, a mixture of stigmatization and medicalization is the typical social outcome of psychiatric disorders, something allowed by their protean character: They do produce more or less unique social/psychological and behavioral symptoms along with social incapacity and eccentricity but also, it must be emphasized, a range of primary neurovegetative reactions that express as bodily symptoms of considerable complexity and ambiguity (Fabrega 1989c, 1990b). Furthermore, given the nature of stress, disability, impairment, and associated problems of sickness, many "secondary" bodily ailments accompany "primary" psychiatric disorders, and vice versa. More or less well defined specialists in the healing of psychiatric disorders probably first evolved in (some) empires and civilizations, although the care of the mentally ill has always been a prominent feature of all societies, except possibly during the early medieval era in European societies (Fabrega 1990a, 1991a, 1991b).

The social problems posed by the interrelations among some chronic mental illnesses, poverty, and disability due to disease and handicaps in general all must be held to be prominent features of civilizations and empires (Mollat 1986). The prevalence and concentration of these general medical sicknesses can be assumed to have had a significant effect on general attitudes and values, social policy, political theory, and religious ideology as well as on purely sickness/healing concerns. An exposition of the cultural, social, economic, religious, and intellectual repercussions of this medical/psychiatric dimension of sickness and healing constitutes a separate story; only a few themes are emphasized in what follows.

Reaffirmation of Somatization as an Idiom of Sickness.   Descriptions of healers pertaining to some civilizations and empires emphasize their selflessness, tolerance, charity, and caring (e.g., Dols 1984a, 1984b; Kakar 1982; Kutumbiah 1969; Unschuld 1979). While these orientations and dispositions are often emphasized for contrasts with the contemporary scene in medicine and need to be judged positively and as reflecting natural altruistic human tendencies, they also have their disadvantages and costs since they may help to reinforce and validate different features of conditions of sickness. In particular, they can accentuate the dependency, passivity, and psychological demoralization that accompanies not only disease and injury but also conditions of social marginality, exploitation, and stress. To the extent that healers are caring, nurturing, supportive, and permissive they can thus contribute (consciously or unconsciously) to the prolongation of sickness of all types and create conditions for the medicalization of a variety of problems that in societies where life is more onerous, demanding, and circumscribed ecologically and economically would be less likely to be validated as sickness.

I would posit that the moral economy of sickness and healing in civilizations and empires was not entirely influenced positively and constructively by the humanitarian, benevolent, and univalently caring demeanor of healers. More specifically, I would contend that the prevailing social conditions pertaining to sickness and healing may have had the effect of influencing the way the manifestations and idioms of sickness came to be shaped and valued as social phenomena.

Attention was already given to the increased role that interpersonal and psychosocial conflicts played in the construction of sickness generally, including, in particular, the human misery and agony that can result from sheer social oppression and exploitation devolving from differences in economic and social power. These are social conditions of civilizations and empires that cannot but have profoundly affected the moral economy of sickness and healing. A more effective medicalization of the distress and suffering produced by such warped social conditions is made possible by a heightening of the importance of textual knowledge of sickness and disease* and of understandings of somatic complaints, more generally. This is so because a cultural effect of such medical texts can be not only a more "scientific" academic orientation but also the promulgation, popularization, and standardization of models for sickness.

All of the preceding must be regarded as a feature of civilizations and empires that reinforced how an individual's basic capacity or trait for medicine (i.e., the SH adaptation) came to be produced (i.e., the SH response). In this context, the way the social environment manages to shape social adaptation, sickness, and suffering/distress more generally needs to be taken into consideration and appreciated.

To elaborate on this point, one can return to the concept of somatization, which, as described in previous chapters, refers to the use of somatic idiom of sickness. I would contend that it constitutes a "natural," basic idiom for the expression, interpretation, and monitoring of the course of sickness and healing. Today, many social scientists and clinicians extend this term so as to refer to a distinct species of medicalization. In other words, "somatization" is all too frequently used to refer not just to somatic presentations of sickness but rather to denote (wrongly, it must be emphasized) medically suspect, if not specious, "psychiatric" exaggerations of bodily aspects of medical, social, and psychological problems. I would contend that this particular category of sickness may have been partially created by the distinctive social medical environment of civilizations and empires.

The high visibility and social importance of sickness and healing, a result of epidemiology and the commercialization of medicine, operated to constrain and shape the effects of the "medical collision" that took place in these societies: The political economy of oppression and the social psychological strains on adaptation met head on with the holistic, psychosomatic, and sociosomatic unity of the biological apparatus that human evolution had created. A prominent result was scenarios of sickness and healing with bodily manifestations reinforced.

The more general point is that the phenomenology of sickness, suffering, and social distress is shaped and configured by the inputs provided by the social and cultural environment. More specifically, given the social medical ecology of civilizations and empires, there developed a tendency toward distinctive sickness pictures with distinctive social valuations. The consequence of specialization among healers, the availability of elaborated ethnopathologies using symbols pertaining to bodily processes and mechanisms, and the commercialization and monetarization of medical healing was that suffering, distress, and sickness came to be manifest in scenarios that contained prominent bodily manifestations, the somatization or somatoform disorders mentioned earlier. Stated baldly, distinctive social environmental inputs gave a distinctive cast to the way the SH adaptation was expressed in relation to perturbations of social and psychological systems as well as to those of the physiologic/immunologic/metabolic systems. This development affected how sickness and healing scenarios came to be valued and estimated as social states from a moral standpoint. To elaborate on the implications of this theme, I need to introduce a separate but related feature of sickness and healing that came into prominence in civilizations and empires (and which was not prominent, not tolerated, or simply not possible given living conditions in less evolved societies).

Possible Stigmatization of the Psychological Components of Sickness.   The prominent, "natural" use of somatization as an idiom of distress and the increasing prevalence of somatization or somatoform disorders as distinct species of sickness had a correlated feature. In these societies, chronic social psychological symptoms manifesting in behavioral dilapidations and deterioration of morale and social competence punctuated scenarios of sickness generally, and insanity and madness specifically. This created conditions that devalued what one may describe as the "mental illness" component of general medical sickness pictures.

I would posit that holistically complex and chronic sickness pictures consisting of somatic and social psychological and behavioral symptoms devolving from social oppression and marginality provided conditions for possible stigmatization of "nonsomatic" symptoms of sickness. The latter types of manifestations were more easily equated with frank mental illnesses (i.e., psychoses) that were clearly stigmatized (Fabrega 1990a, 1991a, 1991b). The social, cultural, and psychophysiologic push toward somatic emphases on sickness resulted from the specter of social marginality (with the inevitable recourse to begging, ostracism, banishment, or frank incarceration) associated with purely "mental" disabilities as well as complex somatic pictures of sickness. In short, social conditions and cultural values in civilizations and empires came together to expand the domain of sickness and healing in complex ways affecting not only the moral valuation of the medical but also its phenomenology.

Cultural Shaping of the Phenomenology of Sickness and Healing. As discussed in chapter 2, evolution promoted a unified, holistic way of coping with stress and environmental insults, with serious, visible symptoms authenticating sickness. This biologic imperative produces a psychosomatic and somatopsychic amalgam, or behavioral template, for the manifestations of sickness. The seemingly "natural" configuration of how the SH adaptation is realized was described in chapter 2. However, for the reasons emphasized in several of the preceding sections, one may posit that a new emphasis on the meanings of the manifestations of sickness and healing was set in motion in civilizations and empires. These meanings may have operated to differentiate types of manifestations, creating special types of disorders (somatization or somatoform), favoring an idiom of somatization, and disfavoring psychologization (Fabrega 1990b; Kirmayer 1984) and also, in some instances, medical politicization (Kleinman 1986).

In summary, a tendency to value the somatic as compared to the psychological component of sickness may have achieved greater emphasis and prominence in civilizations and empires. This was a consequence of negative valuations acquired by the social psychological and behavioral symptoms of sickness now termed psychiatric disorder, by general social and cultural influences on medicine, and by the social impotence of politically exploited individuals and groups. Stated more baldly, idioms of distress and suffering that emphasize the body and its dysfunctions are easier to formulate and "safer" to express than are idioms that underscore political oppression and social exploitation.

It is of course in modern European societies, where mental illness and the psychiatric acquire a prominent social stigma, that one observes a clear overvaluation (and social authentication) of somatic manifestations of sickness as compared to psychological manifestations (and the somatization and somatoform disorders). It is in such types of societies that the intellectual consequences of dualism and the sociological effects associated with the movement toward the asylum operate as important factors shaping sickness and healing. Nevertheless, I am proposing that some of these same tendencies were manifest in earlier civilizations and empires, societies that shared many structural features with modern, contemporary ones.

Dialectical Influences Affecting Culture, Society, and Medicine. An additional but related consequence of the social and cultural ecology of sickness and healing can be entertained, and it underscores the complex interactions that exist among society, culture, and medicine. I have suggested that textual medical knowledge shaped manifestations of sickness and, of course, the conduct of healing. Conversely, the social and psychological components of sickness and healing, posited as a property of the cultural ecology of stress and adaptation of these societies, came to characterize the way knowledge of disease* was represented theoretically.

One notes that many symptoms of mental illness are represented in the knowledge structures of the great traditions of medicine of civilizations and empires. Visceral/somatic and the purely psychological manifestations of psychiatric disorders (such as those now termed schizophrenia, depression, anxiety, dementia, epilepsy, and the like) are all intermingled in descriptions of disease*. This reflects two factors: the holistic, integrated nature of how the human material is constructed and breaks down as a consequence of all forms of stress, and the absence of a strong dualistic tradition (especially in ancient China and India, but even to some extent in Hellenistic medicine). This intermingling of the somatic and the psychological in medical theories can also be judged as constituting a clue about how the social and cultural environment shaped sickness and how it was played out and evaluated as a social phenomenon, specifically, in scenarios that contained mental symptoms as well as bodily ones. Undoubtedly, medical/social/cultural influences together contributed importantly to how pictures of stress, suffering, and chronic sickness were constructed and played out, with a heightening and valuing of all manifestations in the prevailing explanatory models represented in the great traditions of medicine.

In summary, bodily manifestations of social stress and political economic oppression (in marginalized impoverished groups) figure importantly in the social construction of sickness and healing generally but especially in more complex, evolved societies. In concert with considerations elaborated earlier pertaining to social psychological and psychiatric considerations, including a tendency to overuse and overvalue a somatic idiom, one can anticipate a sheer concentration in the population of persons with complex profiles of sickness. All of this enhanced the holistic and multicausal epistemology of disease* that evolved to cope with the high burden of sickness in empires and civilizations. Thus, in these societies, a biocultural factor, the "natural" mix of sickness manifestations, came to be reflected in the epistemology of the prevailing tradition. Although I have emphasized purely intrinsic, social structural and evolutionary factors in the production of medical knowledge structures and social scenarios of sickness and healing, it cannot be doubted that diffusion of information and knowledge pertaining to medicine across civilizations also constituted a factor in promoting more or less similar, elaborate, holistic conceptualizations of disease* and approaches to sickness and healing.

Dynamics of Medical Practice.   An increased social/psychological and behavioral emphasis in the pictures of sickness and healing would also have figured more importantly in the dynamics of what earlier was termed "clinical medicine" and its underlying explanatory bases. Multicausality, comprehensiveness, and holism (psychosomatic and somatopsychic unity) would have been strongly emphasized by healers in their efforts to treat extended conditions of sickness. Social psychological and behavioral/somatic influences were strongly shaped into scenarios of sickness and healing through the "chemistry" of the maturing "doctor-patient" relationship that must be judged as an important feature of medicine during this stage of social evolution. Moreover, factors promoting a holistic emphasis would also have added to the theoretically integrated (psychosomatic and somatopsychic unified) structure of medical knowledge; and vice versa. Finally, the increased load and visibility of "mental symptoms" linked to the importance of interpersonal factors and the high prevalence of psychiatric disorders would have also accentuated the purely psychological component of healing.

In summary, changes in the political economy of healing, the increased role played by interpersonal conflicts, and the high prevalence and visibility of psychiatric disorders, along with related problems of medical dependence and disability in the pool of sicknesses of civilizations and empires, may have had complex influences (1) on the way sickness was played out and the sick role used (in some ways accentuating and in others curbing its excesses), (2) on the actual content of sickness material that merited authentic exculpation through recourse to the role of sickness (accentuating somatization as "valid" because of stigma linked to social marginality and purely social psychological symptoms easily equatable with madness and insanity), (3) on the character of theoretical knowledge (promoting multicausality and holistic interpretations), and (4) on the actual conduct of healing (by emphasizing psychological and emotional needs of the sick).

General Comment.   A complex picture of sickness and healing is found in civilizations and empires. First, persons and populations are vulnerable to experiencing greater amounts of disease, a function of poor nutritional quality, of possibly increased life span among some, of their susceptibility to more infections spread directly by contact and by fecal-oral routes of transmission, and of the apparent increase in chronic diseases. Second, what one can term a social industry of medicine appears to evolve in response to the greater load of sickness made possible by demography, social organization, and the different bioecologic picture of disease. Third, increasing sedentarization, urbanization, and the prominence of practitioners of many varieties made possible by occupational differentiation as well as by ethnic and social diversity of the population contribute a complexly colored supply component to both the sickness and the healing side of the medical equation. There simply are more and varied practitioners who are accessible to the highly diversified populations, and many of these practitioners adopt a more mechanical, practical, systematic, and commercialized perspective on the practice of healing as well as a spiritual or magical orientation, which clearly continues to exist in these societies. Fourth, the expansion and systematization of medical knowledge, the nature of its semantics and epistemology, and the great influence that it exerts on conceptual and social aspects of health and well-being means that sickness will tend to be played out more prominently in response to social and interpersonal tensions and crises as well as political economic oppression. The theories invoke multicausality, which prominently includes social, psychological, and environmental factors. Comprehensive and competing perspectives on sickness evolve, some of which are systematized in texts, which spread to encompass programs of prevention and health promotion. Opportunities for individuals and families to exploit the sick role are enhanced. Fifth, psychiatric disorders become more prevalent and the character of the sickness pictures they produce leads to the evolution of special institutions and, possibly, special emphases to the way all sicknesses are conceptualized and played out behaviorally and dealt with by healers. Finally, bioecologic factors, the nature of medical knowledge, and economic contingencies of healing create a culture and society in which sickness and the medical are more prominent and important in influencing social life and governing the way many different institutions of society operate and function. The latter characteristic has both positive and negative (maladaptational) repercussions: it could enhance positive influences toward healing and health but promote opportunities for exploitation of sickness on the part of persons in compromised medical and social circumstances, and could lead to exploitation on the part of healers.

Sickness and Healing in Modern European Societies

The way sickness and healing are played out in these types of societies constitutes part of everyone's understanding today of "the medical." The societies embody the kinds of social, political economic, and scientific developments that evolved in Western Europe beginning perhaps during the late eighteenth century, continuing especially in the nineteenth century and early twentieth century. The characteristics of these societies affecting epidemiologic profiles, scientific/epistemologic approaches to medicine, and general social cultural emphases are too complex and also well known to require an extensive review here (see Golub 1994 for a recent excellent account), and I will concentrate on selected issues that relate to my specific concerns.

One can say in the way of a brief résumé that salient developments include the epidemiologic and demographic transitions, massive urbanization with its attendant problems, the social effects of liberalism as a political philosophy, the growth of capitalist industrialization, the imposition of compulsory education, increasing secularization, and the development of modern Western biological sciences.

The rise of biomedicine to eminence is associated with a change in the concept of disease. In European societies, throughout the classical, medieval, and early modern periods, sickness was conceptualized as special to the individual considered as a unique whole person. The comprehensive (Euro-Mediterranean, largely Galenic) theory of disease* that prevailed incorporated characteristics of the person's age, sex, social position, and habitual lifestyle as well as (ethno)physiology in explaining a sickness picture. Such a *functional theory of disease** is a hallmark of medical traditions described earlier as associated with empires and civilizations and is found not only in Europe but in India, China, and Islam; the latter, of course, was very much influenced by the Galenic theory.

The new *ontological theory of disease* that came to constitute the hallmark of biomedicine described entities that showed common features regardless of the person's unique characteristics; entities that were believed to have specific causes, manifestations, and courses. The immediate consequences of this approach to disease have received a great deal of attention from comparative and historically oriented epidemiologists. Whether a growth in medical knowledge per se as compared to associated social transformations affecting living conditions, diet, hygiene, sanitation, and general approaches to health (e.g., involving exposure to fresh air and sunlight, exercise, home accommodations) were instrumental in diminishing the levels of mortality and morbidity and contributing to the demographic transition in Western societies is controversial (Golub 1994; McKeown 1988). Nevertheless, that the early modern Anglo-European ontological approach to disease* was fundamental to the eventual development of biomedicine and to its impact on society both epidemiologically and culturally cannot be disputed.

Examined from the standpoint of social evolution, this ontologic emphasis drew on lay, folk, and professional conceptualizations of sickness. Culture-bound concepts about local medical syndromes (i.e., more or less peculiar to Anglo-European societies) that had led to sickness and disease* descriptions became academic, scholarly, scientific, and clinical disease objects as a result of complex sociologic, scientific, and technological developments in the societies in question. These developments were, on the one hand, political economic in nature, and, on the other, involved in the growth of science, public health, scientific medicine, and hospitals. In the process, of course, the changes pertaining to conceptualizations of sickness and healing were *universalized*; that is to say, sickness and healing came to be viewed as entailing natural objects and natural processes and acquired a panhuman relevance.

Viewed from a cultural standpoint, the growth of biomedicine involves a blend between the local cultural approach to sickness of a small array of (Anglo-European) societies and the associated "scientific revolution" in biology that took place in those societies. The stability and success of this amalgam was dependent on the encouragement, support, and outright sponsorship of the state and hence is necessarily linked to distinctive historical and political economic factors.

The growth of biomedicine to a position of cultural hegemony is a consequence of changes in the structure of work of medical subcultures that themselves were yoked to changes in the political economy of the societies in question. These social and cultural changes are integral to the growth of scientific knowledge and to its eventual acceptance and promotion as social policy. They include dialectical changes that span strictly medical/clinical approaches to patients and structural changes in the societies involving the growth of mercantilism, industrial capitalism, and social/philanthropic policies pertaining to the sicknesses of the poor. These changes varied depending on the historical traditions of the European societies, particularly Italy, England, Germany, and France. The changes in question involved epistemological perspectives; approaches to the care of sick persons made necessary by social and political transformations in societies that had led to crowded living arrangements, poverty, and increased morbidity particularly in association with new epidemics; increasing awareness of the causes of these diseases clarified by the developing cultural outlook about sickness; the growth of the modern hospital as a setting in which to treat and observe sickness pictures; and the consolidation of groups of physicians into corporate, professional bodies empowered by the state to deal with sickness problems and meet educational needs for new physicians. These changes are staple themes in the social history of Western medicine and cannot be further elaborated here.

The growth of the biomedical sciences has profoundly affected how sickness was conceptualized and healing carried out. Although the initial effect of biomedicine on the prevalence of disease and general health of the population is a contested matter, it is certainly the case that many acute and chronic infections and a range of bodily ailments have been controlled and in some instances eliminated. The control of infection and the advent of anesthesia had a pronounced effect on the success of surgery and the evolution of the modern hospital, which in many respects is equated with the success and power of biomedicine. Besides the strictly clinical consequences, refinements of surgery laid the groundwork for a more physicalized conception of the self, which has had an enormous impact in the postmodern era (see below). Many other medical and social developments complementary to the technology of surgery have played important roles in diminishing the prevalence of sickness by altering the bioecology of disease and its effects and contributing to altered conceptions of personhood, sickness, and healing.

Biomedical explanations of causes of sickness and rationales of healing have radically altered the logic of explanation in the culture of medicine. This was illustrated above in the discussion pertaining to the ontological theory of disease, which rendered sickness problems the expression of disease considered as a natural object with its own natural history. In medical explanations, the germ theory with its closed systems, unicausal approach to explanation initially dominated but came to be supplemented by the open systems, multicausal emphasis. With the idea of specific cause came the idea of specific treatment, which materialized healing and raised expectations of cure by means of "magic bullets." With multicausality the treatment of sickness and disease was shown to constitute a complex undertaking and, hence, problematized.

Medicine emerges as a dominant profession accorded enormous social prestige. In the modern era, physicians acquired considerable social power and the medical establishment became a corporate organization of arrogated authority that in the postmodern era (see below) has been challenged and chastened. The development of medical colleges and schools and the role of the state in supporting medical education and certifying biomedicine as the official language of medicine are also distinguishing properties. There clearly emerge new ideas about causation, anatomy, physiology, pathology, pharmacology, and the basic clinical sciences of medicine and surgery. There emerge also many types of professional, biomedically oriented specialists who exercise a great deal of influence in the culture, one example of which is the widespread medicalization as played out in the welfare state. The growth of psychiatry and the blurring of mental illness with social deviance is an example of this, although that physicians play an important role in sanctioning sick behavior in many sectors of life is common knowledge.

In summary, in the modern period sickness and healing are marked by the establishment of the cultural hegemony of biomedicine. Several components of this transformation need to be distinguished: (1) the medical enterprise became highly secularized, essentially cut off from religious themes, spiritual considerations, and cosmological assumptions; (2) the preceding was accomplished through a revolution in scientific knowledge about disease, immunology, anesthesia, surgery, and pharmacopedics which promoted a biological reductionism and during its early phase, at least, reliance on a unicausal closed model of disease; (3) emblematic of the special power and regimented culture of biomedicine was the hospital, which became a center of healing and research, with resources and technical means of curing and controlling disease and prolonging life; (4) the categories used to explain sickness, despite their cultural roots in Anglo-European societies, became universalized (i.e., the corresponding diseases came to be seen as pancultural and panhistorical, applicable to and similarly structured in all peoples); (5) the medical marketplace came to be sharply partitioned and formally divided into orthodox (biomedically trained) physicians and unorthodox practitioners, providers of "alternative medicine"; (6) the profession of (orthodox) physicians became unified and organized, its educational requirements and forms of practice regularized and standardized, and its code of healing formalized and legally enforced (e.g., licensing stipulations, examination requirements); (7) many classes of practitioners and specialists were created, and these differed as to training requirements, prestige, status, and economic success. The proliferation of medical specialties reflects and accentuates the parceling and objectification of the body that came to characterize social thinking about sickness and healing. Finally, (8) integral to this process of medical specialization was the growth of the discipline of psychiatry and the increasing importance given to mental illness in the society and in conceptions of social disability, welfare, and crime. These developments, integral to social aspects of medicine during the modern era, constitute a separate story about the evolution of medicine.

The cultural hegemony of biomedicine thus entails three factors, the first a strictly medical/clinical one, which involved the refinement in the scientific basis of medicine, the second a professional one that involved the gaining of a monopoly over orthodox modes of healing, and the third an administrative one in that government-backed legislation promoted and sponsored the preceding two aspects of the modernization of medicine.

In many ways, these developments increased the power of specialist healers as compared to sick persons: what sickness should consist of was stipulated in technical, authoritarian, and expert terms. Healing outside of establishment medicine was suspect, unorthodox, "alternative," and neither condoned nor supported by economic grants or subsidies. With respect to the behaviors of sickness and healing, impersonality, objectivity, rationality, and technical scientific conventions came to characterize the medical explanatory model. How healers behaved and the way sick persons were expected to behave were stipulated by this "model" of the "doctor-patient relationship." In these societies, physicians as experts on the body set the tone and momentum of clinical practice. In other words, they became the dominant agents of medical dialogues.

Sickness/healing in smaller-scale societies was either an egalitarian, family/group-centered enterprise or an enterprise wherein a person or family sought specialist help from a selected member of the group who was connected socially and culturally to the world of the participants. The content of the dialogues and narratives exchanged in sickness/healing interactions contained material of vital concern, interest, and relevance to all participants and was imbued with emotional, spiritual, moral, and religious significance as well as with medical relevance. All of this changed dramatically in the modern period with physician experts dominating and setting the model of how sickness manifested and what it signified. To be sure, some (less striking) elements of social/emotional distance, authority, expertness, and ethnophysiologic emphasis on disease* matters were features of sickness and healing as configured and played out in civilizations and empires; however, in these latter societies patients still shaped transactions. This is not the case in the modern era (Cook 1994; Jewson 1974).

Sickness and Healing in Postmodern Societies

Configurations of sickness and healing in contemporary European and Anglo-American societies are held to constitute an additional stage in the cultural evolution of medicine. It can be conceptualized as reactive to the modern and transitional to a future stage that cannot be fully visualized as yet.

Postmodern societies are characterized by the advanced forms of capitalist and socialist industrialization, with all of its attendant sociological and political economic transformations. Changes in approaches to sickness and healing are difficult to spot because much of the "modern" orientation remains influential and also, obviously, because one lacks the advantages of hindsight. However, distinctive features of the way sickness, illness, and disease are conceptualized and healing carried out today have led many to describe a postmodern phase of medicine.

One dominant factor is the subtle way in which the medical has insinuated itself into almost every facet of contemporary life, thought, and behavior. The high prevalence of chronic diseases, an obsessive preoccupation with health and fitness, and the paradox of a "healthy but sicker" society are part of the postmodern configuration of sickness and healing. The limitations of biomedical reductionism are being appreciated (and widely publicized) and the ethical dilemmas that it raises problematize the meanings of sickness and healing and the purposes of the medical enterprise. At the same time, the sheer momentum of the machinery and technology of biomedicine continues to debilitate and undermine cultural emphases and related humanistic concerns pertaining to human suffering. One consequence of this is an apparent accentuation of interest and pursuit of alternative, unorthodox, Eastern, and holistic healing practices.

Only a few of the many changes that have taken place need to be fully discussed. One can include the following as relevant characteristics: the escalating cost of medicine, pervasive medicalization, increasing abilities to diagnose and control disease and prolong life, the construction of many diseased persons who, when properly "managed," are minimally sick (e.g., those with diabetes, hypertension, cancers in remission), and the advent of transplantation surgery with its promises of increased longevity and physicalization of self, as well as the cosmetic uses of surgery that further illustrate how healing has come to promote aspects of self far removed from standard meanings of sickness. More basically, a commercialization of health, the body, and private bodily functions has become prevalent.

The machinery and functioning of the body are visibly portrayed or narrated in constant bombardments carried in the communications media aimed at informing and persuading. Bioethical concerns concerning the beginnings and ends of life have surfaced in a prominent way, rendering decisions about how technologies derived from healing should be applied in medical contexts that do not conform to the usual idioms of sickness, distress, and suffering.

All of these sociomedical changes have profoundly affected conceptualizations pertaining to the person, health, the body and its functions, disease, death, and the purposes of medicine. The impact of the communications industry has produced widespread knowledge pertaining to health and disease, and state regulation of medicine and health has heightened this. There has developed increasing personal responsibility for one's health. Concerns about well-being, sickness, and disease are pervasive in society. Third-party payment schemes have blunted a transactional element of healing relationships. Social and political changes and an increasing commercial and commodified orientation generally influence what "consumers" expect and demand of healers, and this is reflected in a narrow, narcissistic view of what medical practice should entail with a consequent proliferation of medical malpractice claims. The vulnerability of physicians to malpractice suits has affected relations of healing, producing greater caution and thoroughness, often complemented by the temptation and potential of healers to exploit sickness and healing. Medicine has emerged as the dominant institution of society and concerns about disease eradication and new approaches to the modification of life support systems have created an almost technical, mechanical, and impersonal approach to sickness and dying.

A number of perspectives on sickness and healing differ when compared to modern societies. Whereas health meant the absence or negation of disease, it now constitutes a positively "worked for" or achieved state. Similarly, whereas disease was a denied possibility, it is now a heightened eventuality and sickness a realized preoccupation. A passive, victimlike orientation to disease has shifted toward an active, somewhat illusory mastery of disease through prevention and healthy lifestyles. Yet, paradoxically, there exists the awareness that chronic diseases are not preventable and sickness symptoms are inevitable. A sense of somatic vulnerability and heightened body function/symptom awareness (if not preoccupation) accompanies the active pursuit of health and fitness.

Consumerism in medicine has prompted patient activism and independence from practitioners via a resort to new diets, vitamins, and health remedies obtained from any number of mail order companies and life extension programs. Health consciousness and fear of sickness is of course a universal phenomenon, but that it has been socially dealt with in different ways is clear. As societies have increased in size, differentiation, and urbanization, exploitation of the fear of disease and injury has become a veritable industry. This was observed in civilizations and empires and modern societies. The new twist on this in the postmodern phase is distrust of physicians, the medical establishment, and the agencies of the state that sanction biomedical rationales and practices. All of this reflects the heightened awareness in the population of disease, loss of biologic functions with age, the inevitability and fear of death, the impotency of physicians to prevent this, and the setting of increasing limits of what establishment medicine will condone and validate. Biomedical practitioners and their agents are seen less and less as authoritative, faultless, and well intentioned. In some population segments, a demand is evident for an expanded physician role to include termination of prolonged suffering, leading to a modification of their traditional role. The economic remuneration of specialists and an awareness of their contribution to the cost of medicine is promoting increased state interference in the control of undergraduate and graduate medical education. The structure of medical practice is changing as a result, and solo practitioners give way to managed care among health care conglomerates. Sickness and health have become, if not system/organ concerns, at least highly individualized features of civil obligation and responsibility; conversely, healing and healers are now amalgamated and united in group structures and subject to an increasing political economic regulation by agents of political and economic institutions. In short, pervasive contradictions and complexities regarding health status, perceived health, prevalence of symptoms, and motivations for healing have replaced the older, modern health versus disease orientation. Issues pertaining to psychiatric disorders are discussed in later chapters.

I would judge the increasing regulation of medical practice by administrative state agencies and third-party private corporations as a dominant feature of the ethos of the postmodern phase of the cultural evolution of medicine. The "doctor-patient relationship" and the "science of clinical medicine" are no longer dominated by healers and their specialist/expert knowledge structures and supporting paraphernalia and procedures as in the modern era and, indeed, as in ancient civilizations and empires. More and more, purely political economic directives emanating from other sectors of society shape and condition sickness and healing. The content and processual unfolding of sickness/healing are now forced to accommodate, reflect, and sometimes conform to rules and regulations that often bear little relation to disease and injury but more relation to political economic exigencies. This and related aspects of sickness and healing in postmodern societies are discussed in more detail in later chapters.

5

Culture, Drugs, and Disorders of Habituation

The purpose of this chapter is to present a frame of reference for conceptualizing how drugs are used and the functions they play in human societies. The chapter reviews and integrates literature from anthropology, evolutionary psychology, and the history of medicine pertaining to drugs and rationales for their use. The unique properties of Western biomedicine considered as a cultural system and the meaning of its concept of habit are given special consideration. The chapter seeks to clarify the relationship that exists between drugs, culture, and biology and the role played by the concept of habit in this relationship.

A drug is defined as a chemical substance that is taken to prevent or cure disease or to otherwise enhance physical or mental welfare. The definition implies a *cultural rationale*. The purpose for taking the substance is crucial in the definition, and this clearly means intentionality and embraces cultural considerations about the procurement, preparation, ingestion, and mode of action of the "drug." In addition, since the user wants to enhance his or her welfare, culturally specific ideas about the self, well-being, and illness are also implied. These generalizations apply to all societies regardless of what drugs are prevalent and regardless of their conceptions of illness.

In Western contemporary societies the abuse of drugs, whether these be prescribed or nonprescribed, constitutes an important cause of medical disorders. What in effect one may view as *social adaptations,* namely, evolved cultural rationales and products related to sickness and healing and the enhancement of health, more generally, have become *social maladaptations,* cultural traits that contribute to problems in adjustment and morbidity. The problems resulting from abuse of drugs are commonly thought of as *disorders of habituation.*

The formulation of drug-related disorders as stemming from undesirable habits constitutes a special feature of the contemporary, biomedical epistemology pertaining to sickness and healing. It is made possible because of the integral relationship that exists in this epistemology between concepts pertaining to persons, behavior, physiology, pharmacology, and drugs. This formulation of sickness and healing is to be contrasted with related approaches in societies not governed by this type of epistemology. It is evident that peoples of all societies use "drugs" for medicinal purposes and to enhance well-being and personal experience, more generally. Foraging behavior may be viewed as a biological trait of the human species, and this has always entailed the use of plants as foods and as medicines. Hence it is reasonable to inquire about the distribution of "disorders of habituation" in different societies and to attempt some formulation of the phenomenon in question in the event significant variation in prevalence is found.

A Comparative Approach to Drugs

Ethnobotanists, cell biologists, and ethologists have studied the use of plant materials having medicinal properties in any number of animal species (Clayton and Wolfe 1993). Johns (1990) has provided a general formulation of the relations between animal adaptations and chemical ecology, which involves the study of the flow of energy and chemicals between different trophic levels (e.g., plants, herbivores, carnivores, parasites). His conceptualization of the role of plants in an organism's adaptational economy is pertinent: "It is difficult to distinguish a pharmacological from a nutritional adaptation in most studies of animal behavior" (Johns 1990: 253). The term "pharmacophagous" has been used with respect to insects if they search and use secondary plant substances for purposes other than primary metabolism. The possible use of plants among vertebrates for "self-medication" was proposed by D. H. Janzen (1978). Pharmacognosy refers to the scientific study of the interaction of chemicals and plant substances consumed by organisms, and Eloy Rodriguez (1993) has proposed the term "zoopharmacognosy" to describe the process by which animals in the wild use specific plants for the treatment and prevention of disease.

In chapter 2, I reviewed briefly observations that have been made of higher primates, in particular chimpanzees, that have suggested that some ill members appeared to make special use of certain plants during early phases of illness (Hart 1990; Huffman and Seifu 1989; Wrangham and Goodall 1987; Wrangham and Nishida 1983). The plants were known to have pharmacologic properties that could be said to have improved the condition of the organism. The fact that chimpanzees carefully ingest leaves without apparent mastication is significant since this may allow certain chemicals with medicinal properties to exert their effects. These observations of close relatives of man who are held to show awareness of self and to possess the rudiments of a theory of mind raise the question of a possible chimpanzee "awareness" of illness, of the environment as a resource for healing, and of a "native pharmacopoeia." As I elaborated in chapter 2, the observations suggest that among the many psychological adaptations that natural selection has sculpted into the higher primates and man, one involves the capacity to recognize a condition of sickness and as a consequence search the environment to acquire knowledge about the beneficial effects of naturally occurring botanical specimens.

Culture is generally thought of as a system of symbols and their meanings that is internalized by members of a social group (D'Andrade 1984; Geertz 1973). In contrast to phylogenetically inherited information in the genome, culture constitutes a body of more recently acquired, socially transmitted information that accounts for distinctive senses of self and distinctive world pictures. Enculturation starts very early and includes learning distinctive ways of construing the world, of responding to the physical and social environment, of feeling, and of behaving. Cognition and emotion generally and perceptions of bodily changes more specifically are standard topics in the study of cultural differences (Fabrega 1974; Lutz 1988a).

Ethnopsychology and ethnophysiology refer to the ways in which the culture of a group influences conceptualizations of the self and of the body, respectively. The terms thus imply that culture influences mental and bodily experiences. Ethnopsychopharmacologists more explicitly aim to elucidate the role of cultural factors in patients' responses to psychotropic medication (Lin, Poland, and Lau 1988; Lin, Poland, and Smith 1991; Mendoza, Smith, and Poland 1991). The role of culture in response to drugs is actively being researched. In a number of studies differences in the pharmacokinetic and, in some instances, pharmacodynamic responses of blacks, Asians, and Caucasians have been recorded (Lin, Poland, and Lau 1988; Lin, Poland, and Smith 1991; Strickland, Ranganath, and Lin 1991).

Group differences in pharmacokinetic responses to a drug result from differences in diet or in other kinds of organic substances (medicinal or otherwise) that a group routinely ingests. These effects would influence the way a drug is absorbed, broken down metabolically, and carried in the blood. The result would be mathematical differences in the way the drug is handled by the body, and by implication, differences in the effects of the drugs. Group differences in pharmacodynamic responses, by contrast, can be regarded as a more direct and "stronger" effect of culture. In this instance, the kind of effect that the drug has on the nervous system or the body more generally is called into question. Effects on the target cell (receptor density, transmitter binding capacity, reuptake patterns) and on associated cerebral or peripheral autonomic structures are implicated. Culture can be expected to affect the general stress level of a group; the intrinsic, baseline of nervous system functioning; and the way the body and brain are coordinated physiologically and endocrinologically.

One can regard culture (in the strict, informational sense) as a form of cognitive/emotional indoctrination that in programming an individual's orientations and expectations of necessity also programs his or her nervous system, endocrine systems, and various organ systems (Damasio 1994; Fabrega 1979c, 1981a, 1989a, 1989b, 1989c). The overall result is that a cultural orientation influences the effects that any drug has on behavior. A variety of "cultural" effects have been noted in studies aimed at elucidating the effects of marihuana on behavior (Jones, Benowitz, and Bachman 1976). Subjective "mental" effects of this drug clearly differed depending on the prior cultural experiences of the subjects studied, whereas more objective measures (i.e., changes in pulse rate, salivary flow) did not.

The following factors seem relevant in any consideration of "drug effects" (i.e., special use of substances for medicinal properties) in relation to culture. (1) Ideas pertaining to drugs, including what "drugs" are for, how they are to be prepared and ingested, what they owe their properties to, and how they bring about their effects. This implicates the so-called placebo effect, since folk attributions and expectations about drugs influence their eventual effects. (2) Ideas pertaining to the way the body is constituted and operates, including what the body is made of and how ingested substances allegedly produce their effects. (3) Ideas pertaining to the way the mind and the self are constituted and function, including factors held to govern how bodily experience and awareness comes about and what it means (Damasio 1994). (4) Ideas pertaining to the worldly and otherworldly domains, since drugs can alter an individual's perception of the world and the sense of what is real, imaginary, good, and desirable as opposed to bad and undesirable.

The Relationship of Drugs to Sickness and Healing

A society's pool of information about sickness and healing includes an elaborate pharmacopoeia of herbs and special combinations of them that one can term drugs, given the definition proposed earlier (Fabrega 1974; Johns 1990). In contemporary preindustrial societies, it is very difficult to study the medical conditions for which these drugs are used as well as their effects. First, one must establish that a common body of knowledge underlies the use of drugs and that they are specifically used for clearly identified conditions or purposes. Furthermore, since members of these societies in the third world have easy access to Western pharmaceutical products, one must determine not only what effects the native plant or drug has from a pharmacologic standpoint but also rule out whether any other (Western) drug that may have been used in conjunction with the herb accounts for any effects noted. The study of the efficacy of native folk pharmacopoeias in contemporary preindustrial societies has proven to constitute a complex undertaking because of the difficulty of controlling for these factors (Fabrega and Silver 1973; Johns 1990).

The history of medicine teaches that in earlier periods of Western history botanical specimens and preparations were often used prudently (Garrison 1929). Many of our contemporary drugs are a product of the folk wisdom of earlier Western peoples (see Johns 1990 for a review). What one can term the validity of a native people's folk pharmacopoeia can be assessed from two points of view. First, the pharmacologic effects of a native drug, as prepared and used by a people, are compared to the effects stipulated in the native theory. Here one is interested in determining whether the ethnophysiologic rationale for the drug (i.e., the effect sought) is validated given its known scientific pharmacologic effects. Second, the pharmacologic effects of the native drug is matched with respect to the known, physiologic problem for which it was used, the latter being determined by Western biomedicine. In this instance, one hopes to find out whether the native drug was pharmacologically effective given our (scientific) understanding of the medical problem for which it was used.

Both forms of what can be termed pharmacologic validity have been confirmed for a number of botanical specimens used by the Aztecs (Ortiz de Montellano 1990). Native Aztecans used drugs for distinctive effects in ways that parallel what they themselves thought about their drugs and their conditions and also for conditions for which contemporary medical scientists say their drugs would have been effective. Empirical studies of Johns (1990) among the Aymara of South America and his general review of recent studies of this topic are consistent with a general formulation about the adaptive use of various plants among indigenous peoples of the world. This line of inquiry supports the idea that systems of medicine are universal and incorporate the use of many botanical substances, that groups acquire accurate knowledge of what effects botanical specimens produce, and that there is a universal science of pharmacology and psychopharmacology insofar as the target medical conditions and the herbs used to treat them all conformed to central nervous system processes in ways that were predictable by modern science.

The practitioners of native folk medical systems often use psychoactive substances in the process of healing (Brown 1972; Dobkin de Rios and Winkelman 1989; Schleiffer 1973; Wright 1989). The effects of hallucinations and altered states of consciousness are actively sought and used. (This touches on the question of whether such "drugs" produce "habituation disorders," a topic that will be taken up below.) The experiences are part of the native practice of medicine. These practices are said to allow healers a richer, more elaborate way of communicating with the spiritual, otherworldly domain where healing is supposed to originate; moreover, the psychoactive substances are frequently given to persons who are sick and are used for recreational purposes as well.

Whereas the use of such plant substances has generally been attributed to their mental, stimulant effects, Eloy Rodriguez and Jan Clymer Cavin (1982) have suggested that the indole or isoquinoline alkaloids that are found in hallucinogenic plants might have instead been selected by Amazonian peoples for their antiparasitic properties. This possibility is highly consistent with the formulations of Johns (1990) about the connection between nutrition, herbal practices, and the origins of medicine as a cultural institution. With respect to the line of argument pursued here, Rodriguez and Clymer Cavin's hypothesis underscores the complex interplay between intentions, drug use, drug effects, social practices, and the adaptive significance of "habits." In terms of a scientific epistemology, native peoples might be said to show "habits" of recreational plant use that are pharmacologically effective, reflecting a biological adaptation, but that do not conform to native, cultural understandings (i.e., the "ethnopharmacopoeia").

The Ritual Use of Drugs for Culturally Prescribed Occasions

There exists a large literature pertaining to the use of psychoactive substances (Furst 1972; Harner 1973; LaBarre 1969; Weil 1972) among native indigenous people of preindustrial societies. The Yanomamo of Brazil (Chagnon, LeQuesne, and Cook 1971), as an example, have access to a number of hallucinogens and use them for a variety of social reasons, including leisure, medicinally, and as magical aphrodisiacs. In adult males, the typical users of these drugs, pleasure and excitement combine with active, purposeful elicitation of spirits for purposes of enhancing health and social success in mate selection, warfare, alliances, and the like. The drugs merely afford a means of communicating effectively with spiritual agents that determine (in the Yanomamo worldview) how reality is played out. Teenagers merely seeking pleasure are sometimes found among users, although many of them are in shamanic training. In general, although psychoactive substances are readily available in the habitat of the Yanomamo, the "supply" never exhausting itself, they are not used to excess or in a way that compromises subsistence pursuits such as hunting, gardening, and foraging as well as defense of territory and intravillage activities. This bears on the point made earlier about the possible medically adaptive use of such substances. Rodriguez and Clymer Cavin (1982) suggest, as an example, that features of the mental experiences produced by psychoactive substances among Amazonian indigenous peoples might actually be used as effective dose markers of antiparasitic alkaloids.

Robert C. Bailey (1991) has documented that among the Efe Pygmies of the Ituri Forest in Zaire, cannabis use is extensive and has created a dependence among many group members. Although no interference in social functioning was associated with cannabis use, smokers were significantly more likely to be poor. However, the Efe acquire their "drugs" from nearby agricultural groups as a result of trading. Bailey's monograph suggests that cannabis use is primarily recreational and does not constitute a feature of the physical habitat of the Efe to which their culture had been adapted to traditionally.

In summary, it would appear that in isolated, "pristine" small-scale societies, the availability of psychoactive substances does not result in abuse or in the associated social psychological disturbances found in contemporary industrial societies. As already indicated, the actual "function" or purpose served by such substances is complex and difficult to establish. In this context, one can define abuse as the use of a drug for purely recreational or hedonistic pleasure at the cost of associated neglect of basic subsistence activities and social obligations resulting from the effects of the drug or dependence on it. In other words, the use of the substance becomes so frequent and compelling that the individual seeks its effects for enjoyment, for stimulation, or to ward off any withdrawal effects. In the process, the organism suffers an interference in behavior that is socially dysfunctional and maladaptive.

The lack of indicators signaling "drug abuse" among smaller-scale isolated preindustrial people, what implies a regulated use of these substances, is explained in terms of biocultural adaptation. Culturally prescribed rituals underlie and monitor the use of the substances. In restricting the use of these "dangerous" substances to specific social occasions, often ritually sanctioned (healing rituals, spiritual pursuits, celebration of group achievements, etc.), and in ingesting them in prescribed ways (in combination with other substances and in specially prepared ways), the users seem to be spared the pernicious effects observed in complex modern societies.

An excellent illustration of how culture and society interact to shape behavior in relation to drug use in adolescents is provided by a study by Charles Grob and Marlene Dobkin de Rios (1992). They analyzed adolescent hallucinogenic plant ingestion during initiation rituals among Australian Aboriginal males, Tshogana Tsonga females of Mozambique, and Chumash youth of southern California. In these "tribal" societies, a "psychotechnology" was said to operate to manage successful transitions into adulthood. An institution explicit in its directives manages the transition of adolescents into adulthood by creating altered states of consciousness that promote a kind of death of childhood and a rebirth as an adult. This is accomplished through initiation rituals that elders supervise and monitor and in which plant hallucinogens are used to attain visionary quests. By instructing youth on the consequences of hallucinogenic plant ingestion, the elders are able to induce expectations and in carrying out sometimes painful mutilatory practices they facilitate receptivity in the adolescents. The sacred character of the plants, the honored status accorded the rituals, and the socially valued transition into an adult status that is strongly sought and cherished imbue the whole experience with cultural significance and meaning. The absence of abuse of these substances in tribal societies is emphasized: "Such drugs have been accepted to be of sacred origin and have been treated with awe and reverence. In tribal societies, plant hallucinogens were in limited supply and protected from abuse and profanation by deviants insofar as they remained under adult control and administration" (p. 133). "Thus, psychoactive substances in tribal societies were not abused, but perceived as sacraments facilitating controlled entry into valuable states of consciousness in which 'visions' essential for the continued existence of the society could be assessed" (p. 134).

An integral part of the analysis undertaken by Grob and Dobkin de Rios is to compare the above institution regarding adolescent transition and initiation with happenings in contemporary Western societies. They emphasize the absence of meaning pertaining to transitions taking place in contemporary society during adolescence: "Contemporary society no longer possesses viable, pre-established paths to initiation. The tribal process of initiation culminates as rebirth into a new life, endowed with special qualities and new meaning. The coming of age in non-state level tribal societies was a solemn rite of passage with the initiates consecrated into adulthood. In the absence of such initiations, we are left with widespread alienation and despair" (p. 135). An implication of the analysis is that the erosion of values and purposes in the minds of many contemporary adolescents, the absence of institutions concerned with promoting and managing a culturally meaningful transition into adulthood, and ready availability of drugs possessed of no sacred, socially celebratory functions are key factors that promote substance abuse, a prominent form of contemporary adolescent psychopathology.

The scenario of drug abuse in smaller-scale societies suggests that biology and culture interact to bring about a dynamic, informed, and prudent use of environmental plant and "drug" resources for purposes of nutrition, stimulation, leisure, and healing. A balance is established between internal biological systems and external social cultural systems, hence the term "biocultural adaptation." Evolutionarily selected and genetically transmitted information incorporated in cerebral processes and mechanisms that promote the search for environmental botanical agents is integrated with socially transmitted cultural information pertaining to ecology. The balance and integration in these two systems of information have as a consequence the regulated use of herbs or drugs for adaptive social and medicinal purposes. In contrast, what one observes in contemporary societies in the way of substance abuse reflects an imbalance between these various systems. No longer does culture as a system of symbols for promoting adaptation integrate constructively with biological systems to regulate and control behavior. Instead, the powerful pharmacologic effects of the drug now drive the physiology of the organism at a cost to its competence and that of the society.

Drug Use in an Evolutionary Context

The SH adaptation or trait (see chapter 2) that links sickness and healing ensures that plant specimens in the environment will be used adaptively and not be abused. In conjunction with an evolved cultural rationale of the group about drug lore, the adaptation functions to promote the medicinal and allied social uses of what in actuality are potentially abusing substances in the environment. The SH adaptation is targeted at the environment and although a product of natural selection, is geared to the enhancement of behaviors having a social and cultural rationale. The adaptation depends on internal (motivational) mechanisms, what in effect constitute lower-order adaptations. The latter would include such things as centers subserving taste, pain, fatigue, malaise, nausea, weakness/lassitude, and emotional regulation. Changes in the functioning of these brain centers no doubt activate a sickness/healing adaptation, mediate its physiology, and constitute its organic rationale (to be elaborated in subsequent chapters). The evolutionary basis of such an adaptation means that a determinate role is played by social/environmental cues: These activate the adaptation, engage its psychophysiology, and produce the relevant behaviors. The behaviors subserved by the sickness/healing adaptation are specific and circumscribed to the desired goals of alleviation of symptoms and enhancement of health and well-being.

It follows from the argument above (and discussed in chapter 2) that a changed social and cultural environment capable of locking into the psychophysiology of evolved mechanisms subserving sickness relief and enhancement of well-being can potentially undermine their adaptive functions. By providing access to refined and concentrated preparations of highly reinforcing substrates of naturally occurring substances, substances the physical apparatus has evolved to use adaptively, contemporary society provides the means for the production of psychological states that the apparatus has learned to value during the extended period of evolutionary adaptation. When to this capability is added (1) an erosion of the social and cultural rationales for the adaptive and regulated use of medicinal substances and (2) the substitution of a social and psychological malaise for bona fide medical malaise, conditions are created for (3) the widespread abuse of the substances in question.

In summary, what has been termed a sickness/healing adaptation designed for adaptive and regulated use of substances that can enhance health and well-being can prove maladaptive when activated by cultural environments that do not match conditions found during evolution. The result can lead to behaviors that pose an intellectual dilemma: How can activities seemingly natural and geared to the enhancement of well-being be explained and counteracted when they prove harmful and maladaptive? The concept of habit constitutes a social and cultural invention modern society has used to rationalize this dilemma.

On the Concept of Habit

In contemporary Western industrial societies, disorders stemming from the abuse of drugs like alcohol, cocaine, and nicotine loom as ever more important problems. These disorders are alike in that an individual's habits are said to play an important etiologic role. Moreover, they are difficult to treat and prevent. From a general evolutionary and anthropological standpoint, the use of a concept of habit to explain the cause of illness constitutes a relatively new and unusual category of explanation. To highlight this it will be desirable to compare cross-culturally kinds of explanations for illness. The idea that illness is caused by undesirable habits will be shown to be an integral part of the technology of biomedicine.

For purposes of discussion, the word "habit" will be defined as "a thing done often and hence, usually, done easily; practice: custom, an act that is acquired and has become automatic; hence a tendency to perform a certain action or behavior in a certain way." The word "habituation" signifies the process of bringing into a habit or of being habituated. Finally, the term "excess use" implies a practice that goes beyond the usual, reasonable, or legal limit. When given a medical interpretation, the above concepts mean that the actions facilitate or predispose to the development of a medical disorder. Implied then is a practice of an individual that is harmful in light of a particular theory of sickness, disease*, or medical system.

The history of the various meanings of the concept of habit and habituation are listed in table 2. The table reveals that in ancient Latin, "habit" first denoted physical aspects of appearance and bodily demeanor. Its mental application came later. These meanings were later incorporated into English. By the sixteenth century, the mental aspect of habit was in widespread use in England. In a general way, the use of "habit" with reference to medical themes was prevalent in England during the Renaissance. Its specific reference to addictive drugs seems to have been an American development. This meaning has been traced to the late nineteenth century, when the problems of drug abuse became a prominent public health concern. As will be emphasized, the shift in meaning of the concept of habit to drugs, and eventually to disorders of habituation, illustrates how social systems, in this instance, modern ones, cope with changes in the prevalence of social and medical problems by elaborating a conceptual and linguistic technology.

The general prevalence of the concept of habit among people of smaller-scale preindustrial non-Western societies is not generally known. From reading the literature in cultural anthropology, one gains the impression that in such societies, persons are identified by social categories and what they "do." Societies possess terms that are used to describe persons and their behavior (Lutz 1988b). Researchers have examined universals in concepts of interpersonal

Table 2.   Outline of History of Meanings of the Concept of Habit

---

A. Sense development in Latin

   1. Holding, having, as in the way one holds oneself; the mode or condition in which one is, exists, or exhibits oneself.

      a. Externally, such as demeanor, fashion of body, clothing.

      b. Internally, in mind, such as character, disposition, customary way of acting.

   2. Such meanings were largely completed in ancient Latin.

B. English-language usage involved borrowings from Latin without reference to their original order of development.

   1. Fashion or mode of apparel, dress.

   2. External deportment, constitution, or appearance; habitation.

   3. Mental constitution, disposition, custom.

      a. Way of mental or moral constitution; disposition, character.

      b. A settled disposition or tendency to act in a certain way, especially one acquired by frequent repetition of the same act until it becomes almost or quite involuntary; a settled practice, custom. This meaning was evident in the sixteenth century: "By long studies and great contemplation . . . got an habite and custom to be malancholike," Pettie; "How vse doth breed a habit in a man" (Shakespeare).

      c. Applied to the natural or instinctive practices characteristic of particular kinds of animals, and to natural tendencies of plant.

      d. The practice of taking addictive drugs. This sense appears to be an American development. The first use appears to be 1887. As quoted in *American Speech* 23, no. 246 (1948): 2: "May he continue to wage war against them (sc. Chinese opium dens) until the habit has been swept entirely out of existence." An interesting development is recorded in *Vocabulary of Criminal Slang* (1914): "Habit, current amongst dope fiends. Necessity for opiates; a craving; the condition produced by habitual indulgence in drugs."

      e. Habituation; the action of rendering or becoming habitual; formation of habit, especially the formation of such habits as dependence on drugs. An early medical use as quoted in the journal *Pharmacology and Experimental Therapeutics* (1929): "'Habituation' we interpret to mean a condition wherein one becomes accustomed to but not seriously dependent upon a drug. There is recorded 'the inherent difficulty in establishing a uniform cut-off point where"habituation" becomes "addiction."'"

---

behavior that point to its evaluation (desirable/good versus undesirable/bad) and to force of character (strong versus weak) (White 1985). With respect to the question of behavioral dispositions, such groups have concepts for persons who follow norms and those who don't, and means of dealing with each. Although all people have a vocabulary of personalities (a lay personality trait psychology of sorts), it does not appear to be the case that the concept of habit serves as a common device for explaining what people do. There is no "mental trait" standing between the individual and his or her behavior like our "habits," nor are persons individuated by having various types of "habits" that serve to differentiate and qualify their behavior.

A distinctive (Western) personality theory would seem to underlie the development of the concept of habit: Persons harbor internal entities that govern what they do, and these consist, among other things, of habits. The concept of habit is thus a "social invention" that provides for a means of enriching and diversifying explanations of behavior and an individual's identity. In non-Western societies social structures are often relatively homogeneous and less complex. Moreover, in them, the family, the group, and the community are important pillars of identity and social action. The idea of habit appears not to be necessary to help explain human action. All people are locked into one reality that claims total participation of the whole individual. One can also say that in such societies basic cultural directives have not dictated an emphasis on personal separateness and autonomy. Anthropologists have discussed this in terms of individualistic concepts of personhood, the modern Western case, as compared to more sociocentric concepts, found in non-Western societies (Shweder 1991). This line of reasoning suggests that a distinctive culture as a system of symbols and meanings is what constructs persons as atomized units and ascribes to them individualistic traits like habits to account for discrete types of behaviors.

Both the Chinese and Ayurvedic traditions of medicine, which claimed the allegiance of large civilizations, enjoined dietary prescriptions and made use of an elaborate pharmacopoeia. Since causes of illness included improper regimes of diet and exercise, it might be claimed that at least a concept of harmful medical substances was invoked. However, such a concept, although implicit, did not conform to the modern Western concept of habit. The explanatory systems of the "great" non-Western traditions of medicine were not secular but sacred. The traditions were framed in terms of holistic, cosmological, and moral/religious precepts. Broad programs of living, spirituality, and health promotion were invoked in the tradition, not discrete habits pertaining to drugs and to specific illnesses. Thus an individual's general way of conducting his or her life was brought into question and regulated by the medical tradition. A one-to-one relation between a drug and an illness linked in terms of a mental trait (i.e., habit) did not figure importantly in the medical tradition. Moreover, principles governing use of medicinal drugs were implemented in terms of social practices that incorporated rituals with moral and sacred overtones. Given all of these considerations pertaining to civilizations as compared to small-scale societies, it would appear that the level of complexity of a society is not what creates conditions for the idea of habits to gain prominence; rather, it may be that a culturally distinctive *dualistic* frame of reference is required in order for such a concept to develop.

The Semantics of Medically Relevant Habits

In pointing to behavioral uniformities of a person, habits allow one to partially explain behavior. The explanation that results, however, is vacuous or tautological: Individual *A* behaved that way because he has a habit and one knows he possesses a habit because he behaved that way. Habits also provide one with a means of approving or disapproving of another's (good or bad) actions without necessarily also qualifying the total worth of the person. One can qualify from an evaluative standpoint what an individual does without necessarily condemning their moral worth by indicating they acted "out of habit." This is not easily accomplished in societies that have not invented the concept of habit. The concept of possession, that supernatural spirits caused an undesirable action, is one way around this conundrum of rationalizing an individual's improper behaviors without fully condemning and discrediting them.

The idea of habit thus has an interesting relation to central Western tenets about human psychology. On the one hand, it can be used so as to blunt free will: An individual "acting out of habit" has had his individuality and will neutralized and may, in fact, be held less accountable for his actions. On the other hand, the fact that one has acquired "bad habits" implies one has some responsibility for or role in actions influenced by them and an obligation to "control the habit." The ways in which the idea of habits is used, then, reflects conflicts in how human behavior is rationalized: Are persons truly rational, purposeful, and hence responsible, or are there factors that can override these mental faculties? Dilemmas posed by the Cartesian view of man are thus mirrored in how we use the idea of habit, and these do not arise in simpler, homogenous societies wherein dualism and rampant individualism are not found.

Negative consequences of a person's action pointedly raise the question of motives and challenge a social unit to take action: Why do people do what they do, and what should be done to people who do harm? The preceding discussion has indicated that in preindustrial societies, to explain and deal with persons who are harmful to others (e.g., bad, deviant) the concept of habit is not used, nor is it needed. Ethnopsychological theories and interpersonal descriptors provide a means for understanding socially unwanted actions and social sanctions can be brought to bear on the person. Furthermore, supernatural punishments in response to wrongdoing always render illness a possibility.

In modern Western societies the need to explain harm to self alone may have been a factor that encouraged the medical application of the concept of habit. In other words, since individuals in such societies tend to be viewed as individuated, responsible, purposeful, rational, and inwardly motivated, one is forced to explain their apparent irrationality. The positing of bad "habits" serves to sociolinguistically neutralize or blunt the free and rationalistic will of a person while serving to explain the patent irrationality that leads to self-destructiveness. On the other hand, in settings in which people are viewed as embodiments of outside agencies and easily subject to their control and in which illness rests on sanctified premises and moral imperatives, habits appear redundant. These agencies and the social transgressions or the sinfulness of the person (and not his or her habits) can be held responsible for mysterious maladies.

Disorders of Habituation

Earlier it was mentioned that in small-scale, preindustrial, non-Western societies many substances and activities whose "habitual" abuse would be injurious appear to be held in check (i.e., are diminished in frequency and intensity) by the stipulation that special (ritual, sacred) situations prescribe or sanction them and by the fact that such substances may be serving biological functions that may or may not be appreciated by the people (Johns 1990). In the logic of the argument of this chapter, the society's social guidelines as well as its (sanctified) theory of illness and of behavior generally appear to "protect" against the potential injuriousness of such substances and activities without there necessarily existing an explicit awareness that this is being accomplished (Rappaport 1979). Many other social practices of a people can be singled out which undeniably are "prudent" since they promote and maintain "health," yet the practices may not necessarily reflect a conscious design. In this sense, cultures, which include a people's theory of illness, are like evolved designs for living that are adaptive. This, of course, raises the whole question of how culture is to be understood and the functions that it serves (see Tooby and Cosmides 1992).

An important reason why there exist few of the problems of "bad habits" that one finds in complex societies is that the facilitating, if not the necessary, conditions for them are lacking. Such people do not have the means of technology or the accumulation of resources that allows the production of substances that in concentrated form can be "habituating" or that can be nutritionally injurious. Moreover, lifestyles (e.g., involving diet and physical activity) are such that they do not easily allow "unhealthful habits" to emerge. The relative absence of problems such as obesity, arteriosclerosis, and hypertension as well as "drug abuse" among simpler people underscores the potential harmfulness associated with modernization (Cohen 1989; Eaton, Shostak, and Konner 1988). Using knowledge derived from the social epidemiology of chronic disease in modern societies, one can say that among people of simpler societies, the social system seems to insulate and protect the individual's own psychobiologic systems; in other words, the former's control mechanisms and outputs (in the form of products of technology) pose fewer hazards to the individual.

The preceding issues suggest that the way in which psychobiologic systems function and the way in which they can break down are both conditioned by the way the larger social system is structured and functions. One may hypothesize that the process of evolution yields something like an equilibrium between these two types of systems, an equilibrium that protects the individual and neutralizes the potential noxiousness that society and his or her own behavior can produce. The evolutionarily sculpted "way of life" of family group foragers, mirrored as it is in a distinctive theory of illness and behavior, may partly reflect such an "adaptive" equilibrium. In this light, contemporary changes in lifestyles and in conceptions of persons, and the availability of substances that can be abused, may be seen as results of modernization that pose a new set of hazards to man. The medical problems that have developed reflect a breakdown in the balance between the individual and society. It is as though the social system's link into the individual's systems has become less stable and balanced, and a deregulation has occurred.

Viewed in another light, one can say that the process of cultural evolution has produced scientific, technological developments as well as human behavioral variations that alter the context of natural selection and in this sense can directly affect the process of biologic evolution. As a result of these developments, the social system is forced to develop a way of prudently bringing about a better regulation. Ideas such as habits, lifestyle, the will, and volition—symbolic inventions that are integral to the whole process of Western modernization and to biomedicine—are used so that they can bring about a control of behaviors that can be biologically harmful to the individual.

Comment

The concept of habit as it relates to drugs plays a strategic role in biomedical theory and in contemporary medical policy. However, it also poses special problems both to individuals and to social planners. On the one hand, the concept of habit rationalizes the incongruity that willful actions can be medically harmful, although appeal to the concept is only partially successful in promoting healthful behaviors. On the other hand, the technical language of habits in relation to drugs may shift emphasis onto the individual, but exigencies of treatment raise questions about the institutional control of behavior.

That disorders of habituation are socially stigmatizing further heightens the tension generated by their designation as "medical." One of the social consequences of using a biomedical language is that in speaking of sickness (a social construction of "dis-ease") using a technical idiom one neutralizes the religious and moral implications that sickness/healing has had in earlier epochs. The medicalization of disorders of habituation is obviously only partially successful. It generates special social and psychological problems since disease terminologies now become means of labeling, generalizing about, and depersonalizing individuals.

Nonliterate, small-scale, and contemporary societies are each plagued by a distinctive set of medical problems that their cultural ecology conditions (Barkow, Cosmides, and Tooby 1992; Lee and DeVore 1968). Each type of society also develops a distinctive theory about body states, illness, and drugs that grows out of its cultural ecology context. The maintenance of health and adaptation is an implicit axiom of all such theories. Smaller-scale societies do not have "disorders of habituation," nor do their theories of personhood and illness make use of mentalistic concepts like "habit" that blur the idea of responsibility and rationality. On the other hand, modern biomedical theory provides a view of bodily disorders and a capacity for dealing with them that was obviously not present in earlier historical epochs. Biomedical knowledge is used to develop a perspective on drugs and behavior through elaborations of the concept of habit in order to understand and alter lifestyles and "bad" habits that are created by modern society. An objective is to train and motivate individuals to handle their psychobiologic systems with the compellingness and prudence that natural selection has promoted in the maintenance of health. It requires, as it were, the programming of prudent and healthful behaviors to counteract behaviors and dispositions that society itself has made prevalent.

6

Somatopsychic Disorders in an Evolutionary Context

The previous chapters have outlined how problems of disease and injury are configured and played out in different social types. The material content of the medical, as conceptualized by physical anthropologists, historical epidemiologists, and paleopathologists, has been reviewed briefly for each type of society. It is out of this medical base that sickness and healing as social and cultural activities are fashioned. Salient characteristics of sickness and healing in each social type have been summarized. This has provided a way of conceptualizing how medical institutions related to sickness and healing vary in relation to structural and political economic properties of society. There is a large "ontological jump" from the material (organic/pathological) base of medicine to its social and cultural realization in symbols and practices as sickness and healing. This creates epistemological difficulties for one intending to formulate in an integrated way relations between biological and cultural aspects of medicine.

To better visualize how the medical base of a population gets shaped, labeled, and dealt with as social phenomena in relation to structural and political economic factors it will prove instructive to concentrate on a paradigmatic cluster of medical disorders that are clearly connected causally to social happenings and, in addition, have protean manifestations in behavior as well as psychophysiology. This is the case because such medical disorders, the manifestations of which affect different systems of the individual, provide opportunities for clearer formulations of how sickness and healing vary in relation to social factors. Problems of sickness manifested by prominent symptoms of anxiety, depression, (biomedically) unexplained pain, and other changes in body experience and function (the latter termed "somatoform") constitute important contemporary psychiatric disorders. Because the problems so classified are "mental illnesses" and reflect, show, and contribute to social psychological difficulties marks them culturally in special social ways in contemporary medical practice and society more generally. However, this cluster of medical problems also prominently affects general physiological function and can manifest through alterations in well-being, sleep, appetite, motivation, energy level, and body experience and function in many different systems. The problems are very common in psychiatric and general medical practice settings of contemporary Western European societies, and studies of anthropologists confirm that they also figure prominently in medical settings cross-culturally. Finally, the symptoms and problems of these disorders are well represented in the writings of practitioners and theorists of the great medical traditions of ancient India and China and the Western Mediterranean societies of the classical and medieval era. Because of their complex mixture of body and psychological manifestations, the disorders are referred to here as somatopsychic.

In summary, one can arguably maintain, given what is known about the biology of somatopsychic disorders, that they constitute human universals and would have figured importantly in the sickness and healing experiences of all peoples. Consequently, formulating however tentatively the way in which such psychiatric disorders were likely to have been fashioned, interpreted, and handled in different social types should provide a more concrete, integrated, and diachronic explanation of how sickness and healing have changed during cultural evolution.

Somatopsychic Disorders as Objects of Healing: General Considerations

Psychiatrists and general primary physicians eventually see most of the somatopsychic disorders in contemporary modern societies because of their somatic and psychopathologic manifestations, but many other persons in society are contacted for help as well. Special psychopharmacologic agents, special forms of professionally scripted psychotherapy, and special types of (corrective) social relationships or changes occurring naturally in the social system can attenuate, modify, and even terminate these disorders. Providing individuals with social support, positive ways of redefining themselves and their social world, and constructive strategies for coping with social/interpersonal and work-related hardships are generally instrumental in bringing about improvement. Equally—and in many instances more—important is the resort to special drugs that have the effect of restoring rhythms of sleep, activity, work, and pleasure; levels of energy, motivation, and interest; and capacity to experience pleasure. In the event that effective interventions, either of a social/psychological or pharmacological variety, do not occur, these disorders can take on a chronic course with increasing incapacitation. In the throes of a major depression, for example, a person can be driven to seek direct relief from symptoms (e.g., from doctors, religious personages, secular advisers), to undertake changes in their life (e.g., involving work, family, or group relations), withdraw from social relations, resign themselves to the inevitability of death, or show a complete dilapidation in their behavior. Even if interventions are available and forthcoming, suicide or forms of behavioral nihilism can result from a major depression.

To visualize major depression and other, related somatopsychic disorders in a culture and era different from the contemporary one it is important to keep in mind their salient properties and also the characteristics of the contemporary setting of medical practice. Viewed abstractly and generically, the manifestations of the disorders are a product of disturbances in the overall well-being of the person considered in a holistic, unitary way. Signs and symptoms are multifaceted and reflect disturbances in many systems (e.g., biochemical, physiological, psychological, behavioral). In a contemporary medical setting, general physical complaints will dominate, whereas in a psychiatric one, emotional, cognitive, and behavioral manifestations may occupy center stage. In either instance, a selection or shaping operates. In other words, negative reports pertaining to the person's well-being will be framed in terms of either body function and pain or psychological/behavioral disturbance, described in objective/mechanical terms. This idiom will constitute the person's "chief complaint" and description of the presenting illness. This is so because of the high medical awareness that exists in our society and because a dualistic, exclusionary idiom constitutes the acceptable way of formulating disability in our society and culture.

Another way of making this point is to say that in our society and culture medical practice tends more and more to be disease or illness centered. The rationale of a patient-physician encounter is to focus on these entities as ontological things manifesting in distinctive (i.e., bodily, mental/behavioral) ways (Temkin 1963). Alternatively, one can view this same characteristic of the way the patient-physician dialogue is formulated in terms of the idea of expertness: Physicians and psychiatrists are presumed experts in the machinery underlying the functioning of the body and mind/behavior, respectively, and it is disturbances in these narrow spheres that one is expected to volunteer (i.e., "present") and elaborate in an objective, deliberate, and mechanized way. The dominant influence of the idea of expertness and the correlated emphasis on illness manifestations account for the fact that in contemporary society physicians exert a determinate influence on doctor-patient dialogues (Jewson 1974).

In social settings not dominated by science but rather by different explanatory models of sickness (or idioms of distress) and where the comparable notion of medical expert does not exist, one can expect that disturbances in well-being will be formulated differently (Fabrega and Silver 1973; Farquhar 1992; Jewson 1974; Lewis 1975; Porter 1985; Trawick 1992). Dialogues between healers and patient will not be dominated by a dualistic reductionism, nor will the idea of expertness hold sway. Instead, patients are likely to exert greater control of dialogues and the course of medical treatment. Symbols, meanings, and details drawn from the culture will be used to describe and formulate a person's chief medical complaint. In a complementary way, the model of healer will play a determinate role in how a patient presents and elaborates his or her complaints just like the healer's queries will draw out salient characteristics that bear on his or her conceptualization of medical problems. From a cultural and comparative standpoint, one can say that sickness has little shape or content other than that provided by culturally specific models, although, to be sure, the realities of anatomy, physiology, and neurobiology will shape sickness pictures along specific neurological and anatomical configurations.

An argument can be made to the effect that in societies other than the European of the early modern and especially the modern era, sickness, illness, or what we term "disease" was not the center or focus of a medical dialogue. Instead, something like what we mean by general well-being and "healthy personhood" was the focus (Fabrega and Silver 1973; Harwood 1970; Leslie 1976; Lewis 1975; Ngubane 1977; Sivin 1987; Temkin 1963; Zimmermann 1982). Theories used to explain sickness were in reality theories that explicated how health and well-being *failed to be maintained*; in other words, the dominant concern of a practitioner or healer and patient was maintaining health viewed in a comprehensive frame of reference. What we term "sickness" or "illness" constituted unwanted departures from an individual's expected level of health/well-being brought about by poor regulation of one's life situation and habits. Virtually all aspects of a person's life determined level of health and well-being, and this was expressed in terms of a comprehensive theory or tradition of medicine. Complementarily, practitioners and healers operated as advisers and counselors who were concerned to evaluate an individual's conduct of life with respect to the maintenance of well-being.

This health-centered focus and adviser/counselor orientation has been powerfully demonstrated for European societies in which the Hippocratic/Galenic theory prevailed (Cook 1994; Sawyer 1986; Temkin 1963). The focus and orientation is highly consistent with what is known about other comprehensive medical traditions (e.g., Ayurvedic, Chinese, Meso-American) and can be supported with respect to nonliterate traditions studied by anthropologists, although in this instance the "theory" or tradition of medicine was not explicit and codified in any articulated sense (Fabrega 1974; Leslie 1976; Ortiz de Montellano 1990; Sivin 1987; Zimmermann 1982). As societies increase in social complexity one observes a diversification of approaches to health and the advent of what one can term more empirical approaches, and this, of course, becomes a striking aspect of medicine during the early modern European era. These points of contrast and change are taken up later in this chapter.

In summary, the somatopsychic disorders by definition share a general pathology that embraces different systems of the body and the person. Their manifestations are protean and allow culture wide latitude in conditioning how they are expressed and formulated. Moreover, the disorders readily suggest general impairments in well-being. These factors, together with the tendency for medical problems in traditional, preindustrial societies to be interpreted as departures from health rather than the result of specific disease entities requiring specific expertise, means that somatopsychic disorders are likely to readily conform to cultural models of sickness and disability. They thus constitute test cases for the comparative study of sickness and healing.

Some Heuristic Assumptions

The following assumption is relevant to the analysis pursued in this chapter: The prevalence of somatopsychic disorders such as depression in a society is not fully accounted for by a careful review of how it handles "mental illness" or medical problems more generally. In some respects, this assumption is trivial insofar as field studies in social epidemiology readily inform that many disorders go untreated by psychiatrists or even general physicians (Robins and Regier 1991). But it is another aspect of "untreated" that is of concern here. This has to do with the many ways in which society and culture can conceal and disguise what on strict clinical grounds one would diagnose today as major depression, a somatoform disorder, or mental illness more generally. (For a review of a theory about the psychiatric and the way in which it manifests and is handled in societies governed by different cultural conventions the reader is referred to Fabrega 1992a, 1992b, 1993a, 1993b.)

In a heuristic sense one may conceptualize at least three varieties of untreated somatopsychic disorders. A first variety is one that is merely neglected, namely, a constellation of manifest changes that are clearly recognized as burdensome and disabling, perhaps even as medically relevant, but that simply goes unattended by the relevant parties. A second variety is one that also conforms to external, professional criteria of such disorders but that in the society is handled as a general medical problem and never gets labeled as depression, somatoform disorder, or anxiety. A third variety of "untreated" disorder is one that in a society is defined in terms of conventions that render it not a medical problem of the self needing professional or lay/folk treatment but rather a social, legal, moral, or spiritual problem. These are behavioral disturbances or "afflictions" that the self and significant others (in a formulation made possible by culture) explain as relevant or appropriate to other spheres of social arbitration and resolution. In other words, the disturbances or afflictions are defined as special (in either a positive or a negative sense) manifestations of human conflicts or social perturbations and can propel actors to undertake changes in their life (e.g., religious conversion, divorce, resettlement, accusations of sorcery or witchcraft, etc.) that in no way incorporate the idea of sickness, much less "mental illness."

For discussion purposes one can also assume that the amount or level of somatopsychic disorders in societies of different scope, complexity, culture, and historicity does not vary greatly. What does vary is the way these are categorized in the society. In other words, societies have different ways in which problems thought of today as "major depression" or "somatoform" are interpreted, defined, explained, and even realized in the sense of their taking on a manifest appearance or content. Institutions other than the medical (which clearly constitutes a cultural and historical universal of human'societies) and the psychiatric (which is more recent and culture bound) must be regarded as addressing problems of living that in our contemporary secular and highly medicalized and *psychiatricized* society are labeled as major depressions or somatoform disorders. The assumption of a more or less similar level of these disorders (broadly conceived culturally) is presented heuristically. An obvious objection with respect to major depressions, for example, is the argument pertaining to the so-called secular trend in their incidence. Furthermore, as will be discussed subsequently, there are a host of reasons why societies vary in their rate of problems now termed depression (Giles et al. 1989; Hafner 1985; Kleinman 1986; Klerman 1985, 1988). As an example, the much-publicized secular trend of depression could well be the result of gene-environment interactions, with concomitant increases in "real pathologies," and not solely due to apparent increases in pathologies now accorded medical significance purely because of cultural changes pertaining to social outlook and medical/psychiatric awareness in the contemporary, postmodern situation. Alternatively, the relative absence of comforts of contemporary social life, the overcoming of many earthly challenges, the lessened importance of religious values, and the full flowering of political liberalism with an awareness of the intractability of social problems could be factors contributing to demoralization and "real," increased amounts of major depression and other, related somatopsychic disorders.

In light of the above argument and pursuant to the aim of this chapter, a series of questions naturally come to mind: What labels and meanings were attached to disorders here termed somatopsychic, such as depression, in other societies? How were such disorders handled? Where were they located; that is to say, which social institutions contained them? The latter question can be stated in a more elaborate way: What kinds of social pathways did somatopsychic disorders take, and in what sorts of social stations did they congregate in societies other than the modern Western European one? Other questions can be surmised, all of which would have in common the elaboration of cultural scenarios and scripts that clothed somatopsychic disorders in meanings, discourses, narratives, explanatory models, and interpersonal networks of societies that were governed by alternative cultures and characterized by different forms of social organization.

To properly answer these and related questions would require a review of material well beyond the scope of this chapter. For purposes of discussion one can simplify matters and concentrate on four varieties or types of societies conceptualized from a social and evolutionary frame of reference (Cohen 1989; Fabrega n.d.; Johnson and Earle 1991; McNeill 1976; Parsons 1966; Service 1975): (1) simple/egalitarian/mobile; (2) sedentary/agricultural/tribal; (3) state/ civilizational; and (4) early modern European. Later, I define these types of societies and discuss possible scenarios and scripts pertaining to the way somatopsychic disorders could have been and most likely were played out in them.

An important attribute of somatopsychic disorders is obviously their manifestation in body disturbances. Just like contemporary studies of medical practice draw attention to the ubiquity of emotional psychological problems in general primary care settings, largely a consequence of their neurovegetative and somatic manifestations, so in earlier epochs one must assume that the disorders discussed here had similar medical pathways in the social system. When one discusses disorders such as major depressions from a historical and cross-cultural standpoint, then, one must focus attention not only on the domain of the social psychological and behavioral (reflecting the contemporary version, dominated by emotional and associated cognitive changes) but also (and perhaps more important) on the general, "primary medical care" aspects. The contemporary assumption that a somatopsychic disorder like major depression, somatoform, or anxiety is "psychiatric" and predominantly emotional and behavioral in character needs to be seen as essentially ethnocentric and a product of recent history. It is the somatic manifestations of these and related disorders, and their connectedness to a variety of other problems giving rise to somatic symptoms, that require emphasis.

Somatopsychic Disorders in Simple
Egalitarian Mobile Societies

Given what is known today about the incidence of disorders such as anxiety, somatoform disorder, and major depression, it is likely that during the time span of a particular family-level society or of any individual's life, few such disorders would have been encountered. A population of fifty to one hundred individuals simply does not create a high enough incidence to have rendered such disorders socially problematic. Furthermore, the lifetime of individuals in these societies is comparatively short, with few living well into adult years when a disorder like major depression peaks in prevalence. (The incidence of major depression is generally assumed to be affected by historical factors. What its exact incidence might have been in other types of societies cannot be determined, of course, but the question is being pursued here for illustrative purposes.) Individuals who survived to older ages, if infirm, weak, or unproductive, would have been socially discarded. This also obtains in the case of younger group members whose level of energy and well-being fails to meet the rigorous standards of the group. If vulnerability to somatopsychic disorders is a trait that is behaviorally recognizable very early in life, then some social selection against them might have resulted from the infanticide that small elementary societies are known to practice.

All of this means that a strong motivation to be socially productive and engage in prosocial behavior would have operated to promote social responsibility and, together with this, social organization. Moreover, given the highly integrated character of social life, sustained by a pervasive spiritualization and ritualization of the natural and social world, not to say its strong, mutually supportive familial basis, an occurrence of what today one could term, for example, a major depression was probably not a very likely eventuation in family-level societies. The social support and cohesion that serves to protect against or undo such a disorder (in contemporary society, to be sure) is available as a matter of course; indeed, a social environment "protective" of major depressions and related somatopsychic disorders that result from purely social psychological stressors can be said to be defining of the hunter-gatherer way of life. This is not to say that such stressors producing similar disorders did not exist but merely that they were probably not common because of the high interpersonal connectedness and group pressure toward performance with consequent social support.

As discussed in other chapters, in simple/egalitarian societies one finds an integrated view of social life that incorporates morality, religion, and human conduct more generally. The possibility of sickness and overt responses to its occurrence are framed in a manner that takes into account physical, mental, spiritual, and social well-being. Sickness is very often taken to signify moral and social failures as well as deficiencies or disturbances of the physical apparatus. The causes of sickness dictate healing activities that are geared to the restoration of personal morale, self-worth, and social status as well as to the curing of dangerous symptoms—all, of course, framed conceptually in terms of symbols and meanings having enormous impact on the individual's psychobiology.

Those somatopsychic disorders that did occur more likely than not would have been given general medical significance because of their accompanying prominent somatic manifestations. As emphasized earlier, formal processes of healing in family-level societies can be described as crisis oriented: They appear to come into play when individuals are seriously compromised physically, and they are time bound. By this is meant that healing gatherings (and possible simple "ceremonies") appear geared to negotiate the possible loss and grieving that often results or the full recovery that can come from "successful" cures following the mobilization of healing efforts. The latter are not protracted and diversified, nor do they entail elaborate social inquiries that include the "patient" in the event he or she is critically ill or defined as such by the community. It is generally reported that (mainly, acute) infectious diseases form a dominant part of the medical picture in these societies and this accounts for the "crisis approach" to sickness and healing. It is in terms of this framework that disorders such as depression or somatoform illness would have been interpreted and handled.

A prominent feature of medical care in family-level societies is the short-term mobilization of social support and offerings of care and resources to the afflicted and their families. Healing thus has an enormous sociopsychological impact on the person and involves replacing many of the losses and deprivations that are known to cause somatopsychic disorders, especially major depression. While the significance of this holistic approach to sickness for an understanding of major depressions and related disorders may not be as apparent in simple/egalitarian societies because of the sheer pressures of subsistence, it becomes so in societies that are larger, sedentary, and more complex.

A social theory of psychiatric phenomena consists of general definitions and propositions that explain how psychiatric disorders are distributed and handled in different types of societies (Fabrega 1992a, 1993a, 1993b). It should be evident that were one to develop a social theory about somatopsychic disorders like major depression, the hypothetical scenario of their occurrence and manifestations in family-level societies would loom important. This is the case not only because of the centrality of this form of social organization in human evolution but also because the genetic basis for these disorders would have to be explained in terms of its biologic significance to individuals of such groups. Primate models of disorders like depression and studies of the neuroendocrine and behavioral consequences of separation and loss underscore the biological rootedness of human responses to social and psychological stress. The kinds of losses and stresses found in the higher primates are common in hunter-gatherer groups and suggests that problems interpretable as somatopsychic loomed important. But so, one can contend, did naturally evolved models of holistic healing aimed at restoring social supports and new attachments in the group.

The incidence of somatopsychic disorders like major depression in contemporary populations seems too high to be accounted for simply by random mutations. Instead, it would appear that some value attaches to this genetic predisposition. Thus an important question becomes: What selected for the genetic basis of disorders such as major depression? Does the human genome acquire "advantages" as a result of incorporating a diathesis that predisposes to major depression? Of what might these advantages consist?

Somatopsychic Disorders in Sedentary/Agricultural Societies

As discussed in earlier chapters, sedentary/agricultural tribal societies are composed of families, relatives, and (at their larger extremes) even members of distinctive clans or lineages. By their very nature, then, they contain rival factions that create opportunities for social antagonisms and jealousies. Whether the health status of members of agricultural societies can be characterized as "higher" or "better" is controversial; but that such societies contain a sizable number of individuals of late maturity seems true in general so that the age of maximum accumulated risk for somatopsychic disorders like major depression is commonly reached in the population. The increased life span of individuals means that more of these and related disorders are likely to have become prevalent. The greater size of the societies also means that a disorder like depression, with a lifetime prevalence of roughly four to eight per hundred, would acquire social prominence in the setting of larger settled societies. Thus it is very likely that what we term major depression, anxiety, and somatoform disorder begin to become socially more visible and common medical problems in societies placed in this category (and stage of social evolution).

These societies are also characterized by a great deal of social integration and support, with ritual, religion, and the morality of social life deeply imbuing a sense of purpose and meaning. Nevertheless, poverty and high mortality with its attendant losses are found. Interpersonal strife and its attendant feelings of social condemnation and isolation constitute real and not uncommon eventualities. Hence many of the social psychological factors that are believed to contribute to the outcome and persistence of somatopsychic disorders begin to become medically consequential at this level of social organization. Because social rivalries are more common and persistent in sedentary societies, opportunities are created for the playing out of these rivalries in the idioms of distress and affliction that reflect somatopsychic disorders.

All of this means that at this level of social organization and evolution somatopsychic and related disorders are afforded the opportunity to become social dramas that both constitute and allegorically symbolize the agonies of loss and separation as well as social frictions and antagonisms. This of course provides a way of dealing with disorders (such as major depressions) that are more likely to occur and persist in societies whose members experience social psychological stresses of different varieties. However, a different aspect of somatopsychic disorders needs emphasis. One can reformulate the property of social complexity by saying that conditions for the emergence of a *social role of sickness* become manifest in these types of societies and, as can well be appreciated, become an increasingly attractive option for individuals who for whatever reason are socially maladapted. Any individual experiencing a psychological or biological correlate of a (perceived or actual) loss, separation, or demoralization now has available a better articulated social role through the filling (or exploitation) of which he or she can obtain "secondary" gain in the way of support and compensation. This social option is also, of course, available to persons with symptoms traceable to intercurrent disease states of different types. As reviewed in earlier chapters, all such organismic perturbations can become enmeshed in or constituted by social rivalries and conflicts, and played out in sickness roles. In short, healing (i.e., rituals/divinings/ceremonies) becomes the occasion for the restoration of social support and consolidation of social worth as well as health, construed in a holistic sense. It is not unlikely that many such social exegeses of sickness and healing constitute local varieties of somatopsychic disorders and their therapeutics.

The fact that in sedentary/agricultural societies medicine begins to emerge as a more or less distinct institution with specialized healing roles and more elaborate knowledge structures pertaining to sickness means that the societies acquire social technologies for dealing with extended pictures of sickness that are not immediately life threatening. It is very likely that many such afflictions and their ritualized forms of care encompassed somatopsychic disorders. The medical theories or explanatory models of sickness address important symbols and meanings that promote or disturb social adaptation and psychobiologic well-being.

Finally, in this type of society, and for many of the reasons listed above, madness and insanity (traditional "mental illnesses" involving thought, feeling, and social behavior) become more common eventualities. A review of their manifestations and mode of healing in the medical anthropological literature suggests strongly that many episodes of general medical sickness and ceremonies of healing explained as local varieties of madness constitute ways in which psychotic and purely emotional/cognitive varieties of somatopsychic disorders manifest and are dealt with in the society (Fabrega 1974).

A social theory of somatopsychic disorders would seek to explain how the transformations that brought about this stage of cultural evolution affected their definition and social pathways. Notwithstanding the obvious increased incidence and prevalence of acute and chronic infectious diseases found in large, sedentary societies, it would appear that at this stage human psychosocial conflicts become more relevant to the eventuation of sickness. The conditions of social life render social conflicts and losses of all types more common and provide roles by means of which maladapted individuals can obtain support and validation, and the technology of healing favors protracted efforts aimed at restoring physical and interpersonal connectedness in the group. Societies and their populations become increasingly burdened by social and symbolic systems that while necessary for the articulation and organization of settled, congested life, begin to impinge on the maintenance of social status, social morality, and personal well-being. Conversely, societies begin to acquire medical technologies that are geared to cope with these psychosocial parameters—

clothed, of course, in the idioms and symbols that define personhood and explain human afflictions and distress. All of these factors contribute to a higher prevalence of somatopsychic disorders and render their manifestations and social pathways medically highly visible. The somatic dimension of somatopsychic disorders constitutes their most compelling social feature, although opportunities are also created for an elaboration of their social psychological manifestations.

Somatopsychic Disorders in States and Civilizations

In a strict sociological and anthropological sense, this category of social organization is, like the preceding one, a hybrid, and it is also used because it serves to efficiently incorporate important changes affecting sickness and healing and their possible implications for understanding major somatopsychic disorders. Important characteristics from a societal standpoint are the growth of state bureaucracy and regulation, larger size and concentration of populations, the growth of cities, mercantilism, and the availability in most instances of a well-articulated body of knowledge about religion and the natural world that, in the case of civilizations, is literate. It is debatable whether in these societies the health of the general population is "better" than in those described earlier. What is certain is that one finds social groupings based on level of economic resources and that in these groupings general health varies considerably. Wealthier segments enjoy much better health owing to improved living conditions, sanitation, greater availability of a stable food supply, and better nutrition. In these societies the existence of maritime trade means greater exposure to epidemic diseases (McNeill 1976). It also means that food luxuries in the way of condiments and stimulants of different types are available, along, of course, with imported objects of all sorts. While these are more likely to be found in the wealthier groups, many such items become incorporated in the living styles of city folk more generally. It is possible that the preparation and distribution of pharmacologically active substances capable of altering consciousness becomes more prominent in these types of society given their greater capacity for large-scale production and reliance on a money economy. To the extent that these substances begin to be seen and used strictly for pleasure as compared to occasions of ritual and religious celebration, a potential for abuse of substances is created. (Typically, disorders of abuse are not found in societies described earlier, which are in a "pristine" state; that is, unless they are exposed to modern complex civilizations.)

When compared to less complex societies, then, these show a greater economic stratification and occupational differentiation. Psychosocial burdens and problems of morale can be expected to also vary across groups and for a variety of reasons (e.g., devastation of war, inconstant food supply, unemployment, enforced marriage, increased social regulation). Since vulnerabilities to sickness vary in relation to biologic well-being and social/psychologic well-being, pictures of sickness will vary significantly across groupings but in general will be more prevalent in these societies. Similarly, attractions of a sick role and the ability to have that role supported and authenticated (and to exploit it) can be expected to vary considerably across social groups.

In addition to differences in socioeconomic standing, the populations of these societies are characterized by ethnic pluralism and religious diversity, which can further complexify and problematize social life and the maintenance of a sense of inner stability and authenticity. Religious and ethnic pluralism bring challenges to the established way of defining social and moral status. They also bring intergroup marriages and, more generally, set further conditions for social and moral conflict. That societies at this level of organization have elaborate religious systems means also that opportunities for conversion, pilgrimages, retreat to monasteries, and lives of devotional pursuits to the holy become available as options for those who are psychobiologically demoralized for whatever reason. The implication of all this for social pathways of what today are termed somatopsychic disorders and especially major depression can readily be appreciated. Stated succinctly, conditions are created for the higher incidence and persistence of these disorders and for them to be interpreted and played out as afflictions and sicknesses with widely differing social and psychological meanings.

Societies at this level of social organization show well-differentiated "systems" and "traditions" of medicine that of course are not easily separated from what one could term religion. In most instances, one finds an academic literate tradition (e.g., Ayurvedic in India, the Chinese, the Galenic in Europe, etc.) together with competing "lay" or "folk" traditions associated with other religious and ethnic groupings. Because of factors discussed earlier, chronic sickness pictures become more visible social properties of states and civilizations and there exist many different varieties of healers with beginnings of specialization on types of disorders and patients. The "practice" of medicine becomes increasingly secularized. Thus, although one continues to find spiritual and moral themes dominating responses to disease and recourse to healing, in states and civilizations the concrete manifestations of sickness become more relevant in the way medicine is conceptualized and in the way that diagnosis and treatment are carried out. Sickness pictures become codified in writing, and the comprehensiveness of these systems is underscored by the fact that it is possible to find in them descriptions that conform to our mental illnesses, including, in particular, disorders like the somatopsychic ones, or psychoses, or major depression as well as general medical disease entities.

An important feature of what have been termed the great traditions of medicine (e.g., Ayurvedic, Chinese, Galenic, medieval Islamic) is their holistic, comprehensive approach to health, sickness, and healing. As discussed earlier, the "wisdom" of these literate traditions is in seeing the maintenance of health and well-being (and by implication, sickness) in the light of an individual's psychological, social, physical, and moral circumstances. Healing has a rationale only in the light of the totality of an individual's social standing in his or her family and immediate group and takes into account physical activity, nutrition, social relations, and spiritual/moral strivings. Such a "theory" of health and well-being as well as sickness seems especially well geared to embrace the kinds of social deficiencies and strains that on the basis of contemporary psychiatric theory appear to play an important role in the incidence and natural history of somatopsychic disorders.

The holistic character of social adaptation and the connectedness between biologic systems that constitute health and sickness determine the way a picture of sickness is played out. This interconnectedness is apparent in the way that somatopsychic disturbances manifest today. Indeed, these disorders constitute paradigmatic examples of how genetic vulnerabilities combine with biological and social stressors to produce psychosomatic and somatopsychic (i.e., unitary) disturbances in adaptation. As reviewed in earlier chapters, one can assume that a breakdown in biologic unity as a result of stress has played a significant role in the development of the comprehensive approach to health, sickness, and healing found in all the great traditions of medicine. A psychosomatic and somatopsychic unity provides the backdrop for the way sicknesses unfold in social systems and has probably served as a model for the way they are explained and dealt with. Indeed, one can say that the necessary partitioning of the body, mind, and behavior undertaken by modern science and medicine led to the breaking apart of the unity of thinking about sickness and healing, that is, to the perceived connectedness between phenomena now classified separately as mental, physical, somatic, psychiatric, and the like. A consequence of this partitioning and reinterpretation of social adaptation, sickness, and healing was the invention of "mental illnesses" such as major depression, psychogenic pain syndromes, and somatoform disorders.

In summary, this type of social organization and level of cultural evolution is characterized by important properties that would become influential were one to develop a social theory of somatopsychic disorders such as major depression. These would include conditions for the higher incidence and persistence of chronic sicknesses and human suffering more generally among which one would have found varieties of these disorders.

Besides providing a rich setting for the realization of the somatic pathways of somatopsychic disorders, these types of societies also provide opportunities for the realization of some of their many nonmedical, psychosocial pathways. These would include, in addition to madness/insanity per se (a category that is better articulated and standardized, albeit often disvalued in these societies

[Fabrega 1990a, 1991a, 1991b]), such things as geographic migration, religious conversions, monastic careers, occupational change, and marginal social positions (e.g., vagrant, vagabond witch, beggar, criminal). It is very likely that persons suffering from somatopsychic disorders such as major depression would have chosen or been shunted into roles and careers such as those that are special to states and civilizations. Moreover, the availability of stimulants, intoxicants, and substances that enhance psychological well-being means that demoralized and depressed individuals would have been able to avail themselves of diverse ways of self-treatment with obvious complications.

Somatopsychic Disorders in Early Modern European Societies

The categories of societies described earlier constituted ideal types conceptualized in an evolutionary frame of reference. Specific details of cultural orientations and practices were not discussed in terms of content and meaning but rather generically and abstractly. In this section, societies are described in terms of a distinctive and familiar culture and history. From a strictly structural point of view, namely, that involving social complexity and organization, early modern European societies are similar to those described in the previous sections (Johnson and Earle 1991). Italian city-states of the Renaissance and medieval periods, as an example, essentially preceded early modern societies in time, and are connected in a line of continuity with them. Similarly, in a broad comparative and evolutionary frame of reference, one assumes that Mediterranean states of the classical era as well as ancient Chinese or Indian states, considered as social structures, shared properties with medieval and Renaissance states of Europe (Parsons 1966; Service 1975).

In brief, political economic and cultural changes, especially those involving the growth of science, constitute the crucial difference between states and civilizations considered earlier and the early modern European ones. I will not attempt to discuss in any detail the enormously complex problem of how European or Western societies are different from Oriental or non-Western ones. Or, alternatively, whether and, if so, why science as we understand it today developed in an early modern European setting as compared to a Chinese, Indian, or Islamic one. These topics are not only complex but highly controversial and have been discussed elsewhere (Baechler, Hall, and Mann 1988; Butterfield 1965; Gellner 1989; Jones 1987; Lindberg 1992; Mann 1986).

Early modern European states provided conditions that transformed the way disorders termed somatopsychic were viewed and handled in human societies. In Europe and England during this era, roughly 1500–1800, lay/folk and professional perceptions of sickness generally and what we now term mental illness or psychiatric disorders in particular changed in the direction of what prevails today (Porter 1985; Wear 1992). Since models that explained health, sickness, and personhood more generally changed, so of course did perceptions of sickness including those we might today call psychiatric. One can add that, in important ways, manifestations of disease states changed as well since it is in terms of prevailing cultural models that diseases are experienced, reported, inquired about, and described. A change in orientation toward the "scientific" led to new emphases in what was searched for and found regarding general medical diseases and psychiatric disorders as well. Eventually, the outcome of this process was the emergence of disorders described in terms of contemporary classifications and nosologies. The early modern European period, thus, is transitional to the modern and contemporary one in a cultural and historical sense, and it can safely be so regarded with respect to the kinds of social and clinical pictures of somatopsychic disorders that it produced.

The historical trends of this period are many and complex and were discussed in a previous chapter. The changes involve a lessening of an emphasis on exalted religion, spirituality, and magic; a growing emphasis on things in themselves, scientific understanding, and instrumental effects; increasing urbanization and industrialization; the spread of capitalist social relations; and the growth of consumerism with its effects on value and accountability of objects and social relations. As a general summary, society became more secular in the way problems were explained, objectives were formulated, and institutions, including the medical, functioned. The transition that took place during the period can usefully be summarized by providing different scenarios of major depression as it might have been played out in England.

The notes pertaining to the medical practice of Richard Napier in the midlands of England during the early part of the seventeenth century have been the object of careful analysis (MacDonald 1981). Napier has left material summarizing the tens of thousands of patients that consulted him during his forty years of medical practice. Although less than 5 percent of these presented evidence of a primary psychological disturbance, this accounted for a substantial number of patients (approximately 2,000). Many of these showed prominent symptoms of depression, irritability, despair, anxiety, and psychotic reactions involving hallucinations and delusions. Physical symptoms were integral components of these maladies, although this aspect of clinical presentation was not analyzed. The "clinical material" left by Napier concentrates on the psychological and physical consequence of what today would be qualified as "social stressors" (related to work, farming, physical disease, bereavement, economic hardships, etc.) and interpersonal conflicts (marital difficulties, courtship problems, familial rivalries, problems involving harsh masters or incompetent apprentices, etc.). A psychological language of grief, pain, sorrow, envy, aggression, and violence and the like dominated in the way patients and Napier discussed the "present illness."

A common theme in the way Napier's patients experienced the consequences of these quintessentially secular and contemporary-sounding "stressors" was that of religion, magic, and the supernatural more generally. Napier himself very often formulated his interpretations of "present illness" in these terms as well. A religious idiom (involving such things as temptation, sin, demoniacal possession, and godly as versus ungodly impulses) was an integral part of the psychological language that described the dialogues between Napier and his patients. Although this type of psychological material forms the basis of this particular study, it is important to emphasize that religious and psychological themes were intermixed with somatic concerns involving body functions, body mechanisms, and bodily pain. This is in keeping with the way prominent medical afflictions were formulated in the seventeenth century. Likewise, the treatments prescribed and carried out by Napier involved a gamut of physical procedures and medicines as well as spiritual counseling.

The orientation of Napier toward his patients is important. He presents as a health adviser able to aid the troubled through advice, support, and understanding and the prescription of standard remedies. He is an active participant in the mental and social lives of his patients. His approach is that of what today one might term a general medical practitioner active in primary care, but he functions very much like a psychotherapist, listening and intervening as best he can in the secular and spiritual travails of his patients. In many ways, Napier's was a psychological practice heavily tinged with religion. Given the focus of medical practice during this period and Napier's theological training, that religion, demonianism, and possession should figure prominently in the idioms of distress of patients is understandable. This orientation that Napier showed with patients classified as psychologically disturbed was not different from the orientation he showed with the rest of his patients and indeed could be said to be typical in the medical practice of seventeenth-century England (Porter 1985; Sawyer 1986).

The clinical scenarios described by Napier are characterized by despondency, despair, anxiety, and physical disability in patients of different ages, stations, and gender. The major depressions that underlay many of the problems of Napier's patients can be said to have displayed psychospiritual, psychosocial, and psychosomatic manifestations if it is understood that these qualifications imply phenomena that are conceptualized and experienced as unitary. It is the connectedness between these now separately construed domains that appears to have characterized the way major depressions were realized and dealt with in this period in England. A person's dominant concerns in life and the myriad stresses he or she experienced were considered integral components of sicknesses of the body and the mind; and activities of healing took into account a broad array of medicines, magical practices, and counseling efforts including emotional and spiritual support, all aimed at modifying and ameliorating the complex unity that described the individual in early modern England.

The dominant role played by religious themes needs emphasis. Ideas of sin, temptation, the Devil, possession, and godliness/ungodliness were integral to the maladies brought to the practitioner. Religion figured in ultimate causation (sin, possession), description of manifestations (how pain or bodily malfunctions were experienced and reported), pathogenesis (how ungodly spirits were imposed on the self and altered physiologies), and in the way severity was gauged (whether religious duties and obligations were interfered with). Because Christian symbols and meanings made up how individuals interpreted their predicaments, one can claim that major depressions were strongly colored in a spiritualist, religious psychological idiom.

By the middle of the eighteenth century, a religious language no longer dominated in the way sickness and healing were configured (MacDonald 1981; Porter 1987a, 1987b; Rosen 1968). More and more, the language of the body and its systems and chemicals became the preferred mode of describing and explaining illness. Demonianism became discredited as an explanation of cause. Instead of religious possession, exalted visions, or inspired convictions pertaining to the spiritual and supernatural realm, formulations were cast in the language of altered perceptions and delusions. The stresses that contributed to psychological and physical disability may not have changed dramatically, but the way these were formulated and reported with distinctive mechanisms and processes centered inside the organs and tissues of the person became more prominent. The medical philosophy of ideology, with its empirical reductionism, began to more and more dominate explanations and doctor-patient dialogues (Rosen 1946). This change in medical conceptualization was an integral component of the wide-ranging cultural and political transformations described earlier and affected conceptualizations of sicknesses like the ones produced by major depression and also some of its consequences. As an example, this period witnessed what has been termed the secularization of suicide (MacDonald 1986): Persons were less and less morally/religiously/spiritually culpable for suicide, illness and despondency became more acceptable explanations, and legal moral punishments of surviving family members were relaxed.

This transformation in the mode of conceptualizing sicknesses and social psychological stresses interpretable today as somatopsychic disorders (from religious to secular idioms) is consistent with the changes described by early modern European historians with respect to problems of behavior and responsibility seen as "cases of conscience" (Thomas 1993). Attention has been drawn to the high prevalence and compelling nature of conflicts of morality in seventeenth-century England among both Catholics and Protestants. The increasing application of moral rules to *particular instances of conflict* contributed to the growth of casuistry and the science and practice of this application as forms one can think of as spiritual and moral counseling. It can hardly be doubted that "casuistic counseling" was provided to persons suffering from psychological manifestations of somatopsychic disturbances like major depression.

In other words, the high prevalence of casuistic reasoning and practice draws attention to the likelihood that moral conflicts and scruples constituted idioms through which such somatopsychic disorders manifested during the seventeenth and eighteenth centuries.

As the eighteenth century progressed, there was a decline in casuistry. The reasons, again, are complex but clearly were reflected in changes in the conceptions of morality, with an emphasis on *overall sincerity of intentions and general moral character* as compared to preoccupation with specific transgressions and maintaining consistency among individual acts and moral reasoning. The following quote is appropriate: "Bishop Burnet declared robustly that 'the greater part of those that are troubled in mind' were 'melancholy hypochondriacal people'; they needed medicine, not spiritual advice" (Thomas 1993: 52). Thus a transformation in conceptions of morality led to a more secular, medicalized interpretation of "cases of conscience." Persons who previously were described as morally conflicted and aggrieved because of presumed transgressions and religious doubting, cases of conscience handled through "casuistic counseling," came to be described as medically depressed and in need of medical treatment.

Eventually, this change in intellectual orientation toward responsibility and behavior undoubtedly affected the way somatopsychic disorders like major depression manifested and were explained, not only by the clergy but by physicians, lay practitioners, and the general population as well. An idiom of bodily distress and emotional/cognitive disturbance began to supplant one of moral conflict and spiritual failing; the physiological economy of the individual began to take precedence over moral economy in the explanation of suffering and behavioral failure.

In summary, the cultural and political economic transformations of this period played a decisive role in the way sickness was interpreted and medical practice was carried out. Practitioners now began to be more focused on specific symptoms and signs referable to the body and less so on general aspects of moral behavior and spiritual failings. Instead of advice pertaining to overall aspects of health, dietetics, moral responsibility, and spiritual/religious accounting, it was the presence of signs/symptoms and their location on or "in" the body that counted. The causes of medical problems came increasingly to be seen as more physical or objective as compared to religious/magical. The dialogue between practitioners and patients became more centered on concrete effects of agents directed at specific markers of sickness. Finally, the actual interpretation or explanation of sickness centered more on specific mechanistic and chemical changes involving the body and its parts as versus general states and imbalances involving the humors and temperament. As reviewed in an earlier chapter, it was in these societies and during this period in history that the modern concept of disease was developed (Cohen 1961; Rather 1959; Temkin 1963).

Somatopsychic Disorders in Contemporary Societies

The psychiatric institution that is found in contemporary societies is a product of complex cultural and historical changes. These are generally thought to have been set in motion and acquired the outlines of their contemporary form in the European nation-states during the modern era, namely, the late eighteenth century and especially the nineteenth and the first half of the twentieth century. Historians of psychiatry emphasize positive aspects, such as humanitarian motives, enlightened social reforms, and the growth of scientific insights pertaining to the understanding of behavior, be these psychological or neurobiological. Revisionist, sometimes termed "critical," historians, in contrast, emphasize such things as the expansion of the state, the pressures for social control, unwarranted medicalization, and professional ambition in the context of very limited, if not an absence of, true medical/psychiatric expertise (Castel 1986; Doerner 1981; Jones 1972; Scull 1993).

Both types of historians would agree that complex social and political economic developments unique to modern European nations provided the conditions that created or constituted psychiatry and along with this such things as somatopsychic disorders, psychogenic pain syndromes, somatoform disorders, and major depression. The political economic and cultural changes were reviewed in an earlier chapter. From a medical psychiatric standpoint, they include the development and growth of the asylum; the concomitant growth of attendant forms of behavioral regulation and sequestration (with consequent opportunities for description and analysis) through the prism of medicine, asylum doctors, and eventually psychiatrists and other "behavioral" disciplines; and finally, the progressive forging of expertness, organic determinism, and physician dominance in doctor-patient relations.

Viewed in a cultural and evolutionary frame of reference, psychiatry is the institution or discipline that necessarily resulted (emerged, socially evolved) when ways of handling behavioral dilapidation or breakdowns associated with somatopsychic disorders and the major psychoses assumed their modern medicalized form. As a consequence of political and economic transformations (if not revolutions) that took place in Anglo-European societies, older, time-honored institutions of social control and behavioral regulation linked to the ancien régime lost their power and rationale (Castel 1986; Doerner 1981; Miller and Rose 1986; Scull 1993). The result was secularized, civil libertarian approaches to the interpretation of sickness and behavior with its emphases on social responsibility and obligation. In the society at large, the protection of citizenship became a dominant political concern. In the medical domain, this political dictum translated into the restoration of citizenship through medical treatment. Individuals had a legal right and the state an obligation to restore individuals to their full capacities as citizens, and this had a profound effect on the handling of mental illness (Castel 1986). In parallel with developments in general medical practice and public health involving cameralism, welfarism, medical policing, and the growth of professionalism more generally, the state turned to asylum superintendents and other protopsychiatrists for the regulation, control, and repair of behavioral anomalies (Rosen 1953). Somatopsychic forms of human suffering, classifiable today as anxiety, psychogenic pain, neurasthenia, or major depression, became objects of social and political concern. The increasing secularization of society thus resulted in a change in the way medical problems were conceptualized and medical dialogues were configured. From an emphasis on symbols about the humors, astrological configurations, and spirituality, the language of medicine and eventually psychiatry settled on objective descriptions of bodily function, pain, and behavior/mood.

The evolution of the contemporary concept of major depression can again be used as illustration (Berrios 1984, 1988). Emotion, affectivity, and mood have played a relatively minor role in the growth of descriptive psychopathology, being eclipsed by the heavy emphasis on aspects of cognitive function or rationality/intellectuality. Conceptualization of psychiatric phenomena in terms of emotions and the like is a development that appears not to have received much attention until the middle of the nineteenth century. Disorders now labeled major depression have been accorded different interpretations as forms of madness and behavioral dilapidation. The modern history of major depression involves its interpretation under such labels as "tristimania," "lipemania," "melancholia," and eventually "depression" in the writings of Continental and British psychiatrists. The term "neurasthenia" was in vogue in American medicine and psychiatry and retains meaning in Chinese psychiatry to this day (Kleinman 1986).

Such an account traces the historiographic evolution of the concept of the disorder. In Germany and Britain scientific thinking about psychiatric disorders such as major depression has oscillated prominently between psychological and especially organicist emphases, with the latter becoming dominant late in the nineteenth century. The social trajectory has included the consulting rooms of general physicians for psychological and somatization problems, parish records pertaining to poor and dependent persons for related problems, court records involving the certification of psychotic and suicidal persons, and, of course, the asylum itself in the form of melancholia and puerperal melancholia (Jones 1980; Loudon 1988; Suzuki 1991, 1992; Walton 1985).

Social historians have emphasized that early in the reform movement moral therapy played an important role in the understanding and treatment of psychiatric disorders generally. At this time, then, psychosocial aspects of disorders and major depression in particular probably received explicit attention, no doubt constituting positive influences on their course. On the other hand, during the last half of the nineteenth century, at least in England, there existed a strong tendency toward minimizing the importance of psychological manifestations of psychiatric disorders (Clark 1981; Jacyna 1982). At this juncture, it was the somatic and neurological, brain-related aspects of disorders that counted in explaining their nature. Symptoms, at most (when properly enumerated and classified), could but aid in diagnosis. Since little of what patients experienced, felt, and thought (e.g., the content of feeling states and delusions and the perceived reasons for them) was used in treatment, this suggests that the somatic reductionism that existed during this time may have worked against the constructive handling of the social and psychological conflicts, losses, and separations that contributed to the outbreak and persistence of major depression. In other words, during this "genealogical" phase prevailing conceptualizations of major depression may have worked against the provision of optimal care.

Concluding Comment

The social scenarios of somatopsychic disorders that were reviewed in this chapter constitute descriptions of how a universal psychobiologic vulnerability for sickness could have been played out in different types of societies. Such disorders were assumed to have a medical, social, and cultural expression in categories, roles, explanatory models, interpersonal networks, and behavioral opportunities that were culturally constructed in societies during different stages of social differentiation and evolution. A heuristic assumption was entertained of a more or less equal level of incidence and prevalence of such disorders across types of human societies, with interpretations and locations in the social system constituting a significant variation in the way these were played out and configured as ontological "things." Whether the assumption is supported or invalidated by the discussion pursued here is not considered important. What does require emphasis is that the social picture of these disorders varies considerably across types of societies with respect to labels, meanings, and social significance. The complex interpretation and mode of handling of something like major depression would need to be taken into account in any attempt at constructing a social theory about its relationship to culture and society.

The analysis pursued in this chapter was undertaken with an appreciation of three by no means mutually exclusive positions that challenge it strongly. First, in contrast to standard historiographic accounts of disorders such as melancholia and depression (Jackson 1986), the analysis was admittedly professionally hubristic and Whiggish in the sense that it presupposed the psychobiological validity of the modern conceptualization of these disorders. With the hindsight of contemporary biological psychiatry, an interpretation was offered about genealogical versions of the somatopsychic disorders, in particular, major depression. Conjectures and hypotheses, as compared to empirical data, provided the rationale and method of inquiry.

Second, one could take the position that somatopsychic disorders such as major depression are exclusively modern and postmodern creations. In the light of what is known about their "natural history" in our society, one could say that their incidence and prevalence in any society (with these epidemiological concepts broadly construed culturally) serves as a barometer of social integration and harmony in that society. Stated baldly, the amount of strain, deprivation, exploitation, and stress-producing circumstances more generally (including in particular the way roles are defined, e.g., gender) would play a determinate role in the level of sicknesses including somatopsychic disturbances such as major depression. This would be an argument for a social functional and social conflict theory of these disorders and sickness more generally. The argument would posit that not only is an entity such as "major depression" the result of a modern concept, but the biology of what it signifies is also very much a modern eventuation; social systems displaying more or different varieties of social integration may not have been plagued by the same amounts of major depression. For reasons that are scientifically self-evident this position cannot be fully validated.

Third, one could also take the position that the social and cultural rationale of a society conditions the incidence and prevalence of all sicknesses that the biology of its population and the ecology of its physical environment might produce. On this account, what one on ethnocentric grounds might term "major depression" simply has no currency or meaning about conditions obtaining in that society. This would probably be the position of many historians and anthropologists who endorse a strict version of cultural relativism. They would claim that societies characterized by different cultural rationales contain their own set of strains and dispositions toward problems of sickness and health, their own labels and definitions, and their own theories and practices of healing. A society's "medical" facts, the argument would run, could only be interpreted in terms of the symbols, meanings, and conventions of the prevailing culture. This would be the argument of one committed to a truly cultural medicine or cultural psychiatry.

Although these positions challenge the ultimate validity of the argument of this chapter, they do not detract from its main purpose. This has been to lay the groundwork for a social theory of somatopsychic disorders such as major depression. This enterprise would enlist the efforts of functionalists, conflict theorists, anthropologists committed to all interpretations of cultural relativism, epidemiologists, and psychiatrists.

7

Descriptive Parameters
of Sickness and Healing

In chapter 1 I reviewed previous thinking about the evolution of medicine. In large part, it is the social and cultural evolution that researchers have addressed. One approach has consisted in examining from a historical point of view the prevalence of different diseases in societies of varying size and complexity. William H. McNeill's magisterial work (1976, 1992) can be cited as a classic example of this approach. He drew attention to the role of disease in major transformations of world history. The ecology of disease, the effect of commerce and travel in causing major epidemics and in altering disease pictures more generally, and the social and historical consequences of all of this received central attention. McNeill took a broad, expansive approach, concentrating on the major upheavals in mortality and morbidity occasioned by changes in the epidemiology of disease. These consequence of disease pictures were examined in relation to changes in population size and movements of populations.

I would view McNeill's discussion as laying the foundations for an evolutionary account of medicine. The historical biology of disease in populations of different size and density is described in relation to major historical changes. From this "macroscopic" account it is possible to infer events and processes taking place in actual social contexts, that is, at the "microscopic" level. However, the fundamental behavioral aspects of medicine, what I handle here as sickness and healing, did not receive McNeill's attention, nor can it be said that he envisioned an evolutionary account of medicine considered as a social institution.

Those that have conceptualized medical phenomena from the standpoint of evolution, such as Alland (1970), have done so stressing populational and epidemiological features of specific diseases and have relied on the framework of cultural ecology. It is clear that Alland dealt with the idea of evolution from both a biological (emphasizing population biology) and a cultural (emphasizing the effects of native medical orientations perspective). Cohen's (1989) study is an expansion of this approach. He concentrated in depth on specific disease pictures of prehistoric and historic societies and gave explicit attention to evolutionary questions. However, like McNeill and, to some extent, Alland (who mainly addressed biological concerns), Cohen did not go into details about social cultural evolution of societies except insofar as they might affect epidemiological measures of mortality and morbidity. Finally, the work of Dunn (1976) and Kleinman (1978, 1980) must also be cited for its comprehensive cultural as well as biological (especially, Dunn) emphasis with respect to medicine; however, they did not elaborate on evolutionary questions per se. Only Janzen (1978a) addressed evolutionary sorts of questions (primarily for the modern era and in Africa), but he did not give much attention to biological or epidemiological questions.

Sociologists, most notably Fox (1988a, 1988b), have concentrated on evolutionary implications of disease and medical institutions but from an entirely existential and social psychological standpoint. (The scheme presented by Robert N. Bellah [1964] on the evolution of religion contains a number of ideas that Fox draws on and that are very useful for conceptualizing sickness and healing from an evolutionary standpoint.) The role of medical beliefs and practices in the management of cognitive and existential uncertainty produced by disease, and the interplay between medicine and religion, was the main focus. Fox used rather global categories of societies and did not address specific kinds of diseases characteristic of these categories. The study of Peter Conrad and Joseph W. Schneider (1980) is another sociological work that can be cited which adopts a comparative approach to medicine; however, this one concentrated almost entirely on topics related to social deviance and was limited to the modern era. The analysis pursued in this book and summarized in the present chapter essentially builds on the work of these scholars and could not have been undertaken without their earlier efforts.

A Darwinian approach to medicine stipulates that there exists an evolutionary rationale to the way organisms and their internal systems respond and behave when affected by the varied physiologic changes subsumed under the category "disease" (Williams and Nesse 1991). In other words, the symptoms and signs of disease are not necessarily negative and pathological, requiring eradication or neutralization, but often positive responses of the organism geared to stabilize, limit, or counteract the noxious effects of disease. Given this Darwinian perspective, the task of the physician is to constructively use the evolutionarily based, "natural" responses of the organism so as to promote recovery and restore health. Johns (1990) dealt with the dynamic interaction of plants and humans and also reflected a Darwinian, evolutionary frame of reference. He concentrated on biological aspects of food procurement, dietary preferences, and innate mechanisms regulating the metabolism of plant products and related these phenomena to the use of natural and specially prepared medicinal substances. In his model of human chemical ecology, plant chemicals, parasites, and human activities are seen to interact through various biological and cultural adaptations. He views the origins of (herbal) medicine as linked to natural processes involved in the regulation of an organism's chemical ecology. The formulation about sickness and healing presented in chapter 2 and to be elaborated in this chapter and the following one is consistent with a Darwinian approach to medicine.

I conceptualize sickness and healing as the behavioral expression of disease, injury, and the SH adaptation. Organisms, in other words, are held to possess "innate" knowledge or information that produces a natural tendency to understand and communicate about disease and injury as sickness, to "self-heal" and also to "other-heal." All of this is assumed in the long run to promote inclusive fitness. Sickness and healing are based on and mediated by kin selection and reciprocal altruism and were selected for in the social and cultural environment of the evolutionary line leading from protoculture to culture and man.

The bulk of the biology of sickness and healing was sculpted by natural selection during the Pleistocene epoch. Some modification of the biology of resistance to infection may have occurred since. What, if any, traits of man can have been selected for in so short a time span is controversial. In this chapter the assumption is that by far the most important process and mechanism accounting for the evolutionary changes in sickness and healing are cultural and social in nature. The characteristics of different types of societies, the changes they undergo, the mechanisms accounting for them, and the implications of all this for an understanding of sickness and healing are summarized.

Sickness, Healing, and Cultural Evolution

In earlier chapters emphasis was given to ideal types of societies. The properties of these social types can no longer be said to be fully displayed because of such factors as cultural diffusion and concomitant social transformations, including, in particular, colonialism and modernization, all of which have problematized sickness and healing. Nevertheless, for heuristic purposes, these social types allow us to outline key phases of change in the way sickness and healing have been configured.

A first inclination might be to claim that only healing might possibly have evolved. Such an argument would stress that only during the later stages of cultural evolution has healing really materially changed and evolved to constitute a differentiated and specialized social institution. Such evolution, it would be claimed, should be conceptualized entirely as a product of changes in society and culture. During the existence of fully formed *Homo sapiens,* marked changes in concepts and instrumentalities of healing have taken place. However, there have probably not occurred many behavioral changes in healing that reflect genetic changes in the way organisms are able to read aspects of sickness and adaptively respond so as to self-heal or provide healing to others; what have occurred are changes in conceptual structures and technologies that are properly to be viewed as outcomes of cultural evolution.

In a complementary way, the argument would stipulate that the amount of time enabling a cultural evolution of healing is likewise simply insufficient to have allowed changes in sickness to have taken place. This is especially the case, the argument would run, because sickness is linked to organ structures and systems that register the effects of disease processes. The latter, in being connected to systems anchored in physiological systems and genetically canalized, has simply not had opportunity to change in important ways.

To argue in this way is to favor sickness as a purely biologic category subject to strict genetic evolution and healing as a social and cultural category subject to cultural evolution. In line with the arguments first put forth in chapter 2, this would constitute a false dichotomy because both sickness and healing have been handled as equally biological and cultural. In other words, both of these categories have been configured as biocultural in nature—made up of behaviors that are both learned and symbolic (products of a culturally inherited information) as well as reflecting capacities and dispositions that are genetically based and physiologically realized (in a biology of disease/sickness and of altruism/healing). Hence, to maintain logical consistency, one is entitled to continue to handle sickness and healing as sociobiologically linked or nested categories subject to the same processes and mechanisms of causation and change.

The social and cultural evolution of medicine was described by positing six social types that are held to form a continuum of increasing social complexity and differentiation. The schema employed was derived from the study of Allan W. Johnson and Timothy Earle (1991). It is not clear whether these scholars intend their schema to constitute a veritable stage theory of social evolution or to merely illustrate characteristics of societies showing different degrees of social complexity. I have used their schema because it summarizes considerable thinking in the social sciences, especially anthropology. I have also relied a great deal on the writings of Sanderson (1990, 1994, 1995a), who has not only provided a history and critique of controversies associated with evolutionary theory in the social sciences but also, in the light of his critique, has presented a general theoretical summary of key tenets of evolutionary materialism that is persuasive and has proven helpful. In general, conceptualizing the evolution of medicine from both a biological and social cultural standpoint raises a number of complex issues that have been studied from different points of view.

I visualize social evolution as passing through various stages or phases that I equate roughly with the social typology of Johnson and Earle (1991). Each society or stage, described by me as a social type, constitutes a constellation of economic, technological factors associated with increasing differentiation and complexity. Any particular society (termed by me a "social formation") is held to display characteristics that equate it with a social type and to have progressively acquired its characteristics. I do not assume that these are the only stages of social evolution or that all societies pass through each of the preceding stages. Societies may skip stages or undergo side stages during evolution (Sanderson 1990, 1995a, 1995b).

A society's social and cultural system of medicine encompasses and also determines how sickness and healing are conceptualized and played out. With an awareness of the limitations of the concept of system (Press 1980), I find it useful nonetheless to assume that a more or less distinctive "system" of medicine is associated with the six social types described in the previous chapter. The material on medicine reviewed in earlier chapters summarizes and interprets important characteristics that I feel pertain to a theoretical and evolutionary conception of medicine.

Social scientists have proposed a number of basic factors that function as the motor or engine that propels evolution, and these could have, directly or indirectly, affected the evolution of medicine. Material, technological, and ideological (religious) factors have frequently been cited along with warfare and absorption as prime movers of social evolutionary change. In general, how social evolution originates and the process by which it unfolds is controversial and contested.

Sociologists who study cultural and social evolution usually confine their analyses to descriptions of molar processes and social transformations (see Collins 1988; Lenski 1970; Sanderson 1990). They are less concerned with positing particulate features of societies or cultures that set evolution in motion and less interested in delineating specific mechanisms or details about how cultural evolution works, or in discussing it in comparison with or in relation to biological evolution. (Campbell [1965], who did concentrate on sociological issues and who is a psychologist, constitutes a clear exception.)

Anthropologists and biologists who have addressed cultural evolution have given explicit attention to details and have attempted to conceptualize elements of the evolutionary process and to model it. Particulate units that bring about evolution through mechanisms and processes producing variation, selection, and retention of these units have been proposed; and processes analogous to natural selection, which in effect account for social incorporation, transformation, and inheritance, have been discussed (Barkow 1989; Boyd and Richerson 1985; Durham 1991; Lumsden and Wilson 1981).

Units of Information in the Cultural
Evolution of Medicine

In chapter 8 I will give more attention to the question of "prime movers" of the medical evolutionary process, whether this be thought of as biological or social. Here I am concerned to develop a conceptualization and methodology for understanding medicine from a general and comprehensive evolutionary standpoint. I assume that the evolutionary process operates in terms of units of genetic and cultural information derived from biological and social systems, respectively, and from any number of a society's social organizations and institutions. In chapter 2 I discussed material related to genetic considerations, and a more specific formulation of this will be presented in the next chapter. With respect to social and cultural evolution, I assume that "medical units" play important roles in the social evolution of sickness and healing and that a similar mode of selection and retention operates on them as it does on cultural units of information pertaining to other institutions.

I have found useful the idea of a "meme," introduced and discussed by Richard Dawkins (1982, 1986). He originally used this idea to denote replicators different from but related to genes. He defined a meme as "a unit of information residing in a brain . . . [having] . . . a definite structure, realized in whatever physical medium the brain uses for storing information" (Dawkins 1982: 109). A meme is obviously related to but different from the effects that it produces, referred to as "meme products" or "phenotypic effects," which "may be in the form of words, music, visual images, styles of clothes, facial or hand gestures, skills" (Dawkins 1982: 109).

In the discussions that follow here and in subsequent chapters, this technical distinction between memes and their products needs to be kept in mind. I will be using the idea of a meme to refer to both the brain substrates and to their effects or products in behavior, knowledge, and technology. The context should make evident exactly which meaning of the term is being used.

Using the notion of a "meme" as a unit of cultural information (stored in the brains of persons, communicated and spread to others through their effects, and subsequently learned by them and stored in their brains) one can think of "healmemes" as basic units of information (or instructions) pertinent to an social evolutionary account of healing. As will become evident, a healmeme describes a cultural, medically relevant trait that connects and integrates biology and culture, since my view is that these are best conceptualized as partially linked, connected processes. More about that later. With respect to the social and cultural end of things, medicines, concrete procedures applied to the body, rituals linked to healing, learned behavioral routines that play out sickness or healing, and social practices for organizing healing are all examples of (products of) healmemes. The practices of the Gnau (Lewis 1975) of congregating together and visiting a sick comember to offer advice and exonerate themselves from blame constitute expressions of healmemes, as does also their beliefs about the way the physical habitat needs to be worked to avoid sickness. Likewise, the various herbal and botanical remedies developed by the Aztecs (Ortiz de Montellano 1990) are examples of the phenotypic effects of those healmemes carried in the brains of Aztec healers just as much as are the many "wonder drugs" of the modern era that are carried in the brains of contemporary populations.

Healmemes may all be thought of as units of cultural information that members of a community or population develop, store, and use for purposes of combating the effects of disease and injury. They involve inventions of people that are elaborated with the expectation that they will counteract negative features of sickness (e.g., relieve symptoms, shorten duration, facilitate social processes that hasten or promote healing), neutralize them, or even enhance any positive payoffs that the otherwise negative state of sickness brings. Healmemes are invented and resorted to by members of a community because if implemented they can in theory bring benefits to those who are in a condition of sickness. They are learned and used by persons who, by knowing of and themselves being vulnerable to the manifestations and potential outcomes of sickness, want to minimize its costs and maximize its benefits and outcomes to relatives and other comembers. In the logic of evolutionary psychology, they do so because reciprocated acts of a similar nature will benefit them and their relatives and in the long run this will lead to an enhancement of inclusive fitness.

In the evolution of the medical, it is obvious that treatment factors have played extremely important roles in transforming how sickness and healing were configured and played out, and this is the reason for terming units of the medical "healmemes" (i.e., healing units). However, it should be clear that units of the medical could have also been termed "sickmemes" to draw attention to the fact that they are relevant to the programming of illness as sickness. This gets closer to the biological end of things.

The SH adaptation described in chapter 2 included a machinery and a capacity for coping with disease and injury in meaningful ways expressed as sickness and healing. Thus many of the features that take place as a result of disease and injury and that have communicational, informational value to others of the social environment, *and that are programmed rigidly in genetic terms,* connect with sickmemes. The manifestations of disease and injury are expressed, so to speak, in these units of information for they are what construct sickness as a socially meaningful "thing." In other words, aspects of sickness also change and evolve in response to selection influences. Units and parameters that more purely seem to realize sickness (in ways of behaving, thinking, and orienting) also contribute variation to the evolutionary process. As an example, the units of information that serve to "program" behaviorally a person who is ill with regard to what to make of nausea, vomiting, or abdominal pain, and also what to expect from sickness and what to demand and seek in the way of healing during a condition of gastrointestinal illness, are all also products of sickmemes. As socially shared phenomena they vary in relation to levels or stages of social evolution. Indeed, what a person who is ill can make of a condition of illness, which takes into account the definition, threshold for illness (including behaviors one can equate with a "sick role"), and standards of restoration of "health," is based on units of information that one could term "sickmemes" as compared to "healmemes."

This underscores the reciprocal nature of sickness and healing in socially constructing (i.e., socializing) a medical eventuation. What develops anew in the domain of sickness and what develops anew in the domain of healing each affect the other when the focus is biologically meaningful ("symbolic") material realized in social behavior, habits, and routines related to the medical. Put differently, it can be said that sick persons and healers share a body of (genetic and cultural) information about sickness and healing and they both orient to each other in a given medical context accordingly. This complementarity, if not conjunction, between sickness and healing viewed symbolically in terms of information is the reason why the biological trait (or sets of traits) pertaining to the medical has been handled as unitary and termed SH. In the following chapter this and related themes are developed further.

Conceptualizing Sickness and Healing Holistically

The idea of medical memes (i.e., healmemes and sickmemes) constitutes a way of providing content to the SH adaptation discussed in chapter 2. To recall, the adaptation was held to consist of psychological mechanisms sculpted during human evolution that endow disease and injury with conceptual and behavioral meaning. The adaptation was held to have a biological machinery that promoted culturally meaningful behaviors geared to adaptively coping with disease and injury in the environment of evolutionary adaptedness. It thus furnished the "trait" that enables individuals of a society to learn and enact the behaviors associated with sickness and healing.

The concept of a medical meme was introduced because it will prove analytically useful in the discussions of the social and cultural evolution of medicine in the next chapter. In a sense, medical memes constitute a conceptual bridge for crossing from the biological evolution of medicine to its cultural and social evolution. As units of cultural meaning, the products of medical memes realize or make up the SH adaptation in a particular social and cultural context.

The idea of a medical meme thus serves as an analytic tool with which to begin to develop a comparative and evolutionary account of sickness and healing. The basic adaptive problem that such an account of the medical seeks to comprehend is how different types of societies cope with disease and injury. A step in the direction of explaining medical phenomena using a scientifically satisfactory theory is to describe how different types of societies have configured sickness and healing. Descriptive material was reviewed in the earlier two chapters. The patterns of sickness and healing in the different societies discussed in previous chapters are summarized below.

It is useful at this juncture to state in summary and extended form the seeming rationale of medical memes. In any given social formation this rationale is contextualized in culturally meaningful behaviors of sickness and healing. The following declarative sentences summarize basic directives and imperatives of medical memes associated with sickness and healing. Detect and define the manifestations of disease and injury (registered as a state of illness). Identify and name the condition as a sickness. Ascertain possible causes of the sickness. Estimate prognosis of sickness. Seek to undo the causes, manifestations, and consequences of sickness through healing. Prepare for the process of termination in the event healing is of no avail.

The biological components of disease/injury that undergird and support the sickness/healing response (i.e., the SH adaptation) can usefully be recalled. These *organic, physiological,* and *bodily* components of disease and injury are expressed behaviorally in units of cultural information (i.e., medical memes) that constitute an interpretation of the disease/injury as sickness. When properly understood, the set of medical memes pertaining to an eventuation of sickness and healing allow the self and others to draw inferences about diagnosis, cause, prognosis, course, and healing regimen. The set of medical memes serves to delineate a relevant domain and set of parameters that stipulate what the effects of disease/injury mean and how they should be dealt with.

Bodily aspects of sickness and healing may be based on physiology, but (as discussed in chapter 2) they are expressive and social in nature. To give free play to communicative and interpretive idioms, the underlying rationale of medical memes is stated in the form of imperatives that accompany, monitor, and activate in a reflexive manner the SH response. Some examples of the rationales of medical memes follow (see also chapter 2): (1) relieve pain wherever it is located on the body (i.e., relieve pain regardless of its nature and location, whether it is associated with a physiologic function, whether it is in the body cavities, in the musculoskeletal apparatus, or on the skin and body surface); (2) stop bleeding wherever it occurs on or inside the body; (3) warm the body in the event that it is cold; (4) cool the body in the event that it is warm; (5) relieve and undo abdominal cramps and diarrhea; (6) provide fresh air and ventilation and support upright posture in the event of shortness of breath; (7) relieve and eliminate feelings of nausea and associated vomiting; (8) counteract feelings of weakness and lassitude; (9) replace loss of fluids and nutrients;

(10) stabilize, neutralize, counterpoise, repair, or eliminate changes in the outline, appearance, and structure of the body (e.g., swellings, eruptions, protuberances, dislocations, fractures).

The cognitive and behaviorally expressive components of disease and injury that serve to elaborate the sickness/healing response (i.e., the SH adaptation) need to also be taken into consideration. These, essentially, are medical memes that communicate *psychological* needs and *social* imperatives triggered by disease and injury. These medical memes serve to configure in symbolic terms the sickness and healing adaptation or suite of behaviors. As in the previous instance, the medical memes are held to be communicated in symbolic form and interpreted socially. For purposes of illustration, the rationales of these medical memes will also be stated in general declarative form: (1) provide knowledge/information that is helpful and encouraging; (2) offer emotional/affective communications that promote hope; (3) notify and seek out friends and family; (4) undertake tasks and responsibilities that are negated by the condition of illness and that are vital for continued subsistence; (5) perform rituals of appeal and supplication that elicit moral and spiritual support; (6) seek and consult with specialist healer(s) and diviner(s); (7) select from among alternative remedies proposed; (8) participate in and help carry out the chosen regimen; (9) prepare the sick and family for, and help them cope with, the implications of terminality in the event the sickness is serious and protracted and fails to improve.

As reviewed in earlier chapters, sickness and healing also provide the context for the expression of existential questions. The latter can be viewed as a reflexively central part of the sickness and healing ensemble. The questions draw on and essentially constitute general properties of sickness and healing that when provided with cultural content or meaning articulate its existential importance in the society. In summary, because of its biological significance in signaling vulnerability and impermanence, an event of disease and injury has the potential of expressing existential questions and these also are judged as coded in medical memes. Properly interpreted, they stipulate and elaborate the medical memes reviewed earlier. The following are some examples of elements of sickness and healing that provide the context for the elaboration of basic existential issues that are seen as coded in medical memes: (1) identity and nature of the agents or agencies responsible for cause of sickness; (2) nature of evidence integral to disease and injury that points to a diagnosis of sickness; (3) social and moral implications of sickness and healing; (4) exemptive value of manifestations of sickness; (5) spiritual interpretation of sickness and of healing regimen; (6) social composition and character of healing party; (7) social and psychological implications of the nature and types of actions, medicines, and procedures of healing; and (8) variability of course and susceptibility to healing influences.

The material discussed in this section summarizes basic aspects of sickness and healing that are culturally and behaviorally elaborated in any society. It provides a good focus for the comparison of sickness and healing across social types and formations. In a conceptual sense, this material can be thought to provide the conditions for and also stipulate *elemental medical memes* comprising the SH adaptation, for when examined from a symbolic standpoint and diachronically, they register the transformation in the SH ensemble that take place during biological and social evolution.

Social Patterns of Sickness and Healing

To furnish sickness and healing with theoretical content so as to integrate and explain material covered by these terms we will consider a number of *sickness parameters* and *healing parameters*. Basically, these are social behavioral elements of sickness (or healing) that describe what constitutes sickness as a social and cultural phenomenon (or similarly, what it is that constitutes healing and how it is carried out). The parameters vary across types of societies, reflecting some of the many external factors that can influence sickness and healing and that vary. The prototypical forms of social and cultural organization that were discussed encompass a continuum of social complexity and are often thought of as forming distinctive types, possibly stages, in social and cultural evolution (Campbell 1965, 1975; Fried 1967; Johnson and Earle 1991; Service 1975; Upham 1990). These forms were chosen because they facilitate delineating important changes in the way sickness and healing have been conceptualized and carried out.

What are termed parameters of sickness and healing define aspects of behavior and experience related to disease and injury that can vary across types of societies. Sickness and healing constitute a complex ensemble of perceptions, cognitions, behavioral dispositions, and actions, all of which can be expected to vary as a function of the type of society, including in particular its culture. Since sickness is holistic and healing can constitute a multifaceted effort, it can be expected that any parameters that purport to describe them will not be mutually exclusive but will be related and even overlap conceptually.

Sickness

Social Medical Properties.   The level of general health in members of a social group varies and is a function of many factors pertaining to the group's size, ecology, and physical habitat and personal characteristics, in particular, acquired immunological defenses and nutrition. The preceding influence the volume or amount of sickness in a society, and this might constitute a parameter that could be used to study sickness and healing comparatively. Members of a social group also are vulnerable to many different social medical types of sickness. These vary with respect to rate of onset, duration, and severity. Acute fulminating infections may predominate in one society, whereas chronic and progressive ones may predominate in another. Sickness in one person may or may not be spread to a comember, and epidemics are observed in only certain types of societies. All of these factors pertaining to the concrete sociomedical properties of sickness can be expected to influence how they are conceptualized and handled.

Organismic Manifestations.   The signs and symptoms of sickness are variable. It is debatable whether they should or could be incorporated into a social theory of medicine. In my view, some aspects of these manifestations should be included since I am convinced that social groups make different things of them. Whether sicknesses are conceptualized implicitly as holistic entities or as dualistic is a factor that appears to vary across societies. In the former instance, no differentiation is made between physical/bodily as compared to subjective/mental manifestations, whereas in the latter these distinctions appear to be important. Moreover, and in relation to these distinctions, groups vary in the degree to which they single out as special or different sicknesses that have come to be called psychiatric. Some groups handle "mental illnesses" as no different from other "illnesses," whereas other groups do emphasize these distinctions; that is to say, how these sicknesses are conceptualized and handled on social grounds differs. When holism operates, the overall psychosomatic and somato-psychic unity of the manifestations is emphasized, whereas when sicknesses are subjected to an ontological partition, psychologization and somatization biases are possible, and with this a singling out of "mental illnesses" as special or different. A somatization bias operates to draw attention to bodily manifestations, perhaps even serving to authenticate sicknesses with these types of manifestations; a psychologization bias operates to draw attention to psychological manifestations, singling these out as important and different, perhaps even giving sicknesses in which such manifestations are prominent a special ontological character.

Knowledge.   The formal characteristics of the structure of knowledge (as compared to content; see below) that exists in a given society pertaining to sickness vary substantially across societies. I have in mind here such things as the richness of the inventory of illness types (terms that are available in the society at large to describe sickness conditions), the number of causes that are invoked, and the number, complexity, and consistency of the basic propositions used to explain illnesses. This could be conceptualized as the total number of bits of information devoted to classification and explanation of illness and the degree of redundancy inherent in this pool of information.

The characteristics of this knowledge, for example, its degree of system-atization and separation from other bodies of knowledge (cosmological, reli-gious), differ. Some people have a base of knowledge that is fluid, changeable, and restricted; others show a measure of structuration and organization; still others have a knowledge that appears ossified. The distribution of the knowl-edge of illness in a society also can be expected to vary. In some societies, for example, there may exist esoteric knowledge that only privileged persons might possess; in others the lay populace essentially share an equal base of knowl-edge; in still others the state may control knowledge. In some societies medi-cal knowledge seems to have arrogated authority, whereas in others it is part of the practical everyday reality of a people. In addition, there may exist few or many alternative systems of knowledge associated with different social, reli-gious, or ethnic groupings. Thus one could speak about the degree of pluralism that exists in the society.

Finally, one may draw a distinction between the kinds of concepts used to explain sickness and rationalize healing. Thus what one could term "natural concepts" may predominate: these are concepts that are derived from everyday experience and that are part of the everyday "physical" or concrete reality of people. However, theoretical and abstract concepts may be employed, namely, those that are more conceptual and intangible and based on esoteric and highly inferential assumptions that are specialized and not a part of everyday reality (except for explaining sickness, healing, and related phenomena).

Meanings.   The semantic categories in terms of which a condition of sick-ness is understood is another parameter that can be expected to vary. In some societies these might constitute ritual and moral states of the individual; in oth-ers, purely physical features and functions of the body, a body-centered failure shorn of moral implications; and in still others, taboos and rituals pertaining to the physical habitat may be dominant. Sickness may implicate the status of so-cial relations and reflect the state of psychological health. Thus sickness can be understood and played out in terms of family and community relations or in terms of lifestyle/habits and wellness and exercise programs. Evil intrusions into the territory of the person might underlie illness, or simply physiologic imbalances of forces, fluids, vital essences, or specific chemicals. Sicknesses can be "blamed" on others, on the self, or on no one in particular. They can mean potentially "bad" things about the group, or bad things about the universe or about the intentions of enemies from surrounding groups. Finally, sicknesses might possess uniform meanings or be socially marked; for example, gender or social standing of the person sick may be all-important in determining the significance of the illness. These and related meanings or semantic properties of sickness are potentially important characteristics that could color it as a so-cial and cultural reality.

Responses. The typical actions of a sick person and his or her family and immediate group also differ, being partially an outcome of whether persons view themselves as passive victims or as masters over sickness. Among the Gnau of New Guinea, it sometimes leads individuals to pretend to be sicker than they really are because this might deceive the agents that are believed to have brought it about (Lewis 1975). In some contemporary societies sickness constitutes a legitimate opportunity to evade social responsibilities. In others, it can initiate a review of personal failures, suspected antagonists, or dietary indiscretions. One factor that can vary, then, is the degree and nature of blameworthiness; in some societies it is the self that is mainly blamed, whereas in others it is mainly outsiders. In some societies sicknesses are likely to be minimized, whereas in others they are likely to be accorded great concern and be indulged. Sicknesses can occasion social anamneses aimed at uncovering their causes, whereas in other instances they can lead to warfare. Thus they can be associated with social integration, promoting group cohesion, social divisiveness, enhancing rivalries and fissions, or carry few or no social implications other than occasioning worry and support from significant others. The responsibility for seeking relief can fall mainly on the (adult) self, or it can bring into play the coordinated efforts of others who "take over."

Expectations of and Attitudes toward Healing. A condition of sickness can lead to fatalism or optimism about healing. The possibility of death may be ever-present. In other instances, a promise of purification and social exoneration can promote a sense of positive anticipation. A protracted ritual journey or ceremony might be anticipated. The possibility of healing can be dreaded, it can be indulged in, or it can be viewed as a nuisance. Sick persons can feel a sense of direct camaraderie, loyalty, awe, respect, or partnership vis-à-vis a healer.

Access to Healers and Settings of Healing. Sick persons can have easy access to many healers, both within the family/group and outside it. They might be able to resort to or hire caretakers who function like healers, or they can seek specialists of the community who, in turn, can be few or many. Access to healers can be expected as a matter of course, or they might have to be actively sought. There may exist many varieties of healers, in which case the sick person or his or her surrogate may be required to construct a hierarchy of resort and an elaborated treatment plan. The actual places where healing can or does take place differ across societies; thus healing can take place in private (i.e., the home, within the family), in public (i.e., village setting, outside the home dwelling), or in special places that are ritually (i.e., having religious or moral implications) or officially (i.e., by professional or administrative fiat or stipulation) marked.

Sick Role Conventions.   The models of how sick persons are supposed to behave while sick, including what they can be expected to obtain and receive in the way of resources, be these medicines, social dispensations, or favors, can be expected to vary across societies. Some societies may stipulate highly visible and stringent requirements for the condition of authentic sickness, perhaps punishing exploiters or cheaters. Other societies may stipulate vague and loose requirements, or none at all, leaving the matter of the determination entirely to the sick person—or to others for that matter. Sick role conventions could be explicit, perhaps even formally standardized or systematized, for example, in terms of moral/ritual requirements or economic/legal sanctions. Or, they might be expected to be worked out on an informal basis.

Sick Role Exploitation.   One might think that individuals will be tempted to socially manipulate the condition of sickness in different ways depending on the cultural conventions pertaining to the sick role. However, whether such a temptation is consciously entertained or implemented will depend on cultural conventions, and hence the opportunity for and actual exploitation of the sick role varies as to degree (low, moderate, and high). Social manipulation of the sick role can be pursued consciously or unconsciously on behalf of the sick person or for the benefits of significant others. How the sick role is exploited will obviously also differ across societies depending on a host of factors pertaining to other parameters of sickness as well as characteristics of the society more generally. Whether societies are generous and loose with respect to how the sick role is filled or whether they are strict and punitive will vary across societies; thus sick role exploitation can be easy or difficult.

Stigmatization of Sickness.   It is not unlikely that the availability of a social language of sickness facilitates and reinforces any stigmatization of sickness that may exist in the society. It is when sicknesses are differentiated into disease* types, with some reification if not ontological identity, that they can more easily acquire culturally specific meanings and be used as markers of social identity and worth. In some societies, no sickness is potentially stigmatizing, whereas in others there are some that disfigure or produce mental aberrations. In some small-scale societies it would appear that many conditions of sickness are stigmatizing. In the event certain sicknesses are stigmatizing, the sick person or the family itself is ostracized or discredited.

Healing

Number and Types of Healers.   All adult members of small, family-level societies are potential healers, and they do not appear to differ as to specialization. In these societies it makes sense to say that there exists a large number of primary healers but no specialist healers. In more complex societies, there exist a large number of specialist healers, hence their influence on the course of sickness can assume importance. Societies can also provide paramedical personnel, so that one can speak of a number of secondary and tertiary healers. Healers can be specialized as to type of cause, type of procedure, age of person, gender of person, or type of disease*. The degree of prestige of specialist healers can vary. If their prestige is high, then their judgments tend to be binding. Alternatively, specialist healers can be local folk whose advice is merely solicited on a more or less informal basis, in which case the obligation of compliance is low.

Knowledge of Healing.   This parameter overlaps with its analogue under sickness, above. One thing that it highlights is the degree of separation of expertise between the sick person and the healer, something that becomes relevant in more complex social formations. Knowledge of healing can be limited by cognitive memory structures of the individual or supplemented by textual documents. The degree of complexity and comprehensiveness of what a society regards as authentic, valid, and definitive knowledge of healing can be very large, well beyond the reach of primary healers, whereas in other societies it is not knowledge per se but revelation that imparts validity. The knowledge possessed by a healer might be regarded as valid and reputable or suspect and dangerous. It might be easily acquired or might entail long apprenticeship or formal and extended education. The state or local opinion may determine certification. Knowledge held by specialist healers may be based on cause, gender of patient, age of patient, or type of disease*. Diviners and witches, it would appear, are mainly specialists of cause, although they can and do offer advice and provide treatment. Geriatricians and gynecologists are specialists on sicknesses categorized on the basis of age and gender.

Meanings Associated with Healing.   Healing can be construed as a moral and religious exercise, an inquiry about interpersonal relations, or an impersonal and technical procedure. The scope of a healer's inquiry can be broad to the point of having no boundaries, essentially in violation of ordinary social conventions; or it can be narrow and sharply constrained by them. A healer might be expected to comment about and intervene in all aspects of the sick person's life, or he or she might be rigidly limited in terms of what it is appropriate to pursue and later undertake. In some societies meanings regarding healing can be official and standardized through governmental forms of regulation; in others variety and equality of status of participants seems to determine what general meanings attach to healing. Societies can thus be characterized by having a dominant, official perspective on healing, or they can lack this, sanctioning many different varieties and not valuing them differently.

Responsibility and Accountability.   The conduct of healing, including its outcome, may be shared by primary healers, no one person being held responsible except, perhaps, the person suspected of causing the sickness, who in village or chiefdom societies might be a resident of the community and even a potential healer. In other cases, specialist healers may be held responsible for outcome, a consequence of their expertise, knowledge, or motivation. Responsibility for outcome may be explained as the result of impersonal factors, perhaps chance, in terms of otherworldly agents, or in terms of the moral conduct of the healer, the sick person, or the sick person's family. Responsibility for the outcome of healing might be determined in an informal or formal way, perhaps established via an inquiry or a legal transaction. Healers might be immune from the consequences of an unexpected outcome, or they might be held personally responsible.

Healing Actions.   This refers to the types of activities that healers undertake and the resources they have access to for purposes of healing. It encompasses such things as ritual incantations, prayer, or ceremonies, all of which have moral/religious significance; physical procedures, which can vary in number, scope, and variety; social interventions aimed at probing and resolving family, community, or lineage conflicts; otherworldly dialogues with figures such as ancestors, spirits, or demons; the use of medicines, which themselves can vary in number, mode of preparation, and mode of administration. The degree to which anatomy and bodily functions are the focus varies, not only in terms of overall emphasis but also in terms of whether the body is externally drawn, internally drawn but analytically partitioned, or internally and anatomically partitioned. Healing can encompass comprehensive health management with regulation of habits and lifestyle, or it can be focused and discrete, limited entirely to the neutralization of symptoms or the undoing of specific causes. The procedures that a healer can perform may be limited to massage and manipulation of the external portions of the body, or they might include trephination and elaborate surgical procedures.

Uncertainty and Probability of Relief.   Almost by definition sickness is associated with apprehension and uncertainty. The nature of this uncertainty has been explored in great detail by Fox (1988a, 1988b), who rightfully sees it as pervading almost all of the medical enterprise. I concentrate here on a much narrower conception, emphasizing the likelihood that healing acts will bring relief of the concrete manifestations or indicators (i.e., symptoms) of sickness. This, no less than the broader uncertainty, is an enormously difficult parameter to delineate analytically with sufficient rigor to allow comparison. It can implicate organic factors as well as more subjective and perceptual ones under the sway of cultural conventions about the meaning of sickness and well-being. I emphasize here sicknesses other than trivial, common ones that experience teaches remit promptly; namely, the more protracted enigmatic pictures of symptoms or sicknesses. Furthermore, in all societies persons die from disease, having been unsuccessfully treated, so that a measure of uncertainty tied to sickness can be expected as a matter of course. Nevertheless, in some societies, depending on the mix of sicknesses, healing is or was associated with a high probability of relief and low uncertainty of outcome. In other words, in these societies much of the turmoil of serious and disabling sickness seems to have been reduced, although chronic symptoms of a mildly disabling and serious nature persist and are common. Different reasons can underlie this. In modern and contemporary societies science has managed to provide a great deal of confidence that many diseases can be controlled and undone. However, even without science, a relative degree of high probability, low uncertainty seems to have prevailed (compared to family- and village-level societies) in sedentary, agricultural societies, such as chiefdoms and prestates and especially states and empires, where chronic disease problems appear to have been numerous and a fair proportion of sicknesses were based on and construed in sociological terms, enhancing the likelihood that minor ailments could be played out for social purposes. With states and empires there is the likelihood of therapeutically useful pharmacopoeias whereas in small, village-level societies there existed a low probability of relief. As indicated, in modern and contemporary societies the probability of relief of symptoms of disease is quite high. Indeed, in these societies numerical estimates of probability of relief and ultimate reduction of uncertainty are possible. This does not mean that the broader sense of uncertainty about the ultimate meanings of life is in any way affected. In fact, as Fox (1988a, 1988b) has indicated, medical uncertainty in this more existential sense seems to have escalated.

Relationship with Sick Person. The quality of the relationship that healers establish with sick persons varies. A measure of mutual trust is almost universal; indeed, it seems to be rooted in the biology of altruism: Persons provide help to relatives and offspring, and this expands to include others with the expectation of future reciprocation. Sickness entails a measure of need, vulnerability, and dependence and an expectation that these will be met; the biological complement of this psychological state in the human line and in other species is the offering of help, support, and care (i.e., healing). A biology of healing can be modified by cultural conventions, but (given the contingencies of natural selection) it is unlikely that these will be contravened. Thus a measure of fiduciary bond between a sick person and a healer can be regarded as universal. With regard to more specific aspects of the relationship, one can observe that in small-scale societies they are close, informal, and egalitarian. The more academic, professional, and elitist the healer, the greater the likelihood that the relationship will be formal, neutral, impersonal, and distant. A factor that probably correlates with the preceding is the degree of confidentiality that exists between the "patient" and the "doctor." Healers can be friends, relatives, and even potential antagonists or simply neutral outsiders. Relationships that healers establish with sick persons can be moralistic, condemnatory, exhortatory, or friendly and supportive.

Influence on Sick Role.   Healing can in theory offer an unqualified endorsement of the sick role, essentially ratifying the sick person's definition of the situation. Healing can also be construed so impersonally that it bears no relation to how the sick person behaves. In contemporary, postmodern society, authentication of the sick role is something the healer and the state can influence, and this is classically the case with respect to disability determination.

Competition among Healers.   In small-scale societies, where all adults are potential healers and can participate in the process of healing, offering advice or forgiveness for a possible unintended action that might have caused sickness, the idea of competition among healers carries little currency. As healing becomes an occupation and especially a profession, there exists a high level of competition. In some societies, such as the early modern period in England, there existed intense competition. Conversely, in theory some societies might promote cooperation among healers, even when there are different varieties of them whereas in others government regulation may play a role, perhaps sharpening differences by prosecuting those that violate the official ideology that is stipulated to apply to sickness and healing.

Remuneration.   This varies considerably across societies depending on complexity and political economic structures. Even when remuneration for healing is expected, this can be set by the healer, left at the discretion of the sick person and his or her family, or stipulated by the state. The kinds of resources that are appropriate for compensation can vary; food, property, favors, or money can be expected.

Ethical Codes. These appear to vary directly in terms of the scope of professionalization and specialization that exists among the community of healers. In small-scale societies, there can be said to exist no ethical codes per se, other than the pervasive moral responsibility that group members share with each other and that they display through mutual participation as primary healers. With explicit roles and occupations of healing, a sense of collegiality and organization among healers, and remuneration seems to come the explicit formulation and stipulation of ethical codes. In modern and postmodern societies these are almost statutory, becoming part of litigation procedures, almost constituting criteria for the formal regulation of healing.

Parameters of Sickness and Healing in Different Societies

Each society is characterized by a distinctive picture of sickness that is a result of its profile of disease and injury. The latter is an outcome of the society's physical ecology, social organization, political economy, and culture and the genetic vulnerabilities of members of the population. Archaeologists and epidemiologists who study disease pictures in ancient populations have emphasized the different patterns of nutrition and diseases regularly associated with societies of different levels of organization and complexity. These generalizations were covered in earlier chapters.

With respect to sickness pictures, two heuristic assumptions were made. First, there exist panhuman genetic commonalities with respect to vulnerability to disease; all members of *Homo sapiens* are more or less equally vulnerable genetically to the same infectious agents and to the same disease processes. This generalization allows one to infer that the mix of diseases in a population is not a function of unique, special properties of its genetic structure. Second, the manifestations of any one disease, in particular, the unfolding of its biology, is not an exclusive result of genetic physiological factors unique to an individual. Such organismic factors underpin all sickness and are shared by members of the species *Homo sapiens*. This means that, in addition to the (universal) disease process, the culture of the individual will play a determinate role in explaining differences in the parameters of sickness and healing. These two assumptions allow one to explain the way sickness is configured across societies in terms of differences in culture and social organization and not differences in genetic factors affecting prevalence or physiologic responsivities.

The type of sickness picture and its overall meaning is extraordinarily important in determining how a people's medical knowledge is used. Sicknesses that produce minor symptoms and do not occasion much overall lassitude, weakness, and malaise are far more likely to be explained as "just happening" and naturalistically caused; those characterized by intense and persistent symptoms are more likely to be attributed to existential and moral causes that implicate otherworldly agents. Moreover, were one to record responses to sicknesses that progress and escalate from the mild and trivial to the serious and dangerous, one would see a progression in the types of explanations proffered, namely, from the naturalistic to the otherwordly. Because of the richer way in which the more serious and protracted sicknesses are handled in societies, they are used as reference points in the material presented earlier and in tables 3 and 4. When appropriate and necessary, peculiarities in the way a social formation might handle the more trivial sicknesses are included.

The description of parameters of sickness and healing naturally raises the question of whether sickness and healing could properly be said to evolve. What assumptions about the nature of sickness and healing need to be made in order to speak of their evolution? How does this process apply to phenomena that pertain to something as biological as disease and injury and yet also seem so rule based and intrinsic to cultural institutions? More specifically, accepting the idea of evolution of sickness and healing, how is one to construe the unit of selection? What indeed are the differences between biological and cultural evolution when sickness and healing are the topic of concern? A way of handling questions such as these is facilitated by using the various parameters as units that change and evolve.

Tables 3 and 4 summarize parameters of sickness and healing in each of the prototypical forms of social organization described above. In each table, an entry in a particular cell usually encompasses material in the preceding column of that row. As an example, developments found in village-level societies are often similar to those of the preceding variety, namely, family-level societies; thus, as an example, a description of the nature of responsibility and accountability of healers should be expected to presuppose and elaborate on characteristics found in the preceding social formation, found in the column to the left. In instances when this is the case, the corresponding column includes the entry "same," which indicates persistence of descriptive features. In the event that societies display sharply divergent parameters of sickness or healing, this entry is omitted.

Table 3. Parameters of Sickness in Prototypical Social Organizations

Sickness Parameters	Family-level Societies	Village-level Societies	Chiefdoms, Prestates, and States	Civilizations and Empires	Modern European Societies	Postmodern Societies
Sociomedical Properties	Moderate/high volume; good general health; many acute, short lasting infections (the zoonoses); skin lesions, trauma, high prevalence; little person-to-person spread; no epidemics	Same. More spread, fecal-oral; general health possibly lower	More spread; epidemics (?); signs and symptoms somewhat (?) important; higher volume; slightly more chronic; lower general health; fecal-oral spread high	Same; much spread; true epidemics; volume depends on socioeconomic status; more chronic; lower general health among poor; some "diseases of civilization," signs and symptoms become important	Same; epidemics better controlled; acute sicknesses better controlled; fear of closeness, germs; advent of many chronic diseases	Same; expansion of sickness definitions to include morale, appearance; much better control for many acute illnesses; fear of intimacy (AIDS)
Organismic Manifestations	Holism. Possession explanation for "mental illnesses"; no ontological differentiation; regarding types of symptoms	Same; possession likely explanation for "mental illnesses"; no devaluation of types of symptoms	Holism; possession explanation for "mental illnesses" very common; some ontological differentiation, as mental illness specialists can exist	Same; holism and no ontological differentiation in academic theory; ontological differentiation on social grounds; possession explanation very common	Dualism; ontological differentiation in academic theory and on social grounds; somatization bias; possession explanation minimized	Dualism, with holism also emphasized; ontological differentiation; psychologization bias; many types of personality disorder; widespread somatization
Knowledge	Few illness types; few causes; incon-	Same; some leaders might possess	Some illness types; more causes; more	Very elaborate; basic propositions complex	Same; ontological emphasis; distributed	Health/sickness an obsession; very much

	sistent propositions; not systematized; not separated; widely distributed; many naturalistic concepts; spirits involved also; no pluralism; knowledge equally shared in group	special knowledge; more causes; greater number, more elaborate propositions in theory	consistent basic propositions; some theoretical abstract concepts; greater separation from social; esoteric knowledge; some differentiation across population segments; some systematization; some pluralism	and more consistent; highly systematized, explicitly formulated; many causes, illnesses theoretical and abstract concepts; broadly comprehensive; unevenly distributed; some state sponsorship; esoteric knowledge; pluralistic knowledge systems; functional emphasis	in terms of social classes; less pluralistic; physician-controlled knowledge; state-sponsored knowledge; complex propositions; theoretical and abstract concepts abound	widespread throughout society; less pluralism yet interest in alternative medical systems; state-controlled knowledge of disease; theoretical and abstract concepts dominate; plethora of competing knowledge structures
Meanings (Semantics)	Sickness victimizes; dangerous overtones; probably much ritual, moral but physical/natural aspects important; very little social relations emphasis; environmental taboos possibly important; other or outsider blaming; danger to group subsistence; sicknesses not differentially marked	Same; ritual/moral predominates; some social relations emphasis; environmental taboos prominent; potential threat to group integration	Social relations and environmental taboos very important; physical features of body complement; ritual/moral and empirical/natural both important; sickness/healing played out in family and community relations	Physical features and functions of body very prominent; ritual/moral still found but varied as to social ethnic, religious groupings; social relations still important, but less so; psychological state important; illness types marked	Same; physical features and functions of body dominate; lower social classes and some ethnic groups retain indigenous meanings; psychological state less important; disease a denied possibility; health equals absence of disease	Physical and physiological predominate; psychological states important; social relations important; disease as heightened possibility; sickness as a realized preoccupation; sickness/healing played out in activity and wellness programs; health actively sought

Table 3. Parameters of Sickness in Prototypical Social Organizations (continued)

Sickness Parameters	Family-level Societies	Village-level Societies	Chiefdoms, Prestates, and States	Civilizations and Empires	Modern European Societies	Postmodern Societies
Responses	Usually social integrative to group; individual responsibility for seeking relief, family complements; few or no social implications; little or no interpersonal blaming; persons viewed as passive victims	Same; can also be socially divisive in group; some social anamneses expected; some blameworthiness	Same; social anamneses dominate; illnesses carry strong social implications; family influential in response	More socially integrative; social anamneses less dominant; beginnings of commodification of body; body preoccupations high; illnesses carry strong social implications; individual habits and healthful lifestyle emphases render passivity less prominent	"Germs" and contamination important; individual and family responsible for seeking relief; group social anamneses much less important; denial of disease; patient as passive victim of disease	Habits and social practices important; individual responsible for seeking relief; social anamneses not prominent; dominant commercialization of health, body, sicknesses; individual and communication media regulate; active mastery of disease
Expectations of Healing	Fatalism; possibility of death high; some purification; group ceremonies high; direct camaraderie; passive compliance; profound uncertainty, resignation	Same; greater purification; group ritual ceremonies still high; profound uncertainty and resignation; expect healer to help, his charisma nurtures	Same; death less imminent; more optimism; social exoneration; ceremonies more individualized; curing often a ritual journey; loyalty; beginnings of respect and awe for healer	Same; social variability; optimism high; less social exoneration; persisting invalidism and impaired well-being likely; relief of specific, chronic symptoms important; greater confidence	Same; great optimism; multiple expectations, with death a controllable eventuation; respect and awe; patient subordinate, compliant, passive, respectful; in awe of physician	Same; potentially expanded life; transplantation; death a manageable eventuation; less respect and awe; less optimism; partnership; active pursuit of health by self-healing

Access to Healers and Settings	Very easy, matter of course; public; setting not special	Same; occasionally actively sought; settings can be ritually important	Same; easy access, actively sought; hierarchy of resort; some settings privacy; some settings ritually important	Same; paid nurses, health caretakers; greater privacy; settings vary depending on social grouping; great variability	Less easy access, actively sought; biomedics dominate; privacy almost sacred; official settings; hospitals are doctor's sacred settings; person's identity reduced in hospital	Third party invades privacy; easy access, actively sought; many biomedical types, lay therapists, advisers; alternative systems; official settings for treatment and leisure settings for health promotion
Sick Role Conventions	Vague, loose, sick persons determine; few imposed restrictions; informally worked out; moral/ritual requirements	Same; family begins to influence playing of sick role	Family more influential in articulating; generously elaborated as illness linked to sociological and family/lineage dimension relevant; moral sanctions	Same; perhaps some standardization and formalization depending on socioeconomic level and specialist sought; sick role legitimized	Physician monitors, patient follows; well-defined script in doctor's setting, socially sanctioned publically	Visible, stringent, state/physician regulated and enforced; economic legal sanctions; patient's behavior scrutinized, carefully assessed
Sick Role Exploitations	Very low; little social manipulation; perhaps some unconscious motivation; difficult to exploit	Same, with some opportunity for manipulation; possibly some conscious motivation; difficult to exploit	High potential for social manipulation, conscious and unconscious; easy to exploit	Same; sick role can be incorporated into sickness and social identity; full potential for exploitation, conscious and unconscious	Much sick role indulgences; moderate level of exploitation; mainly unconscious	Harder to exploit; mainly unconscious but conscious important because of economic incentives; chronic symptoms challenge sick role

Table 3. *Parameters of Sickness in Prototypical Social Organizations (continued)*

Sickness Parameters	*Family-level Societies*	*Village-level Societies*	*Chiefdoms, Prestates, and States*	*Civilizations and Empires*	*Modern European Societies*	*Postmodern Societies*
Stigmatization	None	Very little, as moral wrongdoing somewhat important	Some stigmatization; family and personal morality important	Very high, sick person and family; mental illness stigma	Very high, mainly sick person; mental illness stigma	Moderate, mainly sick person; less mental illness stigma

Table 4. Parameters of Healing in Prototypical Social Organizations

Healing Parameters	Family-level Societies	Village-level Societies	Chiefdoms, Prestates, and States	Civilizations and Empires	Modern European Societies	Postmodern Societies
Number and Types of Healers	All or almost all adult males of group; many primary healers; group emphasis enforces compliance	Same; some elders possibly have more expertise; all implement same rationale; same outside village sought	Some specialists; some follow official views of sickness; some more practical, or more discredited; compliance variable; individual healer prestige and influence becomes important	Many types of specialists; prestige determines compliance; individual healer influence very strong	Proliferation of biomedical specialists; many paramedical personnel; high likelihood of compliance since physician very dominant, authoritative	Same; many alternative healers, trainers, therapists; compliance is internally based as physician like adviser
Knowledge of Healing	Knowledge secular and sacred; sick and healers share, no separation; cognitive memory structures, limit; part of social knowledge; not bodily elaborated; not complex or comprehensive; easily acquired	Same; some possibly more insightful, experienced; medical and social knowledge blended	Beginning of specialization; some have revelation, distinctive frameworks for explaining; more comprehensive, elaborate, and complex; acquired through apprenticeship; prestige high among diviners, priests; increase in secular knowledge	Pronounced specialization; diverse systems of knowledge; textual documents; highly elaborate and systematized; language of disease*; literate knowledge among academics; some spreading across healer types; systematic academic training or apprenticeship;	Same; formal, elaborate state schooling; state certified; literate; scientific; specialized; not accessible to sick; biomedical knowledge is expert, compelling, socially influential; pronounced specialization	Same; accessible to sick; spread by communication media; specialized as to disease, cause, age, and gender; widespread preoccupation with health, symptoms; high health, sickness, illness, and disease awareness; biomedical knowledge made public

Table 4.   Parameters of Healing in Prototypical Social Organizations (continued)

Healing Parameters	Family-level Societies	Village-level Societies	Chiefdoms, Prestates, and States	Civilizations and Empires	Modern European Societies	Postmodern Societies
				hereditarily transmitted in some instances; certification sometimes		
Meanings Associated with Healing	Broad public inquiries; threat to group subsistence; little interpersonal; moral and religious when curing instituted; many healing activities drawn from everyday, natural concepts, occurrences; healing is like group liberation; healing entails possibility of failure, death	Same; interpersonal, more prominent; a social and moral crisis as well as threat to life; attributed usually to outside group, occasional intragroup cause many splinter groups	Same; interpersonal very prominent; official religious has higher status, credibility; sociological implications prominent; diverse meanings, depending on ailment, severity, cause; healer can intrude into private matters	Same; less broad inquiries; official academic most prestigeful; other competing systems; impersonal and technical more important; more empirical; comprehensive, holistic view; sickness has many meanings related to social status and lifestyle; functional theory	Same; impersonal and technical dominate; official and standardized; physical engineering problem; mechanistic view; germ theory influential; dependence on specialist; healing undoes, removes sickness and disease (ontological view); some specialists invade privacy	Same; potentially correctable condition; behavior control, healthy lifestyles; healing cannot undo disease; sickness symptoms can be controlled, neutralized; many patients healthy and not sick but worried about disease

Responsibility and Accountability	Shared by primary healers; otherworldly agents; informally worked out; healers passive and weak	Same; perhaps occasional outside healer bears responsibility	Healers gain in strength, hence some responsibility on specialists; moral conduct of person and family; social inquiries through divination	Specialists; moral conduct of person sick	Impersonal; maximally placed on physician	Chance; formally determined, beginning of state determination; regulation; individual also held responsible
Healing Actions	Simple procedures, medicines; ritual incantations and prayer; group ceremonies very prominent; otherworldly dialogues; directed at whole sickness; bodily regions and functions not singled out in a special way but topical procedures present with body viewed from outside (externally drawn); lifestyle incorporates sickness-prevention, reflexively	Same; some social interventions; more elaborate procedures, cures, medicines, procedures; life programs are programs to avoid sickness	Same; more physical procedures; prominent social interventions; directed at sickness; body and its functions more singled out; more elaborate medicines, procedures	Same; very varied; physical procedures, diet, medicines very prominent; comprehensive health management; body prominently singled out; many focused, discrete procedures; directed at sickness and disease*; many medicines; body mainly externally drawn, more important as target but analytically not anatomically partitioned in many societies; anatomy in Galenic system	Same; expansion of surgery; anesthesia; directed mainly at disease; germs controlled; individual psychotherapy through talk; predominance of technological procedures; specialist actions aimed at sick; anatomical body is target	Same; organ replacement; chronic disease management; directed at non-disease also; much self-healing, prevention; diet, behavior, and medicines; group therapy, support

Table 4. Parameters of Healing in Prototypical Social Organizations (continued)

Healing Parameters	Family-level Societies	Village-level Societies	Chiefdoms, Prestates, and States	Civilizations and Empires	Modern European Societies	Postmodern Societies
Uncertainty and Probability of Relief	Very high uncertainty and low probability of relief for internal systemic problems; moderate for localized external lesions, ailments	Same; perhaps slightly higher due to accumulation and greater availability of knowledge of medicines, procedures, but doubtful	Higher; many sicknesses outcome of interpersonal, psychological conflicts that are effectively resolved in many instances	Higher for relief symptoms, some relief for specific diseases*; many chronic, less disabling, psychosocial sicknesses/illnesses "cured"	Very high for acute infections; surgery highly successful; advent of chronic diseases that are managed	Very high, but disease inevitable and physical symptoms of chronic diseases very prevalent; paradox of healthy but "sick" society with symptoms that can only be temporarily relieved
Relationship with Sick Person	Informal, equal, close, all share in treatment; healers are friends and relatives; friendly; supportive	Same; some social distance if outside elder or diviner; healers can be friends, even rivals; friendly; supportive	Depends on healer; some distance as consequence of role specialization and compensation; perhaps some confidentiality; some friends; mainly local folk; some moralistic tone; potentially condemnatory; some healers authoritarian	Same; greater social distance; confidentiality increased; some neutral outsiders; some local folk; some moralistic tone; paternalistic relationship; more authoritarian specialists	Same; neutrality, objectivity; distance, formality; physician active, dominant; marked confidentiality; neutral outsiders; dependence on specialist healers; supportive but authoritarian specialist healers	Same; less dependence on physician, often in partnership with person; confidentiality lessened by state regulation; physician as adviser; media and health industry personnel as advisers and enforcers of health

Influence on Sick Role	Automatic as part of healing; group monitors as part of informal and formal caring; healer has little effect; person determines	Same; perhaps beginning of family influence	Family influence considerable when social relations affected by diagnosis and treatment; family often determines sick role occupancy; special healers can influence	Specialists can formally ratify sickness and sanction sick role behavior; unqualified endorsement	Considerable physician influence; physician monitors	Marked as state intervenes; physician, state impose, determine; somatization promotes exploitation
Competition among Healers	None	None	Sight to moderate	Marked	Less marked but high within and across specialties	Same; regulated
Remuneration	None	Possible minimal gifts if healer outside village	Varied foodstuffs, currency	Prominent, depends on type of practicing	Prominent, depends on specialist and on reputation	State regulated, third party controls
Ethical Codes	Social morality	Social morality and social competition color morality of healing	Rudimentary; informal political hierarchy might supersede	Beginnings of formalization; stipulated in texts, commentaries popular, practitioners informal	Professional body implemented	State implemented

8

An Evolutionary Conception of Sickness and Healing

On the Phylogeny of the SH Adaptation

In chapter 2 I presented a perspective on a genetically based adaptation for sickness and healing. I assume that this adaptation has general biological roots and was perfected by natural selection in the line of evolution leading from protoculture to culture, culminating into *Homo sapiens*. A fundamental property of the adaptation was that of *recognizing* the effects of disease and injury (in the self and conspecifics) and *responding* in such a way so as to promote healing (in the self and conspecifics). The adaptation, then, constitutes a form of *symbolic behavior,* exercises a communicative function, and conveys meaning to the self and conspecifics.

I believe that the material reviewed in chapter 2 supports the assumption that sickness and healing are not "just" or "merely" cultural in nature. In other words, sickness and healing are not purely the expression of general psychological mechanisms subserving social behavior plus elaborations made possible by higher intelligence, curiosity, problem solving capacities, and capacities for existential awareness and spiritual yearning. Sickness and healing have a special, biological rationale; they are special and unique behaviors elicited by disease and injury and shaped by natural selection.

I discussed how the SH adaptation grew out of, elaborated, and no doubt influenced the neural mechanisms that mediate emotional contagion, empathy, compassion, and caring, all of which are integral to social cognition and behavior. In other words, the adaptation, which was naturally selected by the effects of disease and injury, presupposed and enhanced an organism's ability to be self-aware, distinguish self from other, and identify different states of the self and of conspecifics. I have emphasized that language, advanced levels of social cognition, and related "higher" cortical functions were integral elements that promoted and enhanced the overall effectiveness of the adaptation. In short, when complemented by associated cerebral mechanisms linked to the evolution of human intelligence, the adaptation led to more elaborated efforts to cope adaptively with disease and injury through healing.

The argument in support of the evolutionary basis of sickness and healing was constructed on the basis of a synthesis of the literature in general biology and made extensive use of knowledge pertaining to the behaviors of nonhuman primates, especially chimpanzees. I will recapitulate briefly generalizations and related assumptions that were used to argue in favor of a special adaptation for sickness and healing. The following are relevant: (1) caregiving is observed in any number of animal communities; (2) caregiving constitutes a form of social behavior; (3) caregiving is triggered by sickness signals (i.e., a consequence of disease and injury) in a conspecific and, thus, has an interpretive and communicative basis; (4) self-medication also has a phylogenetic distribution; (5) self-medication entails deliberative behavior; (6) self-medication is triggered by a condition of an organism analogous to our "sickness"; (7) caregiving and self-medication are "natural" responses to sickness; (8) sickness, caregiving, and self-healing constitute integrated, reflexive behaviors that are adaptive (i.e., promote longevity and reproduction and group harmony/organization); (9) in nonhuman primates sickness and healing draw on, influence, and in an integrated, dialectical way, relate to mechanisms underlying social behavior and social cognition (e.g., involving self-awareness, perception of psychological states in group mates, empathy) as well as general cognition (e.g., knowledge acquisition, social memory, problem solving); and finally, (10) sickness and healing behaviors need to be viewed not as mere passive consequences of other psychological mechanisms but as influential causes of much of human adaptive behavior (i.e., as having a primary function).

Generalizations and assumptions such as these serve a heuristic purpose. They help to point out how the idea of a special adaptation for sickness and healing (the SH adaptation) "makes sense" biologically, that is, from the standpoint of human evolution. In this chapter I present further material in support of such an idea. My goal is to show how use of this idea of SH can integrate knowledge in the social and biological sciences that pertain to the study of medicine. Support for the validity of an evolutionarily sculpted biological adaptation for medicine will depend on field and comparative studies in general biology and primatology and on further, more rigorous theoretical analyses by scholars from different disciplines.

The Dynamics of the SH Adaptation

The SH adaptation constitutes a mechanism or machinery that produces sickness and healing. The adaptation was progressively forged during the process of human evolution. It is obviously a complex, "higher-order" adaptation: It is held to "sense" when the various "lower-order" physiological and chemical responses (e.g., metabolic, gastrointestinal, respiratory, immunological) of the organism are diseased or injured. When any of these systems breaks down, it brings about local and systemic changes in the organism that signal disordered anatomies, chemistries, and physiologies.

The SH adaptation may be thought to "use" the signs and symptoms of disease and injury to communicate to the organism (and to conspecifics) that illness exists and that healing (self- and other-healing) is necessary. It does the latter by organizing behavior in a biologically meaningful way so that the organism and conspecifics "know" and "learn about" the results of disease and injury. The immediate, proximal function or "goal" of the adaptation is to bring about healing actions so that the effects of disease and injury can be countered.

The SH adaptation was forged in the environment of evolutionary adaptedness that involved the movement from protoculture to culture in man. This environment prevailed during the Pleistocene and consisted of small, group living, family-oriented communities of hunter-gatherers. That the SH adaptation was forged during these conditions is crucial. In such highly migratory groups conditions of living were harsh and competition between groups and with other mammals, especially with higher primates, was very keen.

The effects of disease and injury were immediately registered in behavior and could easily compromise a group's mobility, pattern and efficiency in hunting/gathering, and resourcefulness with respect to competition. These conditions naturally constrained the way sickness and healing could be carried out; in other words, what and how much could be made of disease and injury. The resulting picture of sickness and healing, its parameters given these socioecologic conditions, was described in chapter 2.

How a scenario of sickness is constructed and played out is anchored in the psychosomatic, somatopsychic unity of the apparatus that biological evolution has furnished *Homo sapiens*. In other words, organisms are programmed to respond to disease and injury in a holistic way that encompasses bodily, mental, and behavioral changes. Features of the social and physical environment provide the input to the program and thus influence the form of the SH response.

The dynamism of SH and the protean character of its effects in the form of sickness and healing need emphasis. On the one hand, the SH adaptation essentially commands, psychologically, organisms to attend to the effects of disease and injury so as to identify a state of illness (as sickness) and to heal themselves and significant comembers: the adaptation can be regarded as programming a *language of sickness and healing*. The expressive, message component of the SH language informs about disease and injury through sickness behaviors and its receptive/interpretive component elicits and gives rise to healing behaviors. On the other hand, the social and cultural environment provides an input that influences how the adaptation is finally configured and played out. During human evolution, the environment of evolutionary adaptedness constrained how the SH adaptation would be configured and played out.

As discussed in chapter 2, the exigencies of Lower and Middle Paleolithic living conditions in prehuman groups necessitated short-term, cost-effective investments with respect to sickness and healing. Relief and reversal of the distress of disease and injury were the problems that the SH adaptation was geared to solve. However, the possibility, indeed likelihood, of death was also an integral component of the language of sickness and healing sculpted in the brain by evolution. That disease and injury were dangerous and could kill provided urgency and socially bounded and existentially contextualized the expression of the SH adaptation. Those equipped with the capacity to "speak and understand" the language of sickness and healing also "knew" that these common ubiquitous medical eventuations could and often did kill.

The dynamism of the SH adaptation resides in the imperatives of the expressive and communicative situation created by disease and injury. Organisms are provided with a behaviorally compelling grammar and syntax with which to demand and expect healing, a language that also compels them to provide this healing to themselves and to others. The benefits of the SH adaptation and of the situations created are to restore health and well-being if possible or to ameliorate and assimilate the sense of loss in the event of death. The result is to restore and promote individual and group initiatives (selfish and/or altruistic), including competition, everyday needs, and requirements of living, including, for example, reproduction and social cooperation. The costs are those of having to suspend other pursuits and activities and having to provide resources entailed in healing and medical caring.

Each of the two biologically integrated facets of the SH adaptation, and of the behavioral scenarios it constructed, need to be kept in mind for each can be made the focus of individualistic attention and exploitation, as was reviewed in chapters 3 and 4. On the one hand, in a setting of personal distress and suffering, an individual is equipped with an expressive language that is compelling and that can be used to garner personal, selfish health advantages and resources. It can be used to manipulate the social environment and all of the potential healers in it. The individual is more or less free to make of sickness and healing what it can and has only the group and its culture to contend with. The roots of somatization, psychologization, and medicalization more generally reside in this dynamism and holism of the SH adaptation and its potential for exploitation. This point, already emphasized in the case of empires and civilizations, will be elaborated in a later section.

On the other hand, given conditions of distress and suffering in others, individuals are empowered with a powerful language with which to manipulate them for personal, selfish gain. In providing or promising to provide healing and relief to sick and distressed members of the group, healers purchase advantages and rewards, which, again, the group and its culture make possible. In summary, just how the sickness component of the SH adaptation is constructed depends on biology and culture, and so also does the healing component, and both can be exploited for pure, selfish gain.

On the Material of the SH Adaptation

The question arises as to how best to conceptualize the SH adaptation from an ontological and epistemological standpoint. Is it neurobiological machinery? Is it psychological mechanism? Is it behavior? Is it genetic, or is it cultural? Previous discussions have implicated all of these types of considerations. Furthermore, putting aside the matter of what exactly the adaptation consists of, how can it best be formulated so as to make it conform to a process that entails the variation, selection, and retention of material that somehow evolves? Here, one can think of *medical genes* to better visualize and make epistemological use of the complex, biocultural nature of the adaptation that lies at the root of medicine.

Medical genes, or "medgenes," are what give rise to or program the SH adaptation. They are the units of material that were selected during human evolution and that gave and give rise to the machinery that produces the behavioral ensemble of sickness, healing, and the medical itself. The idea of medical genes is used with the awareness that it encompasses a complex phenomenon that is not easily delimited into well-defined categories. By definition, medgenes are *medical* because they connect with and are part of the effects of disease and injury. Because the SH adaptation was progressively sculpted by natural selection during human evolution, it is under *genetic* control and can be said to consist of or depend on genes. Because the adaptation enables those in possession of it to learn, communicate about, understand, and respond adaptively to the distress and suffering of disease and injury, it has a direct connection with *medical memes* ("medmemes") discussed in the previous chapter.

The concepts of medical genes and memes, then, help to convey the complex meaning carried in the idea that sickness, healing, and medicine are all products of human genetic and social cultural evolution. First, they indicate that medicine rests on a biology of disease and injury: The SH adaptation draws on and makes use of the manifestations of disease and injury so as to signal its owner that sickness and healing are required. Second, the concepts indicate that the adaptation at the base of medicine has been progressively shaped by natural selection and entails mechanisms that program behavior. Third, the concepts indicate that the SH adaptation involves units of biological and cultural information designed to constructively solve the problems of human disease and injury. Fourth, the concepts alert that the phenotypic effects of genetic and cultural information are all complexly implicated in the SH adaptation. Fifth, because cultural information is integral to the adaptation (how it is expressed and handled), the medical memes in particular signal the ease with which details pertaining to sickness and healing can spread within and across groups and generations.

The SH adaptation, constituting an amalgam of biology and culture geared to relieve and neutralize the bodily and mental distress and suffering ordinarily produced by disease and injury, can be used in different ways and for different purposes. It can be used to directly signal manifestations of disease and injury, given conditions of physical, biological, psychological, and social stress, so as to elicit healing. The somatopsychic/psychosomatic unity of SH, its holism, means that human beings are naturally programmed with a capacity to show distress and suffering *regardless of its origins,* although, as indicated earlier, the social environmental "input" plays an influential role in the form that the response takes. Stress occasioned by purely social or political economic hardships can "switch on" or constitute the input for the SH adaptation just as much as can infectious agents or an altered metabolism. The adaptation is integral to the empathy, concern, and caregiving inherent in medical healing, considered in a broad sense. Finally, the adaptation can be exploited by an allegedly sick person or seemingly well-intentioned, would-be but fictive healers for purely individualistic and selfish ends. In this latter sense, medical genes and memes, and the SH adaptation that they realize, make connection with the biology and psychology of manipulation so lucidly depicted by Dawkins (1982).

In the previous chapter a medical meme (i.e., healmemes and sickmemes) was defined as a unit of information that described the content of the material of the SH adaptation in the brain and that was expressed in socially meaningful behaviors or actions related to sickness and healing. The SH adaptation, in effect, is realized through a set of medical genes that are a product of biological evolution and that in conjunction with medical memes provide the basis for different cultural approaches to sickness and healing.

When visualized behaviorally and socially, the products or phenotypic effects of a set of medical memes that are characteristic of a population are what furnish the parameters of sickness and healing of a society with distinctive profiles as summarized in the previous chapter. The ideas of medical genes and memes bear a relation to what have been termed epigenetic rules or psychological adaptations (Lumsden and Wilson 1981; Tooby and Cosmides 1990a, 1990b; Wilson and Lumsden 1989). They are anchored in the evolutionary psychology of *Homo sapiens* but are shaped by and realized in and through cultural conventions.

Since medical memes are in some way a product of cultural and social evolution, they are in some way responsive to mechanisms and processes taking place at the "group" (or societal, cultural) level. However, although learned from "culture and society," the search for, development, use, storage, and ultimate value or purpose of medical memes bear a relationship to the process of natural selection. As units of cultural information stored in the brain and connected to genetic programs of the SH adaptation, medical memes are affected by the process of natural selection operating on medical genes. Thus a heal-meme that in the guise of healing actually involved doing harm and damage to an individual or to his or her body, such as to lead to that individual dying in the long run, would eventually be selected against. In this example, either natural selection or cultural selection might be operating to bring this about. (See later discussion.)

The SH adaptation discussed in chapter 2 can be analogized to a computational theory that was evolved for the purposes of solving problems posed by sickness and healing. Many of the routines and suites of behavior comprising SH can be thought of as products or expressions of basic medical genes that are represented in complex neurobehavioral programs of the brain (the term used by Laughlin and d'Aquili [1974], "neurocognosis," bears a relation to the point discussed here, as well as to the idea of medical memes). The structure and functioning of these basic medical genes cannot be expected to have appreciably evolved in recent history, and they continue to produce universals of behavior integral to sickness and healing. When influenced by medical memes, some of these medical genes can be masked, modified, counteracted, or elaborated as perhaps occurred in later stages of the evolution of sickness and healing. Interactions between medical genes and memes lead to differences in the biocultural manifestations of disease and injury. The more plastic, evolved products of medical genes are comparatively more influenced by learning during enculturation. Medical memes integral to the social and cultural evolution of medicine, although motivated by and instanciated in complex organizations of the central nervous system pertinent to sickness and healing, are part of the more general cognitive imperatives created by diverse behavioral problems, not just those generated by human disease.

Many of the parameters singled out in the previous chapter that characterize sickness and healing embody and reflect medical memes. It is quite likely that some of them may have actually favored (i.e., helped select for, enhanced the inclusive fitness of) individuals who invented them, but the selective advantage of a medical meme to its inventor is not of exclusive interest here. What is equally, if not more, important is their general social and cultural effects. In the event, the immediate adaptive consequence of a medical meme to problems posed by sickness and healing is one determinant of its value or "success."

If the persons who invent a medical meme, or who appropriate it, were in positions of power and thus could have their will imposed on the society, this also constitutes a factor in the "successful" implementation and propagation of medical memes, *at least in the short run*. As a result, others of the society learned them or had them enforced. In time, medical memes become institutionalized, fixed by social structures of organization in the society. As a result, the memes may have lost connections with agents for whom they proved to be initially selective in the strictly biological evolutionary sense or in the social and cultural evolutionary sense. However, because of social inertia or because the medical memes have entered into cultural arrangements of great complexity with significant vested political economic power, they continue to be propagated even though they may in a strict sense prove harmful, thus constituting social maladaptations. Some products of medical memes unquestionably qualify as cultural universals in the sense that, given social formations of certain size and scope, they are very likely to be found in use because they prove advantageous to many individuals (Brown 1991). Either as a result of diffusion or new invention, the medical memes and their "phenotypic" effects (or analogues of them) will be found operating and structuring the way sickness and healing are conceptualized or played out in many societies of the type in which they evolved or in societies showing higher or lower degrees of social organization.

Not all medical memes can be said to carry any differential measure of inclusive fitness to individuals who carry them. At the level of the individual, medical memes that are learned or imposed by others or by "the society" may or may not favor an enhancement of inclusive fitness. Some may be neutral in the sense that they do not differentially (i.e., via natural selection) affect an individual's health or reproduction or that of his or her relatives. On the other hand, some medical memes may in fact constitute maladaptations that have simply been propagated "by custom," without a full appreciation of their individual effects. The tendency to somatize, to exploit the sick role and the potential of the healer, by virtue of the role that evolves for him or her, and to promote or extend sickness were cited as possible examples of medical memes that have led to social maladaptations.

The Ontogeny of the SH Adaptation

All individuals are held to incorporate the SH adaptation. It constitutes an innate structure that produces sickness and healing behavior. The machinery of the adaptation is a property of the mind-brain. It acts as a maturational constraint that programs an individual to attend to, interpret, and act on specific types of information pertaining to disease and injury. The adaptation provides necessary conditions for the activation and execution of a cognitive/emotional/social readiness state that one can think of as an illness. Depending on personal experiences in the family and contingent on cultural representations prevalent in the group, an individual who is diseased or injured and as a consequence of activation of SH perceives himself or herself as ill is held to progressively "learn how to be sick and heal" (itself and others) in a manner conditioned by the adaptation and cultural information.

The SH adaptation matures and unfolds in an individual and the suite of behaviors that it produces is influenced by social experiences with caretakers and group mates. Looked at in a developmental context and neurobiologically, young children already in the first year begin to differentiate self from others and in the second year show behaviors toward distressed others that are held to constitute empathy, concern, and caring (Levenson and Ruef 1992; Stern 1985; Zahn-Waxler et al. 1992; Zahn-Waxler and Radke-Yarrow 1990). This behavioral ensemble allows for attempts to alleviate discomfort in others and has analogues in nonhuman primates, as discussed in chapter 2 (see also Brothers 1989, 1990).

In short, the machinery that evolution has designed to facilitate social cognition and social relations in general is held to constitute the foundation for the more specialized adaptation that eventually produces sickness and healing responses. The SH adaptation, as discussed in chapter 2, constitutes an elaboration and refinement of neural mechanisms and behavior dispositions that, in conjunction with maturational experiences associated with disease and injury as well as other stressful life events, pattern and shape an individual's responses that we term sickness and healing. During childhood and probably into adolescence (Sweeting 1994), individuals' experiences (social psychological and medical) with caretakers, family members, and comembers come to influence how they express and respond to sickness in self and others.

At the most general level, the culture and social organization of the group, mediated by family members, furnish the input that activates and completes the programming of the adaptation, which, in turn, influences the way sickness and healing are eventually configured and played out. The kinds of experiences that individuals have with disease and injury during "critical" periods of childhood thus play influential roles in how the SH adaptation is shaped in the individual. Here, it is possible to visualize two types of emphases or scripts created by the interaction of biology and social environment.

From the standpoint of the individual, experiences with disease and injury (in the self or significant others) during a critical period of development of the SH adaptation can influence how that individual comes to medically orient to sickness in others. Adult, mature expressions of the adaptation can be surmised. It is possible that certain culturally contextualized "successful" experiences with disease and injury in some persons have the effect of reinforcing and heightening innate behavioral tendencies to heal. Healers of a social group, be they physicians, shamans, nurses, diviners, or herbalists, are individuals who, depending on social and cultural circumstances, are characterized by more or less distinctive developmental experiences with disease and injury during a critical period of development. In them, thus, the adaptation unfolds so that as adults they are attracted and drawn to heal others. Conversely, other types of developmental experiences may culminate in a tendency to minimize or withdraw from the effects of disease and injury in others. These are individuals who shun, avoid, or are repelled by disease and injury in others, which leads them away from the healing role.

Other types of critical developmental experiences are held so strongly influence, if not determine, how adult individuals come to behave when they
themselves are ill. Whether the individual comes to exaggerate or underplay a
condition of illness, for example, is a result of how SH constraints are affected
by inputs from the physical and social environment as contextualized culturally.
Thus an outcome of excessive worry or preoccupation with bodily function
and health as well as accentuation of bodily symptoms, roughly analogous to
but less pejorative than our "hypochondriasis," is one possible outcome of
(perhaps negative, unsuccessful) experiences with disease and injury. Related
to this outcome is a tendency to overuse or exploit society's sick role in the setting of disease problems others might judge as not serious. Another outcome is
a tendency to deny, inattend to, or disregard the signals set up in the body in a
setting of disease; that is, the obverse of a worrier or one who easily succumbs
to similar types of signals.

What clinical medicine today conceptualizes as aberrations or idiosyncrasies
in the way some persons cope with disease and injury, "aberrations" that are
defined given the biomedical epistemology and that would not have been socially profiled in earlier epochs, are probably related to special inputs that come
to influence how the SH adaptation unfolds during childhood, adolescence, and
early adulthood. The basis for this claim is the notion that sickness and healing
ensembles are culturally constructed in the context of disease and injury, and
that an individual's experiences with disease and injury during critical periods
of development *in a distinctive cultural environment* are what comes to "fix" or
stabilize the way the SH adaptation comes to operate in the individual.

In terms of the individual, then, early, critical experiences with disease and
injury should be regarded as highly influential in how the innate, genetically
determined SH adaptation is shaped and comes to function in organizing behaviors of sickness and healing. Within parameters set by culture and social
organization, variation in the way the SH adaptation is expressed is a result of
the interaction between genetic loading carried by medical genes and input experiences carried by medical memes. In brief, genetic information is held to
influence how cultural information comes to be encoded in the brain (as medical memes). Here again, as discussed earlier, one notes the integration of biology and culture with respect to how the SH adaptation is realized.

One can also point to the interplay of biological constraints and culturally
programmed input experiences pertaining to disease and injury in terms of groupwide, societal consequences. This can be visualized leading to the formation
of the different parameters of sickness and healing described in chapter 7. In
other words, the distinctive patterns of sickness and healing found in different
social types should be regarded as the result of how innate, biological tendencies to express disease and injury in symbolic idioms are molded by cultural
uniformities. This means that a social group's, society's, or culture's tendency
to somatize or psychologize sickness and healing will undoubtedly be a result
of the kinds of memes prevailing in the group, society, and culture. The pool of

memes of the society essentially realizes the developmental programs embodied in the SH adaptation.

The psychosomatic/somatopsychic capacity to medicalize conditions of distress and suffering *in different ways and with different emphases* may be held to reside in the way members of a society have come to operationalize, using cultural knowledge, the biologically innate information that leads to the formation and expression of the SH adaptation. Human evolution through natural and social selection has fashioned an adaptation that for its expression and final realization requires cultural and social inputs related to disease and injury. A society's pictures of sickness and healing should be viewed as only partially determined by its epidemiology and its familiarity with biomedical "facts" about disease and injury; in other words, the way individuals are "expected to behave" given *biomedical biases* about type of disease/injury and associated mind/body relations constitute but one factor in the way sickness and injury are programmed. Stated baldly, the behavioral character of a society's medical facts is a function of the interplay between innate, universal programs and culturally variable inputs.

In summary, the SH adaptation endows all human organisms with a capacity to respond to disease and injury in a biologically significant way. As a cognitive/emotional/behavioral constraint the adaptation requires information from the environment with which to operate. The developmental trajectory of the SH adaptation in any one person is probably highly vulnerable to "critical" experiences during childhood and adolescence provided by family members and caretakers, all contextualized culturally. Depending on this interplay, more or less distinct "careers" of sickness and healing are constructed in a social group. Healers and health care workers are individuals socially selected or behaviorally shaped because of unusual genetic loading or environmental experiences pertaining to the SH adaptation. In the same way, persons who exaggerate, deny, or delay seeking care for illness and groupwide behaviors that appear to underplay or overplay different facets of sickness and healing are all forged by the interaction of genetic mind/brain constraints and social experiences related to disease and injury that underwrite the SH adaptation.

Conceptualizing the Evolution of the Medical

Viewed in abstract terms, an evolutionary process implies three things. First, an entity or system that changes. In the present case, this entails what one can term a medical system or organization that is made up of particulate units that in their totality shape the social practices related to sickness and healing. All of the preceding, in turn, have an effect on the level of disease and injury in the society. Second, agencies, forces, or processes that perturb or change the system; in particular, changes affecting the level, intensity, and mode of configuration of sickness and healing in a society. The third factor involves the production, variation, selection, and retention of units of the system. Features programming the machinery of the SH adaptation and the information underlying the beliefs and actions related to sickness and healing are seen to be the products of medical genes and memes, respectively, "units" that vary, are selected by agents of some sort, and are differentially "passed on" to subsequent generations as a consequence of their adaptive value or use/utility.

How sickness and healing evolve, indeed, the paths and configurations taken during cultural evolution, was illustrated in a descriptive sense by means of the various parameters of sickness and healing. They are intended to portray how sickness and healing as behavioral phenomena produced by the habits and routines that constitute the expression of the SH adaptation are configured in a particular society or level of social organization/evolution. The particulate units of the medical that are subject to the evolutionary process have been termed "medical memes" to equate them with units of (genetic) information in biological evolution.

That units of cultural information pertaining to the medical are affected by evolutionary processes implies two things. First, and from a general standpoint, it implies that how sickness and healing are configured and played out in a social formation change as a consequence of changes in the prevalence, morbidity, and mortality of disease. Such epidemiological characteristics are all influenced by social, ecological, biological, and cultural factors. Second, evolution of the medical implies that these same types of factors play a role in the invention, evaluation, selection, rejection, or retention of medical memes, which are what structure sickness and healing.

Evolution in medicine involves the selection of particulate units of information of two types and by means of two processes. There is much disagreement about whether biological and cultural evolution constitute two processes, whether they can be equated at all; and given the possibility of the existence of two types of evolutionary processes, there is a disagreement as to whether they can be thought of as taking place at different levels of organization (Sober and Lewontin 1982). The units of selection in either or both processes are highly controversial as well. The most fundamental involves biological evolution, and in this case many hold that the genes (or clusters of them) are the units of selection. Some hold that individuals constitute actual units of selection in biological evolution and others that individuals constitute the vehicles for the preservation of genes, the true units of selection (Dawkins 1982).

As indicated earlier in this chapter, individuals are held to inherit medical genes and with input provided by medical memes elaborate culturally meaningful scenarios of sickness and healing, depending on social circumstances. This means that evolution in medicine also involves the selection of cultural units of information. The units of selection in the cultural and social evolution of medicine are memes. Here again there is controversy; some hold that memes are the proper units of selection, others that individuals are selected, and still others that groups of individuals or larger units, such as social structures and whole societies, are what evolve. In the logic of Dawkins (1982), it would be appropriate to hold that memes constitute the units of selection in cultural evolution and that individuals or larger entities really constitute the vehicles for the preservation of memes. Stephen K. Sanderson (1995b: 14), who is mainly concerned with social evolution, holds that there is no such thing as "group selection" but that "nevertheless, it is groups and societies that do the actual evolving, even if only by virtue of selection and adaptation taking place at the level of individuals."

I have found it useful to sidestep these controversies whenever possible. I hold that genes and individuals and memes and individuals can usefully be thought to constitute units of selection in the processes of biological and cultural evolution, respectively. I also find it useful to think of selection at levels higher than the group in the case of cultural evolution, and whether collectivities are the units selected or the vehicles of memes remains an open question in my mind. In this and in later chapters I elaborate on these issues.

Medical Memes as the Basis for Medical Institutions

Units of cultural information stored in the brain as memes produce ways of orienting to, thinking about, and behaving in the setting of disease and injury. Habitual ways of constructing and patterning sickness and healing bring to mind what social scientists construe as institutions ("settled habits of thought common to the generality of men" [Veblen 1919: 239]). Seen as "an outgrowth of the routinized thought processes that are shared by a number of persons in a given society" (Hodgson 1993: 125), institutions involving sickness and healing are nothing but products of medical memes that are shared by members of a society or group.

This reasoning about medical institutions and about phenotypic effects of medical memes is consistent with current thinking in the social sciences wherein institutions of different types are handled as habits and patterns of thought and behavior of a relatively enduring nature that are intrinsic to and shared by persons interacting in human communities or societies. Institutions vary as to content; and they serve to pattern, organize, and provide meaning to behavior in different areas. The medical institutions impose ordered behavior in the areas pertaining to disease and injury and in this way constitute social conditions of sickness and healing.

In the account presented here, then, the products of medical memes of a collectivity or society are essentially medical institutions. Because these medical institutions are based on particulate units of information, they are easily communicated to others who on learning them come to also play them out behaviorally among persons. Just as memes are inherited, so are institutions. The set of medical memes that is found in a society or collectivity may be held to constitute its medical organization or corporation. A macrosociological description of a medical system as a whole is taken up in chapter 10.

Medical memes, their products, and the integration that exists among these products in the form of medical institutions *mix and compete with* other, nonmedical memes, their products, and the coordination implicit in them as nonmedical institutions of the society. As an example, there exist a variety of economic, political, legal, and religious institutions that operate in a society and that regulate individual behavior and social action more generally. Institutions are based on (the product of) elemental units of information that people internalize cognitively and that serve to standardize behavior in different social spheres and within social organizations or corporations (the latter are often the form that institutions take in complex societies). Varieties of these institutions, and perhaps ordered clusters of them, can be held to be subject to processes of social and cultural evolution as adumbrated by social scientists.

In summary, in social and cultural evolution institutions compete with one another and, depending on their value/utility/function, are differentially selected. Because they are based on particulate units of information that are learned from others (and eventually stored in brains), they spread in the society; and, provided they contribute to adaptation in the short run, broadly construed, they may be passed on to succeeding generations. Selection of institutions entails the selection of underlying medical units (i.e., the medical memes) *in relation to other units of information,* for example, memes involved in the social construction of political, economic, and religious institutions. Thus medical meme products may conflict and compete with each other and with other types of cultural information and institutions (i.e., memes) that are found in a society or collectivity.

Some Further Complexities Attending Medical Evolution

The process accounting for the selection of medical memes, their products, and their integration as institutions, a process complementing biological/genetic evolution, may be provisionally illustrated in a descriptive sense as follows. Using so-called postmodern societies as an example, one can point to a number of different types of institutions that compete with the medical ones. What one could term institutions pertaining to culinary and leisure pursuits (i.e., patterns of thought, feeling, and action that are widely shared pertaining to pleasurable eating and outing) frequently compete with health habits/directives (products of medmemes) involving appropriate foods and lifestyles that have evolved as part of the healing of certain diseases as well as for the maintenance of health and the prevention of disease more generally. In this instance, then, the implementation of certain medical memes conflicts with the implementation of other memes pertaining to related areas of behavior.

Memes, their products and institutions pertaining to a person's vocation or occupation, and the need for the attainment of success/prestige that attaches to all of this can obviously "compete" with medical memes and their products that enjoin rest, relaxation, and leisure. The medical meme that prepares an individual to expect healing and that has been elaborated during cultural evolution to yield the expectation of dyadic healing (i.e., that enjoins an exclusive reliance on a "doctor-patient" relationship) is now competing with newly developed memes and medmemes the products of which urge and enjoin managed care and group medical practices. The result of this is considerable unrest among patients and doctors and may constitute a transitional point in the social and cultural evolution of medicine.

Escalation of the cost of malpractice insurance and disability/negligence litigation alert one to the fact that medical memes can compete sharply with institutions or memes related to prevailing political and legal concerns. Thus the medical memes and their products that have prepared the doctor-patient relationship in a positive light (e.g., enjoining trust, goodwill, commitment, faithfulness) have come to compete (unfavorably, it would seem) with the effects of newer medical memes about healers and with memes and political institutions pertaining to civil liberties, property violation, and freedom in the pursuit of one's self-interest. This competition obviously leads to problems of medical litigation and in the delivery of medical care, and the effects currently suggest a possible transition point in the social evolution of medicine.

In the area of life preservation and terminal illness, one can see complex changes in the way products of medical memes (e.g., professional norms and ethical imperatives) have continued to operate and function. The environment of evolutionary adaptedness sculpted medical memes that enjoined sickness and healing under conditions of group living during the Early and Middle Paleolithic eras. The biological constraints of this social ecology did not allow for sickness exploitation or healing exploitation; nor did it promote protracted healing in the setting of chronic or serious, progressive sickness. In fact, the medical memes of prehuman and early human groups prepared sick persons and healers to anticipate little care given a context of terminality. Sick persons and significant others prepared and planned for death as part of the SH adaptation. However, as a result of medical evolution during phases of states and civilizations—which involved greater leisure, wealth, complexity of organization, and literate medical knowledge traditions—medical memes and their products evolved to prepare individuals to expect continued care and healing well beyond conditions of health that in earlier periods would have been judged as wasteful and unnecessarily costly. A related point is that the temptation to exploit sickness became not only possible but also compelling, and although this cannot simplistically be invoked as "causing" unnecessary, heroic medical efforts and treatments in the context of terminality, it nonetheless certainly bears a relationship to the dilemma of planning prudently for death.

Currently, in the modern and postmodern setting, preparedness for sickness and healing has entailed so costly an enterprise that the responsible medical meme (or a set of them) now competes with memes, meme products, and institutions pertaining to savings, income, property, and the like as when individuals or families are forced to consider making costly trade-offs pertaining to treatment of a chronic or terminal disease. And the medical memes obviously "compete" with memes, meme products, and institutions associated with various industries that make use of science and technology.

A final example of how conflict and opposition between medical and nonmedical memes can potentially affect the evolution of sickness and healing can be illustrated for the contemporary period by considering problems associated with the treatment of chronic medical conditions in persons with mental retardation or brain injury who require hospitalization. Very often such patients, in addition to being unable to care for themselves properly, develop disabling symptoms such as aggressiveness, self-injurious actions, and convulsions. It can be appreciated that in a social environment and ecology that was harsh, punitive, and depriving (such as during the evolution of the human line) these individuals would have been the targets of selective infanticide or neglect. Throughout most of history, individuals such as these have generally been provided with marginal care and little or no healing. Over the course of the cultural evolution of medicine, the medical memes and behaviors of sickness/healing that came to institutionalize such social medical practices have become progressively elaborated and changed so that today special organizations and professionals are available whose primary concerns are the problems presented by mentally and neurologically compromised individuals. Parents or guardians are invariably the persons who constitute the first unit of the appropriate healing party for these individuals. In addition, they are morally and legally empowered to make decisions about medication on behalf of such patients because the latter are intellectually compromised and not fully competent in a juridical sense.

Very often those responsible, although well intentioned, do not grant permission for an identified treatment plan. Reasons given are such things as opposition to a specific psychoactive agent, dislike or distrust of physicians, or disagreement on principle with the medical team's assessment of diagnosis or need for treatment (despite having brought the patient for hospitalization).

The result of such an impasse is that the patients are often discharged improved (when permission is granted to pursue an alternative, less than optimal plan) only to subsequently fail to maintain improvement. That family or guardians are not able to provide a therapeutic setting in the home very often precipitates a readmission just as much as do the limitations inherent in the initially chosen, less than optimal treatment plan.

The readmission initiates a new round of appraisal and discussion that all too often has the same end result as the original hospitalization. A third, "objective" or neutral party who could provide the permission to implement the needed treatment is difficult to obtain in such cases. Other relatives are reluctant to intervene and hospital or social welfare personnel and administrators are unwilling to take responsibility and seek a juridical resolution for the permission to conduct an optimal treatment. The end result of dilemmas such as these is prolonged hardship and agony for patients (as well as their often well-meaning relatives, who are forced to cope with the intractable symptoms) and repeated, costly hospitalizations that consume resources and compromise the welfare of other patients who could be effectively cared for with the inefficiently squandered resources.

In the above example, then, what takes place is a clash in the operation of medical and nonmedical memes and their products and integration as institutions of the society that come to bear in the care of certain classes of patients. This can be conceptualized in terms of opposition among memes. The family, which constitutes the most "natural" segment of the healing audience, brings into play a set of memes (involving spiritual, religious aspects of caring and responsibility) and medical memes (reflecting their interpretation of the sickness) that conflicts with medical memes of the professional members of the healing audience. Similarly, there is a clash between medical memes and political and ideological memes regarding the definition of personhood and autonomy/individuality as these come into play in sickness and healing. The prevailing political memes make it difficult for individuals (relatives, friends, or legal personnel of the hospital) to seek juridical responsibility to ensure optimal treatment. In a free, democratic, and individualistic society, persons (or in special circumstances, relatives) are the ones required to make decisions regarding their sickness and healing, and professional members of the healing audience are reluctant or unable to intervene (except in matters of life and death, which most often do not strictly apply in the circumstances outlined). The result of these clashes in medical and nonmedical memes and their phenotypic effects and integration as institutions is a failure to achieve the consensus that is required for therapy.

The above scenario is not unlike dilemmas such as those that daily confront families and medical personnel that bring to the surface questions of euthanasia, assisted suicide, and efficiency in the use of medical resources. The dilemmas are a staple theme in bioethical conferences and in the writings of health economists.

Several points need emphasis. Medical memes program and prepare individuals to orient, think about, and behave in medically relevant ways. Medical memes integrated with medical genes are anchored by biological evolutionary processes but have always been influenced by purely cultural and social conditions. How sickness and healing are configured and played out in a society reflects the biology of the SH adaptation and the way that the neurocognitive machinery for it is developmentally modified. The scenario for sickness and healing in relation to serious disease and injury has changed dramatically. The changes are the result of social and cultural evolution of medicine and society. As societies and medical systems evolve and complexify, competition among what have been termed medical and nonmedical memes (and their products and integration as institutions) create medical quandaries. In a more specific sense, inconsistency and opposition in medical and nonmedical memes surrounding certain categories of sickness and healing interfere with and militate against the implementation of others. The result could be termed medical stasis or medical devolution. The inefficient use of some resources because of such maladaptations hinders optimal resolution of medical problems and advances in the treatment of others of the society. These are examples of structural constraints in the social system of medicine, in the way of constructing sickness and healing. Such a state of affairs also conforms to what Anthony Giddens (1984: 373) terms "contradiction": "Opposition of structural principles, such that each depends upon the other and yet negates the other; perverse consequences associated with such circumstances."

Clearly, policies are needed to more effectively and efficiently deal with a range of medical problems associated with sickness/healing as this is configured and played out in contemporary "postmodern" society. The failure to effectively resolve such dilemmas, which entails careful deliberation of and decisions pertaining to choices among moral, political, spiritual, and economic directives, hinders the evolution of effective policies regarding sickness and healing. At the base of these impediments or maladaptations (Rappaport 1979) in the social system of medicine are conflicts and quandaries surrounding the meanings and values of memes, healmemes, and their products.

Levels at which Medical Evolution Operates

To comprehend in a relatively clear way the social/cultural evolution of sickness and healing one needs to keep in mind a number of issues, such as which types of institutions compete with medical memes (i.e., the medical institutions), at what level of organization are the nonmedical institutions, the factors influencing social selection of institutions, and how all of this takes place. As I will elaborate in a later chapter, I visualize sickness and healing as evolving along with other social institutions of a society. For example, some social selection is limited to specific, individual institutions and medical memes whereas other forms of selection would seem to involve whole sets of these medical memes, as when indigenous medical traditions compete with biomedicine and are rejected (or at least deemphasized) during the process of modernization.

In small-scale societies, a different type of complexity is found in attempts to visualize and formulate the social and cultural evolution of the medical. For example, in these types of societies it is difficult to determine whether a particular medical meme product, rather than constituting a "pure" medical institution, operates instead as, for example, a religious meme product or institution. In other words, in enacting a particular type of ritual a person in a family-level society may be seeking both medical treatment and spiritual/religious "healing." In seeking to restore a split in group relations a people of an agricultural society may follow simultaneously what one could term both a political institution and a medical one, since doing so may be thought to undo the ritual poisons causing the sickness and promote political and economic security in the group. In these types of societies, in other words, fewer institutions charged with multivalent meanings (i.e., spanning across the medical into the political, religious, etc.) appear to order and regulate social action. Consequently, whether competition and selection takes place between truly distinct *types of institutions* would be difficult to determine precisely.

Selection among units of information, whether these be conceptualized as genetic or symbolic in nature, occurs for different reasons. At the level of genes and individuals, selection and retention of information takes place "naturally" (i.e., natural selection by the physical and social environment) provided that information favors the inclusive fitness of the units selected. At the cultural and social level, it is items of information that individuals originate or learn about and that affect thought and behavior that are selected. These items of information are by definition adaptations in that they are purposively and deliberately selected because they are thought to enhance well-being and satisfaction at least in the short run. At still higher levels of selection, larger chunks of information may be selected. In other words, forms of *group selection* are likely to take place at the level of whole organizations or corporations involving sets of (higher-order) healmemes. This type of selection at levels higher than the individual is much contested (Sanderson 1995a, 1995b; Sober and Lewontin 1982). To complicate matters, a particular medical meme or set thereof can be selected because it constitutes a better way for the person and for the *collectivity* to carry out healing, organize medical care, and/or promote well-being and health. However, as mentioned earlier, sickness and healing can be affected as a consequence of selection of other types of meme products or institutions. Selection of political "memes" or institutions, as an example, can have positive or negative effects on patterns of sickness and healing, and this could in turn have negative or positive effects on the inclusive fitness of individuals or their genes (SH).

In summary, in an evolutionary frame of reference, the medical is seen as a hierarchical structure that describes how genes, memes, individuals, institutions, and societies operate and function. From the standpoint of demography and epidemiology, this "medical structure" accounts for patterns of morbidity, mortality, disease incidence/prevalence, and age and gender distribution. This more material, "infrastructural" level plays a determinant role in the way sickness and healing are configured and played out by constituting a powerful influence on the selection, use, invention, and eventual retention of medical genes and memes. From the standpoint of symbolic, culturally ordered behavior, the medical "suprastructure," one sees parameters of sickness and healing played out among persons and groups of persons. At this level, it is possible that whole sets of medical memes can be selected for the benefit of the collectivity as a result of social and political economic policy that most individuals of the society have little say about. Finally, to the extent that societies can be classified and ordered as to level of complexity and social organization, so too can in theory their medical structures and parameters of sickness and healing.

Not only can the evolution of sickness and healing be conceptualized as taking place at every level of the medical structure, but the effects of selection at one level can affect selection at another level. For example, changes in the genes that affect vulnerability to disease and physiological adaptability more generally will affect how sickness and healing are configured. In other words, sickness and healing will be patterned differently as a result of genetic selection ("strict" biological evolution) affective vulnerability to disease and physiological resiliency more generally. A significant change in this pattern could affect how the medical system of the society functions, and this might in turn affect adaptation and selection at higher levels of (social and cultural) evolution. Conversely, it is possible to conceive of changes taking place largely at the level of institutions (e.g., involving religious practices, marital preferences, leisure pursuits) that will affect how sickness and healing are thought of and carried out. In time, changes initiated at the level of nonmedical institutions could through complex "superstructural" feedback connections influence the configuration of medical genes and memes that undergird the SH adaptation. It is very likely that contemporary populations have differing genetic structures rendering them differentially susceptible to infectious agents, and social and cultural changes associated with complex societies undoubtedly were the prime movers here. Social cultural changes have probably brought about other more "plastic" changes in the SH adaptation and its configuration of sickness and healing (e.g., somatization, manifestations of psychiatric disorders) during recorded history. The degree of autonomy or amount of feedback that exists in the events occurring at different levels of evolution of the medical structure is obviously complex, problematic, and likely to be highly contested. This is so because it involves matters pertaining to atomism, holism, organicism, and reductionism as these affect evolution over which social and biological scientists and philosophers of science have strong differences of opinion.

Making Sense of Evolutionary Transformations of Sickness and Healing

An evolutionary account of sickness and healing implies that the way these medical factors are configured and played out in a social formation changes across time. Moreover, since attention has been given to the parameters that sickness and healing have in different social types, understood as phases of social evolution, it is implied that these social aspects of medicine demonstrate cumulative change. In the event, the following questions are relevant: first, what exactly were the major evolutionary transformations of sickness and healing, and, second, how can one best conceptualize the processes of variation and selection that brought about or realized these changes?

The process of transformation of sickness and healing is difficult to visualize for several reasons. Issues related to the plasticity, systematicity, and seeming complexity of sickness and healing partially account for this difficulty. Given the systemic character of sickness and healing, it may be difficult to conceptualize just exactly how one social type's configuration of sickness and healing (which involves an integrated set of beliefs, expectations, and behaviors) changes and evolves into that of another. One way out of this quandary is to recall that sickness and healing are based on medical genes and memes.

I am most concerned with *general and mainly cultural* aspects of medical evolution. The influence of genetic change on how sickness and healing are configured, and on social and cultural phenomena more generally, is thought to operate on a much longer time line than the changes brought about by cultural inventions pertaining to sickness and healing. Biological anthropologists and geneticists appear to agree that such factors as differential fertility, frequency of inbreeding, marriage patterns, and the size of the basic population breeding unit all together have a pronounced effect on the composition of a group's genetic structure as this pertains to level of health and general survival. Similarly, dietary factors associated with civilization are singled out as having had the most pronounced effect with respect to levels of disease. Furthermore, it is conceded that studies of existing tribal societies are not likely to yield the number of observations that are required to establish relations between specific genes and selective advantages with respect to disease and injury (Neel 1994).

In general, it is also difficult to visualize in a clear way how actual changes in gene frequencies pertaining to disease and injury affect behavioral and cultural phenomena pertaining to medicine. Alland's (1970) pioneering effort touched on this theme, as did also the Dunn's study on malaria (1965). The reflections of Neel (1994) pertaining to his Amerindian studies are particularly relevant also since they involve aspects of health in relation to evolutionary scenarios.

Two more or less interpretable instances of genetic change having effects on levels of disease are those that affect the structure of hemoglobin (e.g., sickle cell trait) and those that affect innate susceptibility to infection (e.g., measles). In both instances, a "positive" consequence can be visualized: as a result of genetic mutation or drift, individuals or an isolated group may be favored by innate acquisition of resistance to infection. The inventiveness and resourcefulness of those naturally selected in this way can be expected to have potentially beneficial effects on the group. If an individual in a leadership position acquires immunological resistance via mutation, this is likely to be especially overrepresented in subsequent generations because of the unique preponderance of their contribution to the gene pool of village and tribal societies. Conversely, the "negative" effects of mutation can be expected to render individuals or groups unusually susceptible to disease with deleterious consequences for the society and culture, should the otherwise "positive" contributions of those individuals or groups be lost or at least lessened. The transformations in human populations described by McNeill (1976, 1992), although mainly involving passive immunity and not necessarily resulting from genetic differences, bear on the general point of the social cultural consequences of genetic differences pertaining to disease and injury.

In none of the briefly discussed examples of genetic changes affecting disease susceptibility are effects on the configuration of sickness and healing as social and cultural phenomena easily accessible or visualized. Stated differently, in these examples genetic differences have direct populational and *general* social cultural consequences as compared to *specific* effects on the institution of medicine itself or in the way sickness and healing are configured and played out culturally. In terms of concepts introduced earlier, it can be said that in these examples the products of medical gene differences are compelling differences in disease susceptibilities rather than changes that appear to integrate with and, hence, produce effects through medical memes on sickness and healing behaviors (i.e., the cultural configuration and meaning of these behaviors). Thus, as has already been emphasized, the effects of genetic changes on *sickness and healing and on medical institutions* are best thought of as having had their main effect on the construction of the machinery for the SH adaptation per se rather than merely influencing its set point or vulnerability.

With respect to purely social and cultural factors pertaining to the evolution of medicine, then, one's task is to delineate the content of medical memes that account for a society's social scripts for and general parameters of sickness and healing and visualize how all of this might have changed during evolution.

The Role of Medical Memes

It has been pointed out in chapter 7 that one might be able to identify a basic set of medical memes, abstractly formulated, that account for sickness and healing in all social types and formations. These can be conceptualized as *elemental* medical memes. As reviewed in the earlier chapter, the sheer need for relief of pain/discomfort, for example, seems integral to sickness and should figure importantly in this respect. There is also the possibility that one could delineate in a more concrete manner medical memes (derived from the more abstractly formulated elemental ones) that seem integral to specific social types. Thus there may exist more or less standard ways of conceptualizing pain/discomfort in family-level societies as compared to states and civilizations. Moreover, conceptualizations of pain obviously interrelate with conceptualizations pertaining to sickness and its causes, consequences, and modes of relief. Thus one should anticipate that medical memes relating to pain are semantically consistent with those involving types and causes of sickness. More generally, one can anticipate that medical memes special to a social type are logically and empirically consistent and, in integrating together, create the distinctive parameters of sickness and healing reviewed in the previous chapter. These parameters impart a unique picture that captures the way sickness and healing are configured and played out in the social type.

In this light, the transformation of sickness and healing from one to another social type entails semantically and behaviorally consistent changes in the cultural content of elemental medical memes (i.e., in the way these are realized and integrated). This touches again on the matter of the systematicity of sickness and healing. In other words, one can posit that the way the core elements of sickness and healing are structured or framed during evolution change in systematic, "organic" ways as a function of other changes that affect the society as well as the human organism.

An emphasis on medical memes raises the question of which ones are retained, which ones are rejected, and which ones are newly invented or acquired through diffusion and then passed on across generations. Ideally, the timing and sequencing of the changes in medical memes during cultural evolution should also be specified. It might be possible to identify one or two elemental medical memes of a social type that play a strategic role in its configuration of sickness and healing. The change in content of one or a few such strategic medical memes during the process of evolution may have a snowball effect on other medical memes, eventually contributing importantly to the new configuration of medmemes of the more evolved social type.

An example may make this point more clear. During social evolution the transformation to agriculture and sedentarism meant that large numbers of persons comprised human groups in relatively close living quarters. In such groups, a different epidemiological profile of medical problems prevailed. Moreover, conflicts and rivalries were more prevalent and thus human antagonisms and jealousies came to figure importantly as causes of sickness. This development, in turn, meant that resolution of conflicts became a requirement of curing rituals. Moreover, since psychosocial conflicts and familial feuds operated as ever-present realities incorporated in sickness and healing, individuals developed the opportunity to manipulate sicknesses or at least to perpetuate them until such personal conflicts were satisfactorily resolved. The possibility of psychosocially exploiting the role of sickness thus became stipulated as a possible medical meme that structured healing practices. In this instance, then, a political economic change involving social organization promoted the invention of a medical meme pertaining to cause of sickness, and this medical meme may have had a snowball effect in the discovery or need for other medical memes resulting in a transformation of the way sickness and healing were carried out.

The previous example points to a related conceptual problem involved in understanding the role of medical memes in the cultural evolution of medicine. As was emphasized in a previous section, one should be able to specify what aspects of the way sickness and healing change stem from and link directly to medical memes per se (i.e., items of cultural information pertaining to disease/injury and its amelioration/prevention/control) and what aspects of changes in the cultural institution of medicine stem from happenings outside the realm of disease/injury and its treatment (i.e., from the indirect medical effects of memes associated with other institutions of the society). In the example presented earlier, memes derived from outside the medical institution, involving political, economic, and perhaps religious/ideological considerations, can be said to have prompted major changes in medical memes, which in turn transformed the institution involved in handling problems of disease and injury.

Integration of Medical Genes and Memes

In light of this discussion, one can posit that evolution equips the human organism with an evolutionary sculptured neural machinery that subserves sickness and healing. In a general sense, this machinery would (1) provide for a physiological and neurophysiological capacity that produced more or less distinctive behavioral routines in the eventuation of disorders of the anatomy and physiology of the body (the core symptoms and signs of disease), (2) allow for plasticity in the mode of operation of this machinery such that when it was suitably activated culturally, it accorded social and cultural meaning to the way the manifestations of disease and injury were configured and played out (e.g., heightened, minimized, modified, qualified symbolically, etc.), and (3) provide a cognitive capacity for organisms to recognize and interpret the meaningfully elaborated manifestations of disease and injury, and to respond behaviorally in ways that attempted to modify and ameliorate their morbid effects either in the self or in others. This, as discussed earlier in the chapter, summarizes the workings of the neuropsychological machinery that results from the programs carried by medical genes and that operates as the substrates for the meaningful behaviors of sickness and healing carried in memes.

The SH machinery can be held to underwrite or constitute the capacity for the learning of medical memes. The machinery embodies the cumulative results of natural selection during evolution of the human line, results that progressively sculpted organisms so as to seek to understand and ameliorate the effects of disease and injury. Indeed, as discussed earlier, the SH machinery and its realization in elemental medical memes can be likened to a special capacity for a language of medicine that enables or equips organisms to meaningfully communicate about and understand the biology of disease and injury as sickness and healing. In other words, the machinery is activated and culturally contextualized according to the accumulated pool of information about sickness and healing that is found in the group.

On the Evolved Content and Architecture of the SH Adaptation

Evolution has sculpted a machinery that equips an individual to expect, search for, delineate, and respond appropriately to disease and injury so as to restore a "basic healthy profile." Thus, with input from the social environment in the form of learned, personal experiences (under the guidance provided by caretakers and comembers during infancy, childhood, and into early adulthood), individuals perfect an ability to determine how disease and injury manifest from a social/behavioral/emotional/communicational and psychological standpoint. They learn, in short, that these medical universals are potentially dangerous, harmful, and in need of correction, they learn to identify them in themselves and others and how to respond to them adaptively, and they learn when to desist from healing with a fatalistic resignation that there are limits to what is humanly possible in the sphere of medicine.

The evolved design of the machinery allows individuals to establish that disease and injury are realized in a person's physical appearance, behavioral physiology, social communication, and psychological or mental theory of the world that constitute a locally acceptable "sense of reality." This would include, as an example, an understanding of what malaise, debility, and suffering look like and imply; what pain means and communicates; what "abnormal" bleeding means (i.e., the culturally acceptable enclosures or confinements of blood); what are the "normal" appearance and configuration of the body (e.g., with respect to coloration, figural outline); what are the physical characteristics of the body's excretory products; what are the different characteristics of arterial pulsations; what is the consequential importance of such things as skin eruptions, itching, ataxia, nausea, aphasia, diarrhea, vomiting, tremors, and convulsions; and insight for determining when beliefs and desires of a comember (inferable from his or her behavior) stray beyond the acceptable rationales and guidelines of the group's behavioral environment (i.e., the ability to determine psychological "normality" compared to "abnormality").

That individuals share an evolved architecture that is expressed "naturally" in (inherent to) the communication of sickness and healing, and that they can understand its logic or rationale, means that there exist meaningful relations among the various medical memes that have been proposed. In other words, medical memes are not just independent items of ("semantic") information but fit together ("syntactically") so as to render more or less coherent behavioral pictures of sickness and healing that inform about the condition and course of disease and injury and how they respond to intervention. In short, it is how an operative subset of these medical memes relate one to the other across time and in light of actions taken by the self and group (i.e., the course of disease of injury) that an inherited "language capacity" for sickness and healing is expressed in the human line. This language is learned, perfected, and used to cope with the burdens of disease and injury in ways designed to enhance inclusive fitness as well as the welfare of the group (since, as discussed earlier, selection occurs at different levels).

The computation of deviations from a "basic healthy profile" is what prompts an average individual to determine illness in the self and others and to respond adaptively by giving medical aid within the realistic limits set by the group. In the environment of evolutionary adaptedness, these limits were undoubtedly calibrated in light of an evaluation of what a particular individual's life was worth to the group and this is regarded as an important attribute of the SH adaptation. In other words, it is very likely that infanticide, neglect, or restriction of healing was "naturally" resorted to in the event of sicknesses in individuals judged as too compromised, aged, or costly, or simply terminally sick. Inherent in the SH adaptation, then, is a capacity to accommodate to the inevitability of death, a capacity the full realization of which requires social and cultural input.

Intrinsic to sickness and healing is the labeling of terminality with its own special requirements in the form of grief and mourning reactions/rituals. Identifying and implementing a complement of universal or "elemental" healing initiatives in light of the meanings attached to sickness, as reviewed in chapter 2, constitute the purely healing side of the SH adaptation (i.e., the healmemes). The result is to instruct individuals to learn about and administer medicaments and implement procedures geared to relieve pain, support and conserve basic energy, stop bleeding, promote needed rest and sleep, and the like.

Explaining Evolutionary Transformations
of Sickness and Healing

For purposes of illustrating evolutionary transformations one can concentrate on selected elemental medical memes that appear to strategically shape and account for a selected part of the variation of sickness and healing across social types. Six illustrative medical memes will be the focus of attention, and these are described as follows: (1) responsibility for cause of sickness, (2) existential intonation or meaning, (3) diagnostic value of manifestations, (4) exemptive value of manifestations, (5) social character of healing party, and (6) course susceptibility.

Responsibility for cause refers to what agents, processes, or mechanisms are held to bring about a condition of sickness. It involves accounting for the condition of sickness in the person and includes actions and changes that pertain to the self, living family relatives, spirits, supernatural beings, or neighbors and other group members. Existential intonation refers to the ideological (e.g., semantic, emotional, and moral) implications that illness has for the self, the family, and the group and would include an account of the kind and degree of vulnerability, victimization, or helplessness that threaten the self and persons connected to the self. Diagnostic value of manifestations refers to an account of how the manifestations of sickness figure in its interpretation (e.g., the ascertainment of cause, healing intervention, and prognosis). Exemptive value of manifestations refers to whether and, if so, which of the different manifestations of illness are accorded special meanings or values in the society. Healing party refers to who, in addition to the sick person, comprises the relevant group that an individual can turn to and expect help from with respect to healing, and it would include what is owed to those persons who participate in healing rituals. Finally, course susceptibility refers to the factors that influence the course of sickness and healing. This would include medicines, procedures, interventions, and social relations that are held to affect the way medical episodes unfold. It encompasses the nature of the dialogues and exchanges that the sick person has with his healing party. In effect, this would also include beliefs pertaining to how the group explains effects on the course of sickness in a social type as a function of the dialogues and actions of the healing party.

Table 5 summarizes how an elemental medical meme is constructed in a particular type of society. By moving horizontally across a row, one obtains a picture of how the social properties of sickness and healing change during the posited cultural evolution of medicine. By moving vertically down a column, one gains an appreciation of how the various social properties of sickness and healing are configured in a particular social type.

Key Transformations in the Cultural Evolution of Sickness and Healing

Family-level Societies

Disease and injury could in some ways be said to happen *to the group* and, correspondingly, to constitute *its* concern: The well-being of all is at stake, and the course of sickness (particularly a serious one) has group implications. One observes the bare essentials of what natural selection has furnished man in the way of showing and coping with disease and injury and, correspondingly, the culturally least elaborated institution of medicine. These societies mark the take-off for the social evolution of medicine.

Medical memes stipulate that the self, ancestors, other supernatural agents, and malevolent actions of person from outside groups are held responsible for sickness. The self is punished because of acts of transgression, although he or she may serve as the mere substitute for punishment of others in the group. Explanations of cause and of manifestations (i.e., ethnopathologies) show little elaboration, and medicines and procedures that persons can draw on are likewise little elaborated. No special healers or shamans are found; among the !Kung Bushmen, all adult males appear to function as shamans. A global, group-felt sense of powerlessness, helplessness, despair, and victimization usually accompanies illnesses that are serious and that persist. The manifestations of sickness have little diagnostic value and are handled holistically, all together signaling a state of undesirable morbidity needing healing. No differential value or meaning is accorded specific sickness manifestations. The family and the group as a whole constitute the healing party, and efforts on its part (usually acting in concert) are held to possibly modify the course of sickness with supernatural help. A great deal of resignation exists in the event of sickness, and the expressed well-being and actions/behaviors of the sick person determine the amount of activity or passivity that is sanctioned during sickness. The sick person, in other words, usually in a way that is acquiesced to by the family and group (given the group's highly integrated character), determines wellness and the end point of occupancy of the "sick role."

Village-level Societies

The demography and political economy condition a culture that makes possible a more elaborated, cumulative pool of medical memes; and because of rudimentary social divisions in the population, they stipulate that persons of greater knowledge and power can influence diagnosis and the course of sickness and healing. Medical memes thus allow that sickness and healing are affected by village happenings. As a consequence of intragroup social conflicts

Table 5.   *The Construction of Elemental Medical Memes in Prototypical Social Organizations*

Strategic Healmemes	Family-level Societies	Village-level Societies	Chiefdoms, Prestates, and States	Empires and Civilizations	Modern European Societies	Postmodern European Societies
Responsibility for Cause	Self, ancestors, gods, outside groups	Same; group co-members possible agents; simple ethnopathologies	Same; group comembers important causes; un-elaborated ethnopathologies	Individual's habits, morality important causes; formulated in elaborate and holistic ethnopathologies	Physical agents and body machinery; ethnopathologies are elaborate and highly partitioned	Emotions and actions of self interact with physical machinery; self is made responsible agent of sickness
Existential Intonation	Overall sense of powerlessness; sick and comembers are vulnerable; all can be potentially accountable and penalized by sickness	Same; family faction is specially victimized	Sick person, family, clan, or lineage being victimized	Sickness has rational ethical/moral basis but more secularized	Personal tragedy	Inevitable eventuation; physical, mechanical breakdown; material change that can be managed
Diagnostic Value of Manifestations	Holistic interpretation; overall morbidity key determinant of sickness	Same	Manifestations offer general clues through divination, but overall morbidity condition is salient	Manifestations critical and influence type of healer; the manifestations are the sickness	Manifestations play determinate role as clue to underlying disease	Same; self-inquiry important; habits and personal stress levels influential

Exemptive Value of Manifestations	Holistic disvaluation of sickness; all manifestations equally disvalued		Same	Insanity symptoms more disvalued; beginnings of social enhancement of somatic manifestations	Physical/bodily symptoms more authentic markers of sickness	State and physician determine validity of manifestations of sickness
Healing Party	Family and group	Family	Family and healer	Family and one or several healers	Self and doctors and nurses	Same; personal actions toward prevention, wellness; alternative healing enterprises
Course Susceptibility	Family advice; group healing rituals; local lore and knowledge	Immediate group and social relations; occasional healer can influence course; local lore and knowledge	Family and extended group; local lore and shared knowledge structures; specialist healers begin to play influential role; self is influential	Many medicines, procedures associated with literate traditions and competing traditions; specialist healers highly influential; self highly influential	Physicians' directives and biomedical science dominant influences; self retains influential role but countered by physician	Telecommunication media; third-party payers, disability boards, alternative medicine programs; self gains leverage outside biomedicine

and rivalries, comembers with whom there is friction become responsible agents of sickness in addition to the other causes found in family-level societies. Medical memes that invoke malevolent actions from neighbors, witchcraft and sorcery from within the group, become possible and persist as possibilities in groups that are more complex. The more differentiated character of these groups also means that the family, and less so the group as a whole, is experienced as the existential target of the malevolent victimization and despair that is experienced during (serious, protracted) episodes of sickness. Likewise, the family, nuclear or extended, plays a more exclusive role in beginning treatment and seeking consultation and help for further healing. Sickness retains its holistic character as in the previous social type, and specific manifestations are not accorded special diagnostic value or social value/disvalue. The sick person, his or her family, and protoshamans constitute the healing party. It is significant that the cumulation of information found in these groups contains more medical memes involving procedures, medicines, and mechanisms of how enemies and competitors can cause sickness and influence healing (what can be thought of as slightly more elaborated ethnopathologies). This means that the individual and his family can begin to use the status of these relationships to influence course by calibrating when and how sickness episodes terminate. In short, exploitation of the sick role is made possible by these types of medical memes that are themselves the outcome of developments outside the institution of medicine. It is also significant that political economic differentiation makes possible the creation of a role of healer since this lays the foundation for the special social and psychotherapeutic influence that specific and charismatic persons who occupy this role can have in the course of sickness and healing. The obligation to reciprocate or remunerate an individual outside the family, and sometimes outside the group itself, is, of course, also conditioned by this new political economy of medicine.

Chiefdoms, Prestates, and States

The distinctive sociological changes noted in village-level societies are accentuated. Medical memes stipulate specialists in the affairs of medicine, meaning that the availability of diversified audiences complexifies both sickness and healing. They also stipulate the need for remuneration of "service" personnel. While these types of medical memes are far more visible and influential in more evolved social types, they make their appearance here. Medical memes are more numerous and specialized with respect to what sickness portends and means and how it can unfold. They allow for different individuals and social circumstances to figure in the equations of sickness and healing as causes, as existential targets, and as individuals to be placated, reprimanded, or ingratiated through more or less scripted rules. Here, memes from other institutions enter into association with strictly medical memes.

In essence, families, clans, and lineages become the responsible agents in the playing out of sickness and healing and the existential import of medical memes encompass these units as well. Medical memes pertaining to the cause of sickness and the efficacy of healing become more differentiated and complex and begin to incorporate distinctive manifestations of disease and injury. While sickness still retains its integrated character with all types of manifestations accorded equal validity, some of these begin to play a more influential role in the ethnopathology, diagnosis, and nomenclature of sickness and the structuration of healing. Although sickness retains its grave, despairing existential import, the greater articulation and systematization of spheres of spirituality and religion with emerging possibilities for perpetuity or rebirth that are found in these societies provide some relief for the existential burdens of sickness. The commitment (or lack thereof) of the family on behalf of the sick person, the influence of specialist healers, and the participation of comembers conceived as causally implicated in sickness all become elements in the working out of curing rituals, allowing sick persons and their families to construct socially rich scenarios of sickness and healing. All of this creates more opportunities for medical memes that allow and facilitate exploitation of the sick role in terms of group interpersonal relationships, the process problematizing the course of sickness, and the perceived and imagined effects of healing.

Empires and Civilizations

It becomes more difficult to speak of a single approach to medicine in these types of societies because of social complexity and differentiation. A large number and rich variety of medical memes are made available to individuals through the literate tradition. While wealthier and politically powerful groups may constitute the principal holders of them, these items of information are widely disseminated in the population and internalized and come to influence how sickness and healing are played out.

Medical memes continue to elaborate religious, especially eschatological tenets, and conflicts with and actions by others as causing sickness and influencing healing. However, the morality, routines, and habits of individuals themselves become important, with these factors contextualized in terms of comprehensive theoretical explanations that prominently incorporate body parts, mechanisms, and functions. Correspondingly, while sickness can continue to be construed as existentially burdening and harming to the family and the immediate group and to reflect malevolence on the part of neighbors and outsiders competing with and jealous of these units, the ill individual comes more to be defined as especially targeted and to embody the existential burden of sickness. Moreover, because of his or her more strategic role, the individual is more influential in manipulating the condition of sickness for his or her own "secondary" needs. The specific manifestations of sickness and injury acquire a more concrete role in the definition and diagnosis of sickness and in the selection and evaluation of healing. Symptoms of mental illness, particularly those reflecting insanity and madness, tend to be highly discrediting in these types of societies (e.g., India, China, medieval Europe, and early modern Europe). Although sicknesses are explained in a comprehensive psychosomatic/somatopsychic frame of reference, medical memes that stipulate a specifically somatic language of suffering and distress become overvalued as markers of sickness because of the influential role of interpersonal conflicts in causation of sickness generally and because of the more visible and compelling stigma of mental illness that characterizes the large urban centers of empires and civilizations. Healing parties are centered more on the sick person, family members, and healers, with group and clan members less important. All of the latter persons are held to influence the course of sickness. However, the fact that in these types of societies sickness becomes more common, persistent, naturalistically construed, and hence secularized as well as the object of competing commercial interests, the individual who is sick, in his or her more strategic position, comes to play a central role in manipulating and orchestrating its course.

Modern European Societies

The way sickness and healing are structured in these societies is strongly determined by factors external to the medical institution per se. Medical memes stipulate biological reductionism, and the power of biomedicine to explain and control disease induces profound optimism regarding the control of sickness and healing. Medical memes create sickness and healing as objective, mechanical, and technical enterprises focused on the body machinery, with healing aimed at its repair, all of this structured in terms of a fee-for-service framework.

Medical memes stipulate that impersonal agents that disturb bodily mechanisms and processes bear the responsibility for sickness, with causes reduced to disorders of the physical apparatus. Sickness is, correspondingly, devoid of spiritual overtones, constituting a physiologically determined dilemma for the individual to work out with support from the family. Indeed, whereas in previous social types medical memes stipulated that the burdens of sick persons and their families were the "objects" or "functions" of healing, the new ones point to the disease entity invading and inhabiting the individual. The memes elaborate that bodily manifestations of sickness are crucial determinants of diagnosis and treatment and that somatized problems that conform to standard biomedical pictures of disease and injury are the valid idiom of medicine. This means that psychological, emotional problems are discredited as unauthentic and "psychiatric." Indeed, the meaning of psychiatry becomes a meme that plays a dominating role in managing mental illness and embraces coping difficulties and problems of living. An expansion of the kinds of problems addressed by medical memes is noted: A medicalization of deviance is a result, a development that complements the enormous power and prestige of the medical profession in the society at large to define sickness. Yet more and more, medical memes stipulate a relatively impersonal healing party with a single type of "doctor-patient" relationship as the standard. Usually under the control of specialists, the hospital becomes the identified physical setting for the conduct of healing. The physician becomes empowered as the arbiter of sickness, validating its duration and authenticating the sick role, with sanctions being brought to bear on persons who do not conform to the standard profiles of disease or respond to accepted remedies.

Postmodern European Societies

The impact of memes from other, nonmedical institutions continues to be strongly felt in sickness and healing. More specifically, the sociologic and political economic developments described for modern European societies persist and deepen. Medical memes stipulate that how physicians, the state, and third-party payers model disease and injury constitute authentic protocols of sickness and injury. The communications industries expand and exert a powerful role in spreading the influence of memes pertaining to biomedicine as the standards of sickness and healing. However, the limits of the power of biomedicine to heal and control disease and its effects become integral to what meaning is accorded to medical memes. These recognize the fallibility of physicians, the need to contain medical costs, bioethical dilemmas, and the need for cost-effective arrangements for "managing" sickness and healing, arrangements that threaten to undermine the heretofore special features of the doctor-patient relationship.

The effects of these developments on the properties of sickness and healing can easily be surmised. Since mechanical failures of the body due to degenerative diseases constitute major underlying causes of disease, medical memes stipulate that the individual's habits and behaviors play a dominating role in the cause of sickness. Hence these memes "blame" individuals for sickness and hold them responsible for genuine efforts to pursue preventive, curative, and rehabilitative services that are legally approved. Medical memes stipulate that healing parties are constituted by teams of different specialists and general physicians, with patients consumers of their services. Disease is stripped of larger existential overtones, reduced to mechanical failures of the body. Memes instruct individuals how to monitor their bodies for clues to the diagnosis and treatment of disease as biomedical knowledge becomes standardized, widely disseminated, and almost public. The state, through the medical policing efforts of physicians, sets the criteria for what come to be viewed as the authentic states of sickness and entitlements to treatment (a consequence of biological reductionism and reliance on its technology). The result is that the state, which literally sponsors and supports much of biomedical education and research, becomes an influential agent in monitoring the course of sickness and the effects of healing in the population. The capacity for individuals to manipulate their role of sickness is further undermined by physicians as agents of third parties who come to exert increasing control of the medical marketplace. Associated with this, one finds dissatisfaction with physicians, with "establishment" medicine, with the escalating costs of a more routinized and procedural approach to healing, and with the tentacles of medical insurance companies. An outcome of this is increasing interest in holistic medical traditions and the growth of health-promoting and life extension industries that compete with orthodox biomedicine.

Maladaptive Medical Memes and the Cultural Evolution of Sickness and Healing

The constructive use of medical memes by sick persons is understandable and unproblematic: The negative valence of sickness can be undone or neutralized by the implementation of medical memes. What needs to be appreciated, however, is that what amounts to a positive valence of sickness can also be enhanced through the use of medical memes. Thus there exist exploitative and deceitful ways in which medical memes can be used by persons motivated by, vulnerable to, or actually in conditions of sickness. For example, medical memes consisting of new insights into the way sickness manifests, or disease* processes operate, can be appropriated by the sick person to enable him or her to more effectively make use of sickness for selfish purposes. Conversely, healers can use and promote medical memes (i.e., those that are idiosyncratic to them) for selfish purposes, in the process gaining advantages for themselves and their genetic relatives. The first of these exploitative uses of medical memes will be considered in greater detail below.

One must realize that the benefits, dispensations, and resources made available to the sick person by significant others can be better appropriated the more closely conditions of sickness conform to models of illness and disease* prevalent in the community. In brief, individuals wanting to effectively model a condition of sickness are likely to be motivated to make effective use of the understandings of sickness, illness, and disease* that are part of that community's traditions of medicine. By these mechanisms and motivations, then, medical memes are appropriated and learned by persons for purposes of "real" and "fictive" sickness and healing. The exploitation of the sick role may of course benefit the individual, even contribute to his or her inclusive fitness. On the other hand, such use of a medical meme may work to the detriment of other evolutionary "units" (e.g., the society, culture).

It can be appreciated that social sanctions can be brought to bear on sick persons so as to thwart exploitative uses of sickness or the sick role that unduly penalize others. Sickness, however, has proven a difficult social category and condition to invalidate. Developments of biomedical technology have proven of great value in refining diagnosis so as to validate conditions of sickness and illness. Researchers who study pain, as an example, have documented facial display patterns that correlate with "faked" pain (Craig, Hyden, and Patrick 1991). Generalizing from this, one can view all contemporary biomedical disciplines as partly engaged in positive healing and partly engaged in negative healing, that is, in helping to undo authentic conditions of sickness and invalidating conditions of unauthentic sickness that involve exploitation of knowledge of medical memes and of the sick role more generally. Quite obviously, in exercising a function of "negative healing" biomedical disciplines are acting on behalf of the society and thwarting the individual. This discrepancy in aims and functions underscores the differences between biologic and cultural evolution of sickness and healing. (With respect to deceptive healers or charlatans, who benefit themselves selfishly by fictive uses of medical memes, it is fellow community residents, fellow healers, or the state that bring sanctions to bear, depending on the type of society.)

In this light, psychiatry during its heyday in the modern European era can be visualized as a discipline, indeed a socially evolved institution, which among other things, in developing a science about the mental and its effects on the body, has prominently appropriated the function of validating conditions of sickness that eluded the capacities of healers of earlier societies and of specialists of postmodern societies. Psychiatrists, in other words, are the healers who in many ways are called on to authenticate the potentially exploitative uses of sickness in modern and postmodern societies. What is termed "malingering" in psychiatry constitutes an intentional presentation of false or grossly exaggerated physical or psychological symptoms. Such a "condition" essentially invalidates in a formal way a claim of illness (by recourse to "expert" determination as to a fictive sickness state). By contrast, in many ways one can view the concept of somatization as an invention that validates sickness pictures that in general medicine do not meet criteria of disease. The irony is that in this instance, validation takes place by medicalization of a psychiatric disorder, a process that can be stigmatizing.

Another example of the maladaptive use of medical memes is that involving the abuse of clinically efficacious substances. Issues considered in the chapter on habits and disorders of habituation are examples of this. Such disorders illustrate the maladaptive consequences of medical memes. From the standpoint of evolution, abuse of sedatives, analgesics, stimulants, and other "mind altering" drugs can be analyzed as developments taking place at a group (i.e., social, cultural) level. Effective medical memes such as drugs are objects that are linked to healing and that when mass produced and made available to members of the population under conditions of poor regulation prove deleterious to the population and society. Maladaptive use of medical memes can also be analyzed from the standpoint of the individual. At this level, it could be said that social and cultural conditions of modern and postmodern societies have created an assortment of new sicknesses of demoralization, depression, or spiritual emptiness. For these new sicknesses and illnesses, whether or not the outcome of unmet (conscious or unconscious) needs, mental regeneration through drugs is palliative. Persons will be "naturally" motivated to seek healing and healers. However, because the drugs in question mobilize powerful genetically based neurobiological mechanisms, they can undermine adaptive behavior.

In addition to exploitative uses of sickness, forms of social maladaptation created by the process of (medical) social evolution, there exist exploitative uses of healing, which are related types of social maladaptation made possible by the social evolution of healing. In earlier chapters some of these were considered. They included the reinforcement and perpetuation of sickness, exploitation of the human motivation for sickness, and economic exploitation for personal gain. Unorthodox or "quack" healers have traditionally elicited sanctions from sick persons and other healers. In modern and postmodern societies, the state has intervened to regulate the practice of healing and the punishment of unauthorized healers.

9

A Broad View of
Medical Evolution

Thus far in this analysis of the evolution of sickness and healing emphasis has been placed on features of the SH adaptation. It has been described as an amalgam of cognitive, perceptual, sensory, and physiological processes and mechanisms that are under genetic and cultural control and that enable individuals to understand and communicate the effects of disease and injury. The SH adaptation connects with and realizes a suite of medical memes, units of cultural information that are stored in the brain, the products of which "communicate" to the self and comembers how one is ill, what it means to be ill, and what can and should be done about it. From a developmental standpoint, the SH adaptation "uses" the information provided by society and culture "in order to" render sickness and healing meaningful to the self and interpersonally. When shared with members of the society, the products of the adaptation constitute medical institutions and form patterns, parameters of sickness and healing, that were discussed in an earlier chapter.

Sickness and healing, however, as previous chapters have illustrated, consist of a great deal more than the SH adaptation. They are quintessentially social and cultural constructions that are the core of medicine considered as a social system of a society. In other words, while the SH adaptation undoubtedly provides the material that is used to construct specific medical episodes of a society, medicine also has a societal dimension. Medical knowledge, procedures, social practices, and associated phenomena can be viewed not only as organizing a specific eventuation of sickness and healing but also as having a structure and constituting an organization of the society as a whole. This is certainly less evident in the case in smaller-scale societies and most prominent with respect to the later phases of the evolution of sickness and healing.

When pictured in a broad societal way, medicine could be said to represent a system of the society. This could also be described as the medical "Institution," with a capital "I," because this term with a lowercase "i" was used in a previous chapter to refer to shared products of memes. In contemporary societies, for example, the medical organization consists of numerous professions, educational establishments, and shared practices and rituals that make use of stored, ever-growing bodies of acquired scientific information about disease and injury. Medicine is also an industry of a society, an industry, moreover, that is connected politically and economically to a host of other industries that support, regulate, and in many ways exploit it. In this extended sense, one can speak of "social systems of medical care that have evolved . . . conceived of as densely populated networks of heterogeneous arrangements and dependencies [which] include hospitals, pharmacies, insurance companies, governmental departments, university faculties, the multinational pharmaceutical industry [and] national regulatory agencies" (Bodewitz, Buurma, and deVries 1989: 243).

In short, the SH adaptation might constitute the (biological and cultural) representation of the medical "in" and "of" an individual as expressed in episodes of sickness and healing, but this adaptation makes use of, realizes, and is variously controlled by knowledge systems and regulatory practices that spread across wide sectors of the society. In this broad and comprehensive sense medicine is linked, through information and material feedback loops, with other Institutions and organizations of the society.

Visualizing the Medical Institution of a Society

For purposes of illustration, one can describe the medical Institution of a society as consisting of five concentric circles (see fig. 1). As will be elaborated presently, the contents of any one of these circles depend on and build on the contents of those included within it. To this space of the medical are connected various nonmedical institutions or "stations" of the society that affect and are affected by what happens in the medical sector.

The three inner circles constitute the basic core of the medical and can be equated with individuals, average persons of a society. The kinds of diseases and injuries that a particular member of a society is prone to experience or undergo is one way of interpreting the material content of these three inner circles. Were one to visualize a very large pool of these "individuals," they would in effect describe the ecologically based and historically contingent epidemiological load of the population of a particular society. This way of conceptualizing the medical Institution will not be given attention in this chapter. It should be understood, however, that distinctive pictures of disease and injury realize the medical sphere of any particular type of society, as discussed in chapters 3 and 4.

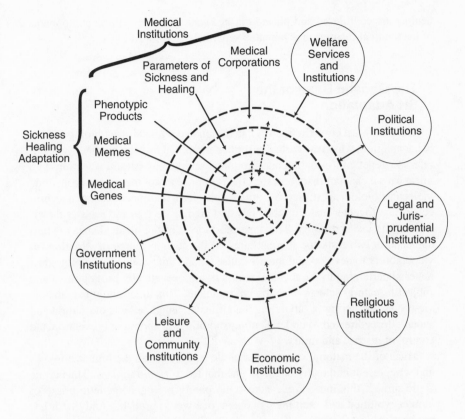

Figure 1. Institutional Structures of Society

The three concentric inner circles are used to provide a descriptive picture of concepts used in previous chapters. The two inner circles describe the information, genetic and cultural, respectively, the products of which determine how disease and injury are configured and played out as sickness and healing in an individual of any particular society. The product of circles one and two is what is found in circle three, the SH response or behavioral output—a social construction or eventuality of sickness and healing.

Circles four and five describe not an average individual but an average society. These circles are thus equated with groupwide aspects of the medical Institution. Circle four is set aside for the society's parameters of sickness and healing. The overall style and cultural rationale inherent in the products of medical memes and institutions make up circle four. Circle five is set aside for the social groups, organizations, agencies, and material products of the medical Institution, all of which enable and in some respects govern the way sickness and healing are configured and played out in a society. Each of these components of the medical Institution is taken up separately in what follows.

The Genetic Base of the SH Adaptation

The innermost circle in figure 1 can be equated with the strict biology of the SH adaptation, what was earlier described as embodying the medical genes. It refers to genetic information and programs sculpted by natural selection. In a linear causal chain of reactions, the effects or products of these genes constitute molecular biological structures, organs, physiological mechanisms, and processes that together make up the body and predispose it to and register the effects of disease and injury. This innermost circle of the medical space is fundamental in two respects: It constitutes (a) the genetic source of variation for vulnerability to develop and manifest disease and injury and (b) the biological material pertaining to the medical that is rigidly, genetically programmed and subject to natural selection by the environment. This inner circle can also be viewed as registering or tabulating the ultimate, genetic effects of cultural and social efforts directed to understanding and bringing about the prevention and control of disease and injury.

Much of the material of the inner circle is shared with the higher primates and was present in the phylogenetic line that led to *Homo sapiens.* Thus if one could project this inner circle across the purely biological/genetic phase of human evolution and examine its content one would probably find that it has not been subject to much expansion or variation. During the later phases of the evolution of *Homo sapiens* there obviously occurred major changes in the character of neural structures enabling language, higher cortical functions, and the character of human experience and behavior more generally. With respect to medical matters, such structures have been influential not only with respect to the signs and symptoms of neurological and psychiatric disease but also in ways of expressing disease and injury generally, as reviewed in an earlier chapter. However, fewer changes have taken place which affect the way other tissues and organ systems of the body are structured and function with respect to disease and injury (e.g., their composition, architecture, metabolism, mode of breakdown).

Since the evolution of *Homo sapiens,* still fewer changes have taken place. The material that regulates the embryology of the body and that leads to the formation of its anatomy, physiology, and biochemistry has simply not varied a great deal and is relatively resilient to environmental influences of all types. There are exceptions to this generalization; for example, during prehistory and historical time genetic vulnerabilities to infectious agents have probably changed, hemoglobin structures have changed in response to the prevalence of mosquitos carrying the protozoa that can cause malaria, and the effects of anoxia at high altitudes have resulted in hematopoietic changes and more efficient ventilatory structures subserving respiration. Of course, some surgical modifications of anatomy and replacements of parts are now possible, but these obviously do not affect medical genes, and rendering them hereditable by means of genetic surgery or therapy is highly controversial. Similarly, although the number of physiological/chemical/pharmacologic interventions that can be brought to bear on the interior of the body and its mechanisms that are under genetic control is very large and seemingly inexhaustible, changes in the nature of how these systems actually unfold during development and come to be programmed and function have been limited, and to date it has not been possible to change the actual genetic systems that affect vulnerability to disease or modification of bodily manifestations of disease and injury.

The Cultural Component of the SH Adaptation

The medical memes make up the second circle of the medical Institution. As individuals during development learn what constitutes sickness and healing and come to store this information in their brains, their medical memes come to program the cognitive/emotional behaviors that together produce sickness and healing behaviors. These programs regulate visceral and cognitive systems that culturally express such things as pain, malaise, nausea, and lassitude so as to communicate sickness and elicit healing.

Circles one and two together, thus, describe the SH adaptation. Since this adaptation is constituted of medical genes *and* memes, a factor that underscores the connectedness between the processes of biological and cultural evolution, the two inner circles of the medical Institution are shown as open and thus continuous one with the other. Moreover, circle two is open and connected with circle three, which describes the actual product of the adaptation in behavior. In conscious, enculturated members of *Homo sapiens* there is held to exist no disjunction between, on the one hand, disordered respiratory and gastrointestinal mechanisms and functions and, on the other, the manifestations of this underlying disease and injury that contribute to shortness of breath, wheezing, nausea, and abdominal pain, *as well as* the associated ways in which all of the latter are expressed behaviorally, interpreted, thought about, and acted on (i.e., as culturally meaningful by the self and/or co-present group members) in eventuations of sickness and healing.

The integrated character of this product of genes and memes in the setting of disease and injury is why the two inner circles have to be formulated as open and connected one with the other: Genes and memes operate together to constitute the adaptation or mechanism that, in turn, produces sickness and healing (see below). All of this underscores the fact that it is very difficult to conceptualize medical evolution with the genetic and the cultural components kept separate.

Compared to the innermost circle, the size and content of the outer, "second" one expands and changes considerably during social and cultural evolution. This is the case because cultural information in terms of which the SH adaptation is expressed accumulates and changes in content and organization during social and cultural evolution. As already mentioned, the variability in the way the SH response is understood, expressed, and "read" culturally, the semantic and existential interpretations of sickness together with the accompanying informational bases for routines and procedures of healing (i.e., medical memes), all have changed substantially and dramatically during cultural evolution, especially during recorded history. Thus, although the genetics of the SH adaptation, how it is materially formed and regulated, has changed very little during human evolution and history, the same cannot be said for its cultural counterpart. It has changed significantly, qualitatively and quantitatively.

The SH Response: Behaviors of Sickness and Healing

Circle three is set aside for the products of medical genes and memes, the contents of circles one and two, respectively. What sickness and healing "look like" in an individual, including its rationale, expressive meaning, psychophysiology, and symbolic form in behavior, are all represented in this third circle. It thus has to be represented as open to and connected with the units of cultural information or the medical memes of circle two that (together with the medical genes, the contents of circle one) produce the SH response. Enactments of pain, shortness of breath, nausea, and other manifestations of sickness, *together with what they communicate and elicit from the self and others* (i.e., their meanings and expressive content), all constitute examples of the material found in circle three. Because the symbolic form of the behaviors that comprise sickness and healing has changed greatly during human evolution and history, the size of this segment of the medical Institution is expansive and viewed across individuals of any one society is highly variable.

Although cultural aspects of sickness and healing, the contents of circles two and three, would appear to have comparatively few semantic and symbolic limits, one could also and in some respects probably should view this interpretive sphere of SH as limited with respect to space and content. This is so because, as shown in chapters 7 and 8, even the more culturally expressive aspects of the SH adaptation could probably be described as consisting of permutations and combinations of a fixed number of fundamental concepts and experiences (i.e., products of *elemental* medical memes, but requiring medical genes) that pertain to the effects of disease and injury and that express sickness and healing in any particular social cultural context. Nevertheless, because it is important to emphasize the changing character of sickness and healing during the evolution of medicine, it is best to depict circles two and three as expansive and variable in size.

The Institutional Components of Medicine

The fourth and fifth circles together refer more properly to the groupwide characteristics of the Institution of medicine. These circles are equated with *average, whole societies* rather than with *average eventuations of sickness and healing* as was the case for the three inner circles. Pictured diagrammatically, the space contained by the two outer circles of the medical Institution has expanded considerably during cultural and social evolution. While both of these outer circles together are held to form societywide characteristics and to demarcate sociological components, they are distinguished on analytical grounds.

The fourth circle in the diagram designates the parameters of sickness and healing discussed in chapter 7. The space of this circle describes the overall style and pattern inherent in the way sickness and healing are configured and played out in a society. A society's parameters vary not only in content but also in heterogeneity, with more complex societies incorporating various traditions and models of sickness and healing. Hence this variable of homogeneity/heterogeneity would need to be represented in the diagram. Circle four is shown as open and connected to the preceding circle because the culturally expressive part of the SH response, that which more elaborately describes the social/cultural construction of sickness and healing in individuals, feeds into, reflects, and draws on the parameters of sickness and healing of the society as a whole; and vice versa. As was described in chapter 7, in each type of society the knowledge base, expectations, and rules that affect how sick persons behave when ill and how they relate to the group and to healers differ, as do the rules organizing the social practices of healing. Thus products of medical memes, when visualized as shared among members of a society, are what give sickness and healing in that society its distinctive overall character. This point can be stated differently: whereas circle three might denote the appearance of a particular "tree" of the medical Institution, the fourth circle denotes the whole "forest" of trees that make up the medical Institution.

The fifth and last circle of the medical is set aside to draw attention to the more structural, corporate, organizational, and material component of medicine. The group of kinfolk that helps manage sickness in Lower Zaire, and the institution that regulates all of this, would be located in this circle (Janzen 1978a). The group of villagers coming together in the Sepik society described by Gilbert Lewis (1975) which focuses on the sick person, which seems motivated by concern, and which shares rules of behavior aimed to deter blame for sickness could also be "located" in this fifth circle of the medical however much its informational basis constitutes a part of sickness and healing it might seem to be. Finally, in this last circle one would find the paraphernalia, associated rituals, and social groupings (e.g., corporate associations) among healers as well as the available medicines, tools, and technical procedures used in healing.

As implied earlier, this fifth sector of the medical Institution is difficult to delimit. There exist many institutionalized practices and man-made objects including medicines and instruments that in some ways are part of the Institution of medicine and would need to be included, yet in other respects they are so far removed from actual episodes of sickness and healing, and under the influence of political and economic factors, that it might seem best to handle them as separate or "nonmedical." To say this is but to affirm again that where the medical ends and its dependencies begin is difficult to specify; and that some imprecision in placing boundaries of concepts is to be expected.

At any rate, a delimited sector is presented in the diagram for analytic and aesthetic reasons in order to describe the part of the medical Institution as a whole that is not exclusively or explicitly tied to behaviors composing sickness and healing but that nonetheless shapes, constrains, enables, and contextualizes them. This space is rendered as continuous with the previous one designating the parameters of sickness and healing. This is the case because the corporate medical structures and physical products of a society impart a distinctive cast to how sickness and healing are configured and played out in a society at large, and traditions about the latter also influence how the medical structures are made to operate. Here, as in any other two contiguous regions of the medical Institution, there exist reciprocal dependency relationships.

In modern societies the corporate, structural part of the medical Institution is very complex. It is made up of such things as learned/scholarly/scientific knowledge structures, technical procedures, and associated physical provisions; knowledge, routines, and resources of "alternative" medical traditions of the society; professional bodies and their rules of operation; institutions involved in the teaching of medicine and nursing; political economic constraints and directives that support practice arrangements; and associated influences from external institutions that structure how medicine is practiced. In brief, the outer circle of the medical encompasses all those structures that render the medical a large corporation and megaindustry that is fed, regulated, and exploited by other corporations and industries of a society.

The two outer circles that comprise the Institution of medicine in effect feed information and material to the three innermost circles (which describe individual eventuations of sickness and healing). As will be elaborated presently, the corporate part of the medical also feeds and receives information and material from the other institutions of the society that in turn will alter parameters of sickness and healing and, ultimately, affect how sickness and healing are to be regulated and shaped. The continued growth and expansion of the medical Institution, especially the fifth circle designating its corporate super-structure, is what poses a powerful challenge to one seeking to understand the direction and end points of the evolution of sickness/healing and medicine.

Control and Regulation of the Medical Institution

Completing the illustration of the medical, one can note by inspecting fig-ure 1 that the concentric and open circles that constitute medicine in its en-tirety are connected to a series of stations. The latter correspond to nonmedical institutions that together describe a whole society from a macrosociological frame of reference. These institutions regulate behavior involving such things as spiritual/religious, political, legal/jurisprudential, economic, social welfare, and leisure concerns.

Each of these separate but integrally connected (to each other and the med-ical) institutions furnishes inputs and receives outputs from the medical. All are interdependent, and happenings in any one institutional sector can reverberate throughout the network of connected organizations. This has been reviewed in earlier chapters. For example, in Zinacantan, Mexico, the political organiza-tion of the community that included the Hiloletik (i.e., native shamanistic healers) as revealed during the annual ceremonies appeared to rank individ-ual healers and this seemed to qualify their repute, affecting tendencies of vil-lagers to seek healing (Fabrega and Silver 1973). In Zulu medicine, as beauti-fully described by Ngubane (1977), the fees charged by diviners are set with respect to the techniques used and the social ranking of the diviner. Here, then, seemingly political groupings and functions and economic factors have an in-fluence on the way healing was carried out. During the medieval period of Eu-rope, as an example, the Christian church played a very important role in how disease* was defined and conceptualized and healing was carried out (i.e., the practices and materials of healing) and hence happenings in the religion insti-tution affected the medical, and vice versa. During the modern and postmodern European phase of medical evolution the influence of the religion institution has all but been eliminated (at least from the biomedical sector) and the legal/governmental and the political/economic institutions have assumed dominance, for these dictate what sick persons can expect and what healers are allowed to do.

In each of these instances, then, corporate, organizational, and material fac-tors pertaining to nonmedical institutions directly influence circle five of the medical, its corporate/organizational sector, and through this effect also influ-ence and constrain the form and style of sickness and healing (i.e., the param-eters). The informational aspects of the way all of this is realized is ultimately represented in how individuals behave, which means that the information is stored in the brain as medical memes. These examples illustrate the reciprocal relations between the nonmedical and the medical institutions. Political economic and governmental developments in contemporary America are increasingly influential in how practitioners orient and conduct practice and also how would-be patients behave in a setting of sickness. Hence, by today's standards of operation, these nonmedical institutions would have to be described as strongly linked to the medical.

In conceptualizing the evolution of medicine as a major Institution of society, I am attempting to depict the more or less systematic changes that have taken place in the way sickness and healing are configured in light of relations among the various other major institutions of society. The diagram reviewed previously provides an illustration of the five interrelated layers of the medical Institution that are implicated in these transformations as well as (some of) the various nonmedical institutions that are dialectically related to the medical during phases of evolution. Obviously, each of the institutional sectors of society can be assumed to be undergoing change in association with changes in medicine. Implicit in my conceptualization of this intellectual problem is that as sickness and healing come to be configured differently during social evolution, society as a whole, along with other nonmedical institutions, is also undergoing evolution.

Stephen K. Sanderson (1990, 1995a, 1995b) offers an excellent analysis of the topic of social evolution and transformation. Factors that are thought to have played a major causative role during these transformations as well as features of society that undergo quantitative or qualitative change are summarized and discussed critically. Notably, archaeologists, anthropologists, and sociologists who address this problem area as a rule do not discuss medical phenomena per se (for exceptions, see Cohen 1989 and also chapters 1 and 2 above). In Sanderson's three books, he reviews the typologies that have been used to depict stages of social evolution. I have used one such typology in my discussion of the evolution of sickness and healing, namely, that of Johnson and Earle (1991).

The general topic of social evolution, its phases and its dynamics, has a long history in the social sciences and is very complex and highly contested. Even a brief discussion of this topic in relation to the evolution of medicine is well beyond the scope of this book. Suffice it to say that in conceptualizing the evolution of sickness and healing (and the medical Institution of a society), I am of necessity putting aside the complex set of evolutionary changes that are taking place in the society as a whole, changes that are causative of, reactive to, and certainly complementary to what is taking place with respect to sickness and healing. For a summary of these issues, the reader is referred to the publications of Sanderson. Figure 1, above, and variants of it that appear later in this chapter propose a way of drawing attention to a small portion of the relatively complex set of changes encompassed by social evolution, namely, those related to medicine.

The Medical Institution Viewed in Terms of Units of Information

A diagram of the medical Institution can be conceptualized from the standpoint of the units of information, the products of which make up and feed into the various circles that constitute the medical. Each circle incorporates and symbolizes the information of those contained within it. The inner circle is composed of genetic information, namely, the part of the genome that programs the apparatus of the body and that furnishes the capacity to become diseased and injured, and which is subject to natural selection. The second circle of the medical contains the units of cultural information that program sickness and healing. Four things need to be kept in mind about these medical memes: (1) their products inform about disease/injury, thus having (2) effects on the self and social environment that (3) elicit self-behaviors and responses from conspecifics aimed at understanding and neutralizing disease and injury and, eventually, (4) feeding upon and leading to innovations in ways of handling sickness and healing—eventually, to inventions, technologies, agencies, and social dependencies. Hence the eventual anatomical and physiological products of medical genes serve as templates for the registration of disease and injury and during development connect with the contents of circle two; the memes of this circle, in turn, produce the SH response of an average person, circle three; and the memes of circle three when examined in terms of their overall stylistic properties, societal characteristics, and material products are found in circles four and five. Finally, happenings in circle five, ultimately regulated and sustained by products of medical memes, affect and are affected by products of nonmedical memes that in effect are what steer and regulate nonmedical institutions.

Most fundamentally, and as elaborated in the previous two chapters, the products of medical genes and memes represent and inform about a condition of disease/injury in informational terms, thereby constructing a sickness/healing routine or ensemble that communicates about its nature so as to elicit efforts at prevention, alleviation, undoing, and, if necessary, resignation to death with attendant preparation for this outcome. I am here emphasizing that the whole medical Institution is a product of, connects with, and is geared to the material substance and behavioral expression of the SH adaptation in sickness and healing, the contents found in the first three circles. There are obviously big distances and logical jumps between genetic programs, pure physiological manifestations of disease and injury, biocultural expressions of this in the form of sickness, "natural" or highly elaborated healing responses from persons of the social environment, social groupings and their modes of operation that organize how sickness and healing are structured, and dense networks of agencies and dependencies that regulate or exploit medicine. The concepts introduced in previous chapters and the frame of reference that was outlined when represented as information constitutes a way of analyzing medicine holistically.

Circle four and especially circle five, then, contain the products of medical memes that involve groups, corporate structures, and material/technological objects, all of which affect how sickness and healing are carried out in a particular society and all of which embody cultural information. How these social practices and arrangements and the man-made objects of medicine are used is influenced and regulated by products of other items of cultural information of the society that reflect political, economic, religious, and jurisprudential concerns. The effects of some of these "memes" might well filter down and come to shape events of sickness and healing and would thus qualify as medical memes, in the sense in which this concept has been defined.

How the Organization of Medicine Changes during Evolution

In contemplating the evolution of medicine as an Institution, each of the previous five compartments of the medical could in theory be expected to change in quantitative size, qualitative content, and (all except the first) in its relations with those medical compartments that are inclusive to it. Furthermore, and as I indicated earlier, since the medical Institution is but one member of an integrated set of major institutions that describe how the society operates and functions—a society that *also evolves*—the kinds of nonmedical institutions that become influential in medicine during different phases of social and cultural evolution differ and change. With all of this one also finds changes in relations between the medical Institution and nonmedical institutions. All of this would need to be taken into account in a broad description of how medicine evolves and is depicted diagrammatically. Given the modest goal of this book, which is to provide a frame of reference and a methodology for conceptualizing the evolution of medicine, all of the preceding types of changes cannot be fully covered. I will limit myself to just a few summary comments.

In *prehuman groups* all of the circles of the medical, especially even circle one, come into existence and begin to expand. The machinery for the SH adaptation becomes defined. Similarly, it is during this late phase of the evolution of *Homo sapiens* that medical memes, the contents of circle two, become defined, elaborated, and relatively focused on the body and the self and become connected with medical genes. The same is obviously true for circle three, which contains the SH response of sickness and healing. Another way of conceptualizing this is to say that although most of the structures and physiological sys-

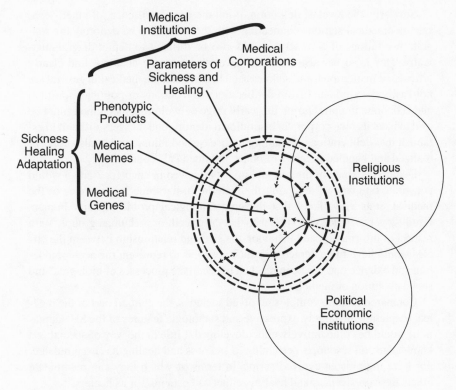

Figure 2. Medicine in Family-level Societies

tems that rendered pre- and early human groups vulnerable to disease and injury were similar as compared to other higher primate groups, the capacity to understand their implications and respond adaptively is posited to have evolved during this earliest stage of human evolution, and this would be marked by the emergence of the various circles that describe the medical Institution.

In *family-level groups* of *Homo sapiens* circle five of the medical diagram, which describes what was termed the corporate, organizational component, would be very small (see fig. 2). There is little that one can point to in these types of societies that qualifies as a separate medical corporation or organization. Sickness and healing are family and group concerns (among the !Kung Bushmen, at least, medical ceremonies are for the benefit of all and seem to have more than just medical purposes; see Marshall 1969), there is little differentiation of roles, little in the way of specialized resources and techniques, and (as described by Holmberg [1969] for the Siriono, at least) a passive, fatalistic resignation seems to often prevail in the setting of a serious, protracted sickness and healing ensemble.

Similarly, the level of definition, if not the actual existence, of outer, separate, nonmedical stations connecting with the medical (i.e., denoting the separate institutions of a society) would also be difficult to depict diagrammatically. This is so because in family-level societies one does not find clearly articulated institutions, and sickness and healing and the medical in general are not easily discriminated from deliberations and actions of political, spiritual, and economic import. During this early stage of evolution, medicine cannot be said to have its own corporate/Institutional identity, and it is very difficult to establish that deliberations pertaining to disease and injury are not also conceptualized and handled in terms of other, "nonmedical" concerns.

Distinctive kinds of disease and injury reviewed in chapters 2 and 3 would constitute one way of depicting the material in the three inner circles of the medical. It is very likely that the epidemiological profile of early human, family-level societies was similar to that described for prehuman groups. With respect to information and behavior, the size and relationship between the circles would have to be depicted in such a way as to represent the accommodation and balance that has been reached between the processes of biological and social evolution of medicine.

Compared to more complex, evolved societies, the cultural part of the medical (depicting the largely expressive and sociologic features of the SH adaptation) would be comparatively underdeveloped. Little in the way of specialized knowledge and resources pertaining to sickness and healing has accumulated, nor have individuals evolved scripts in terms of which they can manipulate others through sickness and healing, either as "patients" or as healers.

Sickness and healing during this phase of evolution reflect most nearly the complementarity among systems descriptive of the human organism. A holistic, biocultural, somatopsychic, and psychosomatic unity characterizes an organism's responses to disease and injury. Moreover, what natural selection has sculpted as an SH response reflects interdependency among group members, runaway social competition with other (prehuman and nonhuman primate) groups, and stringent living conditions. On the one hand, the social environment plays an important function in the way the SH adaptation has been designed, is communicated, and is dealt with; on the other, the individual has evolved so as to configure and play out sickness and healing in a way that balances individual needs with group needs. Although some routines of sickness expression have evolved along with medicines and procedures so as to more effectively cope with disease and injury, these are relatively few in number and exert but limited effects; and although individuals expect help from comembers, imperatives of the group and bare subsistence living render SH deception or exploitation unrealistic, unprofitable, and unacceptable.

For these and other reasons, then, the three inner circles depicting the medical in the diagram should be conceptualized as openly connected with each other and relatively closely placed one to the other and in relation to the fourth circle, denoting the parameters of sickness and healing. This is a way of diagrammatically showing that, compared to more complex societies, in these elementary ones the process of social evolution has not as yet exerted much influence on the way the SH response can be played out behaviorally.

Compared to individuals of family-level societies, the general health of members of *village-level, chiefdom, and prestate societies* is generally regarded as lower due to dietary and nutritional deficiencies, with consequent greater and different vulnerabilities to infections that are transmitted from contaminated foods and objects. Thus some of the material content "inside" the three inner circles of the medical would clearly need to be depicted as different, in an epidemiological sense, accounting for the different mix of infectious diseases and higher general levels of morbidity that are found.

A difference in epidemiological material is complemented by a difference in the sheer construction of sickness and healing because of sedentarism and the increased complexity in the society. To recall, knowledge of and resources for sickness and healing are more elaborated and hence the way the SH adaptation is realized is more varied and complex. This would translate as a larger space and more diversified content that would have to be depicted in circles two and three. The contents of the fourth circle would conform to the parameters of sickness and healing described for village-level and chiefdom/prestate societies in the previous chapter and would likewise (compared to family-level societies) reflect a more varied, elaborated character. In other words, since the patterning of these general aspects of sickness and healing differ from preceding societies, with greater complexity and differentiation evident, the specific area set aside exclusively for circle four would have to be expanded compared to previous social types.

Societies at this level of evolution possess rudimentary forms of what one can term a medical corporation or institution. Consequently, the actual definition and size of the fifth, outer circle of the medical Institution expands and exerts a more distinctive influence on the four inner ones than was the case in prehuman and family-level societies. For example, specialization of practitioners is found in some prestates and healers often show the beginnings of corporate structures. Family management groups are often more influential and institutionalized, and these also would belong in circle five. Furthermore, political and religious concerns, although potentially related to concerns of sickness and healing, are more autonomous, self-sufficient, and explicitly handled than in previous societies. In other respects as well, what one could think of as nonmedical institutions begin to be differentiated. Certainly this is the case for the spiritual/religious and the political but not the legal/jurisprudential, although that one finds more explicit rules and procedures for the resolution of social conflicts is clear. Consequently, in the diagram depicting how these societies operate and function from a medical evolutionary point of view, the outlines that define at least some of the nonmedical stations that "connect" with the medical would need to be enhanced. In eventuations of disease and injury one begins to be able to distinguish, however imprecisely, how activities that have explicit medical, political, economic, and spiritual significance interact.

In these societies, moreover, it begins to be very difficult to provide an average, unitary representation of the first three segments of the medical, the ones that have been held to arbitrarily "contain" the biological and cultural programs of the SH adaptation along with the SH response itself in the average individual. This is so because it is difficult to picture a "typical" eventuation of sickness and healing in any one society at this comparatively higher level of complexity. What one finds is that any one instance of sickness and healing in a particular individual begins to be configured differently from another. This is so because medical events take place and are played out and handled within diverse subgroups and subcommunities of the society. The latter split and segment the society in a complex way. Any two random SH responses taking place in this type of society begin to elicit very different experiences, cognitions, and behaviors because their social and cultural location in the society could differ substantially with respect to kinship structure, lineage lore, rituals, knowledge, and resources. Different sets of attitudes, beliefs, and orientations pertaining to sickness and healing would be involved, depending on the person's social background and access to resources.

These societies would have to have the space of the three outer circles of the medical diagram expanded. For one, more knowledge is available about sickness and healing. This essentially translates as what persons who are sick are able to communicate about disease and injury and how the resulting "messages" or constructions of sickness and healing are capable of being understood and acted on by comembers (e.g., knowledge about bodily anatomy and function and knowledge about medicines and technical procedures). An additional common factor that would account for the greater importance of the outer circles of the medical during this phase of evolution is that the more complex social environment of these societies allows individuals to begin to effectively exploit sickness for individualistic needs; and conversely, specialist healers become differentiated and they gain an ability to manipulate and exploit sickness for their own or their subgroup's needs as well as on behalf of sick comembers. In short, circle four would depict a more diversified design (to account for complexity and heterogeneity of the parameters) and circle five a larger, better-defined outline (to account for the presence of structures, organizations, and elaborated material products).

All of this could also be visualized diagrammatically by recalling that during this phase of cultural and social evolution certain nonmedical, "external," and separate institutions begin to exert a determinate influence on how sickness/healing eventuations are constructed and played out. The arrows connecting certain nonmedical with medical institutions (e.g., the religious and political) would have to be depicted as heavier and more influential. Thus varieties of sickness conditions and their associated causes are likely to be formulated and interpreted in terms of current and past political happenings occurring within and between lineage-affiliated and segmentary groupings. The consultation by a specialist outside healer could also be said to constitute a discernible political input into the medical, as Ngubane (1977), for example, informs about the Zulu. Medical memes developed in one lineage might be imported into another, with a host of political economic implications linked to obligations based on conventions about social exchange and reciprocity. Interpretive schemes and narratives of medical affliction in any one group will naturally expand and become more complex as knowledge structures and social practices pertaining to sickness and healing in a neighboring group or allied lineage grouping are borrowed, expropriated, or simply modified and neutralized.

In societies at this level of evolution that are more centralized and unified, the beginnings of an official, usually sacred version of social order and the justification of norms are found. Such an ideology or religion has obvious medical overtones; it will set reference points for interpretations and contribute some standardization to the way sickness and healing are configured and played out. A more or less standard ideology about sickness and healing can challenge and undermine locally contextualized interpretations, imparting some complexity and positiveness, if not official formality, to how the medical is structured in the society. In the event, sickness and healing configurations could be said to constitute part of an expanding social consciousness about the sacred and secular, a consciousness that begins to distinguish between happenings in separate areas of life (institutional sectors) and between the implications that sickness and healing might have as a consequence of social/political as well as moral considerations (e.g., as devolving from the social standing of the person ill). All of the changes described here would in effect begin to more sharply define what has been described as the outer nonmedical stations of the society.

Essentially all of the changes described for the two previous types of societies are accentuated and more pronounced in societies categorized as *states* and especially empires and civilizations (see fig. 3). This involves in particular (a) pictures of disease and injury, with chronic diseases and disabilities more common (as a result of changes in the ecology and social structure) and also outbreaks of new disease pictures and epidemics as a result of contact with geographically separate societies, (b) the influence of accumulated, literate bodies of knowledge of sickness and healing which greatly complexify medical understandings and behaviors and serve to in part standardize the cultural expression of sickness and healing, (c) the growth of medical "professional" and ancillary corporate structures (e.g., those involved in the invention of medical procedures and the manufacture of special herbs) as well as nonmedical institutions, and (d) the capacity of individuals and different separate groups within

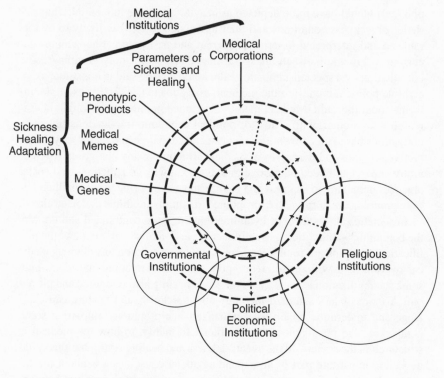

Figure 3. Medicine in Civilizations and Empires

a society to gain power over how sickness and healing are to be played out (e.g., the degree of control as well as social exploitation that is possible for the SH response, regardless of whether one considers its sickness or healing realization).

These types of societies contain separate, well-defined corporate groups, estates, and institutions, and one of these (or a cluster of them, given that different doctrines and traditions pertaining to health are found) can properly be considered as truly medical. These societies are often described as feudal, oligarchic, or "aristocratic" to denote their special combination of particularism (as applies with respect to family-level, village-level and chiefdom/prestate societies) and universalism (as classically applies to modern and postmodern European societies). In other words, individuals are aware of belonging to a specific group or estate (hence their particularistic identifications) as well as "fitting into a universal order of society" (Unger 1976: 148).

For the reasons just discussed, the institutional/corporate sector of medicine, the fifth medical circle of the diagram, would need to be described as well defined, very large, and diversified. Its relative size would naturally expand considerably. Healers are socially differentiated and calibrated as to learning, repute, experience, apprenticeship, specialization, expense, and morality. Family management groups become necessary to negotiate between systems of care that are available. Industries for the manufacture of medicines and sickness/healing paraphernalia of all types become established. The influences of the corporate segment are mirrored in the distinctive parameters of sickness and healing described in a previous chapter. Sickness and healing become more secularized, scientific, and focused on bodily and behavioral manifestations; yet this expanded emphasis on well-being and health continues to have spiritual, moral, and psychological as well as bodily dimensions.

It can arguably be asserted that the strong effects of these corporate, organizational, and material features that serve as quasi standards for the medical (found in circle five) on the contents of circles three and two are unique in the social evolution of medicine. Whereas during earlier phases, the contents and products of memes reflected a balance between individual (disease/injury) centered changes and cultural (spiritual/existential/moral) concerns, during the empire/civilization phase ideological and especially political economic imperatives become highly influential. Similarly, organizational/administrative influences (e.g., municipal or more regional in some states, involving literate, academically trained practitioners in others) begin to play a role in shaping the configuration of sickness and healing. This would show up on a hypothetical medical diagram as expanded material and diversity of content and organization in circle four and especially circle five of the medical Institution.

All of these diagrammatic conventions would symbolize how the Institution of medicine, considered almost as an organization of the society, comes to exert its influence on configurations of sickness and healing. And the latter, to be sure, would be very differently constituted in different sectors of society given its larger size and complexity. Stated briefly, official, scholarly, and either secular (China), sacred (India), or more balanced (Galenic Mediterranean, medieval Islamic) literate traditions of medicine will dominate and strongly influence the SH response by feeding information, material, and expertise that affect how sickness and healing are configured and played out in the many separate ethnic, religious, and social economic groups of these societies, many of which have their own "small" tradition that exerts its own influence. Most, if not all, of the different types of social groups can be expected to subscribe to a folk, indigenous sickness/healing tradition that often functions in opposition to the scholarly, "scientific" one. Moreover, a group can borrow freely from another group's tradition and from the more or less standard, official, literate, and formal one, that is, the "great" tradition.

The large and complex corpus of information, technical resources, and social practices constituting the corporate institution and organization of the medical Institution (the fifth, outermost circle of the diagram) is balanced by the greater definition and influence of nonmedical institutions or stations of the society. Moreover, in states and especially empires/civilizations, the manufacturing, commercial, fiscal, and administrative/regulatory institutions would need to be better defined in the medical diagram than in the less evolved societies, where it was the political and religious institutions that were important. Money payments—to healers and to their assistants for specially prepared herbs, procedures, and complex paraphernalia—now punctuate sickness and healing enterprises. Political and legal/jurisprudential institutions (at least in early modern European societies) begin to regulate and monitor the conduct of sickness and healing. All of these influences, which originate in nonmedical sectors and come to structure the organization of the medical Institution, necessarily influence how sickness and healing are configured and played out in these societies.

The diversity of material and information supplied to the medical Institution by nonmedical institutions constitutes a basic reason why the features of the SH response (the contents of circle three) would need to be depicted as more heterogeneous, more differentiated, and more secularized in the medical diagram of states, civilizations, and empires. In these societies the flow of material and information from outer, nonmedical stations strongly influences circles five and four, and some of it comes to constrain how the SH response is realized (circle three), ultimately coming to be represented in circle two as medical memes.

Developments taking place in societies associated with the later two phases of the evolution of medicine, those termed *modern* and *postmodern,* are illustrated in figure 4. Medicine in these societies naturally involves major changes in the corporate organization of medicine and in the macrosociological architecture of society. But also as a cultural tradition, biomedicine is associated with sharp differences in the way the various "inner" components of the Institution of medicine operate and function with respect to the configuration of sickness and healing. The changes taking place during this phase of social and cultural evolution all reflect, at the minimum, the hardening of secularization, the expansion of scientific knowledge, and the growth of industrial capitalism. They can be equated with the psychological, social, political economic, and jurisprudential transformations associated with modern, liberal, and contemporary, postliberal societies (Berman 1983; Giddens 1984, 1990, 1991; Unger 1975, 1976).

That biomedicine develops a formal, legally official status in the society has several implications. It means, in effect, that all that passes as medically or "clinically" valid must correspond to how the body operates and functions given the biomedical calculus. Now, all "major" traditions of medicine, and many "perhaps even all" of the "minor" ones as well, posit forces, substances, and structures inside the body. However, biomedicine is different. First, it operates in terms of physical anatomical structures and physiological and chemically specified systems and generally this is not true with other traditions of

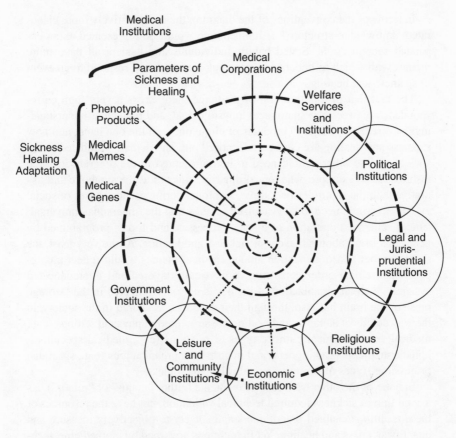

Figure 4. Medicine in Contemporary Postmodern Societies

medicine the anatomies of which are thought of as analytical, functional, and perhaps even metaphorical and the ethnophysiological mechanisms are not always quantified and measurable (although that they can achieve a high degree of specificity is clear, as for example with moxibustion and acupuncture sites in Chinese medicine and specially prepared herbs and foods in Aztec and Ayurvedic medicine). Second, with respect to sickness and healing and compared to other traditions of medicine, biomedicine operates in terms of a highly elaborated, technically based corpus of information about the body and behavior. The scientific understanding of disease and injury (and sickness and healing) may constitute cultural knowledge and is a product of cultural evolution, as is the case with other traditions of medicine. However, its social consequences for the way the institution of medicine operates and functions, as discussed in earlier chapters and now visualized diagrammatically, need to be fully appreciated.

In terms of the conventions of the diagram, the comparatively more elaborated "knowledge structure" of biomedicine would be represented as an expanded second circle. Stated baldly, individuals and healers all have more
memes with which to understand, play out, interpret, and respond to an event
of sickness and healing.

The fact that in this tradition of medicine there exists a very high correspondence between the anatomical, physiological, and molecular understandings of disease and injury (products of circle one), on the one hand, and how
sickness and healing are configured, carried out, and actually validated in the
society, on the other, would need to be represented in the diagram in some
fashion. As an example, what one ordinarily thinks of as the symbolic and fig-
urative material of circles two, three, and four (during earlier phases of social
evolution) would need to be visualized as reflecting the impersonal, universal-
istic, mechanized operation of agents, processes, and forces programmed by
genes that bring about an event of sickness and healing. At the very least, the
sheer number and organization among medical memes would reflect a complex, hierarchical order consisting of physically layered and interconnected
systems. Such an organization of memes is not only reflected in the "storage
bins" of the brain but also, through their products, as shared in the society, in
the way details of sickness and healing are structured in physical settings (e.g.,
medical versus surgical clinics), types of relations (e.g., medical specialists,
holistic medicine practitioners) and in corporate organizations (e.g., specialist
professions, types of supporting medical technologies).

In none of the other traditions of medicine (either "major" or "minor") has
a condition of sickness required technical validation, nor have the resources of
these traditions enabled practitioners and society to objectively measure and
quantify sickness and healing. Yet in traditions governed by biomedicine, technology and physical procedures involving equipment and specialized tests of
chemical reactions, all of which are held to provide "objective" information,
are used to actually render valid and real what in other societies are highly
emotive, socially elaborated, and existentially referenced states of suffering
and distress.

In all societies, of course, the identity given to a sickness and healing ensemble is culturally determined and, in this sense, validated. However, as reviewed earlier, the facts of illness, suffering, and sickness itself have constituted
prima facie evidence of a medical problem. Thus, whereas in other traditions
of medicine personal statements about the self and body and social judgments
pertaining to behavior and experience constitute the "gold standards" about
sickness and healing, in contemporary societies this function is performed by
machines and "experts" of many types, not just healers and certainly not sick
persons. This correspondence between the description of the SH response and
the parameters of sickness and healing (and the actual workings of medical
corporations and nonmedical institutions) might be represented diagrammati-

cally by expanding and more openly connecting circles three, four, and five of the medical diagram and by opening them to the memes of political and economic institutions.

To reiterate this point, in all types of societies there exists a correspondence of sorts between how each of the sectors that comprise the medical is articulated and played out. What distinguishes medicine in the later phases of evolution presently under review is the technologically explicit and detailed way in which the inner circles are delineated and codified, on the one hand, and the determining influence that the material identified in them and the procedures used to measure them have on how sickness and healing are constructed, managed, and processed as socially valid enterprises of the society, on the other.

The corresponding changes in the institutional and organizational aspects of the medical are equally striking. For here, as social theorists have suggested, one finds an effacement of the boundaries between the various corporations and institutions that make up the society (Giddens 1984, 1990, 1991). A merging of state and society is said to take place. The state and its associated influences on other institutions of the society feed and virtually control establishment medicine: public, administrative, and legal directives and rules of the society have an impact on those directives and rules that provide a major rationale of biomedical practice. Scientific and technological institutions outside of medicine become highly influential, not just the political, economic, and commercial ones that operated in civilizations and empires discussed earlier; and technical/expert information germane to these institutions influences how individuals explain their body and its changes during disease and injury. Similarly, the products of service/leisure institutions are communicated in increasingly intrusive ways so that they also come to make up part of every individual's concerns about the body, the self, and health. While all of these nonmedical institutions are separated and somewhat self-governing, hence should be depicted as diagrammatically discrete and autonomous, they are reflexively influential on the individual in a mediated way and thus would appear to be incorporated in the medical memes in the brain, governing preoccupations about health and well-being of individuals of modern and postmodern European societies.

It follows that the sharp boundary that separated the medical from the external, nonmedical stations in the macrosociological diagram of states and civilizations would in some respects be much less visible in the medical diagram of modern and especially postmodern European societies. In fact, it might be necessary to depict these nonmedical institutions as overlapping and continuous with the medical, or at least as connecting freely with it via informational and substantive flows.

This is a way of summarizing the reflexive, mediated impact that general, nonmedical expert/scientific systems, as well as those of other systems of modern society, have on human experience, including medical experience and practice. Although there exist immense differences between modern approaches to sickness and healing and those of earlier societies, the easy traffic across institutional sectors that constitute modernity and postmodernity brings to mind the integrated character of social experiences and situations that is found in the more elementary societies. The difference, of course, is that whereas in elementary societies social experiences surrounding sickness and healing are integrated because the cultural information that creates them is judged as connected to the varied affairs of the group, in modern and postmodern ones the cultural information that creates social experiences is judged as particulate, differentiated, and centered on disease and injury, although relevant to and originating in the separated affairs of the society.

Social theorists (e.g., Giddens) point out that in modern liberal and post-liberal societies social consciousness and the self are profoundly modified by local and distal happenings as a result of rapid information flow and the merging of institutions. Since health and the well-being of the body as well as sickness and healing per se constitute major preoccupations of the self and the latter, in addition, is the focal target of equally compelling and regulative influences from other institutions that serve to promote reflexive monitoring through social mediation, one may begin to get a better glimpse of the complex way in which the many corporations of the society exert control over the configuration of sickness and healing.

Another way of conceptualizing the effect of modernity and its plethora of expert/technical systems on the conduct of sickness and healing is to concentrate on medical memes. In elementary societies, these are few in number and have polyvalent meanings and functions. An item of cultural information pertaining to disease and injury has many simultaneous meanings and implications that incorporate political, economic, and spiritual concerns. In more complex societies, in contrast, the number of medical memes increases and their meanings and functions are more centered on disease and injury. Whereas medical memes in the latter types of societies may have their origin in and repercussions on diverse settings and activities of the society, when brought to bear on sickness and healing their more general meanings and functions are suspended and focused. Yet on the other hand, the context, position, appearance, and manner in which disease/injury is played out as sickness/healing is profoundly influenced by (indeed, assembled and fabricated by) the nonmedical circles or institutions that now come to control sickness and healing.

10

Implications of an Evolutionary Approach to Sickness and Healing

Sickness and healing have not usually been studied from the standpoint of evolutionary theory. One exception is the emphasis on Darwinian medicine (Williams and Nesse 1991). In this instance, what is pursued is how evolutionary theory can sharpen the efficacy of medical practice, rather than how sickness and healing have changed and been transformed. Another exception is the treatise of Johns (1990), which concentrated on the continuity of biological mechanisms involving food ingestion and metabolism and the development of special techniques for preparing and processing plant material. The interplay between biological and cultural adaptations in evolution, seen in relation to human chemical ecology, was the basis for the examination of varieties of human medicine. The search for and use of natural medicinal substances was the focus of Johns's analysis.

In social and cultural studies of medicine a descriptive and more or less static approach has been followed. As summarized in chapter 1, description and comparison of medical traditions, whether cultural or historical, has been a common theme. More often than not, such comparisons are pursued to emphasize peculiarities of modern as opposed to traditional approaches to sickness and healing. Examples of studies that did have an evolutionary focus were discussed in chapter 2. In general, previous studies have concentrated on very general themes and have not handled sickness and healing as phenomena that have shown more or less systematic changes.

Yet evolution deals with change and transformation, and the study of clinical and epidemiological questions can be seen as dominated by these themes. For example, an overriding goal of the biological, clinical, and epidemiological sciences, and even the social sciences applied to medicine, is to eventually bring about change through progressive improvement and refinement of information about the causes and effects of disease and injury. All of these sciences seek to decrease morbidity and mortality, and in some respects this is exactly one factor that natural and social selection in medicine has been posited to accomplish.

Social studies of medicine, then, have characteristics similar to those of an evolutionary approach. What needs to be clarified are the implications of conceptualizing sickness and healing, and the medical Institution itself, as by-products of the twin processes of biological and social evolution and of using concepts pertaining to the respective theories in such an enterprise. The attempt pursued here has provided an interpretation of key concepts and a frame of reference that can be used in future studies. Some of the kinds of topics and questions that an evolutionary approach to medicine makes accessible will be briefly reviewed.

Establishing Links between Biological and Cultural Factors

Sickness and healing have been conceptualized in terms of the two processes of biological and social (or cultural) evolution. The first process involved the construction of a complex machinery and the concomitant refinement of a capacity for the adaptive behavioral expression, recognition, and response to the effects of disease and injury. This process culminated in the line of evolution from protoculture to culture. It occurs within individuals and is held to have led to increased inclusive fitness. Genes are the units of information that control and ultimately determine the transformation of the individual through the process of natural selection.

The second process involved, through social selection, changes in the way sickness and healing were fashioned and carried out as social, cultural, political economic, and technological phenomena or enterprises. This process (more properly, set of processes) is also set in motion by and geared to the effects of disease and injury, but it takes place within social formations and at different levels and in different institutions within them. Memes and products of memes, units of cultural information pertaining to nonmedical institutions, and medical memes, those units of cultural information pertaining specifically to phenomena of sickness and healing, are the objects of selection by means of which the social evolution of medicine takes place.

The social selection of medical memes is construed as an adaptive process since units of information are chosen or invented by individuals for the specific purposes of constructively dealing with the effects of disease and injury. However, it is necessarily (i.e., by definition) adaptive only in the short run, for individuals are assumed to seek corrective action in a rational way. In other words, the desire and the perception that the implementation of a new or different unit of information pertaining to disease and injury will lead or does

lead to decreased morbidity and mortality, or lessening of the social consequences of disease and injury, is what accounts for the social selection of a
medical meme, and it in this respect that it is "adaptive," or at least judged as
such locally. However, selection of a medical meme may not necessarily benefit sick persons in the long run and may, in fact, prove neutral or even detrimental (have maladaptive consequences), whether evaluated locally or by
"external" scientific criteria. In relation to this point, while the process of social
evolution of medicine usually results in increased social complexity or differentiation, like social evolution generally, it cannot always be said to have these
consequences. It may in fact result in stasis or devolution (Sanderson 1990,
1994).

The most evident advantage of studying medicine from an evolutionary
frame of reference is that it can unify and integrate much material in the social
and biological sciences. As implied in chapter 1, many scholars who have
studied medical problems have heretofore pursued narrow disciplinary questions without contributing to the cumulative understanding of medicine as
an Institution of society. An analysis of the material reviewed in the previous
chapters of this book documents that an evolutionary frame of reference pertains to and can potentially enrich knowledge in diverse disciplines. Thus researchers working in the fields of medical anthropology, medical sociology,
historical sociology, human biology, evolutionary psychology, developmental
psychology, paleopathology, historical epidemiology, clinical psychosomatic
medicine, cognitive and social archaeology, and social history of medicine
and political economic institutions all can be viewed as contributing information that bears on the topic of the evolution of medicine. Whether one concentrates (1) on the construction of the SH machinery during human evolution and
its ontogeny during a critical period of development in a particular society and
culture, a topic germane to biologists, anthropologists, and psychologists; or
(2) on the differences in the way societies and ethnic groups manifest disease
and injury, conceptualize these phenomena, and go about seeking relief, a topic
germane to cultural and biological anthropologists as well as sociologists; or
(3) on how societies and institutions change and evolve, a topic germane to historians, economists, archaeologists and sociologists, one is engaged in the pursuit of questions pertaining to the evolution of medicine as this has been formulated in this book.

A rigorous evolutionary account of medicine stipulates that to be effective
medical memes should ideally complement or constructively build on the
genes that program the SH machinery. In other words, in the event of disease
and injury, there should ideally exist an adaptive fit between the programs of
development and function bearing on susceptibility and expression of disease
and injury as cultural phenomena (i.e., as sickness and healing). It is this fit between the products of medical genes and medical memes that links the processes of biological and cultural evolution. Such a fit should prevail in order for
medical memes to be considered adaptive in a scientific sense.

The conceptualization presented by Lumsden and Wilson (1981) pertaining to the link between cultural and genetic factors can be applied to the study of sickness and healing. In this light, the fit between medical genes and memes involves the operation of a sequence of "epigenetic rules" that comprise constraints on development and that influence the selection and use of medical memes (seemingly like "culturgens" in their formulation). An evolutionary perspective implies that individuals and groups select, elaborate, invent, and learn medical memes that in the long run have beneficial effects on inclusive fitness, which is to say, that are consistent with the operation of epigenetic rules. Individuals have imperfect ways of evaluating the long-term effects of medical memes and are often guided by immediate or short-term results (e.g., involving relief of symptoms or restoration of function). However, all members of a society, particularly those identified as healers in complex ones, are held to be involved to a greater or lesser extent in the enterprise of discovering and evaluating the utility of medical memes and their products, thereby attempting to ensure the adaptive fit between the processes of biological and cultural evolution.

There is little need to elaborate in great detail on how the frame of reference and the concepts interpreted in earlier chapters relate to current studies in the social and biological sciences. An important theme in medical anthropology, the social history of medicine and public health, involves clarifying whether, and if so how, "folk" medical practices and the inventory of knowledge embodied in ancient, non-Western traditions of medicine might have been (and still could be, if properly evaluated) effective in terms of contemporary, biomedical standards. A prominent theme in the history of medicine also involves clarifying how earlier medicines or procedures (i.e., products of medical memes) proved injurious, and this merges with the goal of much contemporary clinical research, which is to ascertain which of the medical memes and products now being used and perceived as useful may in fact prove deleterious. Ways in which useful medical memes can also be detrimental and how best to evaluate the efficacy of medical memes is a continuing dominant theme in clinical research. All of these enterprises, actively being pursued in the sciences today, can be said to be based on principles analogous to evolutionary theory and hence require no elaboration.

Challenging Established Medical Practices: What Defines Healers and Their Duties?

An evolutionary account of sickness and healing, such as the one developed here, could be said to be advantageous if it could derive novel questions about sickness and healing and lead to new ways of evaluating medicine as a biological and social enterprise. One possibility is clarifying to what extent a purely individualistic and fractionated way of conceptualizing sickness and carrying out healing, by exclusive reliance on a single, specialist medical practitioner, is truly adaptive. Clearly, this way of configuring sickness and carrying out healing, which seems so integral to biomedicine, has proven beneficial in any number of ways. Moreover, the idea that there exists a natural healing audience to which one can orient and from which one can expect help seems intrinsic to SH. However, in the light of biological and social evolutionary theory, a strict individualistic construction of SH runs counter to the strikingly group-centered approach to medicine that probably existed in the environment of evolutionary adaptedness. Insofar as this was a social environment, among other things, it is possible that the machinery of SH somehow requires a connectedness to and perception of a caring *group*. In other words, this may be the kind of setting that best releases and socially incorporates the SH adaptation. Or alternatively, an important sociocentric focus that blends bodily and existential needs may constitute a natural feature of the SH adaptation.

In summary, one is compelled to ask what exactly constitutes an adaptive realization of a healing audience and is motivated to clarify how "practitioners" of medicine should be used in the enterprise of healing, keeping in mind that exclusive reliance on individual healers is a comparatively late development in the evolution of medicine and one in many respects shaped by factors unrelated to issues pertaining strictly to disease and injury as this operated during the line of evolution leading to man.

Related to the definition of healer is the matter of how healers come to be selected from the social environment. Earlier, it was suggested that healers can be viewed as persons who are a product of the way social experiences of disease and injury affect the genetically based SH adaptation during critical developmental phases of childhood. The similarities and differences in these experiences cross-culturally need to be clarified. Since an emphasis on healing others is one facet of the way the adaptation is realized, it would be interesting to clarify how individual healers come to orient and deal with sickness in the self, the other facet of the adaptation. Studies of shamanism and of characteristics of healing in other societies, a staple theme in medical anthropology, have not ordinarily examined orientations and behaviors of healers to sickness in the self and immediate family. Moreover, the recruitment to the occupation of healer has usually been studied as a purely social and cultural enterprise, rather than one that results from the unfolding of a biological trait or adaptation. Ordinarily, sickness and healing are handled as distinct and separate medical enterprises linked together by local, conventional rules. Conceptualizing them as integrated facets of a single trait or adaptation pertaining to medicine that unfolds as a consequence of the way genetic and cultural information comes to be used during development constitutes a potentially productive way of understanding the influences of disease and injury in human populations.

The Need for Contexts of Healing that Promote Emotional Support and Hope

A related and pertinent question to ask here concerns what has been termed the existential loading of SH. Studies of the way contemporary hunter-gatherers orient to and handle disease and injury suggest that framing SH in an existential context is integral to the biological machinery of SH. Such a realization of the SH adaptation was probably also a dominant component of how disease and injury were dealt with in the environment of evolutionary adaptedness. An issue needing clarification today is how such an existential component of SH is best actualized and whether its expurgation from the arena of practice, as it largely has been in biomedicine, has maladaptive consequences.

A measure of hope, a supportive, group consensus of its limits with respect to sickness and healing, and a way of "naturally" handling terminal states of disease and injury when medical events render hope maladaptive also seem to be integral to the biology of SH. However, it is not at all clear that contemporary approaches to healing emphasize and constructively incorporate these factors into the equation of healing. Obviously, the evolution to social and cultural dominance of the biomedical enterprise has taken place in the context of themes and values pertaining to secularization, individual self-interest, rationality, and strict monetary accounting with consequent commodification of healing.

What needs emphasis is that these are culturally specific values and not natural and intrinsic to the medical enterprise when it is conceptualized in terms of biological and social evolution. The fact remains that the SH machinery requires a suitable existential framing of disease and injury and that this element seems absent from the way SH has been shaped culturally by Western biomedicine. An evolutionary account of SH suggests that to adaptively show sickness is to adaptively communicate it to oneself and others, to adaptively seek to heal it through self-help or by seeking other, group help, to adaptively terminate SH and desist from its exploitation, and to adaptively accept its natural termination in death.

In elementary social types, where the family and the group together with the individual monitor and regulate the way SH is expressed, this appears relatively unproblematic. However, as previous chapters have emphasized, cultural, sociological, and political economic changes seem to have altered this feature of the SH adaptation during the evolution of medicine.

Setting Limits on the Boundaries of the Sick Role

As society becomes more complex, special social psychological aspects of a person's life situation have been highly elaborated in the realization of SH behaviors. Just as there is ample data to suggest that social stress contributes to disease and injury, and may have to be adequately resolved or "metabolized," so is there evidence pointing to the way sickness is perpetuated and social phenomena are unduly medicalized with maladaptive consequences. Indeed, exploitation or cheating of sickness has been an important determinant of the increasing power that physicians and the state have had to adopt, resulting in the attempt to regulate and validate realizations of SH.

The idea of sickness and "wellness" has expanded to include a range of factors connected to body states and perceptions and constitutes a powerful elixir in complex societies, a development that political economic institutions have "capitalized" on and exploited (Kimbrell 1994; Payer 1989, 1992).

This development involving the exploitation of the sick role and its advantages is logically consistent with the abuse of medical memes that enhance well-being and with the appropriation of healing routines and procedures for "sickness" conditions seemingly far removed from the SH machinery, as previous chapters have illustrated. I am referring here to the use of medical technology for purely cosmetic purposes or for purposes of extending lives at the cost of a great deal of pain to individuals and families and of economic resources to the society. In all of these examples, what has evolved during evolution to cope with distinctive types of diseases and injuries, all contextualized in a distinctive social ecologic setting, has expanded far beyond what evolutionary theory would describe as reasonably "medical."

Conceptualizing medicine in terms of biological and social evolution thus provides a way of anchoring it in formal discourse; a new way of analyzing dilemmas of contemporary medical practice; and may facilitate the development of better policy guidelines for constructively dealing with them.

Ensuring Optimal Connections and Communications between Members of the Sickness/Healing Audience

Perhaps the most controversial and complex implication of framing medicine in terms of strict biological and evolutionary theory is that it draws attention to the fact that sickness and healing are two aspects of the same adaptation. In other words, the same adaptation calls for individuals to communicate sickness, seek healing, and render healing. It draws attention to the identity as well as connectedness among members of a society when it comes to medical concerns.

However, in contemporary medicine, types of specialists seem distinct from one another and from generalists, physicians stand apart from "alternative" practitioners, and all of the preceding are conceptualized as different and separate from patients, clients, and consumers. Furthermore, there is, arguably, considerable controversy in contemporary society as to whether the experts and practitioners comprising the healing audience are sufficiently caring. Moreover, the quanta of social power, the motivations, and the codes of behavior of the members of a healing audience, all of which share the same biological imperatives, have become differentiated and specialized, if not opposed. The unity of the SH adaptation has been distorted and fractionated.

During the purely social phases of human evolution, cultural developments connected to political economic changes and imperatives have molded SH into an item or commodity having market value and appeal. A result has been conflicts of interests and opposition in an enterprise that biological evolution informs should be conducted in a cooperative, reciprocal, supportive, and caring manner that complements and reflects the universality of the SH trait.

The preceding points can be phrased differently. Because in an evolutionary context sickness and healing are linked phenomena, this renders medicine an individual group response since the underlying SH adaptation is seen as universal to *Homo sapiens*. Lower and Middle Paleolithic conditions and the hunter-gatherer mode of social organization mean that the family, or group of related families, constituted the environment of evolutionary adaptiveness in which the adaptation was designed. The essence of the adaptation is enlightened, instrumental support and caring in a setting of social understanding, acceptance, shared values and concerns, and mutual obligations. It includes, also, compassion, resignation, and the offering of comfort to the sick as well as his or her family in the eventuality of death (an explicitly recognized outcome of sickness; see chapter 3). In short, those with whom one lives and shares are the ones who heal, and, also, the ones who provide comfort and can be counted on for continued support and care in the eventuality of death.

No one who is realistic can expect that something resembling the social and egalitarian unity of family-level societies could or should characterize the setting of sickness and healing of contemporary societies. Nor should one minimize the power of biomedicine to improve the quality of life in most instances. What an evolutionary frame of reference underscores is how biological imperatives that "naturally" elicit fundamental psychological and existential concerns pertaining to man's connectedness to the social group have been transformed into technical, individualistically centered enterprises that are driven by the momentum of political economic changes. Requirements of technology and of the system of medicine often appear to have greater priority in the equation of sickness, healing, and terminality than do basic functions sculpted by natural selection. An examination of the practice of medicine with a view to restoring the primacy of these functions constitutes a potentially practical benefit of studying medicine from an evolutionary standpoint.

On the Optimal Function of Specialist Healers

With the preceding discussion as background, the model of healing that came with social complexity which involved reliance on a specialist healer (i.e., an "outsider") appears "unnatural" and the one associated with modern European medicine that involved *exclusive* reliance, if not *dependence,* on a neutral, objective, and impersonal physician can almost be characterized as maladaptive. An evolutionary account of medicine emphasizes that the SH adaptation constitutes and provides for a personalized, group-centered scenario of sickness and healing. Relief from the distress and suffering of disease and injury is sought with and from those with whom one has face-to-face, daily relations. On the other hand, modern developments have partitioned SH into an unequal contract between individuals who know each other not at all well (if at all), who very often do not share perspectives on sickness and healing, and who are culturally programmed to expect different things from each other.

Healing is now broken apart into diagnosis and treatment, carried out by different persons/specialists, and both of these "biomedical" concerns seen as entirely separate from the social psychological (and spiritual) support that is needed in the event of continued suffering and possible termination in death. Prevention and health maintenance have been all but shunted out of medical practice. Here again, a property of the political economy of medicine interferes with the evolutionary-based scenario pertaining to sickness, healing, and terminality.

Clarifying the Biological Implications of Somatization

Analyzing sickness and healing from the standpoint of biological and social evolution also provides a new way of conceptualizing medical problems now thought of as "functional" or "psychosomatic" and termed somatoform disorders by psychiatrists (Fabrega 1990b). Such problems of sickness are often stigmatized or seen as spurious in contemporary Western societies.

This way of qualifying and valuing sickness conditions is a result of contemporary cultural values devolving from the way problems of disease and injury are defined and calibrated in biomedicine. Technology or a biomedical construction of the way physiology affects behavior is what certifies a picture of sickness as authentic or valid, and this model excludes pictures of sickness that do not show the requisite changes in anatomy, physiology, and behavior. To somatize too often seems to mean to misappropriate the idiom of embodiment, and to psychologize is to show emotional defects as a result of a failure in coping.

Individuals showing biomedically anomalous sickness pictures are often penalized and denigrated by physicians and other health care workers. In summary, concepts such as psychologization and somatization presuppose that strict conformance to the Western cultural and academically formulated pictures of sickness constitute the "right way" to show disease and injury. An evolutionary perspective informs that the SH machinery conditions sickness and healing as unified and integrated; in other words, there is no special, "bio-medically correct" way in which the idiom of sickness and healing has to be constructed to be judged authentic.

Contextualizing Bioethical Dilemmas in an Evolutionary Framework

An evolutionary approach to medicine may provide a new and better way of conceptualizing ethical dilemmas that arise in contemporary biomedical prac-tice. Some of the problems that are thought of as "bioethical" seem to result from the blurring of the domain of sickness and healing as a result of social and evolutionary developments of biomedicine (Kimbrell 1994).

To clarify this point one needs to recall that the SH adaptation is anchored in and geared to changes surrounding disease and injury and is elicited and set in motion by behavioral changes. In other words, the effects of disease and in-jury on behavior, viewed from a social communication standpoint, are what lead to the "natural" expression of the adaptation. Bioethical dilemmas, to be sure, derive from human problems and needs that are in some way "medical"; at least, they seem constructed as such in our culture. However, the essence of the dilemmas seem to reside in the fact that they entail the application or po-tential application of medical memes to persons who are neither sick nor in need of healing.

Some examples would include the following: (1) cosmetic surgery, (2) the "medical diagnosis" of persons who are not currently sick but seem destined to develop a lethal disease (e.g., asymptomatic carriers of the dominant gene for Huntington's disease), (3) the "diagnosis" of desirable traits using biomedi-cally refined procedures (e.g., amniocentesis for sex determination of a fetus), and (4) the use of advanced procedures to alter human genetic material. In all of these instances, it would seem, the bioethical dilemma resides in the fact that resources and technologies devolving from biomedicine come to be applied to persons who on behavioral grounds cannot be said to be authentically sick. One could say that a particular medical procedure or meme is misappropriated.

Bioethical dilemmas are rendered compelling when one takes into account that in our culture the "medical" seems driven by a technology that has lost its biological connections with sickness and healing. Here again, as discussed earlier and in previous chapters, the link between the biological and cultural evolution of medicine has been uncoupled or dissociated, creating social am-biguities and quandaries.

Medical Evolution as a Topic for the Social Sciences

The emergence, maintenance, and change of social institutions has consti-tuted a staple theme in the social sciences. Thus far, it is mainly general social conventions and norms and such things as commercial and mercantile interests, banking relations, labor relations, and contracts pertaining to the disposition of property that have provided economists and political scientists interested in the emergence and change of social institutions with objects for analysis (Axelrod 1984; Hechter, Opp, and Wipoler 1990; Knight 1992; Schelling 1960). As formulated in the previous chapter, sickness and healing are complementary phenomena and together constitute a social Institution (of medicine). How might material reviewed in that and earlier chapters be reformulated so as to conform to the social science tradition pertaining to the way institutions function and change?

Key areas of emphasis in the social study of institutions are that of their emergence, their transformation, and the ways in which they produce social organization and order. If one were to conceptualize sickness and healing purely as a social and cultural Institution, its evolution would entail an explanation of how the rules and conventions pertaining to problems of disease and injury emerge, get established, and become "functional" in a social formation; and how they get selected and then passed on across generations of members of that social formation. Jack Knight (1992) has usefully classified the development and change of social institutions from the standpoint of their distinctive effects, pointing out that social institutions can be thought to provide collective benefits to the society as a whole or discriminative benefits and advantages to different segments of the society that are in conflict with one another over the resolution of recurring, widely shared problems. Such a formulation clearly applies to the Institution of medicine.

In the previous chapter, rules and conventions pertaining to sickness and healing (i.e., the medical Institution) has been analyzed from both of these points of view: Functional benefits for the collectivity as a whole as well as potential selective advantages to groups in conflict have been covered. Positing a biological adaptation for sickness and healing implies that what a social scientist may term the "medical Institution" serves a function for individuals since their sickness and healing responses are accountable in terms of the processes of kin selection and reciprocal altruism. Thus a biological evolutionary approach can be held to complement the distributional/conflict approach to the study of social institutions that has been used by economists and political scientists.

A strict cultural determinist is likely to explain the emergence and transformation of the social institution of medicine in terms of what a biologist would describe as "group selection," a concept very much discredited in the biological sciences today. Changes in the way the Institution of medicine functioned would be construed in terms of how groups within the society or the society as a whole benefit in the long run. Social conflicts and the optimization of strategies of competition, including social bargaining in mixed strategy situations, all of which come into play in conditions of disease and injury that are costly to a society, would all constitute selective forces favoring groups or the society as a whole. Should "societal needs" come into conflict with self-interests, a group selectionist would be quick to point out that psychological adaptations can and often are neutralized and in some respects even overridden by society and culture. However, as indicated earlier, a group selectionist would need to show that transformations in the medical Institution that reflect selection at the group level do not merely reflect (or can be explained in terms of) epiphenomenal, macroscopic effects of the biology of altruism coming into play with respect to individuals' self-interests and strategic decisions involving disease and injury.

In summary, one can hold that disease and injury constitute ubiquitous, recurring events that pose problems to members of a society which require resolution and as such "challenge" the society and its functioning. All parties to sickness and healing (e.g., sick persons, family members, healers, representatives of any number of corporations) are in some form of strategic conflict with one another the resolution of which requires bargaining with mixed strategies and payoffs. It is in the way that groups compete and bargain with respect to sickness/healing that a medical Institution emerges, functions, and undergoes transformation.

Such a point of view need not conflict with the view that sickness and healing are a product of biological evolution. The SH adaptation set the conditions for a social resolution of the problems posed by disease and injury. From the standpoint of how institutions function and the "needs" of the society, an important question involves the degree to which members of the family and group extend themselves in the event symptoms, weakness, and disability persist and standard healing efforts prove unavailing.

During the early stages of the evolution of medicine, the sheer inability to reverse pathophysiological changes, ameliorate suffering, and promote behavioral stability undoubtedly dampened motivation to pursue long, drawn out, costly, strictly empirical trial-and-error approaches. Alternatively, the heavy costs involved in healing enterprises contributed significantly to arriving at economical strategies highlighted by a fatalistic, preternatural posture toward the prospects of ultimate healing. A social scientist interested in cultural evolution would need to explain these complexities in terms of how individuals, groups, and corporations of a society weighed and priced prolonged sickness scenarios, how they bargained, and how they resolved the corresponding dilemmas with different patterns of costs and benefits in mind.

During the different stages of the evolution of medicine, different types of sickness/healing pictures were produced, each of which had an associated "price," a greater number of competing parties and organizations came into play with different arrangements of costs and payoffs, and different considerations came to affect decisions and behaviors. The challenge for the social scientist is creating a formal, parsimonious, and ultimately mathematical formulation of this evolution of the medical Institution.

Implications for the Development
of Social Theory

The evolution of sickness and healing has been handled with main emphasis given to the hypothetical conduct of key participants in this enterprise. Principal attention has been given to a sick person and his or her attendants (i.e., healers) in situated contexts and locales of copresence that make up the healing enterprise. These participants are seen as constituting a more or less socially integrated unit that embodies rules and resources (material and nonmaterial) drawn from the societies (idealized, to be sure) in which they are assumed to reside.

Medical memes, in this light, constitute the units of information that these participants in strategic interactions of sickness/healing draw on to provide meaning, in the process reflexively monitoring their actions and reproducing, as it were, the underlying tradition and structure.

Sickness and healing, however, constitute more than idealized contexts wherein the problematics of disease and injury are neutralized or composed by social actors in conditions of copresence. Viewed sociologically, sickness and healing are but symbolically organized behaviors that take place in a particular type of institution or social system. As a social system, sickness and healing are made up of structured, institutionalized features that stretch across time and space. As already discussed, such a social system is made up of many attributes that would include (1) characteristics of the culture of the immediate group and larger society, (2) relations of power, based on the distribution of resources among actors of that society, (3) other structural properties of the society including, as an example, its level of social organization/complexity and its political/economic rationales, all of which are finalized in terms of, (4) resources drawn from and relations with neighboring societies and intersocietal systems, all of which embody material (i.e., products of medical memes) that is imported or borrowed and that bears on how sickness and healing can be constructed and played out in more adaptive ways.

The system that encompasses sickness and healing, then, is integrated through reciprocal relations not only among copresent actors involved in dealing with disease and injury but also between representatives (who draw on resources) from different collectivities. In reflexively monitoring their actions, actors reproduce a part of the medical system or institution of the larger social type drawing on knowledge, rules, and material/nonmaterial resources from institutions of a region that extends outside the immediate group and may in fact extend across societies and regions.

An evolutionary framework for analyzing sickness and healing means that what sociologists term episodes have been given attention. Episodes are "sequences of change having a specificable opening, trend of events and outcomes which can be compared in some degree of abstraction from definite contexts" (Giddens 1984: 374). Five episodes involving the institution or system of medicine that realizes sickness and healing have been given attention: (1) from family-centered to village-based social types, (2) from village-based to chiefdom and prestate social types, (3) from chiefdoms and prestates to states and empires, (4) from (premodern) states and empires to modern social types, and (5) from modern to postmodern social types.

Each episode in the social system of sickness and healing involves relations of mediation and transformation of the properties of the institution of medicine. The content and integration of the properties of the social system of medicine change as a result of social, political, economic, and/or purely medical (based on specific inventions of new medical memes) changes. These changes are initiated in different contexts and locales of the society under consideration or in societies that make up the regional intersociety system(s) encompassing any particular society (what Giddens [1984: 377] terms time-space edges: "connections . . . between societies of differing structural types" which are then borrowed or imported. Another factor that influences the evolution of sickness and healing in a particular (type of) social system of medicine is what Giddens (1984: 377) terms world time: "conjunctures of history that influence the nature of episodes."

As can be readily appreciated, when one casts sickness and healing in purely sociological terms this provides an opportunity for visualizing the medical in terms of concepts and propositions of social theory. I have already alluded to this in the present and earlier chapters, and some of the ways in which all of this can be conceptualized can easily be surmised. In any society, from the most elementary to the most complex, the institution or social system of medicine can be clearly separated from other institutions or systems only analytically and then hypothetically. In the event, happenings and processes having political economic and ideological implications, as an example, almost invariably affect the medical and vice versa.

As discussed earlier, the interrelations between institutions and, indeed, the way institutions arise and function is a staple theme in the social sciences (Cohen and Scull 1983; de Swann 1988; Ullmann-Margalit 1977) and one that from a medical standpoint has been and should continue to be mined by sociologists (Abbott 1988; Freidson 1970; Parsons 1951; Scull 1993) and other social scientists. Similarly, aspects of change and transformation or evolution of institutions have been the object of renewed interest in the social sciences (Garland 1985, 1990; Hodgson 1993; Sanderson 1990, 1995a; Upham 1990) and the manner in which what one can term "episodes in the social system of medicine" have unfolded has attracted some sociologists (Bellah 1964; Fox 1988a, 1988b; Jewson 1974; Scull 1993) and anthropologists (Alland 1970; Janzen 1978b). All of this was touched on in chapter 1 and earlier in this chapter.

Suggestive Topics and Themes

Some of the topics and themes that can be pursued in this area of study are the following: the factors that influence how medical memes are invented and their contestation in different social classes; how changes in the level of sickness are affected by memes developed in other, nonmedical institutions; the effects of introducing changes in the political economy of a society that affect the function and organization of healer groups and groups of sick persons (groups of survivors, groups of those terminally ill, consumer advocacy groups, etc.); the way in which folk or popular systems of medicine are influenced by and become modified as a result of political developments in intersocietal systems; and, finally, the properties of elemental medical memes (see earlier discussion) and the way these interact during episodes of change in the configuration of sickness and healing.

In short, whether one chooses to examine social and historical happenings from the standpoint of functional theory, conflict theory, structural theory, deviance theory, cultural materialism, cultural ecology, or as social interaction, it should be evident that framing medicine in terms of sickness and healing and as involving processes of evolution offers a rich opportunity for testing key concepts and generalizations in the social sciences.

Some of the ways in which aspects of the medical can be approached from the standpoint of social and cultural theory have been discussed in other publications (Fabrega 1975, 1976a, 1976b, 1976c, 1979a). More specifically, concentrating on the psychiatric, an aspect of the medical that, to be sure, has special characteristics, I have shown that by calibrating sickness in terms of various concepts or dimensions (i.e., senselessness, acceptability, somatization, and visibility/duration) it is possible to derive generalizations and propositions that take into consideration properties of societies and that are relevant to the topic of social theory (Fabrega 1992a, 1993a). A similar approach should be adopted with respect to sickness and healing more generally.

Sickness, Healing, and the Self

A condition of illness constitutes, by definition, an interruption in the flow of life. It involves a questioning of the implicit assumptions about personal identity and social continuity. In a reflexive way, individuals draw on these assumptions as they monitor and regulate practical affairs. This means that basic existential questions, and the cultural assumptions that render existence meaningful and predictable, are all brought to the fore and critically reexamined during illness (Fabrega 1977).

It follows that conceptions of personhood and the values placed on human life are all woven into and serve to contextualize through cultural symbols the

meanings of sickness and healing. The integral tie that exists between conceptualizations of personhood and of sickness/healing has important theoretical
implications for the study of the evolution of medicine. It means that one interested in charting the stages of this evolution necessarily brings into focus
questions about conceptualizations of mind and personhood that culture and
society make available under different conditions of social organization and
complexity.

The self and its construction has received a great deal of attention from
cultural anthropologists and sociologists. The literature on this topic is vast
and goes deep into the history of these disciplines. During the era when psychoanalysis was very influential in anthropology, for example, the topic of
the construction of personal identity was dealt with extensively, although not
always directly. Similarly, in sociology, the classic studies of Marcel Mauss
([1938] 1985) and George Herbert Mead (1934) on the self and its social construction and the study of Norbert Elias (1978) on the evolution of civility and
manners, the latter conducted also under the framework of psychoanalysis, all
dealt with the question of how individuals saw themselves, regulated their
impulses, and were expected to behave. Sociologists have also concentrated
directly on aspects of personhood and modernity (e.g., Berger, Berger, and
Kellner 1973). However, in none of these studies was the self examined in relation to aspects of disease and injury.

In more recent times, an emphasis on self-construction generally and on the
symbolic organization of various attributes of persons, such as emotional experience, style of interpersonal relating, and group relatedness more broadly,
has been a common theme in these social sciences (Gurevich 1995; Lutz
1988a, 1988b; Shweder and LeVine 1984). However, it is also the case that in
none of these approaches have notions of self been examined with an eye to
clarifying aspects of medicine. More generally, rarely has the study of the self
been examined from the standpoint of a general theory of cultural and social
evolution. Although the topic of self-construction has in many instances been
analyzed comparatively, for example, aspects of personhood in modern and traditional societies, a broader comparison across several types of societies and
the transformations that are entailed in this process have not been the object of
systematic study. Consequently, one intending to use knowledge about the
construction of personhood under different conditions of social organization
and complexity to more graphically portray the configuration of sickness and
healing from an evolutionary standpoint must await future developments in
the social sciences.

It seems appropriate to review some of the ideas of social scientists who
have considered changes in the self and social consciousness as a consequence
of social change. In analyses of the changes from preindustrial through traditional and on to modern liberal and postliberal societies, attention has been

drawn to two major sets of factors: influence of corporate groups on self and behavior and the associated development of individuality and autonomy.

The first factor refers to the increase that takes place in the number of significant groups of the society to which the self relates meaningfully as a consequence of social evolution. According to Robert M. Unger (1976), in smaller, simpler societies, which he terms "tribal," individuals belong to a very small number of significant groups and each collective body tends to play a comparatively large role in identity and behavior. A consequence of this is that a sharp line can be drawn between insiders and outsiders. By contrast, in modern liberal and postliberal societies, individuals participate in a multiplicity of significant groups, the scope of each one of these on the individual's life is more narrowly defined, and because of this familiarity and strangeness attach to the same persons with resulting confusion. "Impersonal respect and formal equality edge out communal solidarity toward some and suspicious hostility toward others. In place of the insider and the stranger, there emerges the abstract other to whom one shows neither love nor hate" (Unger 1976: 144).

How individuals view themselves is said to also change dramatically in relation to social change. With increasing social complexity there is an associated emphasis on self-interests as compared to group interests. Since individuals occupy many roles in society they become preoccupied with how well they play them, and hence roles and how others view the individual's performance of them begin to shape how they view themselves. Moreover, "the reflexivity of modern social life consists in the fact that social practices are constantly examined and reformed in the light of incoming information about those very practices, thus constitutively altering their character. . . . In all cultures, social practices are routinely altered in the light of ongoing discoveries which feed into them. . . . But only in the era of modernity is the revision of convention radicalized to apply (in principle) to all aspects of human life, including technological intervention into the material world. . . . What is characteristic of modernity is not [only] an embracing of the new for its own sake, but the presumption of wholesale reflexivity" (Giddens 1990: 38–39).

A summary interpretation of the evolution of medicine that emphasized purely qualitative, symbolic factors pertaining to the self would begin with the generalization that in prehuman groups and in family-level societies of fully evolved *Homo sapiens,* the self is defined and experienced as more or less connected with and integrated to others of the worldly and otherworldly environment and is consequently not alone in facing and handling the most personal of crises that is posed to itself by disease and injury. The self interprets, experiences, and communicates sickness/healing in a language that signifies through meaningful symbols and behaviors the communitarian character of the medical at this stage of evolution. More elaborately, during this phase sickness and healing (1) constitute a challenge to and response of the self, the family, and the group, all of which (2) are expected and called on to meliorate an eventuation that (3) entails reciprocal obligations among comembers to cooperate with efforts at renewal and to attempt to live through the pain and suffering that is entailed, in the event the group deems this appropriate, and (4) to go along with the group's decision to neglect and hence allow to terminate an ordeal should this be deemed appropriate.

Especially during the later phases of cultural and social evolution there takes place a progressive psychological encapsulation and estrangement of the self, with the individual coming to increasingly shoulder directly the ordeal, burden, obligations, and social costs of sickness and healing. As individuals become more atomized and less powerful in relation to larger, more impersonal corporations of the society (both within and outside the medical Institution), the actual and potential influence that outsiders can have on the meanings, determinants, and outcomes of sickness and healing is correspondingly increased. The self also comes to develop increased resources and skills to exploit a condition of sickness and healing for its own individualistic and selfish needs. It does so by manipulating the healers/specialists, institutions, and knowledge structures that the group and society itself have made available to the person. The culmination of these developments pertaining to the exploitation of sickness and healing is that the state through its agencies is required to intervene in the interests of its own efficiency, eventually having to arbitrarily arrogate to itself the prerogative of validating and controlling how disease and injury are to be configured and handled as sickness and healing, and how their course is expected to progress and terminate.

The Development of Sound Medical Policies

Medicine constitutes a social and cultural Institution that is based on biological phenomena, namely, on problems devolving from disease and injury that are shaped as sickness and healing. While the latter are socially and culturally constructed and hence variable, they are no less biological for this, *because* they depend on an evolved, internal machinery or architecture (which has been termed SH). The study of medicine is thus situated at the crossroads of the natural and social sciences: To fully examine and study the way the institution of medicine operates or "functions" is to necessarily evaluate how knowledge, practices, and policies affect basic biological imperatives sculpted during human evolution and elaborated by developments that have taken place during social and cultural evolution.

The sciences geared to the study of the Institution of medicine are classically thought of as "social." They include, for the most part, anthropology, economics, history, psychology, and sociology. An implication of the argument developed in this book is that decisions and interventions involving how sickness and healing are to be configured and played out in contemporary society, enterprises that are quintessentially social and cultural in nature and that occupy center stage in our consciousness and in the communications media, must be made in the light of how they affect human lives examined from the standpoint of the theories of biological and social evolution.

The sciences of anthropology, ethology, behavioral ecology, evolutionary psychology, and human biology more generally need to be vigorously deployed in the study of human evolution. A basic goal should be to clarify, on the one hand, the mode of operation of the evolved mechanisms implicated in sickness and healing. This would involve not only the study of sickness and healing among nonhuman primates but also the study of the way the SH adaptation unfolds during critical periods of human development. The social careers of individuals exposed to different developmental experiences involving disease and injury during childhood and adolescence should be studied to clarify how biology and environment shape the final products of medical genes and memes.

In the same way, the nature and characteristics of what have been termed *elemental* medical memes need to be specified and their mode of operation clarified. This involves refining our understanding of how organisms respond to disease and injury, more specifically, of how sickness and healing are manifested behaviorally and of the mechanisms and effects of "natural" as well as socially constructed behaviors geared to undo the effects of disease and injury. On the other hand, all of this needs to be analyzed in the light of how they affect not only individual well-being and fitness but also populations and the social collectivity.

In summary, rational social policies affecting the Institution of medicine need to balance benefits to the sick individual, in light of his or her inclusive fitness (i.e., benefits to relatives and to social welfare more generally), with benefits to the group. As reviewed in previous chapters and earlier in this one, the evolution of medicine has enhanced the capacity to deliver at high cost special services to a small minority of the population. These services include the manufacture of life, cushioning the effects of devastating congenital and acquired defects and handicaps, preventing and meliorating the effects of disease, reconstructing socially undesirable anatomies and appearances, and, ultimately, delaying death. The provision of these services, however, heavily limits what can be offered to many others of the population who are in need of more basic, less specialized services. Dilemmas are created because of clashes between medical and political economic traditions and goals. The social quandaries that result require decisions that involve the best efforts of ethicists, biologists, and social scientists as well as physicians and that take into account insights derived from the biological as well as the social sciences.

11

Toward an Evolutionary Philosophy of Medicine

Elements of a Medical Epistemology

I have defined sickness and healing as a single entity: It is one "thing." Each side of the "medical coin" constitutes but a different expression of the same material. The sickness side announces, communicates, and expresses the sufferings of conditions of disease and injury; the healing side is but the response aimed at comforting, undoing, relieving, fixing, minimizing, and, if necessary, drawing to a close that suffering. Both aspects are meaning centered or "symbolic." Experiences conditioned by modern interpretations of medicine, symbolized by such terms as patient versus doctor (or afflicted/sufferer versus healer/practitioner), create a tendency to divide and handle as separate the two sides of the medical coin. But one must follow the implications of the evolutionary insight that sickness and healing are really like "medical isomers."

Both sickness and healing at the same time constitute an interpretation of morbidity and an interpretation of (a possible eventuation in) mortality. On the one hand, sickness tells about a condition of suffering, and in the telling there is already incorporated an interpretation of and an initial effort directed at melioration through an understanding of the phenomenon; and, given that the essence of the medical is disvalue, sickness carries with it elements of undoing, self-healing, and, when necessary, resignation. On the other hand, healing could be viewed as a separate phenomenon, simply directed at sickness; but this would be to fall into the trap of dualism so explicitly concretized by our notions of patient and doctor. More properly, healing reflects or carries with it a realistic, often empathic understanding of the suffering of disease and injury and with this a desire/intention/need/program to make better the suffering (so easily understood); and if the latter is not possible and the suffering becomes unendurable, to bring it to a consolatory end. Each side of the medical coin, in short, incorporates essential aspects of the obverse.

What is sickness and healing composed of? I have entertained different answers to this question. Just three of these complementary (i.e., not mutually exclusive) answers will be discussed here briefly. Sickness and healing constitute instructions carried in information: genetic information connected to, layered over by, or contextualized through cultural information. One source of information is distal, coming from phylogeny, the tree of life as it came to be differentiated in the environment of evolutionary adaptedness of *Homo sapiens*. The other source of information is more proximal, derived from the environment as coded in interpretive acts of group mates and inscribed in the mind/brain of an organism as a (set of) meme(s). It is this feature of sickness and healing that I have equated with the origins and machinery of the SH adaptation.

Sickness and healing have also been thought of as a behavioral ensemble, a response elicited by an instance of disease or injury, expressed and manifested by an organism located in a distinctive social, cultural, and historical setting. This is the phenotypic expression or product of the SH adaptation that is shaped during the development of individuals as a result of local, contextual factors. In this picture, sickness and healing constitute a form of symbolic behavior or action; which is to say that it has or carries meaning and that it has effects in a social and cultural context. While sickness/healing is expressing features and remnants of primal human biology, it is also expressing recently acquired interpretations and constraints pertaining to itself. In other words, in its behavioral form sickness/healing expresses three sets of influences: (1) manifestations of the impact of disease/injury on structures produced by genes (e.g., altered anatomies, physiologies), (2) how products of medical memes interpret those same manifestations, and (3) what nonmedical memes emanating from political, economic, or legal/jurisprudential concerns (to consider just three nonmedical domains) make of sickness and healing and how they order and regulate its expression. All of the latter memes become influential in shaping, constraining, and regulating what sickness/healing means and how it is to be dealt with in the group. This leads to the third of my examples about the constitution of sickness and healing.

Sickness/healing has also been viewed as exemplifying a social institution or set of interrelated social institutions. In this picture, sickness/healing is a social construction with a rationale that is widely shared in a society. Societies develop and refine social institutions and pass them on across the generations of members of the population, modifying them in the process; the institution of sickness and healing is no different. In the event, any social institution including the medical has an individualistic and a collective use, purpose, or function. Societies construct sickness/healing so as to be able to assimilate it, normalize it, cope with it, and prevent, undo, or limit its pernicious social effects. The collective thrust or goal of the sickness/healing institution is to accommodate individualistic needs associated with sickness and healing (to be described presently) and to not allow them to impair or harm others of the collectivity, or the collectivity itself as an emergent entity. Societies aim to protect themselves and thus must regulate, control, or police its members' use of the sickness/healing institution, at the same time seeking to not deprive them of some reasonable, prudent autonomy to fulfill their needs.

The individualistic emphasis on or function of the sickness/healing institution is also complex and multipurposed. Some individuals seek to only minimize the sufferings and costs of sickness and healing (e.g., the morbidities, incapacities, lost opportunities) and others to maximize its potential benefits (e.g., seeking attention, nurturance, support, dispensation). These individuals are forced to negotiate this balance through the directives entailed in the institution. Other individuals must negotiate between the altruistic directive of helping/relieving and the selfish, greedy one of profiting through the political economic rewards that come from helping others in distress and thus creating dependencies.

Sickness/healing as a social institution, then, is an amalgam of three sets of connected, complementary, but potentially opposed influences: those of individuals wanting the relief from suffering but also wanting the social advantages that this can bring; those of healers programmed and motivated to help but also to exploit; and those of, on the one hand, individuals negotiating their various needs and, on the other, collectivities (mediated in the decisions and actions of leaders) attempting to regulate and control individuals, at the same time seeking to protect their own interests without unjustly depriving and coercing members of the population.

All of this implies that when individuals become sick they are showing what their biology has designed, what their sufferings and needs urge, and what their group licenses and makes acceptable. In short, impersonal directives carried in genes and memes, personal wants and needs harbored by more or less selfish and needy individuals, and dictates of group mates devised and demanded by political, economic, legal, and welfare exigencies of the society all come together and realize a particular instance of sickness and healing. An evolutionary frame of reference with respect to medicine informs that sickness and healing are expressions of codes of information, private longings and needs generated by disease and injury (and other medically consequential forms of suffering), and social constraints imposed by the members of the collectivity as well as by the collectivity on its own behalf.

In family-level societies, "medgemes" most nearly express the original design of medical evolution—a balancing of the needs of individuals with those of group mates not to be overly burdened by that suffering, with consequent resignation about the outcome, in an epidemiological context of relatively good nutrition and health. In larger-scale societies, village level on through chief-doms, prestates, and states, medgemes do not appreciably alter the level of in-evitability and resignation about disease and injury, but allow greater freedom to individuals to build on, improvise, and better profit from the biologically de-signed adaptation yet do so in an epidemiological context of great variety and overall inequality of nutrition and health, with much greater medical burdens on the many. In civilizations and empires, medgemes provide individuals with extremely variegated and plentiful resources with which to cope with and de-rive benefits from the heightened epidemiological burden of disease and injury that social organization imposes, but most of these resources are primarily so-cial and psychological and not epidemiological in the strict sense. Further-more, things are unequally available and sometimes unavailable to most of the population who are essentially oppressed, excluded, and powerless. Finally, in modern European and especially postmodern European societies, medgemes have aroused, only to then dampen, great optimism about disease and injury in a highly different epidemiological context; but the excesses inherent in the ad-vantages made possible by more evolved medgemes have given rise to a series of socially troublesome quandaries and to increasing controls and constraints designed to limit those advantages, in the process all but robbing sickness/heal-ing of its individual, private, and existentially comforting meaning.

In each social type, then, sickness/healing is at least three things at once, namely, genetic/cultural information, symbolic behavior/action, and social con-struction/institution. Three different yet interrelated ontologies can be roughly equated with these three epistemologies: subindividual units or nets of infor-mation programmed into the central nervous systems of organisms; individ-uals displaying the behavioral effects of this information; and shared, interper-sonally situated habits that regulate, constrain, and pattern how sickness and healing are to be configured and played out in the light of political economic and other prominent and compelling social cultural influences in the society.

Ideally, one could say that the "best" realization of the SH adaptation is when these three epistemologies and ontologies, if one may be afforded some license here, operate and function in a dialectically satisfactory manner. The information of sickness and healing should be expressed in a behavioral form that does not totally negate either the purpose of its content or its designed product in the adaptation of individuals; and both of the preceding should ide-ally heed the needs of group mates as well as those of the collectivity itself. The awkward phrase "dialectically satisfactory manner" is used to accommodate the embarrassing fact that the three essentials of sickness and healing are in a state of tension and influence each other in complex positive as well as nega-tive ways. The themes of conflict and opposition as well as of exchange and resolution have indicated this in the earlier discussion. It should be clear that it is not possible to accommodate all of the directives inherent in templates of information, needs, and actions of individuals and constraints stipulated by interpersonal and larger collectivities. It would seem that, at most, what it is feasible to strive for is a balance, regulation, and control of the differing influences that shape sickness and healing, influences that cannot really be integrated and much less harmonized since they often oppose one another.

Evolutionary Thinking and Contemporary Medical Policy

Studies of nonhuman primates living under natural conditions suggest high prevalence of disease and injury (Cheney and Seyfarth 1990; Goodall 1986). In addition to toxicities and infectious diseases of various types, intraspecies aggression and predator assaults were common sources of lacerations, fractions, contusions, head injuries, and death. Studies also underscore the social complexity of these groups, with elaborate dominance groupings, rivalries, complex alliances, and hostile competition for food and living space frequent occurrences. Clearly, the presence of disease and injury strained these already "tense" social relationships and alliances.

The "social stress" that can be attributed to the living conditions of nonhuman primates under natural conditions cannot but have been rendered more prominent in members of evolutionarily more complex groups of individuals who are more intelligent, in particular, in pre- and early humanlike groups. Social stress can be the cause of physiological disorders and can lower resistance and increase an organism's susceptibility to disease. All in all, then, problems of sickness and healing must be accorded a prominent feature of social life in the environment of evolutionary adaptedness of *Homo sapiens*.

This type of social environment was the setting in which the SH adaptation is held to have been perfected. The high degree of interdependence among members of families and kin groups rendered disease and injury social crises that interrupted the flow of life and the mobility of the group. A shared obligation and responsibility to "carry one's load" undoubtedly prevailed, rendering protracted scenarios of sickness and healing very costly and risky affairs. Moreover, the closeness of living arrangements rendered the agonies of sufferings highly visible, as it no doubt also did to the deteriorations produced by advanced age and terminal illness.

Under such living conditions, then, an ethos that defined sickness and healing as an undesirable burden and actual threat to the group prevailed, associated with a perhaps hopeful but nonetheless fatalistic resignation that it could lead to the demise of the individual. All members of the group learned these "facts" about what disease and injury meant. Consequently, an individual's motivation to medically deceive group mates and manipulate sickness for personal advantage or, conversely, provide opportunities for others to fraudulently exploit the sick would not have been prominent and in fact very likely not only not tolerated but repudiated and censured.

The social and biological consequences of this type of selective environment "designed" the SH adaptation. It constituted sickness and healing as an individual and group concern and it no doubt scoured and winnowed its properties down to their essentials. These "essentials" can be assumed to have consisted of physiologically and anatomically compelling details, as reviewed in chapters 2 and 3.

It was in this manufactory of sickness and healing that (at least precursors or analogues of) what today is meant by "somatization" was constructed. In other words, such a "medical laboratory" would not have readily authenticated or validated as sickness (deserving of healing) manifestations, for example, dominated by problems of psychological morale and social dependency. Evidence of the critical, pernicious, and fearful sufferings resulting from disease and injury fashioned the properties of the SH adaptation.

Social and psychological stress, as human universals, must be presumed to have prominently contributed to conditions of disease and injury; moreover, sickness pictures undoubtedly contained emotional and psychophysiological expressions of such stress. However, what one can regard as the natural syntax and semantics of sickness and healing emphasized bodily disturbances and associated states of debility, lassitude, pain, behavioral incapacity, and general suffering. Whatever psychological/emotional correlates attached to conditions of disease and injury were most likely to have been phrased in a strongly articulated somatic idiom since this latter medium is what individuals see depicted in group mates and in competing organisms of the ecology as a result of predation, hunting, and warfare as well as serious and terminal states of disease.

Such a somatic idiom undoubtedly included existential and spiritual tenets, guilt over moral transgressions, accusations of wrongdoing, directed at outside agents, and recriminations about imputed punishments. Nevertheless, it must be assumed that a language that drew attention to the physiological, anatomical, and prominent behavioral impairments devolving from biological disruptions and dilapidations is what framed the SH response in the human environment of evolutionary adaptedness. Moreover, contingencies pertaining to meanings of disease and injury in this social ecological setting constitute natural correlates of the SH adaptation. I believe that this constitutes an important generalization about the biological evolution of sickness and healing that requires emphasis because special tenets associated with living conditions of modern and postmodern societies are what have conditioned our approach to disease and injury.

An implication of this emphasis on the story of the origins of sickness and healing is that a relaxation of the sheer Sisyphean labors of extremely onerous and irksome living conditions creates conditions for the potential influence of human deception and human exploitation in the construction of sickness and healing. Indeed, any set of social conditions that made possible a sustained lessening of the intense interdependency and ecologic marginality of human groups would also have rendered possible openings for medical deception and exploitation as I have discussed this in earlier chapters.

I have dealt with deception of sickness and healing as exploitation of the sick role and the presentation of fraudulent healing. With respect to healing, such things as compassion, comfort, caring, lessening of the sufferings and agonies of disease and injury, and the resignation, preparation, and facilitation of death were all phenomena "prepared for" by biological evolution. I would contend that many of the "advantages" of modern medicine have entailed a beclouding, if not obliteration, of these natural, adaptive, and no less human features of the biological trait for medicine. More to the point, there is no lack of information in contemporary societies about the actions and motives of caregivers and associated members of a society's health care industry that point to sheer exploitation of healing. Some of the implications of this have already been discussed. The basic point needing emphasis is that deception and exploitation in the area of healing, not only because of its intrinsic, natural tie to sickness and self-healing but also because of the stern and severe context of life, would not have had much opportunity to develop, perhaps even manifest.

With regard to sickness itself, and continuing the theme started earlier, it would seem that somatic manifestations would loom as important elements in the presentation of deceptive sickness. In other words, behavior pictures that draw attention to exaggerated or fictive states of bodily distress would seem to constitute "natural" avenues for the deception of sickness. Here, the formulations of Randolph M. Nesse and Alan T. Lloyd (1992) about the evolution of psychodynamic mechanisms are relevant. These scholars emphasize the importance for the individual of masking his or her deceptive stratagems designed to socially exploit group mates for whatever reasons. (The focus of their essay is not medicine in the strict sense but applies to the theme under discussion here nonetheless.) In this moral economy of self-interest, repression and the unconscious production of behavior and psychological states become relevant, including in particular, behaviors the manipulative intent of which is even hidden from the perpetrator. Nesse and Lloyd (1992), undoubtedly motivated by efforts to validate psychoanalytic ideas in a general biology, nonetheless provide one with a way to visualize how the "unconscious" production of sickness may have figured in initial attempts to deceive group mates for special resources and dispensations. Indeed, an unconscious, somatic expression of personal strains and conflicts constitutes a recurring postulate of psychosomatic formulations of sickness. In this regard, it is relevant that some of the observations of ethnologists with respect to manifestations of injury in chimpanzees raise similar questions of conscious as compared to unconscious deception of sickness behavior (de Waal 1986). It is interesting that exchanges suggesting "proto" fraudulent healing and medical helping have not been described. On the other hand, in their review of the literature about what the minds of nonhuman primates might be like, Cheney and Seyfarth (1990) describe instances when various individuals may have used grooming as a possible deceptive ploy to immediately exploit others. Analogous actions involving the showing of compassion and the provisioning of help, support, and care in the setting of disease and injury can readily be visualized.

If a heavily somatic idiom of sickness constitutes a natural product of the SH adaptation and if it seems prudent to reinstate this idiom and its implications in a rigorous way, then this in many ways supports the drift of contemporary medical practice and political economic policy of advanced capitalist industrial societies. As previous chapters have suggested, an often seemingly blind emphasis on cost containment in medicine more and more has led to exclusive reliance on technology for the grounding and validation of medical diagnoses in all of medicine including primary care; and more and more aspects of psychiatric practice and general mental health care have been expunged from society's medical budget (a neurobiological determinism with respect to psychiatric practice).

A change in the ethos of medicine, social welfare policy, and mental health practice toward a strict biomedical accounting of sickness and healing, provided it does not exclude human caring, cannot be easily faulted using the logic of an evolutionary perspective on sickness and healing and medicine more generally. However, the strict application of this logic is problematic if there does not also operate in society institutions and nonmedical "memes" designed to help those marginalized, excluded, and in need of basic social services including health services of all types that devolve from exploitation and other social maladaptations of contemporary societies. This directive pertaining to biomedicine clearly merges with directives that are integral to social policy, social welfare, political economy, and religion. It points out how an evolutionary perspective on sickness and healing and medicine more generally cannot but raise important questions about social thought and a social philosophy of medicine.

Challenges to Contemporary Medicine

While social and cultural evolution has led to the generation of newer and, in some instances, better products of the SH machinery (i.e., institutions, practices, procedures, medicines, etc.), it has radically altered the grounds of medicine and created special and socially challenging dilemmas. Success in the prevention and treatment of acute infectious diseases has inspired confidence in biomedicine. However, the high incidence of chronic diseases and an appreciation of the role of personal habits and new lifestyles in their etiology and in the maintenance of healthy body states have brought about a growing awareness of increased personal responsibility for one's health status and resignation of the inevitability of disease and injury.

The limits of biomedicine in preventing diseases of civilization and a trusting, unsuspecting acceptance of its technology for biological imperfections and nonmedical "problems" of appearance and morale reflect ambiguities and inconsistencies in our contemporary constructions of sickness and healing. Any number of questions reflect the limitations of medicine in the postmodern era. What do sickness and healing mean? In what forms should medical resources be consumed? How can the monetarization of medical care be reconciled with the humanitarian imperative of caring? How can physicians and the economy of medicine be encouraged to teach prevention when it does not really pay them to do so? What kind of balance between individualistic as compared to social needs should be pursued in the rationing of health and medical care? Who should be allowed to live? When is a fetus a person? When, how, and why should an individual be allowed to die? These are only some of the kinds of questions that the elaborated, highly advanced products of the SH adaptation have compelled, with obvious associated dilemmas in medical practice. In addition, an expansion of the sick role and monetarization of medical care created opportunities for the exploitation of sickness and healing on the part of patients and medical care practitioners and representatives of various corporations (e.g., pharmaceutical companies, hospital administrations, attorneys).

The changes in social conditions and in the meanings of medical memes have brought about a radical transformation in the way the SH adaptation is expressed. What is conceptualized as a naturally selected integrated machinery and language capacity to communicate, understand, and respond adaptively to effects of disease and injury could be said to have become "dis-integrated" by the conditions that were created during the later stages of the social and cultural evolution of medicine. In communicating sickness to others, individuals have made use of the dynamism of the SH adaptation or language to obtain personal advantages and resources. At the same time, in responding to the communications of sickness of others, individuals have capitalized on the SH adaptation and language by providing healing acts of different meaning and form, in the process acquiring personal resources and power. A third party, the state, has had to intervene in the social and moral economy of sickness and healing. While many of the scientific advantages of biomedicine can hardly qualify as evidence of a dis-integration of a human capacity to communicate and respond to disease and injury adaptively through evolutionarily designed ensembles of sickness and healing, the exploitation of the roles of sickness and healer that human evolution created certainly does, as do also the sheer inefficiency, wastefulness, and maldistribution of healing resources that are associated with the contemporary construction of the SH adaptation.

From a perspective made possible by evolutionary theory one can thus point to a quandary in medicine. Advancements in the understandings of sickness and healing and in medical practices have brought unparalleled success in the control of a small set of diseases and injuries but at the cost of promoting a plethora of medical and bioethical dilemmas that have no solutions and the awareness that the promises of the biomedical dream are based on illusions. The quandary can be stated more formally in the language of memes: Cultural evolution has led to the production of medical memes that achieve ever better control over certain varieties of sickness and healing; a consequence is that such medical memes also enable a refined understanding and regulation of vital structures and functions that control life itself; but in enabling a better control over the underlying factors that mediate sickness and healing, these newly developed memes have also radically exceeded the purposes for which the adaptation was designed during human evolution.

How can an evolutionary understanding of medicine help resolve some of the dilemmas that medical evolution has burdened us with? Can evolutionary theory serve as a guide in terms of which it may be possible to decide what are appropriate conditions for the implementation of selected medical memes? Can this theory provide guidelines for how to avoid, if not resolve, conflicts between the effects of implementing sharply divergent and competing medical as opposed to nonmedical memes? Could an evolutionary account of medicine yield a set of rules and a calculus that could point a way toward a prudent realization of the SH adaptation in modern and postmodern society? These are but a few of the questions that an evolutionary formulation of sickness and healing raises. Studies by social scientists, social philosophers, legal scholars, policy analysts, and physicians sensitive to the socially and philosophically complex aspects of sickness and healing and to the complex mode of operation of social and political economic institutions are needed to cope with the crisis of medicine today.

At the root of the crisis in medical care are several interconnected tenets that have created a social trap that the contemporary, evolved, biomedically interpreted SH adaptation has foisted on mankind. First, is the blinding emphasis on the negative effects of disease and injury rather than on their postponement, avoidance, or prevention. The curing of disease, the technical repair of the machinery of the body, and the illusion that most, if not all, diseases can be undone, cured, or eradicated are guiding imperatives rather than a sensitive appreciation of the inevitability of sickness and a furtherance of caring for the suffering it entails. Political economic factors have seductively seized on existential imperatives devolving from the curing/elimination emphasis that biomedicine has itself derived from the SH adapatation. The fear of disease and the myth that it can be technically undone garners monies for research and teaching in medicine rather than the comparatively uneconomical venture of preventing its occurrence, planning for the promotion and maintenance of health, coping with the realities of chronic terminal diseases, and preparing individuals to die with integrity and relative comfort. The biomedical establishment continues to find it politically and economically profitable to emphasize disease, curing, and eradication rather than teaching and helping to instill attitudes of self-reliance that promote healthy lifestyles and a measure of resignation about the inevitability of disease and suffering.

A second, related and equally injurious tenet of the biomedical interpretation of the SH adaptation is its elitist distinctions between patient and medical worker/practitioner, on the one hand, and members of the "medical care team," on the other. An evolutionary perspective on medicine compels an appreciation of the dictum that doctors, nurses, social workers, and informed alternative health maintenance planners are not only not "really" different from each other but also are not "really" different from diseased patients and would-be consumers interested in maintaining their health. All of these individuals are operating on the basis of the same adaptive mechanism. Differences in social experiences and background and resources account for differences in the way they have come to express and contextualize their adaptive trait for medicine. As long as physicians and those under the seductive sway of biomedical reductionism are deans of medical schools, chairpersons of departments, government representatives on research funding agencies, board members of third-party reimbursement plans, and leaders of the medical establishment and "care teams," their vision of the SH adaptation will be foisted on eager students, ambitious practitioners, and gullible patients/consumers all too motivated to obtain the resources and benefits that they see in and that are espoused by their role models. With division of resources come differences in power and economically inspired competition among workers in the health care field, with a selfish momentum to exclude and lessen the contribution of all but those in power who invariably are individuals trained or under the tutelage of physicians wedded to the traditional biomedical interpretation that emphasizes disease and its curing and eradication. The task facing medicine and society in the next century is for all to pool their efforts and resources so as to unify knowledge, experience, and health planning directives to bring about an evolutionarily informed interpretation and construction of sickness and healing.

A third tenet of the ensnaring biomedical paradigm centers around its neglect of and impotence to face up to a central characteristic of the biologically derived adaptation for medicine. This involves the imperative not only of meliorating sickness and healing but also, and perhaps equally important, of arranging for socially and psychologically satisfying ways of coping with advanced age and with the inevitable failure to avoid the ultimate consequences of disease and injury. So long as political economic privileges remain integral to the biomedical interpretation of the SH adaptation, dealing constructively with the terminal phases of sickness, healing, and life itself, including, in particular, their ultimate terminus, will be pushed aside, minimized, or left to "the family" or "social welfare" and religious institutions. Caring for suffering and arranging for comfortable ways of dying are integral features of the evolutionary design for coping with disease and injury (along with meeting the exigencies of sickness and healing). This rationale is far removed from the dominating one operative today, namely, that of repairing organs, maintaining vital signs, and normalizing chemical indicators of functioning bodies that now persist in vacant, wasted residues of persons. The biomedical regime centered around its interpretation of the SH adaptation has appropriated an enormous percentage of resources; but it has failed to provide for effective ways of enabling individuals to fade out with dignity and relative comfort. Only by rethinking the rationale and goals of "scientific" medicine and by reorganizing and restructuring its education and practice arrangements in all facets of life bearing on health and adaptation will a prudent and satisfying way of improving the quality and quantity of services for all be achieved.

A fourth tenet of the biomedical trap is its persistent, selfish territoriality with respect to sickness and healing. The biomedical version of the SH adaptation persists in separating the concerns of medicine from those of society as a whole. In promoting its vital "scientific" but no less political and economic interests pertaining to curing and repairing, biomedicine obscures and denies that only pronounced social, political, economic changes in society can bring about a better formula for coping with the consequences of disease and injury in human populations. All of the previously described tenets of biomedicine, and their corollaries, have as their consequence a relative neglect and trivialization of social, psychological, and cultural influences in health, well-being, sickness, and healing—and the corresponding necessity for social change in the way the SH adaptation *should be constructed and implemented*. An evolutionary perspective on medicine underscores the connectedness between the biological and the cultural and the vagaries of reductionism in any form. In forcing one to concentrate on the basics of the SH adaptation, why and how it evolved, evolutionary theory renders more transparent the maladaptive features of contemporary policies and practices as well as the costs of pursuing myths devolving from the biomedical trap. Attention to the basics can lead the way to a conceptualization more removed from the detours, deviations, and encumbrances produced by the strictly interpreted biomedical mystique. An emphasis on the evolutionary basis of medicine offers a better frame of reference from which to plan and organize for effective ways of coping with disease and injury.

Implications of an Integrated Trait
for Sickness and Healing

Disease and injury, by definition, create a personal state of pain, discomfort, and malaise. A natural concomitant is the need for relief and corrective action. There are associated emotional responses to all of this. Emotional states connoting apprehension, agony, discouragement, preclusion, interruption, and avoidance or retreat, given ordinary circumstances, come to mind as natural resultants of a condition of disease and injury. Permeating all of this is the awareness of privacy and estrangement, even a sense of aloneness (of being trapped in a state of suffering), with an associated need for support. One could judge the above as hallmarks of a condition of disease and injury in the self.

Built into this condition of disease/injury is an imperative to attempt to heal oneself and to seek and turn to another who, by virtue of his or her "wellness" and intactness, can offer help, support, and some form of healing. A dualism cries out in this narrative: Sickness reaches out for Healing. We can reverse the flow of events. Starting from an individual's awareness of a state of relative health and intactness and, adding to this, his or her perception that another is diseased or injured, one assumes that a "natural" understanding results through a projection to the diseased/injured person of what the picture of the other communicates to the self. Here again, a dualism cries out; this time from Wellness/Healing reaching to Sickness.

The above scenarios, phenomenological narratives seemingly intrinsic to medicine as we understand it today, might be judged as universal and, hence, natural. These scenarios underscore a dualism that incorporates difference, divergence, contrast, and complementariness. Not far away from this dichotomy, I would contend, is the idea of opposition. The alternative pairs of being in this dichotomy connote, on the one hand, negativity, lack, and need, and on the other, positivity, presentation, and contribution (leaving aside complications associated with more selfish pursuits that can enhance and problematize opposition).

I contend that the scenarios just reviewed constitute not universal features of sickness and injury, the natural products of a biological adaptation, but, rather, social psychological constructions of the political economy and culture of complex societies generally and of the possessive individualism incorporated in European, Western biomedicine especially. There are good and "natural" reasons for sickness and healing to have separate, distinct expressions, and these will be reviewed presently. However, for now it is important to emphasize that historical contingencies associated with biomedicine have had much to do with the social construction that overestimates dualism, dichotomy, and opposition: Sickness as opposed to Healing, with each identified in different but complementary beings.

In contrast to this picture of bifurcation, I have indicated that what natural selection has designed is an integrated diathesis or disposition. It has been described as a capacity or language designed to learn about and interpret the effects of disease and injury. Learning and interpretation when instantiated by disease and injury mean to self-heal or to other-heal, whatever the appropriate context might be. Thus a machinery (the SH adaptation) that produces a *unified and integrated response* is at the base of medicine.

Sickness and healing are the two names one can give to the product of this machinery. These names also label two different actors or players in the response produced by disease and injury, and that the response should instantiate a social relationship is clearly significant and revealing: It underscores the sociality of *Homo sapiens*. However, one must not lose sight of the fact that this social relationship is built out of one and the same material. In other words, the same human material or biological substrate is responsible for the behavior of the sick person and that of the healer; different realizations of this material just happen to be centered or expressed in separated beings. What we term healing is but the expression in another of a response natural to the self who is ill. What comembers (i.e., healers) do for the sick person is what that person should do for himself or herself if he or she were experiencing sickness.

It is certainly likely that in many instances the other-healing response will be more effective than the reflexive self-healing one that the self might be able to generate on its own behalf. In conditions of serious and prominent disability, such a dichotomization both maximizes and enhances the effectiveness of the healing response and better defines the sickness response. In medical crises when an individual's resources and capacities are overwhelmed, the separation of sickness from healing makes obvious sense; in fact, it is "natural" as the discussion in chapter 2 has indicated. In these kinds of eventuations, the SH adaptation is enhanced or maximized since its components are allowed separated expression in distinct subjects, and this form of expression physically, logically, and psychologically can facilitate the realization of a more dispassionate, constructive resolution of the problem that the adaptation was designed to solve, namely, the consequences produced by disease and injury. However, it needs to be kept in mind that duality and complementariness do work best for only those certain kinds of sickness problems (e.g., medical crises) that overwhelm the individual, that the adaptation for medicine does constitute an integrated disposition that binds the individual and the group, and that there are potential disadvantages if unequal relations of power are established between the individual and the healing audience.

The preceding formulation has implied that medicine is not an Institution built around naturally occurring, distinct, and contrastive states of being (i.e., sickness versus healing), each with a logic of its own, which is free to be manipulated separately and relatively free of constraints. Rather, medicine constitutes an organization of social life layered on a machinery and adaptation designed by natural selection that is responsive to distinctive human needs that involve individuals, families, and group mates. All participants in the drama elicited by disease and injury share an adaptation that contains an agreement about what disease and injury mean and portend and how sickness and healing are to be handled. Individuals *and* group mates have a stake in how medical eventuations are to be resolved, and all must guard against the possibility of undue deception and exploitation.

This formulation implies that group mates need to guard against all influences that can shape the biological adaptation for medicine, including influences far removed from the immediate consequences of disease and injury. While suffering produced in the body and mind of human beings constitute basic ingredients of the sickness/healing adaptation, the latter's expression is influenced by a number of other factors. Biology programmed *Homo sapiens* with a trait, capacity, or adaptation for coping with disease and injury, but social groups have evolved differing solutions for these problems. The solutions have tended more and more to divide and separate the effects of disease and injury into more or less distinct, complementary parts, but that these parts are derived from and conditioned by an integrated material needs emphasis.

The reason that emphasis must be given to the unity and integration of the biological material at the base of medicine is because political economic factors extrinsic to sickness and healing have beclouded and distorted this fact so thoroughly. The needs or goals of medicine do relate to epidemiological facts that plague individuals, but this can mystify by creating the illusion that (diseased and injured) individuals are the sole and rightful recipients of what medicine has to offer. What has been deemphasized and beclouded in this narrative is how medicine as an Institution feeds on and can parasitize sickness and healing. It has partitioned a natural human diathesis into component segments—and has done so sometimes more for its own needs than those of its clients. The momentum of social, political, and economic exigencies that have fostered this partitioning of the SH disposition has robbed the individual and the group of some of its benefits. Stated differently, the needs of individuals pursuing political economic agendas, needs expressed through a variety of nonmedical memes that erode and blur the basic requirements and existential correlates of sickness and healing, and more and more what govern and determine the way medicine is practiced. The needs of corporations and organizations and not those of individuals all too often seem to energize the momentum of the economy of medicine. An important task for researchers and policy makers involved in the theoretical study of medicine is to better define and help realize solutions to the problems of disease and injury that natural selection has designed.

A natural question that arises is whether, and if so, how, a postmodern society's evolved information about sickness and healing can be realistically used so that individuals are afforded an optimal way of realizing their adaptation for medicine and thus develop strategies that prevent and best overcome the consequences of disease and injury. To address this question, several things need to be kept in mind. The SH adaptation constitutes a disposition and potential in all individuals, a potential that begins to unfold in infancy and during childhood and that requires social influences during more or less "critical" periods of development and into adolescence. It follows that evolved medical information should be supplied early in the life cycle. The factors that promote and affect health, the natural concomitants of disease and injury, the availability of a variety of medicines (natural and synthetic) and procedures that can control its sufferings, and the "natural" though regrettable certainties that attend advanced age and terminal infirmities would need to be systematically and appropriately instilled in all individuals as a matter of course. Elementary school programs of instruction could instill not just information about "health and sexuality" and "first aid" procedures, but, equally important, a biologically informed awareness of sickness, healing, and dying. This would include, for example, the causes and consequences of disease/injury, how altered biological processes can compromise performance, the consequences of failure to follow a health-promoting lifestyle, the natural behavioral consequences of disease and injury, the socially deleterious implications of exaggerating sickness or deceiving through fraudulent healing, health implications of advanced age, and one's responsibilities to others with respect to the certainty of dying. What in modern Western societies has been constructed in the form of fears of the body's malfunctions, passive dependencies of sickness, prestations of healing, and terror at the prospect of dying would need to be transformed into active and responsible behavioral dispositions that reflect a biologically informed understanding and interpretation of sickness and healing. The goal of such a program of enculturation about SH would be to instill in all individuals an obligation and resignation, if not a willingness, to participate in an informed way in all facets of the sickness/healing cycle, including its fatal termination.

The Stalemate in Postmodern Medicine

The SH adaptation integrates individuals since it comes into play on behalf of the self and on behalf of group mates. It also integrates individuals and the group since the former refine the adaptation by availing themselves of accumulated knowledge produced by the group. In both instances, the rationale of the SH adaptation underscores the social character of *Homo sapiens*: It functions to enhance individual fitness at the same time that it benefits the group. These generalizations imply that an optimal cultural construction of the adaptation should favor both its subject and its object. A basic contention of this chapter is that the unitary character of SH has been obscured by cultural evolution and especially by the way biomedical science and contemporary postmodern culture have shaped the medical institution.

An additional contention of this chapter is that the discord and opposition that exists between the medical institution and other institutions of society that influence how sickness and healing are configured and played out create predicaments and entanglements that not only operate against the achievement of an optimal medical policy but also appear to be insurmountable. One way to dramatize this particular contention is to review what an evolutionary social philosophy of medicine might entail.

Knowledge derived from the biological and social sciences should ideally be part of the content of a society's standard package of medical information. The latter should indicate that persons who are sick are entitled to obtain the benefits that the community has evolved with respect to knowledge about SH but are obligated to have their health interests balanced against the interests of the society. Similarly, specially trained healers are entitled to derive benefits from the application of knowledge about SH but are obligated to use it for the benefit of the society as well as sick persons.

Ideally, excessive profit should be expunged from activities geared to SH. This implies that sick persons should endeavor to reverse sickness and need to be motivated to counteract inequitable gains of sickness; and also that healers should endeavor to apply their expertise competently and need to be motivated to counteract inequitable gains of practice. Since disease and injury constitute crises to individuals and societies, all of societies' institutions should be employed complementarily to counteract their effects.

Individuals have the freedom to resort to the healing tradition of their choice. However, if the needs of society are to be given significant weight in health decisions, individuals should in fairness be held responsible when the standardized package of medical information of the society is not heeded. Similarly, individuals have the freedom to resort to nonmedical institutions when diseased or injured but, ideally, should be held responsible when the standardized package of information about SH is not heeded. All of the preceding implies that spokespersons and official corporations of civil society are obligated to evaluate and, when necessary, test all claims to knowledge about SH, to regard claims that are valid as part of the official, standard package of medical information of the society, and to use the effects of applying portions of that package equitably in the political economic evaluation of the course of disease and injury occurrences.

If the unitary character of the SH adaptation was to be truly heeded, then individuals should conceptualize healers not as elitist experts but simply as persons more informed than themselves on matters pertaining to disease and injury and ways of combating its effects, all of which would be conceptualized in biological and social terms. Thus there exists no warrant for the claim that specially trained healers are entitled to levels of compensation that exceed those calculated for equivalent investments on education and work specialization of other members of the society and taking into account the value placed on SH by all members of the society. Ideally, the Institution of medicine would be apportioned resources as a result of a social consensus about the importance of sickness and healing balanced against resources needed for handling other needs of the society.

Persons need to engage in informed deliberations about the medical burdens they are willing to tolerate in themselves and their family members. This implies that an informed consensus about the significance of SH should come to characterize health-relevant behaviors of members of society. Ideally, the level of investment of resources pertaining to medicine that individuals themselves and social groups are required to set aside for future SH conditions should be determined taking into consideration the medically relevant habitual behaviors of the individual.

With respect to actual medical care practices, individuals need to be socialized to feel entitled to obtain appropriate healing and support when sick and should know the standard, expectable end points of healing of the sickness that they manifest. Similarly, individuals should feel naturally obligated to resume work obligations and social responsibilities commensurate with the degree of restoration of function made possible by optimal application of evolved information pertaining to SH as presented to them by specially trained healers or social advisers. Conversely, specially trained healers should handle all of society's disease/injury conditions, and they should be obligated to assign resources to healing that take into consideration biological and social costs/benefits as well as the individual's own health behavior history. As implied earlier in this chapter, individuals should be socialized to expect that realistic personal and social limits are to be placed on conditions of suffering resulting from disease and injury and healers should be responsible for educating their (sick) clients about such matters. Finally, individuals should be socialized to expect that in instances when they are unable to participate in their own SH decisions, a socially prudent consensus on matters pertaining to level of suffering, degree of disability, cost of healing, duration of condition, and actual and potential level of possible effective social functioning will determine how their medical condition will be handled by appropriate representatives of the family and social group who are to decide such matters fairly and with good intentions for all parties concerned, including the society itself.

There are obvious reasons for feeling less than sanguine about efforts to arrive at even a significantly muted version of something like an evolutionarily inspired social philosophy about medicine. One needs to keep in mind that such a philosophy would consist of at least two sets of memes: those applying to self-interest and those applying to group interest with respect to disease and injury. To effectively combat the agonies and sufferings of disease and injury, the best directives derived from biomedicine, from alternative medical traditions, and from the currently evolving life extension programs should ideally be a part of such a philosophy. To effectively minimize wasteful expenditures of (medical and human) resources now squandered on permanent or deteriorating medical dead ends, principles that stipulated the conditions for resolving wasteful and hopelessly painful and disabling terminal disease/injury conditions should also ideally be a part of the philosophy. However, each of these two desiderata would be almost impossible to achieve in postmodern societies: the first because of the power differentials, to say nothing of the incommensurability of worldviews espoused by members of the competing medical traditions; the second because of similar intractable oppositions that characterize political economic and religious institutions and corporations of postmodern social formations. Furthermore, even if in principle it were possible to arrive at these two or any other ensemble of memes that could effectively articulate an evolutionarily sound social philosophy of medicine, what would it take to have its directives equitably and consistently implemented? It seems obvious that the mix of competing memes relating to how civil society should be governed, memes favoring individualism and political freedom, those raising the specter of and sharply opposing central political control (memes articulating the danger of the various "isms"), and those related to traditional religion, create such tensions that they render the achievement of even a watered-down version of an evolutionarily based social philosophy of medicine a chimerical myth. Furthermore, if one takes into consideration the poor track record of recent public health campaigns geared to changing "unhealthy" behaviors, a record that documents group and individual incapacities to carry out well-attested principles pertaining to good health, one is faced with the conclusion that postmodern social formations have evolved a culture and set of social practices that render the development and implementation of something resembling an evolutionary social philosophy of medicine highly problematic.

The SH adaptation "should" promote a medical consensus. It declares that persons have a responsibility for their health and the health of group mates, and should expect social/moral/economic benefits and penalties as a consequence of following or not following the dictates of the adaptation. The adaptation incorporates an expectation of socially realistic self- and other-healing in the event of socially realistic pictures of sickness, all of which must be arbitrated fairly. Handling the problem of terminality in a socially prudent and humane way is integral to the adaptation. A group or subgroup that claims realistic knowledge about the causes of disease and injury and their handling should have that claim appropriately and fairly validated by public corporations of the society. Results of the validation constitute the adaptation. Subgroups whose claims are not validated have the option of resorting to private ways of implementing them, but their members are obligated to also support the publically validated adaptation.

Appendix:
Outline of the Evolution
of Sickness and Healing

I. Nonmedical Concepts

    A. Individual: Person comprising population of a society or social formation.

    B. Gene: Unit of genetic information comprising an individual's genome or genetic structure.

    C. Society or Social Formation: A historically specific group, system, or unit made up of individuals and described in terms of culture and political economy.

    D. Culture: The system of symbols and their meanings of a particular social formation.

    E. Meme: A unit of cultural (i.e., symbolic) information comprising a society's culture.

    F. Political Economy: The social practices and power arrangements governing subsistence and economic production; includes the relations and means of production.

    G. Social Type: A specific kind or category of social formation characterized in terms of size, social complexity, and social differentiation; may be descriptive of a specific social formation or constitute a distinctive category or distinct phase of social evolution.

II. Medical Concepts

    A. Illness: A state of perceived ill health; subjectively experienced and defined and socially validated in the immediate family/group.

B. Disease (and Injury): A pathological condition associated with disturbances in the anatomical, physiological, and chemical systems of the
body described in terms of biomedical science.

C. Disease*: A medical condition described in terms of a society's dominant, official medical tradition.

D. Sickness: The social construction of an episode of illness; the way illness is handled as a social cultural entity and the way it is dealt with in
the society; reflects the cultural presuppositions that provide meaning
and organize action with respect to an illness as well as the ideology associated with the political economy of the society and its medical tradition; takes into account ideas and efforts associated with healing.

E. Healing: The social processes and actions brought to bear in the attempt to counteract a condition of disease/illness; since it reflects cultural and political economic factors of the society, it constitutes the therapeutic complement of sickness; involves actions and dispositions of
members of family and group including persons/agents/resources used
in curing (e.g., healers, folk practitioners, physicians, medicines, surgical techniques, social practices and conventions).

F. Medical Gene: A unit of genetic information that codes how biological systems of the body respond to disease and injury, the products of
which elicit a condition of illness in an individual.

G. Medical Meme: A unit of cultural information that serves to give meaning to sickness and healing; produces the habits and beliefs and underlies behaviors related to sickness and healing; the set of medical memes
of a social formation or type provides the meanings and guides actions
about sickness and healing.

H. SH Adaptation: The biological adaptation or trait that programs individuals to learn about disease and injury, interpret the illness that arises,
and communicate its meanings, and programs the self-healing and
other-healing response of individuals.

I. SH Response: The behavioral response of the SH adaptation given an
eventuation of disease and injury; the product of medical genes and
medical memes.

J. Medical Institutions: Products of medical memes that are shared by
members of a society.

K. Parameters of Sickness and Healing: The overall, societywide style and
patterning of medical memes and institutions; the social and cultural
characteristics of medicine of a social formation or social type; the
way sickness and healing are configured and played out in a social formation or type as a result of the enactment of medical memes.

III. General Assumptions and Principles

    A. Individuals (biological organisms) undergo change across time in their organization and mode of functioning, and such changes can be explained using the theory of biological evolution (i.e., involving genetic variation, mutation, physiological and psychological adaptations, and natural selection).

    B. Social formations or societies undergo historical transformation across time that can be theoretically explained using the research strategy and accompanying theories of evolutionary materialism.

    C. There exist prototypical forms of societies, social types, that differ with respect to differentiation/complexity, and such social types can be conceptualized as constituting phases of social evolution.

    D. Societies show general and repeatable patterns of social evolution that conform to the processes of parallel and convergent evolution.

    E. Social transformation (i.e., evolution) is a change in the structure and complexity of a social formation, and it comes about as a result of deliberate and purposive acts of selection of individuals of new and improved ways of coping with social conflicts and problems (i.e., social selection of memes); acts of individuals are, for this reason, adaptive and reflect changes in habitual ways of thinking and feeling (see I.E).

    F. Natural selection affecting genes is the ultimate cause of biological evolution and operates on a much longer time scale than social evolution; it can result from a particular social transformation or phase of social evolution; societies can evolve socially and culturally, but the individuals in them need not evolve biologically.

    G. Illness and disease are recurrent phenomena in social formations; they bring about healing; and the manner in which illness is interpreted and handled as an eventuation, the specific parameters of sickness and healing determined by the society's set of medical genes and medical memes, reflects the society's culture and political economy.

    H. Characteristics of sickness and healing and the ways these are played out, the parameters of sickness and healing, are a product of nonmedical factors (e.g., ecology, demography, social organization, level of social differentiation, location in an intersocietal nexus of cultural diffusion and political economy) as well as medical factors (e.g., epidemiology, level of morbidity of disease, level of mortality).

    I. The parameters of sickness and healing differ in different social formations and social types.

IV. Medical Evolutionary Assumptions and Principles

A. The state/condition of illness is psychologically and socially undesirable and prompts a (natural) response to self-heal and other-heal (i.e.,
it gives rise to a need for corrective action) through the use and refinement of old medical memes and the development/invention of new
ones. (The use and search for medical memes is a natural concomitant
of illness and hence intrinsic to human societies given the ubiquity of
disease.)

B. Medical genes and memes constitute a medical adaptation or "trait" of
individuals termed the SH adaptation; this programs individuals to
understand and communicate about disease and injury and respond
adaptively through healing efforts; individuals search for and develop
medical memes (i.e., new information about sickness and healing) that
are believed to promote health and heal illness; the implementation of
these medical memes can lead to improvements in levels of morbidity
and mortality; the functions of medical genes and medical memes are
to lessen the negative effects of illness/disease and to facilitate prevention and treatment of disease.

C. Sickness and healing evolve: the beliefs, attitudes, and social practices
related to problems of disease change in systematic ways in association with changes in the content of medical memes and changes in social structure.

D. Changes in the level and character of morbidity and mortality constitute major factors promoting the refinement of old and invention of
new medical memes (new disease pictures, epidemics, or an augmen-
tation in the level of old disease pictures create human crises that com-
pel the refinement of old medical memes and the search for and invention of new ones).

E. Changes in the ecology, demography, culture, and social structure of a
social formation are associated with changes in pictures of morbidity
and mortality and hence constitute the initial, more basic factors promoting the development of medical memes and the evolution of sickness and healing (i.e., material factors play a primary role in affecting
disease pictures and instigating changes in behavior practices related to
sickness and healing).

F. The invention and learning of specific new medical memes constitute
the more proximal, immediate factors promoting the evolution of sickness and healing (medical memes are what directly affect how sickness and healing are configured and played out and, hence, whether,
and if so how, these evolve, but [as per IV.E] material factors as well as
medical/epidemiological factors initiate the search for medical memes).

G. The factors that lead to the production of new medical memes and the rejection of old ones are complex and originate at different levels of the individual/social/intersocietal nexus.

H. Different social types, different phases of the evolution of social formations, display different parameters of sickness and healing; the content of the medical memes of a social type or phase of social evolution differs in systematic ways from that of other social types and phases.

I. Medical memes are readily learned and imitated by members of a society; if judged efficacious in the short run, they are learned by others of the same generation and passed on to succeeding generations; if judged inefficacious in the short run, they are discarded or rejected.

J. Individuals constitute adaptive units; in inventing new medical memes, learning old medical memes, and passing on medical memes, they promote the propagation and inheritance of medical memes; and, as a result of the temporal and spatial summation of a society's medical memes, sickness and healing (i.e., the parameters of sickness and healing) change and evolve in systematic ways.

K. In the long run medical memes can bring about a state of adaptedness or maladaptedness (which includes aspects of morbidity and mortality of disease) in some or all of the individuals of a social formation.

L. Medical memes create and underlie parameters of sickness and healing, and these can undergo stasis, devolution, and extinction as well as progressive evolution; some medical memes are universal (e.g., desire to be rid of the pain of illness, desire to relieve a comember's pain associated with illness) and some are culturally specific (e.g., choice of suitable healer, use of specific medication).

M. At different levels of social complexity/differentiation, and at different stages of social evolution, the distal and proximal causes of the social evolution of sickness and healing differ.

N. The ultimate causes of the evolution of sickness and healing are biological; in other words, psychological and physiological adaptations of individuals encoded in genetic information constitute the capacity for life and promote the search for new and better ways of coping with environmental contingencies, and this underlies social evolution; such adaptations also underlie and account for the search for and use of medical memes; the degree of connectedness between genetic and cultural changes associated with the development and implementation of medical memes is difficult to establish (and is much contested).

V. Medical Evolutionary Generalizations

  A. Family-level societies

    1. Nomadism, smallness of group, and absence of social differentiation determine the way sickness and healing are played out.

    2. All members of the immediate group as a whole experience the burden and consequences of sickness and share in its healing.

    3. The individual (in consultation with immediate family/group) determines (is the arbiter of) the boundary between the conditions of sickness as compared to wellness.

    4. To a varying extent, all group members participate in sickness as healers, although more talented, older, more experienced ones may play a special role.

    5. Sickness constitutes a crisis to the individual and his or her family and the society; explanation of illness as sickness is tailored to the individual (i.e., special attributes of his or her biography and circumstances in the group/community are crucial in explaining illness and rationalizing healing).

    6. Mental and somatic components of sickness are not differentiated or accorded different meanings, values; there exists a holism, psychosomatic/somatopsychic unity, regarding how sickness is constructed socially.

  B. Village-level societies

    1. Sedentarism modifies and strongly shapes the conduct of sickness and healing.

    2. Individuals in nearby, competing groups influence the way sickness and healing are interpreted and played out and are often held to play a causal role.

    3. The status of an individual's social relationships in the group begin to play a role in perceived causation of illness; and they exert a greater influence in determining the boundaries between conditions of sickness and well-being although the individual remains the final arbiter.

    4. Village leaders or more gifted, talented group members ("proto-healers") may be consulted for special roles in healing rituals.

    5. Sickness constitutes a crisis to the individual and his or her immediate family and relatives, but explanation of its cause/meaning remains centered on the individual.

    6. Same as A.6.

C. Chiefdom and prestate societies

1. Social differentiation and complexity influence the way sickness and healing are played out; kinship, clan, and other social groupings have available alternative ways of explaining sickness and carrying out healing, but the general epistemology (e.g., ways of conceptualizing causation, "clinical efficacy") about sickness and healing reflects a common semantic matrix of ideas.

2. Availability of specialist healers becomes influential in the way sickness and healing are played out (e.g., in affecting the course and interpretation of sickness); sickness is an opportunity for social exegeses.

3. The diversity of categories and explanatory mechanisms pertaining to illness, what can be termed sickness narratives, increase in number and complexity; and intragroup dynamics provide important material for these narratives (i.e., affecting the definition, interpretation of, and justification for sickness and healing).

4. Sicknesses are more common and socially more complex and begin to be differentiated semantically as to type (e.g., causation, severity, manifestations), and only certain varieties constitute crises to the individual and his or her family; however, sicknesses for the most part retain a spiritual/sacred/mysterious dimension and remain tailored to the individual.

5. The unity (i.e., holism) of illness and sickness are preserved (mental and bodily manifestations are equally valorized), although mental illnesses become discernible sickness types, but there is little stigmatization and devaluation of psychological components of sickness.

D. States and civilized societies

1. Marked differentiation of population into groups and classes with members of each showing differing levels of health and availability of alternative, even truly contrastive (epistemological), traditions for explaining illness and carrying out healing; great complexity and variety in how sickness and healing are configured and played out in the society as a whole.

2. The services and resources of urban centers become highly influential in the way sickness and healing are conceptualized and played out (e.g., they play a role as a center for diverse types of healers, the production of medicines, education/apprenticeship of specialist healers).

3. Literate medical traditions enhance the complexity of sickness and healing narratives and the way these are interpreted and played out, and its practitioners come to play an overarching validating though highly contested role as more knowledgeable, moral/ethical interpreters of sickness.

4. The healer specialist plays a determinate role in the unfolding of sickness; the number and type of healers in a society is greatly increased; healing becomes a specialized role and full-time occupation; payment of money becomes the standard way of formalizing the healing contract, sickness becomes more secularized but remains individually tailored.

5. Sickness and healing become more secularized and the object of commercial and industrial enterprises in the society.

6. The status of an individual's social relations and the nature of his or her habits and lifestyles become socially incorporated explicitly in explanations of sickness and healing and in the technology for the maintenance of health; literate traditions provide the means for explaining illness and disease* in complex ways that incorporate psychological and physiological factors.

7. Mental illnesses become highly visible in the society, associated with stigmatization and beginnings of devaluation of psychological components of sickness (i.e., relative positive valorization of somatizatic manifestations).

E. Modern European societies

1. Biomedical science plays a dominant role in the way sickness is explained as disease and healing is played out.

2. The state establishes biomedicine as the official approach to sickness and healing and plays an influential role in supporting it and sponsoring its products; it is constituted as the valid interpretation of sickness and healing.

3. Sickness and healing are constituted as natural phenomena devoid of spiritual/moral components; the individual replicates through sickness the behavioral structure of disease that unfolds itself in the person; and naturalistic forces/agents/processes constitute the true reality behind sickness.

4. Biomedical physicians defined as medical experts exert a dominant influence in healing, patients become passive recipients of care, fee for service becomes the dominant mode of structuring the healing relationship, third-party agencies finance medical care.

5. Great optimism surrounds the naturalistic explanation and treatment of disease.

6. Psychiatry emerges as an important medical discipline; mental illnesses are highly stigmatized, and social psychological factors and components of sickness and healing become considerably devaluated (i.e., high valorization, validation of somatic components of sickness).

F. Postmodern societies

1. Advanced monopolistic capitalism exerts a dominant role in the way sickness and healing are rationalized and carried out; money value and the profit motive exert a powerful influence on the definition, objectives, resources, and ingredients of sickness and healing; the latter come to be viewed as commodities and are highly commercialized.

2. Great proliferation of biomedical knowledge and rapid communication of its content and implications in the society strongly influence the way sickness and healing are understood and played out; the society shares much of a public language of sickness as disease.

3. The confidence in and power of biomedicine declines, its hegemony in the society is challenged, and the distribution of its limited resources becomes contested and controversial; alternative health/wellness and life extension industries compete in the medical marketplace.

4. Persons become responsible for and empowered with respect to understanding the nature of sickness and production of healing and health; persons become active, rational, self-interested consumers in the marketplace.

5. The validity of medical knowledge becomes problematic, and the goals and end points of healing become blurred and contested as a consequence of scientific/technological breakthroughs and bioethical dilemmas.

6. The exclusivity of the doctor-patient relationship is weakened and undermined by political, economic, and medical developments in the society as group practices and managed care alliances play a determinate role in structuring and rationalizing sickness and healing.

7. Psychiatry becomes highly medicalized, mental illnesses are less stigmatized, and emotional and psychological components of sickness

are socially more acceptable but economically expendable and become the objects of nonbiomedical disciplines and practitioners.

VI. Medical Memes Programming Sickness and Healing in Social Types

A. Family-level societies

1. An individual's awareness in self (or perception of another) of high sense of physical distress, weakness, lassitude, fatigue, pain, and physiological disturbances (i.e., what can be termed "physical" symptoms) constitutes necessary and sufficient conditions for illness and signal the need for healing. (If I feel very weak, with pain and aches and body symptoms, then I am ill and need healing.)

2. The state of illness and the perceived need for healing is associated with a high sense of apprehension, discouragement, victimization, inadequacy, sociomoral disarticulation, existential crisis, and deepening despair (what can be termed "psychological" or "mental" symptoms). (Since I am ill, the conduct of my life is being questioned, my prospects loom bad, my future looks gloomy, and I may not recover.)

3. Sickness is a condition that entails/requires a legitimate abstention from ordinary/everyday responsibilities. (Because I am sick and need healing, I cannot carry out my responsibilities and am not expected to do so.)

4. Self is the final arbiter of sickness and wellness. (It is up to me to determine when I am well and when my illness is over; I will be able to decide when or if I am well again.)

5. Sickness has a holistic (i.e., psychosomatic, somatopsychic, sociomoral, spiritual) identity and valorization (i.e., no part of the sickness picture is overvalued or disvalued). (All of my symptoms, my body ailments and my worries/fears, make up my illness and make me feel gloomy and bad.)

6. A sense of victimization associated with sickness and healing is experienced as total, global, and more or less explicit: self/others/ancestors/spirits are at fault; however, specific comembers are not explicitly singled out. (Because I am sick, I am being singled out, disvalued, and punished by all; the whole world has turned against me; the authenticity of my life is being questioned by the world.)

7. Self and group members and even ancestors are held to be implicated in the fate of sickness. (My sickness means that me and my whole family-world are potentially at fault and imperiled.)

8. A sense of crisis, threat, mystery, fearfulness, and possibility of impending termination is a necessary, private and public component of sickness (illness requiring healing). (I am on a dangerous course with an uncertain future as a result of my sickness, and my family and friends know this.)

9. Dependence, passivity, and a sense of helplessness with consequent anticipation of group intervention and support is a "natural," moral/ethical, socially visible component of sickness. (As everybody knows, my sickness has rendered me relatively helpless and unable to take care of myself, but I know that my family and friends will help out as best they can.)

10. Resignation to a possibly uncertain short-term future marked by worldly nonexistence or full integration into the group with restoration of well-being is intrinsic to the state of sickness and the pursuit of healing. (I may recover fully from my illness, or I may not live very long and be able to carry on with my family and friends as a result of this sickness.)

11. High sense of group/communal burden, obligation, and responsibility in the immediate group is associated with sickness and healing. (We have an obligation to help him or her because he or she is sick; I can expect help from others because they owe me this and I would do the same for them.)

12. Sickness and healing are confined to the home environment. (We will leave him or her alone and resting while he or she is sick and is being healed by us.)

13. Possibility of sickness is always high and so is a sense of powerlessness that it can be prevented or undone (e.g., low optimism). (Neither I nor anyone can expect to avoid the condition of sickness, and there is not much that can be done about it once it hits one; I know that if I do not get better I might be abandoned and left to die.)

14. Options and resources associated with healing are limited and finite. (There are only a few things that can be done for me during this sickness and all of them will be tried in due course if need be; we will try our usual remedies and rituals on him or her.)

B. Village-level societies

1. Medical memes 1–14 in A above continue to operate.

2. Sense of being victimized from outside the group becomes relevant and in some instances dominant. (My sickness means that someone outside of this group could be/is singling me out and attacking me.)

3. Some heightening and narrowing of dependence on the immediate family and expectation that it will support and heal, with consequent lessening of dependence on the group as a whole. (Since I am ill, I can expect most help from my immediate family and less help from others in the group.)

4. Some explicit recognition or awareness that intragroup happenings may be causal in a condition of sickness. (It could be the case that someone in my village/group is causing me this sickness/harm.)

5. Potential for intragroup blame is present in a state of sickness. (I and my family could hold someone in this group responsible for my illness; anybody in my group could have caused this sickness.)

6. Some dependency on and expectation of help from a socially designated person of the group (or of one nearby) who is held to possess special strength/power/insight, a protohealer, for healing and resolution of social/moral and existential ambiguity associated with sickness; options and resources of healing are thus enhanced. (I know that in my sickness my family can call on help from someone who has had more experience with sickness and who has more power to undo or combat the cause of my sickness.)

7. Group/communal obligation and responsibility are lessened and negotiated by the healer and the family. (Self: There is a limit to what I can expect of others of the group during my illness. Group member: His or her family is mainly responsible for healing and our [my] obligation is limited.)

8. Some healing is moved to special locations, but the home setting retains primacy. (Because I am ill, I may be taken to a special place to undergo healing, but I am likely to return here to my place.)

C. Chiefdom and prestate societies

1. Most of the preceding medical memes continue to operate, but medical memes 1–3 are less binding; as an example, a high sense of physical distress and malaise is sufficient for perception of illness, but not always necessary; sickness can be a less "awesome" condition and associated with more optimism; family members and healers gain some influence over the course and social definition of sickness. (I am not feeling well or up to things, and may be sick; I feel down and have lost some of my energy, so I am becoming ill; some medicines and help from my family may get me over this sickness.)

2. The sense of victimization linked to the condition of sickness is less global and total and more differentiated; the sense of existential despair and annihilation is less dominant; there is less resignation to a possible termination (greater optimism, less pessimism). (My illness is worrisome and makes me feel badly; why I am ill is a puzzle; there can be several reasons why I am ill; there can be any number of causes and consequences to my illness; I or others may be at fault with respect to causing my illness; I can anticipate this illness may cause me and my family to search for reasons and undo them.)

3. Members within the group become important sources of illness, and conflicts in intragroup relations begin to explicitly enter into the constitution of sickness; the social construction of sickness incorporates ongoing social relationships and happenings in the group and affects the ill person. (A spirit/ancestor may be attacking/punishing me through this illness, but someone in my group may also be doing me the evil and bringing on this illness.)

4. The self is more important as a specific object or target of illness; a sense of personal vulnerability/responsibility is more integral to the condition of illness as a result of possible actions of others in the group; sickness is more sociological or constituted along interpersonal lines as a result. (That I am sick means that I am in some way responsible or being singled out; persons in my distant family/lineage or neighbors/group might be implicated in my illness; it is very possible that my illness is a result of bad actions on the part of others whom I or my family know which are directed at me.)

5. A condition of illness and its social construction as sickness becomes a more deliberate, singular eventuation: more contingent on situational factors connecting to self, less contingent or purely physiological failures, less contingent on global preternatural factors. (Recent or more remote happenings, something I did or failed to do, circumstances pertaining to my life and that of my family, and the like, are most likely causing me this illness; spirits, others, or physical factors may be causing this illness, but what I have done recently or in the past may be the "real" or underlying reason I am now ill.)

6. Sickness retains a holistic identity and valorization but discrete (somatic/behavior) manifestations begin to acquire importance to self and family as clues of causation, social typification, and possible stigmatization; semantics and vocabularies of illness and sickness expand. (That I have these types of symptoms means

that I am sick in a specific way; the specific symptoms that I am having are clues to what ails me and what brought it about and how I should go about healing myself; my illness resembles [or does not resemble] illnesses that I have had before and that others in my family/group have [or have not] had.)

7. Options and resources of healing are enhanced significantly; the role of healer is well defined and beginnings of differentiation as to type, emphasis, mode of diagnosis, and treatment are apparent. (There are several ways in which I and my family could deal with this illness; there are several persons we could consult for advice and healing.)

8. Characteristics of the illness state, including physiological manifestations, become important in choices of healing. (Because I am ill in this way, or because I have these types of symptoms, probably means that I have been hurt/injured/attacked in this particular way, or by this specific type of agency; the way in which my illness manifests influences what type of healer I or my family consult, or influences what particular healing regimen I follow; my illness can mean many different things, and I have different ways of ascertaining what is wrong with me, how I should obtain/seek healing, what kind of healing I should follow in the light of the way my illness shows itself in my body.)

9. Exploitation of sickness (i.e., of sick role) for personal, social gains becomes an important contingency/possibility of illness and healing. (When my problems are resolved, I will get over this sickness/begin to feel better; if my problems are acknowledged, I will begin to feel better; my problems need attention and understanding, if not resolution, in order for me to be relieved of illness.)

10. There is high dependence on healers for outcome. (The healer that I or my family consult will advise me and give me the right kind of treatment; I need the help of a particular type of healer to get better; the kind of healing I receive will play an important role in how my sickness turns out.)

11. Beginnings of competition among healers are evident. (Self: I need to balance what this healer says in relation to what the other healer says; a healer may emphasize certain things about my sickness because of the way he or she understands illness; because healers need/want my commitment he/she/they may slant things in a particular way. Healer: I must impress on this sick person my particular strengths to elicit his confidence, otherwise I may not be able to cure him or her.)

12. Healers acquire responsibility for the outcome of sickness and play a crucial role in negotiating (validating) sickness. (What my healer says and does is very influential in what happens to me; my healer plays an important role in the outcome of my illness; if I get better, I can thank my healer; if I do not get better or worsen, my healer may be responsible; I need the advice/support/help/care of my healer to get well.)

13. Greater power and autonomy are ascribed to healers. (A healer plays an important role in affecting the outcome of anybody's sickness; what the healer says and does is crucial in affecting the outcome of my sickness.)

14. Healers begin to be compensated for efforts and blamed for failures. (If I get better, I will have to pay/recompense my healer; if I do not get better or worsen, I can hold my healer responsible.)

15. Healer's quarters or special locations are often frequented by the sick person during ceremonies/rituals of treatment. (To obtain advice and help from a healer, I may have to go to his or her quarters; while I am obtaining healing I may have to live in my healer's quarters.)

D. State and civilized societies

1. Illness is still constituted as a holistic entity with its spiritual component important, but the mystery, danger, and existential annihilation/despair are less frequent concomitants; less pessimism attaches to conditions of sickness. (My illness can mean many different things and have any number of outcomes; illness is something from which one frequently recovers; that I am ill does not necessarily mean that I am being singled out/punished/maligned/attacked, nor does it necessarily mean I am at fault/guilty/blameworthy/bad/sinful.)

2. Illness is a common eventuation, thought of and experienced as more commonplace, quotidian; it becomes more secularized; physiological failures (as in the two earlier social formations, intense weakness, fatigue, pain, physical symptoms) constitute sufficient but not necessary conditions for illness. (Illness is something that a lot is known about and for which healers have acquired special, accumulated understandings and treatments; illness is something common that one can expect as a matter of course; an illness can be serious and long lasting/permanent, but often it is not serious and is short lived; everybody gets sick and sicknesses are varied in their symptoms and causes; I can anticipate/expect that this illness may very well be healed/cured successfully.)

3. The sociological dimension of sickness (i.e., the link of illness and healing to intergroup relations and situations) remains important. (My sickness and its healing will involve me with several people and healers; my family will be involved in my healing; I can anticipate that my family will play a role in my healing; problems that I or my family are having in the community/at work are influential in causing me to get ill; the problems I am having in my life plague and weaken me and make me vulnerable to illness; my illness comes from my many problems and conflicts at work, with family, neighbors.)

4. Expectation of healer intervention is high; the healer plays a dominant role in shaping, validating, explaining, and resolving the condition of illness. (I will need to get specialist help if my and my family's remedies do not help; the healer I or my family consult plays a crucial role in how my illness turns out; only through the help of my healer will my sickness, if it persists, go away and his or her efforts are/will be crucial in how all turns out; my healer is my ally in this condition of illness; how my healer behaves toward me and what he or she does and thinks of me and my illness are influential in whether I will recover.)

5. Chronic sickness problems are common and qualities of illness are crucial in determining the labeling of illness and choice of healer. (My illness may linger; I can expect that some of my symptoms, my malaise and pains, will stay with me for a while; it may be a long time before I am fully recovered; what my symptoms mean and just what type of illness I have will be determined by healers who have great knowledge and understanding.)

6. Knowledge structures pertaining to illness and healing are elaborate, influential, and diversified and become literate, complex, and intricate. A "functional" theory of illness and disease* is in play. The model of sickness is thus multifactorial and personalized. Specialist healers treat and prevent sickness. (The illness that I have most likely can be eventually identified by specialist healers; the knowledge accumulated by healers and written about in the books gives them understanding for developing the kind of treatment that will get me well; the advice of healers can keep me healthy and keep me from getting ill and also get me over this sickness.)

7. The self as an individual becomes a more active, self-conscious consumer of health care and healing, although the family retains an important role in selecting and seeking the healer and in monitoring healing. (In the event I get ill, I can count on the help and

advice of many different persons; there are things I can do to keep myself healthy and to heal myself when I get ill; my family can and will help me choose the right healer, but I am not totally dependent and can influence what is done during my illness and how it all turns out.)

8. Options and resources of healing are greatly expanded and diversified; a greater number and variety of healers allows differentiated choices by self and family; social, religious, and ethnic group membership is very influential in choices, forms, and quality of healing. (In the event I get ill, I can draw on several different medicines and choose from among several different types of healers; the remedies that my family and I know about and the healers who are experienced in the kinds of illnesses we have can provide special help should I or my family get ill.)

9. There is a hierarchy of healers as to repute, knowledge, competence, and modality of healing, and high competition among healers. (There are many different types of healers I and my family can visit for help when illness strikes; illnesses can be mysterious, dangerous, and difficult to figure out, but fortunately there exist sacred knowledge in the books and many different types of healers and remedies; some healers are truly knowledgeable and powerful and can get to the bottom of things provided I stick with them; not all healers are equally good; some healers can make one worse; it's crucial to get the right kind of healer and the right kind of medicine.)

10. Healers are still seen as "curers," but some also assume an important role as adviser on health and preventer of illness; persons, not just sick persons, become "patients"; the (sick or well) person's partnership with the healer is crucial in monitoring, planning, and promoting health, and preventing and undoing illness; illnesses acquire concrete identity as sickness types and disease* types, although functionally explained (i.e., not ontologically), and these are importantly shaped by the healer (partially manufactured, commodified; see 13, below); sickness begins to be defined as a longitudinal entity (i.e., acquires a temporal dimension). (My healer is my adviser; he or she can help me stay healthy and lead a safe life; I can count on him or her for help in many different ways; the sickness that I have is special to me and understood by my healer because he or she knows what I am like physically and morally; I intend to "heal with him or her" throughout my illness, which may linger for a while; I anticipate that it may take time for me and my healer to get control of my sickness and return me to health.)

11. Unregulated exploitation of sickness by the self is possible and frequent through sanctions of the healer, use of varieties of healers, awareness of differences and the personalized nature of sickness, and availability of different ways of healing. (As long as I am not feeling well and feel ill I know I can count on help from my healer; if this healer does not fully help me to get perfectly well I know I can also see another healer who will help me and get me over my illness; there exist many different ways of healing and many different types of medicines, and these might all need to be tried to get me well again.)

12. Organizations, corporations, and confraternities establish places of residence for the housing of the ill and settings of healing. (My guild, my church, the monasteries, our group fellows, the fellowship of my friends, and relatives can see me through this illness; if necessary, I can stay in a special place that they will provide for me where I can be offered special treatment.)

13. Despite functional and personalized theories of illness (i.e., as compared to ontological ones), health, well-being, and states of sickness (named/explained in terms of sickness/disease* terminologies and narratives) become more materialized, almost objectified, and like commodities that are willfully sought after, pursued, purchased, negotiated over, modified, shortened, or lengthened. The healer plays a crucial role in constructing sickness, but the self remains the ultimate "gold standard" for the condition of sickness. (Illness is a condition or possibility that is recurrent and common and that requires vigilance, healing, medicines, changes in diet, and special ways of doing things and routines; it is almost inseparable from life; there exist many types of illnesses and diseases* that learned healers can identify and about which there is much wisdom and knowledge; I know that by seeking the right kind of healer my illness will be properly identified and dealt with; my illness is special to me, but I know that there are special kinds of illnesses/diseases* that I and other people can develop and about which there exists special knowledge in the texts.)

14. Sickness and healing activities constitute a dominant economic enterprise in a society; healing becomes a full-time occupation; the Institution of medicine is virtually industrialized. (Illness is something about which much is known and for which one can do many things; special medicines, treatments, procedures, and "cures" exist in the city for the relief of my and other people's symptoms of illness; I and my family can shop around for different medicines and healers; advice about sickness is plentiful; provided I

and my family have the necessary resources, we can find the right kind of healer.)

15. Sick persons and families bear the responsibility for payment of healing among the well-to-do; confraternities, religious institutions, lay organizations, and in rare instances the state sponsor/support and defray costs of healing in the socially needy and marginal. (I know that if I seek healing for my illness, it may cost me and my family plenty; fortunately, there are special groups/persons/organizations I and my family can draw on for help in getting healing; there exist places and persons I can turn to in the event of illness and get healing and help in coping with my problems/responsibilities during the time I am ill; depending on my and my family's resources, it may not be possible to visit many different types of healers.)

16. Healers become organized into professional associations and stipulate ethical codes that articulate formal responsibilities and obligations. (There exist rules and standards for the right ways to do healing; I can turn to special healers who are members of medical societies that adopt/follow high standards; that some healers adopt/follow/subscribe to ethical codes/standards is a reminder that many do not but that there exist some guidance/regulation/conventions that good healers should follow; I must be on the lookout for good/moral/responsible healers and guard against and avoid those who are out to only make a living.)

17. Mental illness as madness/insanity becomes a distinct, more visible, and more prominent form of illness in the society. (Persons who make irrational statements, hold strange beliefs, become emotionally out of control, or show a breakdown in their behavior are ill, and there exist medicines/healers who can improve them; there exist places where these persons can be kept or groups/families that will look after them; craziness, conditions of irrational behavior and emotional excitement/dyscontrol, is a kind of illness that can affect persons and for which there exist ways of healing.)

18. Stigmatization of mental illness is prominent in most societies. (Craziness is a shameful condition of illness; I would not want my friends to know that a family member of mine is ill with craziness; I would feel singled out and inferior if I developed the illness of craziness.)

19. The literate tradition articulates a comprehensive, holistic interpretation of illness and sickness with an emphasis on the body (i.e., a focus on somatic-physical symptoms), although accompanying

mental/emotional symptoms are given importance as well; the bodily/physical as compared to the purely mental/emotional aspects of sickness are integrated in sickness narratives, with the former weighted more heavily. (In conjunction with 18: To be ill is to have many different types of symptoms, but to be sick purely with craziness means that one is sick in a way different from being sick in a "bodily" sense; craziness symptoms are embarrassing to have, whereas ordinary "physical" symptoms are not.)

20. Sickness is made a more commercial object, its manifestations shaped and regulated by healers and its valorization influenced by the type of physiological and behavioral manifestations. (There exist many ways in which one can get sick, and there are correspondingly many different ways of obtaining relief and healing, but the kinds of symptoms one has and the kinds of healing needed affect what others think of me and how I would feel about myself.)

21. Sickness can be a product of or caused by any number of special factors that implicate the person's biography and life habits as well as ethical/moral and spiritual status. (That I am sick may be due to many different things; my healer will make it clear how the conduct of my life and the conditions of my body and past life could be causing my sickness.)

E. Modern European societies

1. Knowledge structures of biomedicine operate as powerful scripts that program illness and healing, constituting sickness as a physically altered condition of the person brought about by objective, mechanical, ontologically separated disease objects that alter/disturb physiology; the condition of sickness as disease is thus rendered a discrete entity, concrete in its properties and knowable, explainable, and curable naturalistically. (The science of medicine tells me that my illness is a result of specific physical changes in my body organs and systems brought on by a specific disease entity that can be diagnosed and treated effectively.)

2. Biomedicine becomes the dominant ideology/tradition in society and is sponsored, certified, and regulated by the state. Principles of biomedicine are implemented as social policy; biomedical principles regulate social life. (What the science of medicine teaches about disease is the final word about sickness, and this is the reason the government sponsors research and doctors urge the right kind of health practices.)

3. Options and resources of healing are greatly expanded by the creation of medical specialties based on physiological systems and types of disease under the governance of biomedical sciences. (There exist many different types of doctors and specialists who deal with specific types of diseases; what kind of symptoms I have or what kind of disease I have determines from whom I seek help.)

4. Sickness and healing become fully secularized; the spiritual component of sickness/healing is disallowed; sickness is rationalized, objectified, and materialized in concrete terms. (Sickness is really due to physical disease changes in the body and is not a spiritual or religious matter; there are specific physical causes of disease.)

5. Sickness is transformed into expressions of disease objects having defined natural histories and standardized treatment protocols under the control of physicians. (If I follow my doctor's orders regarding medical treatment, then my disease will be controlled/cured.)

6. The full control, prediction, and elimination of disease become possible social realities pertaining to sickness and healing; the burden, suffering, and outcome of sickness is balanced by great optimism regarding the scope and possibilities of biomedicine. (The march of science will eventually make most diseases a thing of the past, and thus sickness and getting ill will be much less common.)

7. The existential annihilation/despair linked to a condition of sickness becomes meliorated and blurred; great optimism is associated with individual states of sickness. (Sickness is something that can be understood and cured; my sickness interferes with my life, but as a worthy person I am not discredited because I am sick; I am confident that although I am sick, the cause of my condition will be found and treated successfully.)

8. The causes and experiences associated with sickness become focused on and limited to the individual, and in this sense sickness can be said to become individualized; the conduct of healing also becomes individualized; the "doctor-patient" relationship becomes exclusive, determinate, and contractual. (Sickness is a result of the way my body is functioning and what physical causes are operating; sickness is my business, and if I put myself in my doctor's hands [i.e., follow my doctor's advice and cooperate with him] I will get well.)

9. Physicians are defined as technical/scientific experts and acquire full autonomy and power as arbiters of (i.e., validate) sickness;

they dominate dialogues of sickness/healing; they are accorded full responsibility for the outcome of sickness; their role as advisers on health/well-being diminishes. (My doctor always knows best, and I should always follow his or her advice if I intend to get well; doctors are scientific experts in the way the body functions.)

10. Sick persons become dependent "patients" and full "consumers" of physicians' services/products; in theory, they begin to acquire formal, socially validated, and legal rights to blame physicians in the event of failures. (The right kind of doctoring should be able to make me well, and if I do not get well it could be/is my doctor's fault.)

11. The cost of sickness and healing is transferred to third-party organizations, including the state. (The cost of my treatment is something I need not worry too much about as someone/somebody/my insurance/the government will take care of it.)

12. Sickness (and the "sick role") becomes the object of social regulation, with the state an important and influential agency operating through the surveillance of physicians who determine what constitutes illness and wellness; a model of illness is stipulated by the mechanism of disease that underlies it; motivations for illness become possible options that are identifiable as disvalued features of the self that are defended, denied, and rendered transparent or opaque depending on specifics of the doctor-patient relationship; motivations for illness and sickness as well as wellness become negotiable via the intercession of physicians. (I am not supposed to stay sick and I should cooperate with my doctor and get well; my doctor will tell me when I am well and can go back to work/ resume my usual activities; I am told by my doctor that I am not really ill [i.e., diseased]; I have an obligation to see a doctor and follow his or her advice.)

13. The mind/body dualism is crucial in identifying types of illness. (Physical bodily symptoms are due to body diseases, whereas emotional symptoms and problems in making decisions and coping are due to mental problems/illnesses.)

14. Mental illness as insanity/madness is important, but there is significant broadening of the meaning of mental illness with the development/expansion of the discipline/specialty of psychiatry; the somatization component of sickness becomes highly valorized; psychologization of sickness is denigrated; psychosomatic illnesses and diseases become distinct entities, objects of psychiatric intervention. (If I have physical symptoms I am really ill, but if I have

mental symptoms it is doubtful that I am really ill and it may be my fault; if I have mental symptoms this means I am mentally ill and might have to see a psychiatrist; physical diseases are real and mental/emotional problems are suspect, reflect a failure/weakness on my part.)

F. Postmodern societies

1. Persons are highly informed of technical advances in medicine as biomedical knowledge becomes public knowledge through expansion of communications and health promotion industries. (The news keeps me informed as to the latest developments in medicine that are approved by the government.)

2. Persons and families have a plethora of options pertaining to health and well-being; physician specialty types expand, holistic physicians and practitioners of alternative systems proliferate, and health extension industries create options and promote new opportunities for self-healing. (How to stay healthy and heal the body and mind is important, and there exist many ways of accomplishing this; determining what is the best medical advice is difficult since there are many ways of doing this and some ways are at odds with others.)

3. State and economic institutions reinforce the centrality of health and personal responsibility for the causation of illness; sickness is thus constituted partially as self-victimization and hence the self can be and is blamed for conditions of illness and impaired health. (If I get ill it is partly my fault; the right kind of living will keep me healthy; I should follow the known rules and practices for staying healthy and living a long life.)

4. Passivity, dependence, and helplessness associated with sickness are blunted, discouraged, and eschewed as sick persons are held more accountable for their state of health; failures and limitations of physicians are magnified and rendered objects of condemnation; trust in physicians diminishes; litigation surrounding the efforts of physicians and consequences of healing becomes a prominent recourse. (It is up to me to stay healthy; doctors are not perfect and make mistakes; doctors are mainly interested in curing and doing procedures; I should get a second opinion to check if what that doctor says is right; who knows best is sometimes difficult to determine since doctors differ in what they think is best.)

5. Persons acquire awareness that illness (as biomedically validated) must have a disease state to explain it; state and economic institutions using knowledge structures of biomedicine begin to stipulate

the valid configurations of illness (what will count as a legitimate and reimbursable sickness picture); thus the self or the immediate social group no longer can fully validate states of sickness, only the physician and ultimately the state acquire this power; paradoxically, the self is a more knowledgeable, more active consumer but judged less truthful by the official Institution of medicine (i.e., as personified by physicians and third-party and state operatives). (The doctors say that my symptoms are not due to a real physical disease; apparently, I do not have the right kind of symptoms that point to a real disease; the doctor seems to feel that I am not really ill; even though I feel ill, apparently I am not entitled to being sick [missing work]; in the final analysis, it is up to the doctors, the insurance companies, and the government to decide if I am really sick and deserve compensation/sick leave.)

6. Biomedical knowledge structures pertaining to health, sickness, and healing become highly elaborated, easily communicated and learned, and highly influential in regulating social life. (By reading magazines and hearing/seeing the news I can stay up with the latest developments in medicine and learn about what to do to avoid those diseases that are possible given my age, social conditions, and lifestyle.)

7. The pursuit of health, the avoidance of illness, and the resort to healing are made features of self-definition and self-regulation and come to constitute personal civic religions. (Nothing is more important than one's health; I should/must eat right, take vitamins, avoid stress, and exercise regularly.)

8. Individual states of illness are less common and less feared and the self feels more empowered about their prevention/control; the experience of sickness becomes naturalized; yet paradoxically, sickness becomes defined as inherent in the human condition, universal, inevitable, immanent, uncontrollable. (Not feeling right and developing an illness is common and nothing to worry about as there are medicines that will make one feel better and get over illness; illnesses and diseases will never be eliminated; with changes in the way people live, new industrial products/hazards, and the possibility of cancers and new infections, getting ill is always a possibility; diseases and the problems of aging are inevitable.)

9. Sickness and healing, like health/well-being, are experienced as material/mechanical conditions and processes that the self has more control over, hence they are more fully commercialized and commodified. (My body is like a machine that I should be able to control; I should be able to control the way my body functions and,

hence, whether I get sick; by buying the right kind of foods, taking the right kind of vitamin supplements, and exercising in a rational way I can stay healthy; there are special ways to relax and avoid/cope with stress and stay mentally healthy; the right kind of living will keep me healthy.)

10. Limits of the biomedical enterprise in controlling and eliminating disease are widely appreciated. (There is just so much that the science of medicine can do; doctors do not necessarily know all there is to know about disease and treatment; doctors are more interested in disease than in health.)

11. The domain of sickness and healing expands to include attributes of physical appearance, personality, and behavior. (My appearance and behavior can be controlled by using doctors or following the advice of medical/health practitioners; whatever bothers me should be able to be corrected by the right kind of advice/action; there are many ways to improve one's health and well-being.)

12. Benefits and possibilities of medical care are defined as limited and finite; the cost of healing becomes a dominant component of the experience of sickness; there is growing skepticism/pessimism about the power of biomedicine and the scope of its capacity to control sickness and health. (Not everybody can get the best kind of medical care since it is expensive and there are limited resources; some people, depending on their age/work/lifestyle/wealth will get special treatment when it comes to medical care; my insurance company may not pay for this treatment; what my medical insurance stipulates is what I can expect in the way of reimbursement; I realize that I am stuck with what is available to me in the way of medical care; the "sky is no longer the limit" when it comes to medical care.)

13. Persons seek new ways to validate illness and sickness and the capitalist health/medical industry correspondingly expands as alternative medical traditions, wellness pursuits, and life extension programs become important industries and sought-after enterprises that compete with biomedicine in the medical market; this contributes to the undermining of biomedicine as the official ideology pertaining to sickness; thus as physicians and the state begin to constrain the (valid) boundaries of sickness, alternative medical industries capitalize on the individual's awareness of illness and need for validation, providing new options and opportunities for sickness (i.e., a dialectical process affecting individual health needs and profit [societally/culturally determined] imperatives). (There are many different ways of staying healthy; there are many different

types of healers and systems of medicine through which one can heal oneself; doctors are not the final word on health and illness; doctors are too concerned with giving drugs and doing procedures/surgery and do not emphasize prevention enough; doctors have a closed mind when it comes to understanding how people can stay healthy.)

14. Health/wellness industries provide alternatives of and for sickness; possibilities for sickness also increase as the boundaries of sickness/healing become blurred and inchoate; cosmetic surgery, elective treatments, and lifestyle parameters are medicalized; physiologies become programmable; personalities and lifestyles become manipulable. (Health and wellness is everybody's business and following the right kind of living style will keep me healthy, and protect me and afford a long life; I can keep my body functioning right by following the right kind of diet and controlling my level of stress.)

15. The proliferation of "official" biomedical knowledge and knowledge structures of alternative medical/wellness traditions profoundly increases the items of relevant medical information (the number of potentially relevant healmemes); the validity of items of medical information is subject to variation and change and is highly contested; the maintenance of health, the prevention of disease, and the pursuit of healing become highly problematized. (The way medical knowledge changes, it is hard to know exactly what is best for one's health; I know my diet is important, but it is hard to know what is the "right" diet anymore; I am confused as to what exactly is the best course of action with respect to staying healthy; I think a chiropractor can help, but doctors say they could actually do harm.)

16. Bioethical implications of "healing" pertaining to the materialization of body parts/functions and alteration of states of sickness loom as social and psychological dilemmas that confuse and create ambiguities about the meaning of sickness, health, well-being, and the valid and ethically justifiable beginning and end of life. (If I need it, I could get a heart/liver transplant; I can have my wrinkles removed if I want to (or get a hair transplant); under what conditions I want to stay/be maintained alive is a worry for me; I want to know the sex and health of my fetus before I decide whether to keep it; I need to think about the way I want to die.)

17. The script of official biomedical healing becomes public and visible as the state and professional and private/lay organizations be-

gin to sponsor efforts aimed at standardizing medical practice and defining the boundaries, limits, and rationing of biomedicine. (By checking the guidelines set aside for my disease by the government/insurance company, I can determine if the doctor is giving me the right kind of treatment.)

18. Persons become highly rational and challenge the authority of physicians; health extension/wellness industries actively compete with and challenge the biomedical industry. (I have to look after my health because doctors can only treat disease and give drugs/ do procedures/surgeries; by reading health reports and staying informed about "new" developments regarding sickness and health maintenance, I can look after myself best.)

19. Persons mentally ill experience and anticipate less social stigma, as mental illnesses and mental health problems become more naturalized and regularized components of sickness and healing; many emotional problems associated with medical diseases and mental illnesses become increasingly medicalized, more strictly controlled by the medical professions; psychiatry as a medical specialty narrows and contracts to a neurobiological emphasis. Correspondingly, there occurs an expansion in lay support groups and alternative mental/emotional therapies for help with psychological problems associated with medical illnesses and eating/alcohol disorders and specific disease support groups. (I have a psychiatric illness and I am being treated with medications for this; mental illnesses are like other illnesses; doctors tend to see the worries and conflicts about having a disease as problems also requiring medicines; if I need help and information for coping with my disease or life problems, I know I can attend an appropriate support group.)

20. In official biomedicine, the doctor-patient relationship becomes less exclusive; the "quality of doctoring" becomes identified as a determinant feature of medical practice that is desirable and important but interpreted in terms of the meaning of officially stipulated standards of treatment protocols and minimal competencies of practice; relationship with a specific physician becomes less central and groups of affiliated physicians become identified as units of healing. (I would like to have a caring doctor, but the one my group/insurance stipulates will have to do; I will have to depend more on formal practice arrangements to get my treatment; so long as I am a member of a good provider group I am well cared for; my health/medical care with doctors depends less on what I may want and more on what my insurance/employer/government makes available.)

References

Abbott, A. 1988. *The System of Professions: An Essay on the Division of Expert Labor.* Chicago: University of Chicago Press.

Ackerknecht, E. H. 1942a. Problems of primitive medicine. *Bulletin of the History of Medicine* 11: 503–521.

———. 1942b. Primitive medicine and culture pattern. *Bulletin of the History of Medicine* 12: 545–574.

———. 1945a. On the collecting of data concerning primitive medicine. *American Anthropologist* 47: 432–437.

———. 1945b. Primitive medicine. *New York Academy of Sciences, Transactions* 2(8): 26–37.

———. 1946a. Natural diseases and rational treatment in primitive medicine. *Bulletin of the History of Medicine* 19: 467–497.

———. 1946b. Contradictions in primitive surgery. *Bulletin of the History of Medicine* 20: 184–187.

Alexander, R. D. 1979. *Darwinism and Human Affairs.* Seattle: University of Washington Press, 197–277.

Alland, A. 1967. *Evolution and Human Behavior.* New York: Natural History Press.

———. 1970. *Adaptation in Cultural Evolution: An Approach to Medical Anthropology.* New York: Columbia University Press.

Amundsen, D. W. 1977. Medical deontology and pestilential disease in the late Middle Ages. *Journal of the History of Medicine* 23: 403–442.

Armelagos, G. J., T. Leatherman, M. Ryan, and L. Sibley. 1992. Biocultural synthesis in medical anthropology. *Medical Anthropology* 14: 35–52.

Axelrod, R. 1984. *The Evolution of Cooperation.* New York: Basic Books.

Baechler, J., J. A. Hall, and M. Mann. 1988. *Europe and the Rise of Capitalism.* New York: Basil Blackwell.

Bailey, R. C. 1991. The behavioral ecology of Efe Pygmy men in the Iture Forest, Zaire.

Anthropological Papers, Museum of Anthropology, no. 86. Ann Arbor: University of Michigan.

Barkow, J. H. 1989. *Darwin, Sex, and Status: Biological Approaches to Mind and Culture.* Toronto: University of Toronto Press.

Barkow, J. H., L. Cosmides, and J. Tooby. 1992. *The Adapted Mind: Evolutionary Psychology and the Generation of Culture.* New York: Oxford University Press.

Barnard, A. 1992. *Hunters and Herders of Southern Africa: A Comparative Ethnography of the Khoisan Peoples.* Cambridge: Cambridge University Press.

Batson, C. D. 1987. Prosocial motivation: Is it every truly altruistic? *Advances in Experimental Social Psychology* 20: 65–122.

Bellah, R. 1964. Religious evolution. *American Social Review* 29: 358–374.

Berger, P. L., B. Berger, and H. Kellner. 1973. *The Homeless Mind: Modernization and Consciousness.* New York: Vintage Books.

Berman, H. 1983. *Law and Revolution: The Formation of the Western Legal Tradition.* Cambridge: Harvard University Press.

Berrios. G. E. 1984. The psychopathology of affectivity: Conceptual and historical aspects. *Psychological Medicine* 14: 303–313.

———. 1988. Depressive and manic states during the nineteenth century. In A. Georgotas and R. Canero, eds., *Depression and Mania,* 13–25. New York: Elsevier.

Bickerton, D. 1981. *Roots of Language.* Ann Arbor: Karoma.

———. 1990. *Language and Species.* Chicago: University of Chicago Press.

———. 1995. *Language and Human Behavior.* Seattle: University of Washington Press.

Bizon, Z. 1976. The adaptation patterns of the medical system and social change. In M. Sokolowska, J. Holowka, and A. Ostrowska, eds., *Health, Medicine, Society,* 331–342. Boston: D. Reidel.

Black, F. I. 1975. Infectious diseases in primitive societies. *Science* 187: 515–518.

Bodewitz, H. F. H. W., H. Buurma, and G. H. deVries. 1989. Regulatory science and the social management of trust in medicine. In W. E. Bijker, T. P. Hughes, and T. Pinch, eds., *The Social Construction of Technological Systems: New Directions in the Sociology and History of Technology,* 5th ed., 243–259. Cambridge: MIT Press.

Boesch, C. 1992. New elements of a theory of mind in wild chimpanzees. *Brain and Behavioral Sciences* 15(1): 149–150.

Bourdieu, P. 1977. *Outline of a Theory of Practice.* London: Cambridge University Press.

Boyd, R., and P. Richerson. 1985. *Culture and the Evolutionary Process.* Chicago: University of Chicago Press.

Boyden, S. 1987. *Western Civilization in Biological Perspective: Patterns in Biohistory.* Oxford: Clarendon Press.

Boyden, S. V., ed. 1970. *The Impact of Civilization on the Biology of Man.* Toronto: University of Toronto Press, Australian Academy of Science.

Brothers, L. 1989. A biological perspective on empathy. *American Journal of Psychiatry* 146(1): 10–19.

———. 1990. The neural basis of primate social communication. *Motivation and Emotion* 14(2): 81–91.

Brown, D. E. 1991. *Human Universals.* Philadelphia: Temple University Press.

Brown, F. C. 1972. *Hallucinogenic Drugs.* Springfield: C. C. Thomas.

Bullough, V. L. 1966. *The Development of Medicine as a Profession*. New York: Hafner.

Butterfield, H. 1965. *The Origins of Modern Science*. New York: Free Press.

Bynum, W. F., and R. Porter. 1987. *Medical Fringe and Medical Orthodoxy*. London: Croom Helm.

Caldwell, M. C., and D. K. Caldwell. 1966. Epimeletic (caregiving) behavior in cetaceans. In K. Norris, ed., *Whales, Dolphins and Porpoises: International Symposium on Cetacean Research*, 755–785. Berkeley: University of California Press.

Campbell, D. T. 1965. Variation and selective retention in sociocultural evolution. In H. R. Barringer, G. I. Blanksten, and R. W. Mack, eds., *Social Change in Developing Areas: A Reinterpretation of Evolutionary Theory*, 19–49. Cambridge: Schenkman.

———. 1975. On the conflicts between biological and social evolution and between psychology and moral tradition. *American Psychologist* (December): 1103–1126.

Castel, R. 1986. *The Regulation of Madness*. Trans. W. D. Halls. Berkeley: University of California Press.

Chagnon, N. A. 1977. *Yanomamo: The Fierce People*, 2d ed. New York: Holt, Rinehart and Winston.

———. 1992. *Yanomamo: The Last Days of Eden*. San Diego: Harcourt Brace Jovanovich.

Chagnon, N. A., P. LeQuesne, and J. M. Cook. 1971. Yanomamo hallucinogens: Anthropological, botanical, and chemical findings. *Current Anthropology* 12: 72–73.

Chase, P. G., and H. L. Dibble. 1987. Middle paleolithic symbolism: A review of current evidence and interpretations. *Journal of Anthropological Archaeology* 6: 263–296.

Cheney, D. L., and R. M. Seyfarth. 1990. *How Monkeys See the World*. Chicago: University of Chicago Press.

Chiu, M. L. 1990. "Mind, Body, and Illness in a Chinese Medical Tradition" (UMI Dissertation Information Service). Ann Arbor: University of Michigan Microfilms International.

Cipolla, C. M. 1976. *Public Health and the Medical Profession in the Renaissance*. Cambridge: Cambridge University Press.

Clark, M. J. 1981. The rejection of psychological approaches to mental disorders in late nineteenth-century British psychiatry. In A. Scull, ed., *Madhouses, Mad-Doctors and Madmen*, 271–312. Philadelphia: University of Pennsylvania Press.

Clayton, D. H., and N. D. Wolfe. 1993. The adaptive significance of self-medication. *Trends in Ecology and Evolution* 8(2): 60–63.

Cockburn, T. A. 1971. Infectious diseases in ancient populations. *Current Anthropology* 12: 45–62.

Cohen, H. 1961. The evolution of the concept of disease. In B. Lush, ed., *Concepts of Medicine*, 159–169. New York: Pergamon Press.

Cohen, M. N. 1989. *Health and the Rise of Civilization*. New Haven: Yale University Press.

Cohen, M. N., and G. J. Armelagos, eds. 1984. *Paleopathology at the Origins of Agriculture*. New York: Academic Press.

Cohen, S., and A. Scull. 1983. *Social Control and the State*. New York: St. Martin's Press.

Cohn-Haft, L. 1956. *The Public Physicians of Ancient Greece.* Smith College Studies in History.

Collins, R. 1988. *Theoretical Sociology.* San Diego: Harcourt Brace Jovanovich.

Connor, R. C., and R. A. Smolker. 1990. Quantitative description of a rare event: A bottlenose dolphin's behavior toward her deceased offspring. *The Bottlenose Dolphin,* 355–360. New York: Academic Press.

Conrad, P., and J. W. Schneider. 1980. *Deviance and Medicalization.* New York: Merril.

Cook, H. J. 1986. *The Decline of the Old Medical Regime in Stuart London.* Ithaca: Cornell University Press.

———. 1994. Good advice and little medicine: The professional authority of early modern English physicians. *Journal of British Studies* 33: 1–31.

Cooter, R. 1988. *Studies in the History of Alternative Medicine.* New York: St. Martin's Press.

Craig, K. D., S. A. Hyden, and C. J. Patrick. 1991. Genuine, suppressed and faked facial behavior during exacerbation of chronic low back pain. *Pain* 46: 161–171.

Craig, K. D., K. M. Prkachin, and R. V. E. Grunau. 1992. The facial expression of pain. In D. C. Turk and R. Metruck, eds., *Handbook of Pain Assessment,* 257–274. New York: Guilford.

Craig, T. K. J., A. P. Boardman, K. Mills, O. Daly-Jones, and H. Drake. 1993. The south London somatization study. I: Longitudinal course and influence of early life experiences. *British Journal of Psychiatry* 163: 579–588.

Cripriani, L., D. Cox, and L. Cole. 1966. *The Andaman Islanders.* London: Weidenfeld and Nicolson.

Crone, P. 1989. *Pre-Industrial Societies.* Cambridge: Basil Blackwell.

Crosby, A. W., Jr. 1972. *The Columbian Exchange: Biological and Cultural Consequences of 1492.* Westport, Conn.: Greenwood Press.

Damasio, A. R. 1994. *Descartes' Error: Emotion, Reason, and the Human Brain.* New York: G. P. Putnam's Sons.

D'Andrade, R. G. 1984. Cultural meaning systems. In R. A. Shweder and R. A. Levine, eds., *Culture Theory: Essays on Mind, Self, Emotion,* 89–108. Cambridge: Cambridge University Press.

Darwin, C. 1869. *On the Origin of the Species by Means of Natural Selection, or the Preservation of Favored Races in the Struggle for Life.* London: John Murray.

Davidson, I., and W. Noble. 1989. The archeology of perception: Traces of depiction and language. *Current Anthropology* 30(2): 125–155.

Dawkins, R. 1982. *The Extended Phenotype: The Long Reach of the Gene.* New York: Oxford University Press.

———. 1986. *The Blind Watchmaker.* New York: Norton.

———. 1989. *The Selfish Gene,* 2d ed. New York: Oxford University Press.

Dennett, D. C. 1987. *The International Stance.* Cambridge, Mass.: MIT Press.

———. 1995. *Darwin's Dangerous Idea: Evolution and the Meanings of Life.* New York: Simon & Schuster.

de Swann, A. 1988. *In Care of the State.* New York: Oxford University Press.

de Waal, F. 1982. *Chimpanzee Politics: Power and Sex among Apes.* Baltimore: Johns Hopkins University Press.

———. 1986. Deception in the natural communication of chimpanzees. In R. W. Mitchell and N. S. Thompson, eds., *Deception: Perspectives on Human and Non-Human Deceit,* 221–244. Albany: State University of New York Press.

——. 1989. *Peacemaking among Primates.* Cambridge: Harvard University Press.

——. 1996. *Good Natured.* Cambridge, Mass.: Harvard University Press.

DeWoskin, K. J. 1983. *Doctors, Diviners, and Magicians of Ancient China: Biographies of Fang-shih.* New York: Columbia University Press.

Dibble, H. L., and P. Mellars. 1992. *The Middle Paleolithic: Adaptation, Behavior and Variability.* University Museum Symposium Series, vol. 4. Philadelphia: University Museum, University of Pennsylvania.

Dobkin de Rios, M., and M. Winkelman. 1989. Shamanism and altered states of consciousness: An introduction. *Journal of Psychoactive Drugs* 21(1): 1–7.

Doerner, K. 1981. *Madmen and the Bourgeoisie: A Social History of Insanity and Psychiatry.* Oxford: Basil Blackwell.

Dols, M. W. 1984a. Insanity in Byzantine and Islamic medicine. In J. Scarborough, ed., *Symposium on Byzantine Medicine,* 135–148. Washington, D.C.: Dumbarton Oaks Papers, no. 38.

——. 1984b. *Medieval Islamic Medicine.* Berkeley: University of California Press.

——. 1987. Insanity and its treatment in Islamic society. *Medicine in History* 31: 1–14.

Donald, M. 1991. *Origins of the Modern Mind: Three Stages in the Evolution of Culture and Cognition.* Cambridge, Mass.: Harvard University Press.

Dube, K. C. 1978. Nosology and therapy of mental illness in Ayurveda. *Comparative Medicine East and West* 6: 209–228.

Dunn, F. L. 1965. On the antiquity of malaria in the Western Hemisphere. *Human Biology* 37: 385–393.

——. 1968. Epidemiological factors: Health and disease in hunter-gatherers. In R. B. Lee and I. DeVore, eds., *Man the Hunter,* 221–228. Chicago: Aldine.

——. 1976. Traditional Asian medicine and cosmopolitan medicine as adaptive systems. In C. Leslie, ed., *Asian Medical Systems: A Comparative Study,* 138–158. Berkeley: University of California Press.

Durham, W. H. 1991. *Coevolution: Genes, Culture, and Human Diversity.* Stanford: Stanford University Press.

Eaton, S. B., and M. Konner. 1985. Paleolithic nutrition: A consideration of its nature and current implications. *New England Journal of Medicine* 312(5): 283–289.

Eaton, S. B., M. Shostak, and M. Konner. 1988. *The Paleolithic Prescription: A Program of Diet and Exercise and a Design for Living.* New York: Harper and Row.

Eisenberg, L. 1977. Disease and illness: Distinctions between professional and popular ideas of sickness. *Culture, Medicine and Psychiatry* 1: 9–24.

Eisenberg, N., and R. A. Fabes. 1990. Empathy: Conceptualization, measurement, and relation to prosocial behavior. *Motivation and Emotion* 14(2): 131–149.

Ekman, P., and W. V. Friesen. 1975. *Unmasking the Face: A Guide to Recognizing Emotions from Facial Clues.* Englewood Cliffs, N.J.: Prentice-Hall.

Ekman, P., W. V. Friesen, and P. Ellsworth. 1972. *Emotion in the Human Face.* New York: Pergamon Press.

Elias, N. 1978. *The Civilizing Process.* Oxford: Blackwell.

Elkin, A. P. 1977. *Aboriginal Men of High Degree.* St. Lucia, Queensland, Australia: University of Queensland Press.

Endicott, K. 1979. *Batek Negrito Religion.* Oxford: Clarendon Press.

Engel, G. 1977. The need for a new medical model: A challenge for biomedicine. *Science* 196: 129–136.

Evans-Pritchard, E. E. 1940. *The Nuer.* Oxford: Clarendon Press.

———. 1956. *Nuer Religion.* Oxford: Clarendon Press.

Fabrega, H., Jr. 1974. *Disease and Social Behavior: An Interdisciplinary Perspective.* Cambridge: MIT Press.

———. 1975. The need for an ethnomedical science. *Science* 189: 969–975.

———. 1976a. The biological significance of taxonomies of disease. *Journal of Theoretical Biology* 63: 191–216.

———. 1976b. Towards a theory of human disease. *Journal of Nervous and Mental Disease* 162: 299–312.

———. 1976c. The function of medical-care systems: A logical analysis. *Perspectives in Biology and Medicine* 20: 108–119.

———. 1977. Disease viewed as a symbolic category. In H. T. Engelhardt and S. F. Spicker, eds., *Mental Health: Philosophical Perspectives,* 79–106. Boston: D. Reidel.

———. 1979a. The scientific usefulness of the idea of illness. *Perspectives in Biology and Medicine* 22: 545–558.

———. 1979b. Elementary systems of medicine. *Culture, Medicine and Psychiatry* 23: 167–198.

———. 1979c. Neurobiology, culture and behavior disturbances: An integrated review. *Journal of Nervous and Mental Disease* 168: 467–474.

———. 1981a. Culture, biology and the study of disease. In H. Rothschild, ed., *Biocultural Aspects of Disease,* 53–94. New York: Academic Press.

———. 1981b. Cultural programming of brain behavior relations. In J. Merikangas, ed., *Brain, Behavior Relationships,* 1–63. Boston: Lexington Books.

———. 1989a. Language, culture and the neurobiology of pain: A theoretical exploration. *Behavioral Neurology* 2: 235–259.

———. 1989b. Cultural relativism and psychiatric illness. *Journal of Nervous and Mental Disease* 177: 415–424.

———. 1989c. An ethnomedical perspective of Anglo-American psychiatry. *American Journal of Psychiatry* 146: 588–596.

———. 1990a. Psychiatric stigma in the classical and medieval period: A review of the literature. *Comprehensive Psychiatry* 31(4): 289–306.

———. 1990b. The concept of somatization as a cultural and historical product of Western medicine. *Psychosomatic Medicine* 52: 653–672.

———. 1990c. An ethnomedical perspective of medical ethics. *Journal of Medicine and Philosophy* 15: 593–625.

———. 1991a. Psychiatric stigma in non-Western societies. *Comprehensive Psychiatry* 2: 534–551.

———. 1991b. The culture and history of psychiatric stigma in early modern and modern Western societies: A review of literature. *Comprehensive Psychiatry* 32: 97–119.

———. 1992a. The role of culture in a theory of psychiatric illness. *Social Science and Medicine* 35(1): 91–103.

———. 1992b. Culture and the psychosomatic tradition. *Psychosomatic Medicine* 54(5): 561–566.

———. 1993a. Towards a social theory of psychiatric phenomena. *Behavioral Science* 38: 75–100.

————. 1993b. A cultural analysis of human behavioral breakdowns: An approach to the ontology and epistemology of psychiatric phenomena. *Culture, Medicine and Psychiatry* 17: 99–132.

Fabrega, H., Jr., and D. Silver. 1973. *Illness and Shamanistic Curing in Zinacantan: An Ethnomedical Analysis.* Stanford: Stanford University Press.

Farquhar, J. 1987. Problems of knowledge in contemporary Chinese medical discourse. *Social Science and Medicine* 24: 1013–1021.

————. 1992. Time and text: Approaching Chinese medical practice through analysis of a published case. In C. Leslie and A. Young, eds., *Paths to Asian Medical Knowledge,* 62–73. Berkeley: University of California Press.

————. 1994. *Knowing Practice: The Clinical Encounter of Chinese Medicine.* Boulder, Colo.: Westview Press.

Fiennes, R. N. T.-W. 1978. *The Environment of Man.* New York: St. Martin's Press.

Filliozat, J. 1964. *The Classical Doctrine of Indian Medicine: Its Origins and Its Greek Parallels.* Delhi: Navchetan Press.

Foucault, M. 1965. *Madness and Civilization. A History of Insanity in the Age of Reason.* New York: Random House.

Fox, N. A. 1989. Psychophysiological correlates of emotional reactivity during the first year of life. *Developmental Psychology* 25(3): 364–372.

Fox, R. C. 1988a. Medical evolution. In *Essays in Medical Sociology,* 499–531. New Brunswick: Transaction.

————. 1988b. The evolution of medical uncertainty. In *Essays in Medical Sociology,* 533–571. New Brunswick: Transaction.

Frankel, S. 1986. *The Huli Response to Illness.* New York: Cambridge University Press.

Frankenberg, R. 1980. Medical anthropology: A theoretical perspective. *Social Science and Medicine* 14b(4): 197–207.

————. 1986. Sickness as cultural performance? Aroma, trajectory, and pilgrimage root metaphors and making of social disease. *International Journal of Health Services* 16: 603–626.

Freidson, E. 1970. *Profession of Medicine: A Study of the Sociology of Applied Knowledge.* New York: Dodd, Mead.

Fried, M. H. 1967. *The Evolution of Political Society: An Essay in Political Anthropology.* New York: Random House.

Furst, P. F., ed. 1972. *Flesh of the Gods: The Ritual Use of Hallucinogens.* New York: Praeger.

Gallup, G. G., Jr. 1970. Chimpanzees: Self-recognition. *Science* 167: 86–87.

————. 1985. Do minds exist in species other than our own? *Neuroscience and Behavioral Reviews* 9: 631–641.

————. 1991. Toward a comparative psychology of self-awareness. In G. R. Goethals and J. Strauss, eds., *The Self: An Interdisciplinary Approach.* New York: Springer-Verlag.

Gamble, C. 1993. *Timewalkers: The Prehistory of Global Colonization.* Cambridge, Mass.: Harvard University Press.

Garcia, J., W. G. Hankins, and K. W. Rusiniak. 1974. Behavioral regulation of the milieu interne in man and rat: Food preferences set by delayed visceral effects facilitate memory research and predator control. *Science* 185: 824–831.

Garcia-Ballester, L., M. R. McVaugh, and A. Rubio-Vela. 1989. *Medical Licensing and Learning in Fourteenth-Century Valencia.* Transactions of the American Philosophical Society, vol. 79, pt. 6.

Garland, D. 1985. *Punishment & Welfare: A History of Penal Strategies.* Brookfield: Gower.

———. 1990. *Punishment and Modern Society.* Chicago: University of Chicago Press.

Garrison, F. H. 1929. *An Introduction to the History of Medicine,* 4th ed. Philadelphia: W. B. Saunders.

Geertz, C. 1973. *The Interpretation of Cultures.* New York: Basic Books.

Geist, V. 1978. *Life Strategies, Human Evolution, Environmental Design.* New York: Springer.

Gelfand, T. 1980. *Professionalizing Modern Medicine: Paris Surgeons and Medical Science and Institutions in the Eighteenth Century.* Westport, Conn.: Greenwood Press.

Gellner, E. 1989. *Plough, Sword and Book.* Chicago: University of Chicago Press.

Gibson, K. R., and T. Ingold. 1993. *Tools, Language and Cognition in Human Evolution.* Cambridge: Cambridge University Press.

Giddens, A. 1984. *The Constitution of Society: Outline of the Theory of Structuration.* Berkeley and Los Angeles: University of California Press.

———. 1990. *The Consequences of Modernity.* Stanford: Stanford University Press.

———. 1991. *Modernity and Self-Identity: Self and Society in the Late Modern Age.* Stanford: Stanford University Press.

Giles, D. E., H. P. Roffwarg, D. J. Kupfer, A. J. Rush, M. M. Biggs, and B. A. Etzel. 1989. Secular trend in unipolar depression: A hypothesis. *Journal of Affective Disorders* 16: 71–75.

Glick, L. B. 1963. Foundations of a primitive medical system: The Gimi of the New Guinea highlands. Ph.D. dissertation, University of Pennsylvania.

Golub, E. S. 1994. *The Limits of Medicine: How Science Shapes Our Hope for the Cure.* New York: Times Books.

Good, B. 1977. The heart of what is the matter: The semantics of illness in Iran. *Culture, Medicine and Psychiatry* 1: 25–58.

Goodall, J. 1986. *The Chimpanzees of Gombe: Patterns of Behavior.* Cambridge: Belknap Press.

Goody, J. 1977. *The Domestication of the Savage Mind.* Cambridge: Cambridge University Press.

———. 1986. *The Logic of Writing and the Organization of Society.* Cambridge: Cambridge University Press.

———. 1987. *The Interface Between the Written and the Oral.* Cambridge: Cambridge University Press.

Gould, S. J., and R. C. Lewontin. 1979. The spandrels of San Marco and the Panglossian paradigm: A critique of the adaptationist programme. *Proceedings of the Royal Society of London* 205: 581–598.

Grob, C., and M. Dobkin de Rios. 1992. Adolescent drug use in cross-cultural perspective. *Journal of Drug Issues* 22(1): 121–138.

Guarnaccia, P. J. 1990. A critical review of epidemiological studies of Puerto Rican mental health. *American Journal of Psychiatry* 147: 1449–1456.

Gurevich, A. 1995. *The Origins of European Individualism.* Oxford: Blackwell.

Gwei-Djen, L., and J. Needham. 1980. *Celestial Lancets: A History and Rationale of Acupuncture and Moxa.* Cambridge: Cambridge University Press.

Hafner, H. 1985. Are mental disorders increasing over time? *Psychopathology* 18: 66–81.

Haldipur, C. V. 1984. Madness in ancient India: Concept of insanity in Charaka Samhita (1st Century A.D.). *Comprehensive Psychiatry* 25: 335–344.

Hallowell, A. I. 1965. Hominid evolution, cultural adaptation and mental dysfunctioning. In A. V. S. deRueck and R. Porter, eds. 1965. *CIBA Foundations Symposium on Transcultural Psychiatry,* 26–54. London: Churchill Press.

Hamburg, D. A. 1968. Emotions in the perspective of human evolution. In S. L. Washburn and P. C. Jay, eds., *Perspective on Human Evolution,* vol. 1, 246–257. New York: Holt, Rinehart and Winston.

Harner, M. J. 1973. *Hallucinogens and Shamanism.* New York: Oxford University Press.

Harris, M., and E. B. Ross. 1987. *Death, Sex, and Fertility: Population Regulation in Preindustrial and Developing Societies.* New York: Columbia University Press.

Hart, B. L. 1988. Biological bases of the behavior of sick animals. *Neuroscience and Biobehavioral Reviews* 12: 123–137.

———. 1990. Behavioral adaptations to pathogens and parasites: Five strategies. *Neuroscience and Biobehavioral Review* 14: 273–294.

Harwood, A. 1970. *Witchcraft, Sorcery, and Social Categories among the Safwa.* London: Oxford University Press.

Hechter, M., K.-D. Opp, and R. Wipoler. 1990. *Social Institutions: Their Emergence, Maintenance, and Effects.* New York: Aldine de Gruyter.

Herzlich, C., and J. Pierret. 1987. *Illness and Self in Society.* Baltimore: Johns Hopkins University Press.

Hodgson, G. M. 1993. *Economics and Evolution: Bringing Life Back into Economics.* Ann Arbor: University of Michigan Press.

Holmberg, A. R. 1969. *Nomads of the Long Bow: The Siriono of Eastern Bolivia.* Garden City: Published for the American Museum of Natural History by Natural History Press.

Howell, S. 1989. *Society and Cosmos.* Oxford: Oxford University Press.

Hudson, R. P. 1983. *Disease and Its Control: The Shaping of Modern Thought.* Westport, Conn.: Greenwood Press.

Huffman, M. A., and M. Siefu. 1989. Observations on the illness and consumption of a possibly medicinal plant *Vernonia amygdalin* by a wild chimpanzee in the Mahale Mountains National Park, Tanzania. *Primates* 30: 51–63.

Huffman, M. A., and R. W. Wrangham. 1994. Diversity of medicinal plant use by wild chimpanzees in the Wild. In P. G. Heltne and L. A. Marquardt, eds., *Chimpanzee Cultures,* 129–148. Cambridge: Harvard University Press.

Ingold, T. 1993. Tool-use, sociality and intelligence. In K. Gibson and T. Ingold, eds., *Tools, Language and Cognition in Human Evolution,* 429–445. Cambridge: Cambridge University Press.

Jackendoff, R. 1994. *Patterns in the Mind: Language and Human Nature.* New York: Basic Books.

Jackson, S. 1986. *Melancholia and Depression.* New Haven: Yale University Press.

———. 1988. Introduction. In W. Pargeter, ed., *Observations on Maniacal Disorders,* ix–xi. New York: Routledge.

Jacquart, D., and C. Thomasset. 1988. *Sexuality and Medicine in the Middle Ages.* Cambridge: Polity Press.

Jacyna, L. S. 1982. Somatic theories of mind and the interests of medicine in Britain, 1850–1879. *Medical History* 26: 233–258.

Janzen, D. H. 1978. Complications in interpreting the chemical defenses of trees against tropical arboreal plant-eating vertebrates. In G. G. Montgomery, ed., *The Ecology of Arboreal Felivores,* 73–84. Washington, D.C.: Smithsonian Institution Press.

Janzen, J. M. 1978a. *The Quest for Therapy in Lower Zaire.* Berkeley: University of California Press.

———. 1978b. The comparative study of medical systems as changing social systems. *Social Science and Medicine* 12: 121–133.

Jenkins, J. H. 1988. Ethnopsychiatric interpretations of schizophrenic illness: The problem of nervios within Mexican-American families. *Culture, Medicine and Psychiatry* 12: 301–329.

Jewson, N. 1974. Medical knowledge and the patronage system in eighteenth-century England. *Sociology* 8: 369–385.

Johns, T. 1990. *With Bitter Herbs They Shall Eat It: Chemical Ecology and the Origins of Human Diet and Medicine.* Tucson: University of Arizona Press.

Johnson, A. W., and T. Earle. 1991. *The Evolution of Human Societies: From Foraging Group to Agrarian State.* Stanford: Stanford University Press.

Johnson, R. H. 1982. Foodsharing behavior in captive Amazon River dolphins. *Cetology* 43: 1–2.

Johnson, T. M., and C. F. Sargent, eds. 1990. *Medical Anthropology: Contemporary Theory and Method.* New York: Praeger.

Jones, C. 1980. The treatment of the insane in eighteenth- and early nineteenth-century Montpelier: A contribution to the prehistory of the lunatic asylum in Provincial France. *Medical History* 24: 371–390.

Jones, E. L. 1987. *The European Miracle.* Cambridge: Cambridge University Press.

Jones, K. 1972. *A History of the Mental Health Services.* London: Routledge and Kegan Paul.

Jones, R. T., N. Benowitz, and J. Bachman. 1976. Chronic cannabes use: Clinical studies of cannabes tolerance and dependence. In R. L. Dornbush, A. M. Freedman, and M. Fink, eds., *Annals of the New York Academy of Science* 282: 221–239.

Kakar, S. 1982. *Shamans, Mystics and Doctors: A Psychological Inquiry into India and Its Healing Traditions.* Boston: Beacon Press.

Karlin, C., and M. Julien. 1994. Prehistoric technology: A cognitive science? In C. Renfrew and E. B. Zubrow, eds., *The Ancient Mind: Elements of Cognitive Archaeology,* 152–164. Cambridge: Cambridge University Press.

Katz, R. 1982. *Boiling Energy: Community Healing Among the Kalahari !Kung.* Cambridge: Harvard University Press.

Kimbrell, A. 1994. *The Human Body Shop: The Engineering and Marketing of Life.* San Francisco: Harper.

King, L. 1963. *The Growth of Medical Thought.* Chicago: University of Chicago Press.

Kirmayer, L. J. 1984. Culture, affect and somatization. *Transcultural Psychiatric Research Review* 21: 159–188.

Kleinman, A. 1978. Concepts and a model for the comparison of medical systems as cultural systems. *Social Science and Medicine* 12: 85–93.

———. 1980. *Patients and Healers in the Context of Culture*. Berkeley: University of California Press.

———. 1986. *Social Origins of Distress and Disease*. New Haven: Yale University Press.

Kleinman, A., L. Eisenberg, and B. Good. 1978. Culture, illness and care. *Annals of Internal Medicine* 12: 83–93.

Klerman, G. L. 1985. Birth-cohort trends in rates of major depressive disorder among relatives of patients with affective disorder. *Archives of General Psychiatry* 42: 689–693.

———. 1988. The current age of youthful melancholia: Evidence for increase in depression among adolescents and young adults. *British Journal of Psychiatry* 152: 4–14.

Kling, A., and H. D. Steklis. 1976. A neural substrate for affiliative behavior in nonhuman primates. *Brain, Behavior, and Evolution* 13(2–3): 216–238.

Knight, C. 1991. *Blood Relations: Menstruation and the Origins of Culture*. New Haven: Yale University Press.

Knight, J. 1992. *Institutions and Social Conflict*. Cambridge: Cambridge University Press.

Kohler, W. 1925. *The Mentality of Apes*. London: Routledge and Kegan Paul.

Kopp, C. B. 1989. Regulation of distress and negative emotions: A developmental view. *Developmental Psychology* 25(3): 343–354.

Kudlien, F. 1970. Medical ethics and popular ethics in Greece and Rome. *Clio Medica* 5: 91–121.

Kutumbiah, P. 1969. *Ancient Indian Medicine*, rev. ed. Bombay: Orient Longmans.

LaBarre, W. 1969. *The Peyote Cult*. New York: Schocken Books.

Landy, D., ed. 1977. *Culture, Disease, and Healing: Studies in Medical Anthropology*. New York: Macmillan.

Laughlin, C. D., and E. G. d'Aquili. 1974. *Biogenetic Structuralism*. New York: Columbia University Press.

Laughlin, W. S. 1961. Acquisition of anatomical knowledge by ancient man. In S. Washburn, ed., *Social Life of Early Man. Viking Fund Publication in Anthropology* 31: 150–175.

Laughlin, W. S. 1963. Primitive theory of medicine: Empirical knowledge. In I. Gladston, ed., *Man's Image in Medicine and Anthropology*, 116–140. New York: International Universities Press.

Lee, R. B. 1993. *The Dobe Ju/'hoansi*, 2d ed. New York: Harcourt Brace College Publishers.

Lee, R. B., and I. DeVore, eds. 1968. *Man the Hunter*. Chicago: Aldine.

———. 1979. *The !Kung San: Men, Women and Work in a Foraging Society*. New York: Cambridge University Press.

Lenski, G. 1970. *Human Societies: A Macro-level Introduction to Sociology*. New York: McGraw-Hill.

Lesch, J. E. 1984. *Science and Medicine in France: The Emergence of Experimental Physiology, 1790–1855*. Cambridge: Harvard University Press.

Leslie, C. 1976. *Asian Medical Systems: A Comparative Study.* Berkeley: University of California Press.

Levenson, R. W., and A. M. Ruef. 1992. Empathy: A physiological substrate. *Journal of Personality and Social Psychology* 63(2): 234–246.

Lewis, G. 1975. *Knowledge of Illness in a Sepik Society: A Study of the Gnau, New Guinea.* New Jersey: Humanities Press.

———. 1993. Some studies of social causes of and cultural response to disease. In C. G. N. Mascie-Taylor, ed., *The Anthropology of Disease,* 73–124. New York: Oxford University Press.

Lieberman, P. 1991. *Uniquely Human: The Evolution of Speech, Thought and Selfless Behavior.* Cambridge, Mass.: Harvard University Press.

Lienhardt, G. 1961. *Divinity and Experience: The Religion of the Dinka.* London: Oxford University Press.

Lin, K.-M., R. E. Poland, and J. K. Lau. 1988. Haloperidol and prolactin concentrations in Asians and Caucasians. *Journal of Clinical Psychopharmacology* 8(3): 195–201.

Lin, K.-M., R. E. Poland, and M. D. Smith. 1991. Pharmacokinetic and other related factors affecting psychotropic responses in Asians. *Psychopharmacology Bulletin* 27(4): 427–439.

Lindberg, D. C. 1992. *The Beginnings of Western Science.* Chicago: University of Chicago Press.

Lloyd, G. E. R. 1978. *Hippocratic Writings.* Trans. J. Chadwick and W. N. Mann. London: Penguin Group.

———. 1979. *Magic, Reason and Experience: Studies in the Origins and Development of Greek Science.* Cambridge: Cambridge University Press.

Lopez Austin, A. 1980. *Cuerpo humano e ideología: Las concepciones de los antiguos Nahuas.* Mexico: Universidad Nacional Autónoma de México.

Loudon, D. M. 1988. Puerperal insanity in the nineteenth century. *Journal of the Royal Society of Medicine* 81: 76–79.

Lovejoy, C. O. 1981. The origin of man. *Science* 211: 341–350.

Lumsden, C. J., and E. O. Wilson. 1981. *Genes, Mind and Culture.* Cambridge, Mass.: Harvard University Press.

Lutz, C. A. 1988a. *Unnatural Emotions.* Chicago: University of Chicago Press.

———. 1988b. Ethnographic perspectives on the emotion lexicon. In V. Hamilton, G. Bower, and N. Frijda, eds., *Cognitive Perspectives on Emotion and Motivation,* 399–419. Dordrecht: Kluwer.

MacDonald, M. 1981. *Mystical Bedlam.* Cambridge: Cambridge University Press.

———. 1986. The secularization of suicide in England, 1660–1800. *Past and Present* 111: 50–100.

Mann, M. 1986. *The Sources of Social Power.* Boston: Cambridge University Press.

Marshall, L. 1969. The Medicine Dance of the !Kung Bushmen. *Africa* 39: 347–381.

Mascie-Taylor, C. G. N., ed. 1993. *The Anthropology of Disease.* New York: Oxford University Press.

Mauss, M. [1938] 1985. A category of the human mind. In M. Carrithers, S. Collins, and S. Lukes, eds., *The Category of the Person,* 1–25. Cambridge: Cambridge University Press.

McKeown, T. 1988. *The Origins of Human Disease.* New York: Basil Blackwell.

McNeill, W. H. 1976. *Plagues and Peoples.* New York: Anchor Press.

————. 1992. *The Global Condition*. Princeton: Princeton University Press.

Mead, G. H. 1934. *Mind, Self and Society*. Chicago: University of Chicago Press.

Meggitt, M. J. 1955. *Djanba among the Walbiri*. Anthropos, L., 375–403.

————. 1965. *Desert People: A Study of the Walbiri Aborigines of Central Australia*. Chicago: University of Chicago Press.

Mellars, P., and C. Stringer. 1989. *The Human Revolution: Behavioural and Biological Perspectives on the Origins of Modern Humans*. Edinburgh: Edinburgh University Press.

Mendoza, R., M. W. Smith, and R. E. Poland. 1991. Ethnic psychopharmacology: The Hispanic and Native American perspective. *Psychopharmacology Bulletin* 27(4): 449–461.

Miller, N. E. 1985. Learning of visceral and glandular responses. *Science* 163: 434–445.

Miller P., and N. Rose. 1986. *The Power of Psychiatry*. Oxford: Polity Press.

Milns, R. D. 1986. Attitudes towards mental illness in antiquity. *Australia: New Zealand Journal of Psychiatry* 20: 454–462.

Mollat, M. 1986. *The Poor in the Middle Ages*. Trans. A. Goldhammer. New Haven: Yale University Press.

Murdock, G. P. 1980. *Theories of Illness: A World Survey*. Pittsburgh: University of Pittsburgh Press.

Nadel, S. F. 1954. *Nupe Religion*. London: Routledge and Kegan Paul.

Nash, J. 1967. Death as a way of life: The increasing resort to homicide in a Maya Indian community. *American Anthropologist* 69: 455–470.

Needham, J. 1970. *Clerks and Craftsmen in China and the West*. Cambridge: Cambridge University Press.

Neel, J. V. 1994. *Physician to the Gene Pool: Genetic Lessons and Other Stories*. New York: John Wiley and Sons.

Nesse, R. M. 1990. Evolutionary explanations of emotions. *Human Nature* 1(3): 261–289.

Nesse, R. M., and A. T. Lloyd. 1992. The evolution of psychodynamic mechanisms. In J. H. Barkow, L. Comides, and J. Tooby, eds., *The Adapted Mind*, 601–624. New York: Oxford University Press.

Ng, V. 1990. *Madness in Late Imperial China: From Illness to Deviance*. Norman: University of Oklahoma Press.

Ngubane, H. 1977. *Body and Mind in Zulu Medicine*. London: Academic Press.

North, D. C. 1990. *Institutions, Institutional Change, and Economic Performance*. Cambridge: Cambridge University Press.

Nutton, V. 1983. The seeds of disease: An explanation of contagion and infection from the Greeks to the Renaissance. *Medicine in History* 27: 1–34.

Ohnuki-Tierney, E. 1981. *Illness and Healing Among the Sakhalin Ainu: A Symbolic Interpretation*. Cambridge: Cambridge University Press.

Omran, A. R. 1971. The epidemiologic transition: A theory of the epidemiology of population change. *Milbank Memo Fund Quest* 49: 509–538.

Ortiz de Montellano, B. R. 1990. *Aztec Medicine, Health and Nutrition*. New Brunswick: Rutgers University Press.

Park, K. 1985. *Doctors and Medicine in Early Renaissance Florence*. Princeton: Princeton University Press.

Parsons, T. 1951. *The Social System.* London: Routledge and Kegan Paul.

———. 1966. *Societies: Evolutionary and Comparative Perspectives.* Englewood Cliffs, N.J.: Prentice-Hall.

———. 1975. The sick role and the role of the physician reconsidered. *Milbank Memorial Fund Quarterly* 53: 257–278.

Payer, L. 1989. *Medicine and Culture: Notions of Health and Sickness in Britain, the U.S., France and West Germany.* London: Victor Gollancz.

———. 1992. *Disease Mongers: How Doctors, Drug Companies, and Insurers Are Making You Feel Sick.* New York: John Wiley and Sons.

Pfeiffer, J. E. 1982. *The Creative Explosion: An Inquiry into the Origins of Art and Religion.* Ithaca: Cornell University Press.

Phillips, E. D. 1973. *Greek Medicine.* London: Thames and Hudson.

Pinker, S. 1994. *The Language Instinct: How the Mind Creates Language.* New York: William Morrow.

Pinker, S., and P. Bloom. 1990. Natural language and natural selection. *Behavioral and Brain Sciences* 13: 707–784.

Plotkin, H. 1994. *Darwin, Machines and the Nature of Knowledge.* Cambridge, Mass.: Harvard University Press.

Polgar, S. 1962. Health and human behavior: Areas of interest common to the social and medical sciences. *Current Anthropology* 3(2): 159–205.

———. 1963. Medical problems from an evolutionary view. *Journal of Social Research* 6: 11–20.

Porkert, M. 1974. *The Theoretical Foundations of Chinese Medicine: Systems of Correspondence.* Cambridge: MIT Press.

———. 1983. *The Essentials of Chinese Diagnostics.* Zurich: Chinese Medicine Publications.

Porkert, M., and C. Ullmann. 1988. *Chinese Medicine: Its History, Philosophy and Practice, and Why It May One Day Dominate the Medicine of the West.* New York: William Morrow.

Porter, R. 1985. *Patients and Practitioners: Lay Perceptions of Medicine in Pre-Industrial Society.* Cambridge: Cambridge University Press.

———. 1987a. *Mind Forg'd Manacles.* London: Athlone.

———. 1987b. *A Social History of Madness.* London: Weidenfeld and Nicolson.

Povinelli, D. J., and L. R. Godfrey. 1993. The chimpanzee's mind: How noble in reason? How absent of ethics? In M. H. Nitecki and D. V. Nitecki, eds., *Evolutionary Ethics,* 277–324. New York: State University of New York Press.

Premack, D., and G. Woodruff. 1978. Does the chimpanzee have a theory of mind? *Behavioral and Brain Sciences* 1: 515–526.

Press, I. 1980. Problems in the definition and classification of medical systems. *Social Science and Medicine* 148: 45–55.

Price, T. D., and J. A. Brown. 1985. *Prehistoric Hunter-Gatherers: The Emergence of Cultural Complexity.* San Francisco: Academic Press.

Prkachin, K. M. 1992. The consistency of facial expressions of pain: A comparison across modalities. *Pain* 51: 297–306.

Radcliffe-Browne, A. R. 1922. *The Andaman Islanders.* Cambridge: Cambridge University Press.

Rappaport, R. A. 1979. *Ecology, Meaning and Religion.* Berkeley: North Atlantic Books.

Rather, L. J. 1959. Towards a philosophical study of the idea of disease. In C. McBrooks and P. F. Cranefield, eds., *The Historical Development of Physiological Thought,* 351–373. New York: Hafner.

Riese, W. 1960. The impact of nineteenth-century thought on psychiatry. *International Record of Medicine* 173: 7–19.

Riley, J. C. 1989. *Sickness, Recovery and Death.* Ames: University of Iowa Press.

Rinpoche, R. 1973. *Tibetan Medicine.* Berkeley: University of California Press.

Robins, L. N., and D. A. Regier. 1991. *Psychiatric Disorders in America: The Epidemiologic Catchment Area Study.* New York: Free Press.

Rodriguez, E. 1993. Zoopharmacolognosy: The use of medicinal plants by wild animals. In J. P. Runco, ed., *Recent Advances in Phytochemistry.* Vol. 27: *Phytochemical Potential of Tropical Plants.* New York: Plenum Press.

Rodriguez, E., and J. C. Cavin. 1982. The possible role of Amazonian psychoactive plants in the chemotherapy of parasitic worms: A hypothesis. *Journal of Ethnopharmacology* 6: 303–309.

Rommanucci-Schwartz, L. 1969. The hierarchy of resort in curative practices. *Journal of Health and Social Behavior* 10: 201–209.

Rosen, G. 1946. The philosophy of ideology and the emergence of modern medicine in France. *Bulletin of the History of Medicine* 20: 328–339.

———. 1953. Cameralism and the concept of medical police. *Bulletin of the History of Medicine* 27: 21–42.

———. 1968. *Madness in Society.* Chicago: University of Chicago Press.

Rozin, P. 1976. The selection of food by rats, humans, and other animals. *Advanced Studies of Behavior* 26: 21–76.

———. 1980. Acquisition of food preferences and attitudes to food. *International Journal of Obesity,* 4: 356–363.

Russell, A. W. 1979. The town and state physician in Europe from the Middle Ages to the Enlightenment. In August Bibliothek Herzog, ed., *Sonderband 17.* Hamburg: Wolfenbuttel.

Ruey-Shuang, L. F. 1989. The 'silent art' of ancient China: Historical analysis of the intellectual and philosophical influences in the earliest medical corpus (UMI Dissertation Information Service). Ann Arbor: University of Michigan Microfilms International, 1989.

Sanderson, S. K. 1990. *Social Evolutionism: A Critical History.* Cambridge: Blackwell.

———. 1994. Evolutionary materialism: A theoretical strategy for the study of social evolution. *Sociological Perspectives* 37: 47–73.

———. 1995a. *Macrosociology: An Introduction to Human Societies,* 2d ed. New York: HarperCollins.

———. 1995b. *Social Transformation: A General Theory of Historical Development.* London: Blackwell.

Sawyer, R. C. 1986. Patients, healers, and disease in the Southeast midlands, 1597–1634. Ph.D. dissertation, University of Wisconsin.

Scarborough, J. 1969. *Roman Medicine.* London: Thames and Hudson.

Schelling, T. C. 1960. *The Strategy of Conflict.* Cambridge, Mass.: Harvard University Press.

Schlanger, N. 1994. Mindful technology: Unleashing the chain operatoire for an archeology of mind. In C. Renfrew and E. B. Zubrow, eds., *The Ancient Mind: Elements of Cognitive Archaeology,* 143–151. Cambridge: Cambridge University Press.

Schleiffer, H. 1973. *Sacred Narcotic Plants of the New World Indians*. New York: Macmillan.

Scull, A. T. 1993. *The Most Solitary of Afflictions: Madness and Society in Britain, 1700–1900*. New Haven: Yale University Press.

Serov, S. 1988. Guardian and spirit-masters of Siberia. In W. W. Fitzhugh and A. Crowell, eds., *Crossroad of Continents*, 241–255. Washington, D.C.: Smithsonian Institution Press.

Service, E. R. 1975. *Origins of the State and Civilization: The Process of Cultural Evolution*. New York: W. W. Norton.

Shafton, A. 1976. *Conditions of Awareness*. Portland: Riverstone Press, 1976.

Shryock, R. H. 1969. *The Development of Modern Medicine: An Interpretation of the Social and Scientific Factors Involved*. New York: Hafner.

Shweder, R. A. 1989. Cultural psychology: What is it? In J. W. Stiger, R. A. Shweder, and G. Herdt, eds., *Cultural Psychology: The Chicago Symposia on Culture and Human Development*, 1–43. New York: Cambridge University Press.

———. 1991. *Thinking Through Cultures*. Cambridge, Mass.: Harvard University Press.

Shweder, R. A., and R. A. LeVine. 1984. *Culture Theory: Essays on Mind, Self, and Emotion*. New York: Cambridge University Press.

Singer, M. 1989a. The limitations of medical ecology: The concept of adaptation in the context of social stratification and social transformation. *Medical Anthropology* 10: 223–234.

———. 1989b. The coming of age of critical medical anthropology. *Social Science and Medicine* 28(11): 1193–1203.

Singer, M., H. A. Baer, and E. Lazarus. 1990. Critical medical anthropology in question. *Social Science and Medicine* 30(2): v–vii.

Siraisi, N. G. 1990. *Medieval and Early Renaissance Medicine: An Introduction to Knowledge and Practice*. Chicago: University of Chicago Press.

Sivin, N. 1987. *Traditional Medicine in Contemporary China (Science, Medicine, and Technology in East Asia 2)*. Ann Arbor: Center for Chinese Studies, University of Michigan.

———. 1992a. Text and experience in classical Chinese medicine. Paper presented at Conference on Epistemology and the Scholarly Medical Traditions, McGill University, May 13–16.

———. 1992b. Science and medicine in Chinese history. In P. S. Ropp, ed., *Heritage of China*. Berkeley: University of California Press.

Sober, E., and R. C. Lewontin. 1982. Artifact, cause and genic selection. *Philosophy of Science* 49: 157–180.

Spiro, M. E. 1986. Cultural relativism and the future of anthropology. *Cultural Anthropology* 1(3): 259–286.

Stern, D. W. 1985. *International World of the Infant*. New York: Basic Books.

Strickland, T. L., V. Ranganath, and K.-M. Lin. 1991. Psychopharmacologic considerations in the treatment of black American populations. *Psychopharmacology Bulletin* 27(4): 441–448.

Stringer, C., and C. Gamble. 1993. *In search of the neanderthals*. New York: Thames and Hudson.

Suzuki, A. 1991. Lunacy in seventeenth- and eighteenth century England: Analysis of Quarter Sessions records, pt. 1. *History of Psychiatry* 2: 437–456.

————. 1992. Lunacy in seventeenth- and eighteenth-century England: Analysis of Quarter Sessions records, pt. 2. *History of Psychiatry* 3: 29–44.

Sweeting, H. 1994. Reversals of fortune? Sex differences in health in childhood and adolescence. *Social Science and Medicine* 40(1): 77–90.

Tainter, J. A. 1988. *The Collapse of Complex Societies.* Cambridge: Cambridge University Press.

Temerlin, M. K. 1972. *Lucy: Growing Up Human. A Chimpanzee Daughter in a Psychotherapist's Family.* Palo Alto: Science and Behavior Books.

Temkin, O. 1963. The scientific approach to disease: Specific entity and individual sickness. In A. C. Clembie, ed., *Scientific Change,* 629–647. New York: Basic Books.

Thomas, K. 1993. Cases of conscience in seventeenth-century England. In J. Morrill, P. Slack, and D. Woolf, eds., *Public Duty and Private Conscience in Seventeenth-Century England,* 29–56. Oxford: Clarendon Press.

Tooby, J., and L. Cosmides. 1990a. On the universality of human nature and the uniqueness of the individual: The role of genetics and adaptation. *Journal of Personality* 58(1): 17–67.

————. 1990b. The past explains the present. *Ethology of Sociobiology* 11: 375–424.

————. 1992. The psychological foundations of culture. In J. H. Barkow, L. Cosmides, and J. Tooby, eds., *The Adapted Mind: Evolutionary Psychology and the Generation of Culture,* 19–136. New York: Oxford University Press.

Topley, M. 1970. Chinese traditional ideas and the treatment of disease: Two examples from Hong Kong. *Man* 5: 421–437.

Trawick, M. 1992. Death and nurturance in Indian systems of healing. In C. Leslie and A. Young, eds., *Paths to Asian Medical Knowledge,* 129–159. Berkeley: University of California Press.

Trinkaus, E. 1989. *The Emergence of Modern Humans.* Cambridge: Cambridge University Press.

Trinkaus, E., and P. Shipman. 1992. *The Neanderthals: Of Skeletons, Scientists, and Scandal.* New York: Vintage Books.

Trivers, R. L. 1971. The evolution of reciprocal altruism. *Quarterly Review of Biology* 40: 35–57.

Turnbull, C. M. 1961. *The Forest People.* New York: Simon and Schuster.

————. 1966. *Tradition and Change in African Tribal Life.* Cleveland: World.

Turner, V. 1963. *Lunda Medicine and the Treatment of Disease.* Publication of the Rhodes-Livingston Museum, Livingston, Northern Rhodesia. Lusaka: Government Printer.

Ullman, M. 1978. *Islamic Surveys II: Islamic Medicine.* Edinburgh: Edinburgh University Press.

Ullmann-Margalit, E. 1977. *The Emergence of Norms.* New York: Oxford University Press.

Unger, R. M. 1975. *Knowledge and Politics.* New York: Free Press.

————. 1976. *Law in Modern Society: Toward a Criticism of Social Theory.* New York: Free Press, 1976.

Unschuld, P. U. 1979. *Medical Ethics in Imperial China: A Study in Historical Anthropology.* Berkeley: University of California Press.

————. 1985. *Medicine in China: A History of Ideas.* Berkeley: University of California Press.

—————. 1986a. *Medicine in China: Nan-Ching, the Classic of Difficult Issues.* Berkeley: University of California Press.

—————. 1986b. *Medicine in China: A History of Pharmaceutics.* Berkeley: University of California Press.

Upham, S. 1990. *The Evolution of Political Systems: Sociopolitics in Small-Scale Sedentary Societies.* Cambridge: Cambridge University Press.

Veblen, T. B. 1919. *The Place of Science in Modern Civilization and Other Essays.* New York: Huebesch. Reprinted 1990 with a new introduction by W. J. Samuels (New Brunswick: Transaction).

Von Staden, H. 1989. *Herophilus: The Art of Medicine in Early Alexandria.* Cambridge: Cambridge University Press.

Wadsworth, G. 1984. *The Diet and Health of Isolated Populations.* Boca Raton: CRC Press.

Walton, J. 1985. Casting out and bringing back in Victorian England: Pauper lunatics, 1840–70. In W. F. Bynum, R. Porter, and M. Shepherd, eds., *The Anatomy of Madness.* Vol. 2: *Institutions and Society,* 132–146. New York: Tavistock.

Ward, R. L. 1977. Curing on Ponape: A medical ethnography. Ph.D. dissertation, Tulane University.

Ware, J. R. 1966. *Alchemy, Medicine, Religion in the China of a.d. 320: The Nei P'ien of Ko Hung.* Cambridge: MIT Press.

Warren, D. 1974. Disease, medicine, and religion among the Techiman-Bono of Ghana: A study in culture change. Ph.D. dissertation, Indiana University.

Wear, A. 1992. *Medicine in Society.* New York: Cambridge University Press.

Weil, A. 1972. *The Natural Mind.* Boston: Houghton Mifflin.

White, G. 1985. Premises and purposes in a Solomon Islands ethnopsychology. In G. M. White and J. Kirkpatrick, eds., *Person, Self and Experience: Exploring Pacific Ethnopsychologies.* Berkeley: University of California Press.

Wilkins, W. K., and J. Wakefield. 1995. Brain evolution and neurolinguistic preconditions. *Behavioral and Brain Sciences* 18: 161–226.

Wilkinson, G. S. 1984. Reciprocal food sharing in the vampire bat. *Nature* 308: 181–184.

—————. 1988. Reciprocal altruism in bats and other mammals. *Ethology Sociobiology* 9: 85–100.

Williams, G. C. 1966. *Adaptation and Natural Selection: A Critique of Some Current Evolutionary Thought.* Princeton: Princeton University Press.

Williams, G. C., and R. M. Nesse. 1991. The dawn of Darwinian medicine. *Quarterly Review of Biology* 46(1): 1–22.

Wilson, E. O. 1975. *Sociobiology: The New Synthesis.* Cambridge, Mass.: Harvard University Press.

Wilson, E. O., and C. J. Lumsden. 1989. *The Human Revolution: Behavioral and Biological Perspectives on the Origins of Modern Humans.* Princeton: Princeton University Press.

Winkelman, M. J. 1984. A cross-cultural study of magico-religious practitioners. Ph.D. dissertation, University of Wisconsin.

Woodburn, J. C. 1959. Hadza conceptions of health and disease. In East African Institute of Social Research, *One-Day Symposium on Attitudes to Health and Disease among Some East African Tribes,* 89–94. Kampala, Uganda: Makere College.

Woodburn, J. 1970. *Hunters and Gatherers: The Material Culture of the Nomadic Hadza.* London: British Museum.

Wrangham, R. W., and J. Goodall. 1987. Chimpanzee use of medicinal leaves. In *Understanding Chimpanzees.* Chicago: Chicago Academy of Sciences.

Wrangham, R. W., and T. Nishida. 1983. Aspilia leaves: A puzzle in the feeding behavior of wild chimpanzees. *Primates* 24: 276–282.

Wright, P. A. 1989. The nature of shamanic state of consciousness: A review. *Journal of Psychoactive Drugs* 21(1): 25–33.

Yanchi, L. 1988a. *The Essential Book of Traditional Chinese Medicine.* Vol. 1: *Theory.* New York: Columbia University Press.

———. 1988b. *The Essential Book of Traditional Chinese Medicine.* Vol. 2: *Clinical Practice.* New York: Columbia University Press.

Yerkes, R. M. 1943. *Chimpanzees: A Laboratory Colony.* New Haven: Yale University Press.

Young, A. 1976. Some implications of medical beliefs and practices for social anthropology. *American Anthropology* 78: 5–24.

Zahn-Waxler, C., and M. Radke-Yarrow. 1990. The origins of empathic concern. *Motivation and Emotion* 14(2): 107–130.

Zahn-Waxler, C., M. Radke-Yarrow, E. Wagner, and M. Chapman. 1990. Development of concern for others. *Developmental Psychology* 28(1): 126–136.

Zimmermann, F. 1982. *The Jungle and the Aroma of Meats.* Berkeley: University of California Press.

———. 1987. *The Jungle and the Aroma of Meats: An Ecological Theme in Hindu Medicine.* Berkeley: University of California Press.

Index

Designer: U.C. Press Staff
Compositor: Prestige Typography
Text: 10/12 Times Roman
Display: Helvetica
Printer & Binder: Thomson-Shore, Inc.